Making It in the Market

Books by Richard Ney

The Wall Street Jungle, *1970*
The Wall Street Gang, *1974*
Making It in the Market, *1975*

Making It in the Market

RICHARD NEY'S LOW-RISK SYSTEM FOR STOCK MARKET INVESTORS

RICHARD NEY

McGraw-Hill Book Company

New York St. Louis San Francisco Düsseldorf London Mexico Sydney Toronto

Book design by Marcy J. Katz.

123456789DODO798765

Library of Congress Cataloging in Publication Data

Ney, Richard.
Making it in the market.

1. Investments. 2. Stocks. I. Title.
HG4521.N45 332.6′7 75-25979
ISBN 0-07-046460-X

Charts reproduced in this book are
courtesy Trendline, a division of Standard
and Poor's Corporation, Securities Research
Company, Francis Emory Fitch, Incorporated,
and Standard and Poor's Corporation.

To

Ben Rous and Jess Kemberling

in friendship, in admiration, and with the great affection I share with everybody who knows them

Acknowledgments

As an author, I am an apprentice in a craft in which I have only to look at my bookshelves to see my masters. If my writings have enjoyed any success it is because others whose gifts are equal to or greater than mine have enabled me to make the best and the most of my talents.

I have already acknowledged how much the wordly wisdom and common sense of my associate, Mei-Lee, helped in the preparation of my second book, *The Wall Street Gang*. Once again I am guiltily aware that thanks to her sovereign good sense and indefatigable industry I have been able to be sinfully free of responsibility as I wrote the present book and gave it to her to edit and organize. Only a few of my ideas marched in single file; most of them pressed in a crowd for attention. She gathered all of them together and, with her great gift of seeing things as they are and as they should be, arranged them into a coherent whole—and she did all this while simultaneously conducting her investment counseling and banking activities as our company's executive vice president.

I must also express my warm gratitude to Gladys Carr of McGraw-Hill for her skillful management of the book from its inception through publication.

Contents

Ney's Axioms

I. He Who Controls the Man Controls His Money

II. Better a Steady Dime than a Seldom Dollar

III. Successful Investing Consists Less in Acquiring Good Habits than in Learning the Specialist's

IV. When We Learn What a Man Is Most Anxious to Hide, We Also Learn Why He Wants to Hide It

V. It Is Not Public Demand That Creates Rising Prices, but Rising Prices That Create Public Demand

VI. Every Decline Provides the Investor with a Chance to Learn That Changes in the Market Are Due Not to Outer Events but to Inner Conditions

VII. He Who Sells and Runs Away Will Live to Buy Another Day . . . Tra La

VIII. The Pain Comes Later. It's Called Hindsight

IX. What Nobody Wants Everybody Gets

X. To Understand What You Do, You Must Only Do What You Understand

XI. A Man Must Learn to Avoid Losing What He Has Today before Thinking of What He Hopes to Get Tomorrow

XII. There Are Few Patient Investors Who Do Not Soon Weary of Their Patience

Making It in the Market

Introduction: He Who Controls Money Controls the Man

Ney's First Axiom: He who controls the man controls his money.

The investor is like a chicken unaware he is about to become a broiler. Awareness usually results from an accumulation of errors. Not, however, in the case of the investor. Decade after decade, he continues to attribute his losses either to unpredictable economic circumstances or to his own incompetence. Yet in reality the investor's losses are caused by the infinitely elaborated controls exerted over the investment process by the big-money insiders of the Stock Exchange. The scandal of the age is that mass education turns investors into puppets, the media fasten the strings, and the Exchange then hangs them.

The public's carefully engineered images of the investment process are rooted in its assumptions about the integrity of its political, financial, and media institutions. Lacking legitimate insights into the motivations of those who head these institutions, investors are unaware that, as aspects of the investment process, they too are controlled by the big-money forces that dominate the Exchange insider establishment.

This book has been designed as a sequel to my earlier books but can be read and understood independently. *The Wall Street Jungle* and *The Wall Street Gang* were written primarily to provide investors with realistic concepts of the stock market which are suppressed by the Stock Exchange establishment. The experiences and experiments of more than a decade as an investment adviser have made clear to me the characteristics and typical procedures of Exchange insiders and the complex of conditions that enable them to dominate the investor's decision-making processes.

My objective has been to break down the age-old traditions of the Exchange establishment by placing investors on the frontiers of experience—by helping them to see that their losses in the market can be attributed to beliefs and practices that serve as the principal instruments to control them. Most investors are so preoccupied with theories and values that *ought* to exist that they pay no attention to what actually *does* exist. Thus they spend their time analyzing destabilizing economic forces, interest rates, or corporate earnings instead of practices that are internal to the Exchange. Once investors begin to think more about the way they think, they will see that what they *think* the market is, or ought to be, determines their style as investors.

The Stock Exchange establishment includes not only the stock exchanges but the eastern banking establishment, the major investment banking houses, and the regulatory agencies that serve as guardians of the establishment. Because the investor fails to perceive the magnitude of this establishment's power, or the manner in which it has immobilized his resources, he fails to see that he is looked upon as an object rather than a person, a commodity to be consumed rather than a consumer.

In "The Emperor's New Clothes" it is a child not yet conditioned by the environment who recognizes that the emperor is naked. Only when the child points this out do others realize that custom has distorted their vision. In a similar manner the investor fails to recognize the true nature of his environment.

Few men have acquired a larger mass of valuable knowledge about the Exchange or are more intimately acquainted with its techniques than former Assistant Secretary of State and former ambassador to Brazil Adolf Berle. Berle was a professor of corporate law when I was a student at Columbia University. Having explored the personalities of the luminaries of the Exchange and the vicissitudes to which their processes subject the individual and the economy, he drew the following picture of the territory in his book *The American Economic Republic:*

> Properly analyzed stock markets only have a distant relation to real investments, that is to actual application of savings as capital to new business construction and operations. . . . Stock markets have relatively little direct connection with the business of accumulating savings and applying them to the capital needs of the country. The economic system could probably get along quite adequately without them.

With few exceptions those who dominate the Exchange's centers of power are neither cruel nor heartless men. They are merely individuals dedicated to an enterprise handed down to them by their forebears in an ever-expanding process that has made most of them multimillionaires. One and all, they have become so acclimated to doing their thing on the Exchange's merry-go-round that it is unlikely any of them will ever get off or—if they can prevent it—let anyone else on. They would rather risk the loss of everything than give up anything. The issue of morality does not arise. In the existing moral climate it would be as pointless to expect them to change their habit patterns as it would be to expect the manufacturers of cigarettes to ask their customers to stop smoking in order to avoid the risks of cancer. The whole enterprise is merely a game that has been passed on from one generation to the next, the father teaching the son, the son the grandson.

When a change occurs in the structure of an institution like the Stock Exchange—whether it be in establishing negotiated commissions or creating a central market—the change is always in the direction of greater control for Exchange insiders. When, for example, a legislative program was instituted for a central market in 1975, everything proceeded according to plan until, at the last moment, the Exchange discovered that its specialists would have to sacrifice their dominant control over the short sale. At that point there was suddenly a mysterious reversal in the attitude of the Exchange toward the legislation. A central market will come into existence only when the Exchange is able to assert its continued monopoly power over the short sale—an environmental process that gives its specialists first crack at placing their brand on the herd.*

Government has the authority to institute fundamental changes that could improve the investor's lot. The fact is, however, that the unprecedented magnitude of the Exchange estab-

*On June 13, 1975, it was reported in the press that the "SEC [had] adopted a previous proposal to tailor its short sale rules to new conditions under the consolidated ticker tape." In other words, working in harness with the Commission, the Exchange had finally managed to devise a plan whereby it was able to maintain its total control over stock prices within the framework of the previous proposal.

lishment's coercive powers long ago reached into government to establish its sources of control. Perhaps the most distinctive feature of democracy in the United States is the extent to which the financial establishment dominates the mechanics of government. In my judgment there is little possibility of reform or criminal prosecution of Exchange insiders. There can be no punishment when government is your bedfellow.

After publication of *The Wall Street Gang*, many investors began to develop systems based on my theories. Many called or wrote in order to check out their progress. I found that many of them had come upon problems that needed to be solved, and I was glad to be brought into closer touch with their concerns and needs. Certainly, if I am to be of any help to the small investor, who is least able to suffer losses in the market, I must be fully aware of the problems he encounters; after all, it is primarily for such investors that my books are written.

This was also a learning process for me. My readers' questions made it necessary for me to formulate in simple terms the specifics of what had become my educated intuitions. Because questions came in from all over the country, it was impossible for me to cope adequately with the various problems on a one-to-one basis. The magnitude of reader interest made it obvious that only a practical and explicit book on the subject could provide answers for the investor in Dallas and for the investor in Minneapolis.

This book, then, is an attempt to provide answers to the questions of investors who have discovered that a new approach to making money in the market is needed if they are not, like lemmings, to continue in their habitual paths to self-destruction. The book methodizes the principles, practices, and information that should enable the investor to choose wisely from among the many options always opening up before him. Although risk is inherent in any money-making venture, I will show the investor how I, as an investment adviser, seek to achieve maximum investment returns consistent with minimum risk.

A minimization of risk requires more than a re-evaluation of the market as presently defined in terms of conventional theory. What is wanted and what I employ on my clients' and my own behalf is an investment philosophy capable of limiting the competitive advantages of an insider bureaucracy. It is characterized by a commitment into the market based on a philosophy of preservation of capital and the attainment of long-term capital gains.

Recognizing that events may occur that cause one to withdraw from the market earlier than anticipated, it has nonetheless been my experience that only by focusing on the principle of long-term capital gains can one minimize the hazards of unexpected and inconsistent events that limit the potentials for maximizing gains. However, I have designed this book to accommodate as well the needs of those who prefer to trade.

With these objectives in mind, I will provide investors not only with insights into insider strategies that persuade them to make badly timed investments but with insights as well into courses of action, values, and risk-limiting disciplines that will enable them to time their purchases and sales according to the techniques I employ. *These techniques underlie the only system I have discovered in more than fifteen years of research which allows me to maximize profit potentials while minimizing risk.*

Within the limits fixed by their material conditions, time, and capacity, investors *can* learn to compete successfully against the insider by following the transactions of the specialist for his own accounts. It is really quite remarkable how successful the investor can become at solving his investment problems once he can keep in his head simultaneously two entirely different concepts: the market as the specialist wants you to imagine it is, and the market as it is because of past and present specialist intent.

Here again the plan of *Making It in the Market* marks a strong departure from that of my earlier books. It is inevitable some things will be stated that I have commented on before, since some sort of recapitulation is necessary for the reader coming to my writings for the first time. I do not, however, again focus on the larger issues of justice, fair play, and reform. My primary purpose here is to prescribe practical investment principles for the guidance of investors.

The specialist is the man who, in the exercise of his role at the center of the market, acts as your broker's broker on the floor of the Exchange. At the same time, he is also acting as both an investor and a trader for himself. We will investigate the specialist's role more fully in the text. For present purposes, it is sufficient to point out that, in the exercise of his role, he is able to determine the long- and short-term movements of the stocks under his supervision.

Many people I know have been surprised and disturbed because although a specialist may seem to do very badly for his customers, he may do very well for himself. Yet it would seem that this is what one should expect. When the specialist can totally control the price movements of his stocks, how can he be expected to deny himself opportunities for maximizing his personal profits while trading against his customers? Nothing human is without self-interest. Why should anyone expect the stock market specialist to behave any differently from any merchant who sells at retail what he has bought wholesale?

If investors are to establish profits in the market, they must learn to use the information available regarding the specialist's activities. I have grown aware, however, that it is not enough to set down the specialist's practices and principles in a primer of basic usage. What the investor requires is the education that comes from the day-to-day experience of a professional in the market. It has occurred to me that nothing could better assist the investor than excerpts from the daily diary I keep on the market. In this way the investor can come into close contact with actual events in which both parties to the confrontation—investors on the one side and specialists on the other—can be clearly identified and the market pattern recognized through which they are moving.

I find most financial writing a coming together of helplessness and hope that is either too technical or too utopian to supply guidance in the development of an effective investment system. It would be difficult, however, for the average investor to jump from the traditional assumptions of most financial writing to the kind of shorthand analysis I do for my daily diary. For this reason, I have used excerpts from my diary to emphasize points in the text it supplements.

In my opinion there is only one reliable method by which investors may predict the future course of stock prices. This method is based on the premise that the market's major trends are known to specialists a long time in advance. It is for this reason that, in determining the relevance of a specialist's past merchandising practices to his present practices, investors are able to determine what events are necessary for the attainment of the specialist's *future* merchandising objectives.

To illustrate this principle, the reader will be situated within a framework of stock market activities during the last quarter of 1974 through the first half of 1975. In the course of examining this period of time, the reader will be presented with practical and profitable alternatives to cumbersome and useless traditional theory.

The two major points of departure between my system and traditional theory can be briefly summarized: Traditional analysis totally ignores the existence of the specialist. It concentrates instead on the assumption that the average investor's success in the market depends on selecting those stocks whose underlying economic fundamentals will cause them to become the objects of public demand and that public demand will cause an advance in stock prices. On the other hand, the basic principles of my system are rooted in the assumption that specialists, as the active core at the market's center, determine a stock's and the market's trends because they are in a position to manipulate public supply and demand. In this connection my system insists that heavy demand by the public—once it is exhausted—enables specialists to drop stock prices profitably, whereas heavy selling by the public—once the selling dries up—provides the specialists with the incentive to advance stock prices. Nothing could better distinguish the opposition of my approach to the market to that of traditional theory.

The second major difference between my system and traditional analysis involves an understanding of the decisive role played by specialist short selling. Short selling not only enables the specialists to establish a ceiling to the market's advance—and short covering, a floor to its decline—but provides them with the financial incentives to create a bear market when their short sales have been established at the market's highs and to create a bull market once they have "covered" their short sales to establish a market bottom. Traditional theory ignores specialist short selling.

The dimensions of the specialist's power are such that he can be said to be the only individual in the market truly endowed with the power of choice. Since this is so, the priorities embalmed in traditional theory are merely abstractions in which profits are an unrealizable ideal. Indeed, they are the solvent that liquidates the resources of investors who employ them. The power of the specialist can be most effectively exercised by investors when they recognize that if they are to achieve success in the market they must gain insight into the direction of specialist thought patterns. This then enables investors to anticipate the decisions of the specialist. For although the specialist is the dominant agent in the market's affairs, the investor is able to avoid the consequences of this domination once he is able to predict his course of action.

So the investor does have a choice: He can either remain an automaton—behaving as specialists want him to behave—or he can become a successful investor by following the paths and precepts of this book to self-determination of his financial destiny.

1

Selecting Your Portfolio or The First Step in Moving Money from the Stock Exchange's Pocket to Yours

Ney's Second Axiom: Better a steady dime than a seldom dollar.

The best things in life are simple. This is true in nature, in art, and in the stock market. In each, simple propositions and principles are ascendent. In the market, the investor generally causes unnecessary complications for himself with the assumptions he employs in the selection of his portfolio. Put together in hope and in fear, the portfolio of most investors embodies a clumsy arrangement of imperfections and inconsistencies. The improbability of consistent gains should cause investors to question the assumptions on which their investments are based. Instead, it would seem that these assumptions have a momentum all their own.

It has been made abundantly clear to me that nothing contributes more to an investor's misconceptions concerning the structure of his portfolio than the influence of market professionals and business schools. For the most part, they misinform because they too have been conditioned to believe in the theory that different investors have different needs. Hence they emphasize the requirements of different age groups, personalities, and financial situations. Widows must supposedly have portfolios different from doctors' and lawyers', who, in turn, should have needs that call for an adjustment to the market different from that of a twenty-five-year-old just starting out with a small inheritance. The professionals divide people in many ways, mostly *from* their money.

It is my view that we should not operate on the assumption that different individuals have different portfolio needs or that some should be aggressive investors and therefore require a growth portfolio, while others should be defensive and require income. The needs of those who enter the market should be the same. Moreover, only those who do *not* need income from their investments should enter the market. An individual whose sole objective is income should invest only in income-producing instruments (such as banker's acceptances, certificates of deposit and treasury bills) in which principal is protected against loss. The same is true for those who need income to provide for daily necessities but who maintain they also desire growth. In my opinion it is incompatible with the realities of the marketplace to seek to tie in growth with income. If the individual must live on income from investments, preservation of capital is the first economic priority. Under these circumstances one cannot afford the risks or traumas of the market.

On numerous occasions I have been consulted by investors whose advisers have said roughly this: "What does it matter what happens to the price of your stock? Your income is the same." Although fictions such as this avoid dangerous admissions of failure, they also sustain dangerous misconceptions about investments. When he has big losses, the investor finds such words reassuring, and they provide the adviser with collateral against which he can increase the already heavy overdrafts against his credentials. As for the investor converted to this kind of investment philosophy, he may be caught with stock that has become worth less than half what he paid for it when (1) he may be suddenly forced to liquidate his position because of an emergency or (2) the dividends are cut when the stock is at its low. At this point, the investor generally wakes up to realize that his adviser doesn't know his business, and without mincing words, he tells him so. The adviser is then quick to point out that it's too bad he "has to sell now because his stocks are sure to come back." Then, pacing up and down his office, the adviser plays his ace. In the market's poker game, it generally wins every trick. He points out that he had the very best stocks in his portfolio; that it was "a well-balanced portfolio"; that his losses are due to economic forces inexorably beyond the reach of anyone's control; that he need only look about to observe that "everyone else is in the same boat." The customers of Wall Street's best banks, brokerage houses, and advisory services have done no better, the client is told. They too have seen their dividends cut and lost their clients' money in the same stocks. Although the ace being played can be seen to have no more merit than the two of clubs, it serves its purpose. Misery loves company, and the investor is comforted when it is brought to his attention that others have suffered equally great losses. The adviser then places his hand on his client's shoulder, utters a few sympathetic noises, and ushers him out of his office as quickly as possible. Regrettably, what is needed is the rent money, not words of sympathy.

Only if one doesn't *depend* on income from investments should one be in the market. And if one *is* in the market, then one's sole objective should be growth of capital. This can best be achieved when investments are made in stocks that offer maximum growth potential coupled with minimum risk. The stocks in this category are the Dow industrial stocks—Eastman Kodak, General Electric, General Motors, for example. As important elements of the Dow Jones industrial average, they enjoy a strategic position at the summit of the specialist's pyramid of power.

Although the historical conditions may no longer exist that once established the Dow as being representative of the supercorps that dominates America's processes of production, this exclusion has nothing whatever to do with the functions of this index. Let us say that the Dow declines 5.92 points. What *is* important about this decline is that the specialists in IBM and Xerox (and all other stocks) now have an alibi that allows them to drop their stocks' prices "in sympathy" with the Dow—and, not incidentally, enrich themselves if earlier they had sold their stocks short. Thus the specialists in more than 1,500-odd common stocks on the NYSE (like the specialists on the AMEX, the Midwest Exchange, the Pacific Coast Exchange, etc.) are able to command profits for themselves not because the earnings of the corporations they represent have added (or lost) value, but because a fluctuation in the Dow has allowed them to employ their wealth-producing processes in order to maximize profits.

Without a trump card in his hand, it is possible for an investor in Dow stocks to take every trick. For in acquiring a selection of these stocks, he has acquired the very stocks that influence the investment decisions of all specialists. This automatically protects the investor from many of the crises of the marketplace. For while it is possible that the investor who *attempts* to buy these stocks at bargain prices may subsequently see them decline further in price (he who swims against the current shouldn't expect it to change direction), he is in the very stocks which, in the next bull market, will be among the leaders on the upside. I should point out that although I have sought to discourage investment in common stocks when the individual's needs insist on income, income is an element also provided by most Dow stocks.

Although I follow each of the 30 stocks in the Dow average on a daily basis in order to keep tabs on the market's trend, when investing for the clients of my investment advisory service, I invest only in a select number of these stocks. This is because the internal characteristics of the most important Dow stocks command greater institutional interest than others. One can relate institutional interest to the amount of shares outstanding in a company. Thus, not all Dow stocks have the capitalization to qualify for major institutional interest. Eastman Kodak, for example, has, at this writing, 161.5 million shares outstanding; General Motors has 287.6 million. The high capitalization of these stocks makes for active trading and ease in buying and selling shares in large quantities. By the same token, the average investor stands a much better chance of being able to buy and sell his shares without causing an immediate price change. It is a simple matter to see why with a company with 11.9 million shares outstanding it would be difficult for institutions to execute large block transactions without being obliged either to take a big drop in price or to pay a big fee for "protection."

Institutional portfolio managers also like to invest in stocks that have demonstrated their great appeal for other institutional portfolio managers (the herd instinct works among this group as it does among investors). One reason Dow stocks possess this appeal is that if they do decline, the declines are occurring in stocks that have established antecedents in terms of longevity and earnings. This provides the portfolio manager's reputation with some measure of protection against potential criticism. Moreover, these stocks generally offer fairly high yields, thus providing the portfolio manager with a built-in cushion against possible losses.

I place great importance on selecting stocks that are institutional favorites, because the meticulous grading of priorities on the Stock Exchange allows these stocks to enjoy the prerogatives of greater favor. For one thing, institutional portfolio managers are willing to pay special fees to specialists and investment bankers to buy and sell these stocks for them in large quantities. Furthermore, once a specialist has accumulated stock at the bottom for an institution and has received his portion of the fees, it is then in his interest to acquire investment accounts for himself in this stock since he now has a built-in incentive to advance its price in order to sell out his institutional clients at a later date—again for a fee. Thus, because of the enormous profits they yield to specialists, these stocks are sheltered behind the ramparts of power. What this means for the investor is that once a major trend has been established, these stocks are less likely to deviate from that trend. Although self-interest exists everywhere, on the floor of the Stock Exchange it is a well-organized way of life.

Despite the safeguards provided institutional stocks, institutions have, generally speaking, racked up appalling performance records. For example, in the October 10, 1974, issue of *The Wall Street Journal* it was reported that "three pooled stock funds managed by . . . [Morgan Guaranty Trust Company] dropped more than $1 billion, or more than 50% in value in the year ended September 30." Morgan Guaranty should by no means be singled out for its poor performance record. Most bank-managed and other institutional portfolios performed equally poorly during that period of time. One reason institutional portfolio records are so dismal, despite the fees paid to specialists, is that specialists are not always able to buy and sell stock for them at optimum price levels. There are limitations on how much stock the public can consume. Thus, because of the tremendous increase in the number and size of mutual funds, hedge funds, offshore funds, and other large trust, pension, and profit-sharing plans, it is impossible for specialists and their investment banker associates to unload onto the public anything but a small percentage of these large portfolios when stocks are moving toward their highs or are at or near their highs. Hence, Exchange insiders tend to gravitate to a limited number of enduring favorites among institutional portfolio managers. But even here, most institutions, because of the size of their financial resources, must invest in hundreds of different stocks. In consequence the great majority of them are unable to liquidate a sufficient number of their stocks at a profit in order to show good performance records.

When we survey the whole picture of institutional portfolio management, we find that among the big advisory services the great majority of bank-managed portfolios tend to have the worst performance records. This state of affairs is peculiarly indigenous to the banking establishment because of the special obstacles the nature of its business places in the path of good performance. These obstacles can be attributed to the highly questionable influences to which bank trust departments and advisory personnel are exposed. In his desire to conform to his bank's business goals, the adviser may seek to create among the heads of a corporation an atmosphere favorable to his bank in order to obtain that corporation's banking business. This factor can weigh heavily in the selection of stocks and bonds that a bank's portfolio manager will buy and sell for a customer's portfolio. For example, if a bank wishes to handle a corporation's pension fund and/or its banking business, or if its trust department wishes to maintain good relations or improve relations with a corporate customer, the desire to "get that business" can shape the decision-making processes of a bank's investment officer, whose major objective is to hold onto his job. Thus he might suggest the use of a private placement of a corporation's bonds.

These bonds would then find their way into the portfolios of the customers for whom the bank, or its subsidiary, is acting as investment adviser.

Another frequent practice for banks that do not wish to lose the business of corporate customers is to place a "hold" on those stocks in customer portfolios which the bank is well aware should be sold. Regrettably, bank customers include the bank-managed trust accounts of individuals as well as institutional portfolios (which of course ultimately affects individuals). However inexperienced in the market the investor may be, in most cases he would still be better off managing his portfolio himself than relying on the discretion of a bank's advisory service or trust department. Granted, old-fashioned New York banking houses have all the tradition and status of the past behind them; their trust departments are like old-fashioned grandfather clocks whose sounds are very impressive but which fail to keep the right time.

Even though the performance records of most institutional portfolio managers can be characterized as incompetent, some of these managers' activities help solve some of the investor's most important problems. One of the attributes of institutional participation in Dow stocks is the manner in which they simplify the investor's problem of timing. Countless stocks will establish their highs in one day and then fall off precipitously. Because of the large distribution of Dow stocks among institutions, however, much more time is required to unload these shares. This provides the investor with more time to recognize the process of distribution and to solve his most important investment problem: when to sell.

In addition to the Dow 30 I follow other stocks that are all "blue chip" corporations in terms of their reputation and position in their industry. Obviously, however, these other stocks do not fulfill the functions of Dow stocks. When they meet the additional requirements of capitalization and institutional participation, however, we have enough examples to show that you can make just as good gains in these stocks when you understand timing and the fact that the worth of most stocks seldom outlasts a bull market. Some of the additional stocks I follow are: Avon, Burroughs, IBM, American Home Products, Xerox, Minnesota Mining, Bristol–Myers, Citicorp, Chase Manhattan, Caterpillar Tractor, Deere, and Coca–Cola.

I would nonetheless recommend to those who employ my theories that they keep their situation as simple as possible by sticking exclusively to Dow stocks. No accumulation of knowledge about stocks, about the specialist's methods, about the machinery and operation of the Exchange can be any substitute for the manner in which these stocks will serve to protect the average investor from the market's changing conditions. For his immediate purposes, the average investor should limit the number of selections for his portfolio to four or five in order to assure adequate supervision. Many investors will feel they require many more stocks. I would point out that I feel I can service a portfolio of $250,000 with no more than five carefully selected stocks. Obviously an investor with $5,000 to invest should be satisfied with no more than three or four stocks. I should also point out that in any event he should acquire *no less* than three.

A list of the 30 Dow stocks follows, along with asterisks to note the issues I believe merit particular investor consideration. The reader can consult a Standard & Poor's monthly "Stock Guide" to determine the capitalization and the latest figures for institutional participation.

Alcoa (Aluminum Co. of America) (AA)
Allied Chemical (ACD)
American Brands (AMB)
American Can (AC)
*American Telephone & Telegraph (T)
Anaconda (A)
Bethlehem Steel (BS)
Chrysler (C)

*Du Pont (DD)
*Eastman Kodak (EK)
Esmark (ESM)
*Exxon Corp. (XON)
*General Electric (GE)
General Foods (GF)
*General Motors (GM)
Goodyear Tire & Rubber (GT)
International Harvester (HR)
International Nickel (N)
*International Paper (IP)
Johns-Manville (JM)
Owens Illinois (OI)
*Procter & Gamble (PG)
*Sears (S)
*Standard Oil of California (SD)
*Texaco, Inc. (TX)
*Union Carbide (UK)
U.S. Steel (X)
United Technologies (UTX)
Westinghouse Electric (WX)
Woolworth (Z)

A selection of stocks from the foregoing list can provide the investor with a giant step along the road to success in the market. Granted, other stocks may make percentage gains that are far greater than anything obtainable by an Eastman Kodak or an Exxon. But there is no question that when alternatives like Dow stocks are available that can provide more consistent gains, the intelligent investor should opt for a steady dime instead of a seldom dollar.

Many professionals (and investors) seek to participate in the profit potentials associated with "growth" stocks. They search for new companies that will one day be what IBM, Xerox, or Eastman Kodak are today. Obviously, of the thousand or more stocks that have started out with such high prospects, only a small fraction manage to fulfill their promise. Thus, once these highly touted growth stocks are manipulated to their highs by insiders who then sell, investors are left holding the bag.

We live in the age of the oligopolist, and it is very difficult for the growth of any new company to proceed very far before entering into competition with the distribution facilities of the Fortune 500. Further, new companies are generally so capitalized that there is very little stock outstanding. This means they do not enjoy consistent institutional favor and that major reversals in their stock's price trends can occur overnight. For these reasons I consider growth stocks high-risk situations more suitable to crapshooting than investing.

Another area of trading that has sold itself into the mind of the public is the buying and writing of options. Public relations has riveted their attention to the surface event that they can get more action in options for $500 than they can in stocks for $5000. The obvious enchantment of this idea has led to an explosive growth in popularity for a device that is fraught with high risk (and high commissions).

In my opinion, they do not belong in the portfolios of average investors. Although they may offer certain advantages to highly sophisticated investors and institutional traders, they have proven to be sources of serious financial loss to most of those investors who have sought to trade in them. Beyond the simplest application, they tend to be difficult for the average person to understand and utilize with low risk. One SEC official with whom I talked commented that he regarded the whole options market as a "commissions gimmick" for the brokerage industry, and "a major source of losses for people who can't afford them." He wondered aloud why the commission hierarchy had sanctioned them. I refrained from telling him.

Briefly stated, an individual can buy an option (a call) for which he pays a premium which gives him the right to purchase 100 shares of the stock covered by the option at a specified price within a specified period of time. Or he can write an option, in exchange for a premium, against stock which he may or may not own which obligates him to deliver the stock upon the assignment of an exercise notice within a specified period of time for the receipt of a specified price. An individual is also free to establish positions in combinations of the two. Before the Chicago Board of Options Exchange (CBOE) opened for business in April, 1973, options were handled exclusively by put-and-call dealers. Now that they are also traded on the CBOE, investors can buy and sell the options themselves, in addition to exercising them. While this helps limit the risk inherent in options, it does not protect the individual against large losses.

The greatest risk the buyer of options assumes is the possible loss of his entire investment in a relatively short period of time. I have heard advisers tell their clients that options limit risk because they limit the amount of loss to the premium paid for the option (or, in other words, the entire investment). I wonder what such advisers would have to say to the investor who wrote me asking if there was any way he could get some of his money back from his broker, who had persuaded him to buy ten options for $6000 instead of 100 shares of a $60 stock. The stock immediately fell to 58, declined further and then traded between 52 and 58, and closed at 57 the day the option expired. If he had purchased the stock as he had originally planned, he'd have had a paper loss of $300, minus commissions. Instead, he wound up losing his entire investment of $6000. This investor might have been able to somewhat limit his loss by selling his options before they expired, but he did not have the knowledge or experience in this area to know what to do.

It should be pointed out that a writer of options against stock, or a "covered writer," can assume huge losses. One of the riskiest transactions in the options market, however, is the writing of what are called "naked" or "unhedged" options, in which the writer of the option does not own the underlying stock. A local investment house recently went bankrupt writing "naked" options. The writer of the "naked option" assumes the same obligation of delivery within a specified period of time as does the "covered" writer. As in short selling, if the price of the stock rises, the "naked," or "uncovered," writer's losses can be horrendous.

There are hedging techniques for options trading that can be useful, but as I mentioned earlier, they are complex and tend to be only for the highly sophisticated speculator with the financial capacity to sustain large losses. Since we are concerned here with what is most profitable for the average investor with minimum risk, I would most certainly urge the investor to purchase outright only the highest-quality stocks in the Dow rather than the options for these securities. The purchase of options obviates most of the important advantages that the purchase of such stocks provides.

This severely clinical approach to portfolio selection will not appeal to the pioneering spirit of many investors. Remaining faithful to the spirit and ideology of free enterprise, they would rather leverage themselves out with options or acquire 200 shares of some little-known company that they've been told has the prospect of becoming another Sears, than acquire 50 shares of Sears. Creatures of emotion, they exhibit the congenital disposition of the average investor to spend his money on junk. It becomes even more of a vicious cycle when one considers that stockbrokers oftentimes have no alternative but to exploit such a customer's greed. If they could, there would be occasions when they would sell him General Motors or Procter & Gamble, but when they mention the names of such stocks, the customer either falls asleep or departs for some other, more enterprising stockbroker with a livelier story. It is for the reader to decide whether he wants to be an investor or to accept the high risks of being a gambler.

How far you go in life and in the market depends very much on the quality of the company you keep. But once you have selected your stocks, of equal importance is the insight required to time the purchase and sale of those stocks properly. A fundamental change has taken place in the stock market that insists on a transition from an investment strategy based on long-term trends in the market, such as we saw in the fifties and through 1961, to a strategy in which long-term capital gains must be established during a six- to nine-month period. The most important factor here is preservation of capital. Expertise in the timing of tops and bottoms is required to preserve capital and see it grow in these new circumstances.

Investors usually make their investment decisions on the basis of the advice of those who, like well-trained parrots, can only repeat the same old phrases. They buy or sell according to the crises caused by earnings announcements, the raising and lowering of interest rates, wage and price policies, wholesale price levels, inflationary developments, gold prices, and a host of other economic complexities. It is no wonder that survival in the market is an uphill battle. If you are to observe procedures that help you meet your investment goals, you must transform yourself from a creature whose constant unconscious temptation is to invest your savings on the Exchange's behalf instead of your own.

While it has been possible to make a brief statement of the kind of portfolio the investor should have, it is impossible in a few pages to provide the information that will give him the ability to time his purchases and sales properly. This I can best do by placing the investor in my shoes and leading him through a day-to-day analysis of the market's actions. In becoming aware of the various strategems and deceptions the market insiders engage in as they raise and lower stock prices, the investor will gradually be able to anticipate these practices and objectives so effectively that he will not be content to observe my play but will grab up the cards and play them on his own behalf.

2

The Specialist & You or How $400 Billion a Year Is Pumped Out of the Economy

Ney's Third Axiom: Successful investing consists less in acquiring good habits than in learning the specialist's.

There are more than 33 million investors in the United States today. Most of them are losers. Not only do they lose their money, they lose their self-confidence, their security, and the chance they had at one time to use their money to make a killing in the market. Yet the fact is that to get the money needed to invest in the market, most of these people had to be fairly successful in their chosen career. As doctors or lawyers, for example, many of them had demonstrated an ability to think clearly, to make plans for the future, and to carry them out. Why then, employing the same intelligence, do they go wrong when they try to make money in the market?

In point of fact their problems as investors are worsened by their ability to move about in their professional territory more or less successfully in the course of their everyday routine. They do, as a matter of course, research the stock they are considering buying in order to acquire the information they think they need to make an intelligent investment decision. Unfortunately, although the information they acquire might be useful in the business world, it will be of no use in the market. It lacks *predictive ability*. However brilliant an individual may be, if he attaches predictive potentials to information that has no predictive ability, he is using the wrong set of data to forecast market events and is bound to foul himself up.

For example, in his role as a businessman, a corporation executive will seek to minimize future risks. Thus, if he is thinking of joining several other executives in order to invest in a local supermarket, he will try to determine what the past earnings of the supermarket were. If the earnings were good, while he has no way of being *certain* they will continue to be good, information about the past is *useful knowledge*. It relates in a very dynamic sense to the future. If the supermarket's accounts show that its earnings increased steadily every year, it is reasonable for him to assume that if he and the other executives buy into this business the earnings will be maintained in future years and they will all make a profit.

It is understandable why the executive might assume that the decision-making process that provided results in the case of the supermarket has a specific relationship to the conclusions upon which he can base his predictions in the stock market. In each instance he uses what he thinks is the raw material from which he can make a valid prediction about the future. The fact is that what passes for knowledge in the area of the supermarket is an opinion about future earnings which may be relevant under the given conditions. The danger, however, is that one may assume that those same opinions are valid in a situation where they have no legitimate application.

The conditions with the supermarket differ from those with the stock market in two ways: (1) The owner of the supermarket can lay claim to part of the assets of the supermarket; an investor in the stock of a corporation listed on the Stock Exchange has no claim to any of the assets of that corporation. (2) The value of ownership in the supermarket is totally dependent on the sales and earnings of the supermarket; the value of shares in the stock market has only a theoretical connection with the sales and earnings of a company's stock. Because good earnings can validate an investment in a supermarket, the assumption is often made that the earnings of a corporation listed on the NYSE tell the whole story about the conditions under which an investment can safely be made in a corporation's stock. To think this way is a mistake, though a common one.

Investors confuse words with conditions, not realizing that only identical initial conditions can lead to identical results. The crucial point here is that words that are perfectly satisfactory for use in one environment may carry implications that are factually wrong in another. The use of such words as "good earnings," for example, with the assumption implicit that they are an aspect of rising stock prices, tends to warp judgment. Consequently, it is impossible for most investors to identify a contradiction between *right* thinking and *their* thinking when they buy stock on the must only be considered as maps." The average investor's errors announcements. Because they equate words with conditions, investors come to be ruled by words.

In his book *Science and Sanity* the semanticist Alfred Korzybski stated: "If we reflect upon our languages we find that at best they must only be considered as maps." Theaverage investor's errors of judgment are a product of a distorted understanding of situations caused by inadequate and misleading verbal maps. His failures are a consequence of trying to use the same verbal maps that carried him successfully through one territory to carry him through another, altogether different territory.

For practical purposes, therefore, if the investor wishes to change his emotional reactions to market situations so that he can profit instead of lose in the market, he must be able to discard his old verbal maps and acquire the skills and intuitions that allow him to make new maps. In order to do this, the investor must learn to break with custom. This will be difficult, since individuals tend to be ruled by custom. What most investors have done is collect an inventory of routines and procedures that they associate with making money in the market.

For instance, it is customary for the investor to accept information secondhand from his stockbroker, a newspaper's financial page, or textbooks. He *assumes* they are well qualified to provide him with reliable information. Thus he fails to use his own senses to survey and research the environment in order to corroborate or discount the value of observations passed on to him by others. Customs such as these cause the investor to move through the market along well-trodden paths. It can be said, in fact, that virtually all the investor's actions conform to the formulas of custom. This condition is of course marvelous for Stock Exchange insiders, since the more the investor can be depended on to conform to established routines, the easier it is for insiders to anticipate and exploit him. It is hardly surprising, therefore, that as investors charge into the market at a rally high, a Stock Exchange's specialist is always there ready to ambush them as he meets them at the pass.

One of the investor's principal problems is that he has been trained to believe that he is investing in an auction market. He is unaware that the Stock Exchange's dominant tradition is deeply at variance with its dominant practice; that for the whole of the twentieth century there has been a fundamental conflict between the theory of an auction market and the whole scheme of the NYSE. Playing according to the rules of a game that has been rigged against them, investors have failed to recognize that they are the victims of Stock Exchange insiders who, unknown to them, completely control the market. As the market is now set up, investors are involved in a system of financial relationships that are not mediated by the laws of supply and demand but controlled by forces beyond the investors' control. Instead of being in an auction market, investors are confined within the framework of an internal operation manipulated by Stock Exchange insiders purely for their own profit. Its functions and limitations establish it as an institution whose processes are actually opposite to those of an auction market.

Thus, when the public buys stock, their demand is turned into a self-defeating financial weapon that beats down stock prices. Public buying has enabled Exchange insiders not only to divest themselves of their inventories of stock but then to employ practices that enable them to drop stock prices profitably in order to reaccumulate an inventory of stock at lower prices. Conversely, when the public sells, they sell to insiders who, firmly anchored in self-interest, will, once they have "filled their shelves" with an inventory of stock, raise stock prices in order to set the process in motion that will allow them to divest themselves of their inventories profitably. Obviously, such an institutional process in no way reflects the structure of an auction market.

Once specialists have established their stock's trend, their control over stock prices is such that neither the government, the corporations whose stock they supervise, nor their customers have the economic muscle to alter the internally controlled direction of that trend. Indeed, the specialist system is like a cartel whose members have divided among themselves the proprietary ownership of the stocks of the American corporate complex along with the exclusive right to determine the upward and downward movements of these stocks in the interests of their own merchandising objectives. That's money power enough to stagger the night thoughts of any Mafia leader.

Most investors will probably never make money in the market over the long run unless they learn to look at the market as a merchandising operation in which specialists manipulate stock prices in order to sell at retail what they bought at wholesale price levels. If investors wish to preserve their savings and see them grow, they must scrap traditional approaches to the market and learn how to time their transactions so that they buy when these insiders buy and sell when they sell.

It is necessary, therefore, to begin with a brief description of who these specialists are and how they dominate the market. There are approximately 360 specialists who operate on the floor of the NYSE. The role of the specialist would be easier to define if he had only one function. But as it happens, he has two, and neither is consistent with the other. In one he is involved in a concrete situation in which, according to theory, he is a fiduciary with all the obligations and responsibilities pertaining thereto. He acts as your broker's broker to facilitate the execution of your transactions. Accordingly, if you wished to buy or sell 100 shares of a stock, you would place the order with your broker. Your broker would then wire your order to his firm's broker on the floor of the Exchange. He in turn would then proceed to the post where the specialist registered in the stock you wanted to buy was located. Since the specialist presumably does not know whether your broker wants to buy or sell, his response to your broker's request for a quote is to give him the highest bid (to sell) and the lowest offer (to buy). In this instance the specialist might quote your broker 60½ bid to 60¾ offered for the stock. In an effort to get a better price for you, your broker might then offer

$60\frac{5}{8}$ in the hope he could save you $\frac{1}{8}$ of a point. Failing that, he would raise his bid to $60\frac{3}{4}$, at which point the specialist would call out "sold"! He then "gives up" to your broker the name of the broker who entered the sell order and sends a report of the sale to the seller's broker. Rules and regulations supposedly circumscribe the specialist's conduct as he functions in this capacity.

But the specialist, as it happens, has another role in which he is happily free to abandon his responsibilities as an agent with its specific fiduciary obligations to the public in order to trade or invest for himself in competition with the public. What does it matter if the specialist's quote is $60\frac{1}{2}$–$60\frac{3}{4}$ today if tomorrow, in order to satisfy his hasty capriccios, you must pay $65\frac{1}{2}$ or 70, or accept $55\frac{1}{2}$ (or even 29)? There are few investors who trade with him when he serves them as an agent who are not trod into the dust when he invests for himself in competition with them.

To the specialist his role as a broker's broker is in many ways a by-product of his function as an investor for himself. He looks upon his function as a fiduciary as a side issue (albeit, highly profitable) that is conducted in order to grant a semblance of legitimacy to his more profitable activities as an investor and trader for himself. When they learn of his dual functions, there are few investors who do not immediately express the wish that they would like to spend the rest of their lives as specialists. Thus, on first learning of his existence, almost the first question the investor asks is: "How do you become a specialist?" My answer is never too encouraging: "By being born the son of a specialist."

The financial activities of specialists are exceedingly diverse. Some operate their businesses as individuals; others as partnerships, corporations, or other kinds of joint venture. Subject to the same market conditions or situations, they will often react in different ways. There are at times incompatibilities of outlook, based on differences of interpretation, on how best to maximize profits or on whom should be given new listings. But always, in the pursuit of profits, the specialists have one thing in common: They are the owners of the Stock Exchange. This means they are the owners of an institutionalized system that, more than do the stockholders, directors, or officers of the companies under their jurisdiction, determines the overall direction of these companies' most important profit-making instrument—their stock prices.

Only under the most extraordinary circumstances would one specialist ever impair the financial interests of another specialist. Thus while the specialist conducts his affairs as he pleases, he does not conduct them as if he had no one else to account to. He conducts them according to the direction of the syndicate—of which he is one of the principal members. Recently, specialists have been putting pressure on the Exchange hierarchy for ever greater representation on the board of directors of the Stock Exchange Corporation. Late in 1974 they formed their own trade group. Believe it or not, they called it "The Association for the Preservation of the Auction Market." *The Wall Street Journal* of March 12, 1975, stated:

> According to the association's president, Harry M. Jacobson (who is a partner of Adler, Coleman & Co., one of the Exchange's largest specialist firms), the board needs more floor members because "*we are the owners of the business, and our livelihood depends on what the board does.*" Mr. Jacobson also has a few thoughts on Mr. Needham's role at the Exchange. "Mr. Needham's rapport with membership could stand for much improvement," he says, adding that he and many of his floor colleagues were rankled because Mr. Needham was at an international financial conference in Paris for the week preceding the board's historic meeting on whether to sue the SEC on rates.

Needham was probably conducting a search for courage on the Champs Elysées. As a former commissioner of the SEC, Needham, it is obvious, would have preferred to be absent rather than place himself in the anomalous position of suing the agency whose steadfast assistance had enabled him to get the chairmanship of the New York Stock Exchange.

Specialists who control important and highly active stocks can turn the market into a powerful instrument for the maximization of their profits and financial resources. In his mid-twenties Michael Meehan was a very popular theater ticket agent on Broadway. Then in 1918 he joined the Wall Street fraternity as a member of what was then called the New York "Curb." It later became known as the American Stock Exchange. In less than two years, like many other of his associates, he demonstrated he had the ability to adapt himself to the realities of his new business by buying a seat on the NYSE. That was in 1920.

The beginnings of Meehan's enormous fortune were largely his acquisitions in the stock of Radio Corporation of America. These began in 1924, when RCA became listed on the NYSE. Because of his heavy accumulations in this stock, Meehan became recognized as the "specialist" in RCA. As the 1929 bull market moved to its peak, it is alleged that his trading in the stock of RCA brought his profits to in excess of $25 million. (The RCA he had acquired at $40 rose to the equivalent of $570 in 1929.) His seat on the Exchange employed eight different people, and his nine offices more than 400.

It is also alleged that, in 1929, Meehan was one of the masterminds in one of the largest of the pooling operations that took place in RCA. Most of these transactions went through Meehan's firm, whose commissions were supposed to have totaled $853,000. The five principal members of the pool, each of whom deposited $1 million, were Mrs. M. J. Meehan, Nicholas F. Brady, Thomas J. Reagan, W. F. Kenny, and John J. Raskob.

In *Mystery Men of Wall Street*, published in 1930, the author, Earl Sparling, wrote at length about Mike Meehan, who was then still the specialist in RCA:

> In ten years he had garnered somewhere from $5 million to $25 million, had pushed his way into the ranks of stock market immortals and his firm had salted away eight Stock Exchange seats—some $2,400,000 worth of them, the largest number ever held by a commission house. . . .
>
> . . . There probably isn't a person in the country who knows ABC about stocks who doesn't know the story of Meehan and Radio—how he, the newcomer, engineered that equally new, untried, non-dividend stock into more than a 500 point rise, including 61 points in four spectacular days. . . .
>
> . . . There were rumors in Wall Street that he got caught in the crash. It can be stated authentically that he didn't. . . .

A logical investigation of the specialist's economic power will reveal that when he's a Meehan, one of the principal attributes of his role as a specialist is that he is never caught in a down market.

The nature of the society into which Mike Meehan had fitted himself satisfied his ambitions until the SEC was forced by public outcry to separate him from the NYSE. As I stated in *The Wall Street Jungle* (page 10):

> After an investigation into the shifting subleties of Michael Meehan's activities in July, 1937, the SEC alleged that his activities were in violation of the law. The SEC stated its decision regarding Meehan in these words: "The gravity of his conduct leads us to conclude that the penalty should be expulsion from all the national securities exchanges of which he is a member. An order to this effect will accordingly be issued."

But there are always more institutionally suitable ways for overcoming the chaos of a specialist's passions than a jail sentence. Hence it was decided that Meehan would be allowed to resign. However, lest it be assumed his firm's operations were in any way inferior to the operations of other specialist companies, the Exchange allowed the Meehan firm to continue under the aegis of his sons and heirs, Bill and Joseph Meehan. Following is a current list of stocks under the firm's supervision:

Amerada Hess (AHC)
Amsted Industries (AD)
Commercial Solvents (CV)
Deere & Co. (DE)
Elixir Industries (EXR)
Ethyl Corp. (EY)
Citicorp (FNC)
Georgia-Pacific (GP)
Ideal Basic Industries (IDL)
Jim Walter (JWC)
Louisiana Pacific (LPX)
Matsushita Electric Industries ADR (MC)
NCR Corp. (NCR)
Oklahoma Natural Gas (ONG)
RCA (RCA)
Richmond Corp. (RCP)
Texas Eastern Transmission (TET)
Wheelabrator-Frye (WFI)

Money is Aladdin's lamp. Not surprisingly, therefore, wherever big money is involved, trouble moves with it like a cloud of flies around a steer. Not the least of life's evils, then, and for which there is small help, is that it should be the source of trouble between brothers who also happen to be specialists. In any event, faced with an oppressive situation allegedly caused by policy differences, Joseph Meehan parted company with his brother William in May 1971. *The New York Times* said he

> left the firm in what Wall Street sources described as a policy dispute with his brother. . . . the Wall Street sources said the breakup would have no impact on the markets and the securities involved. . . . in addition, Joseph Meehan's son, Michael, left the Meehan firm earlier this year to join Salomon Brothers. . . . according to reliable sources . . . disagreements were said to have cropped up as early as 1962, although in the past they were always patched up. . . .

Joseph moved across the floor to establish himself and a community of interests at Post One with the 110-year-old specialist firm of Henderson Brothers as vice chairman and director. It is doubtful if anyone ever performed more handstands than Charles Henderson, who at this time holds specialist books in 40-odd companies. "Mr. Meehan brings to the management of our company broad experience and a distinguished record of achievement. . . ." In addition to the Ford Motor Company, Joseph Meehan also brought to Henderson Brothers the specialist books in Fairchild Camera, Southwestern Public Service, and Oklahoma Gas & Electric. Following is a current list of stocks under the supervision of Henderson Brothers, Inc.:

Arlen Realty & Development (ARE)
Armada Corp. (ABW)
Aro Corp. (ARO)
Bache & Co. (BAC)
Bankers Trust N.Y. (BT)
Bausch & Lomb (BOL)
Bendix Corp. (BX)
Benguet Consolidated Class B (BE)
Bobbie Brooks (BBK)
California Financial (CFI)
Callahan Mining (CMN)
Continental Mortgage Investors SBI (CMI)
Crane Co. (CR)
Fairchild Camera & Instruments (FCI)

Ford Motor (F)
General Host (GH)
Great Northern Iron Ore (GNI)
H & R Block (HRB)
Honeywell, Inc. (HON)
Intercontinental Division (ICD)
International Multifoods (IMC)
Interstate Brands (IBC)
Loral Corp. (LOR)
Meredith Corp. (MDP)
Molycorp, Inc. (MLY)
New England Telephone & Telegraph (NTT)
Northwest Industries (NWT)
Oklahoma Gas & Electric (OGE)
Overnite Transportation (OVT)
Parker Pen (PKR)
Peabody-Galion (PBD)
Penn Central (PC)
Penn Fruit (PFR)
Pennsylvania Co. (PNV PR)
Peter Paul (PPI)
Ponderosa System (PON)
Reading Co. (QRDG)
Richardson Co. (RCS)
Robertson, H. H. (RHH)
Rochester Teleprompter (RTC)
Sangamo Electric (SGM)
Southdown, Inc. (SDW)
Southwestern Public Service (SPS)
Tishman Realty & Construction (TIS)
U.S. Home (UH)
Wometco Enterprises (WOM)

Between them the Meehan family can be said to control the stock prices (and the destinies) of more than 60 of the industrial complex's major corporations.

A Zen handclap should go to young Meehan, since the value of his seat on the Exchange and family connections rated him a partnership with Salomon Brothers. Now when Salomon Brothers wishes to distribute a stock registered with either Meehan & Company or Henderson Brothers, they have an insider who is a master of the routines and has the ear and the confidence of both specialist units along with whatever information he needs to do a good job.

People who invest in the market usually don't spend much time thinking about the specialist, why he is important and why he should be very carefully supervised and regulated—until there is an awesome crash in the market. At such times the public clamors for an investigation of the stock market. Since most of those in government doing the investigating are beholden to the Stock Exchange in one way or another (via campaign contributions or through their law firms), or hope (if they are commissioners and chairmen of the SEC) to be employed in the securities industry at some not too distant date, nothing ever comes of these investigations. Those in government charged with the administration of the securities industry and who conduct these investigations are fully aware that since the turn of the century the findings of such investigations have centered on the fact that the deep and inexorable crises of the stock market are caused by the failure of specialists to operate the market in a fair and orderly manner when acting as dealers for themselves while in competition with the public. According to the "Report of the Special Study of Securities Markets and Exchange Commission" of 1963:

> Specialists are at the heart of the problem of organization, management and disciplinary procedures of the exchange. . . . the misuse of their role in the operation of a fair, orderly auction market and the breakdown of regulatory and disciplinary controls over them— . . . are part of a complex pattern of interlocking causes and effects. It is for

this reason that any program of reform must concentrate heavily on the dominant role of the specialist.

In the past even the most public-spirited investigation of the specialist system, which was the 1963 Report, declined to acknowledge the exact manner in which specialists employed their merchandising strategies to maximize profits for themselves. Part of the reason is that specialists are not bound by either the rules of the Exchange or the SEC to inform the public or anyone else about the specifics of all their transactions. The SEC's report did, however, pointedly insist that the specialists' conduct did not conform to the established code. Where their most important practices were concerned, specialists employed techniques which were impossible for the public to follow because of the specialists' unwillingness to provide the public with information concerning the details of their activities. In particular, it singled out the specialists' use of the short sale.

Under ordinary circumstances, an individual buys stock in anticipation of a subsequent rise in price which will enable him to sell it at a profit. When an individual sells short, he reverses the process by first selling the stock in anticipation of a subsequent *decline* in price which will enable him to then buy it back at a lower price. His profit (or loss) is the difference between the price at which he first sells the stock and the price at which he later purchases it. When an investor wishes to sell short, i.e., to sell stock he does not yet own, his brokerage firm will normally arrange to "borrow" the stock from their or another brokerage firm's pool of securities, with the understanding that at a later date the investor will return the shares. This investor is then able to make delivery with his borrowed stock to the party to whom his broker sold it. When the investor later makes his "covering" purchase of the stock, he is then able to return the shares he borrowed to clear his obligation. The act of selling stock which an individual does not own is called "short selling," while his subsequent purchases are referred to as "short covering."

When a specialist uses the short sale, the process is basically the same. There is, however, one important difference. When an individual sells a stock short, he *thinks* the price of the stock will decline, whereas the specialist's short sale is based on the certainty that he intends taking the price of the stock down. The power of the short sale can be seen in the manner in which this instrument allows specialists to control completely the forces of supply and demand so that ultimately they can raise and lower prices at will. In the hands of the specialist the short sale is a triumph of human ingenuity. Thanks to the nature of the instrument and its paradoxical functions, the short sale enables specialists to determine the short-, intermediate-, and long-term price objectives of their stocks.

Examples of how short-sale rules have been distorted for the benefit of insiders with the aid of the SEC can be found in *The Wall Street Gang*. In 1938 the Commission enacted a short-selling rule that prohibited Stock Exchange members from "demoralizing the market" by effecting short sales at or below a price lower than that of the last sale. This rule was meant to prevent "short sellers from accelerating a decline by exhausting all remaining bids [offers to buy—RN] at one price level, causing successively lower price levels to be established. . . ."

The Wall Street Gang presented documented evidence showing that the SEC provides specialists with a loophole that allows them to "demoralize the market by selling short on downticks" (without having to report these transactions as short sales) whereas the public can only sell short on upticks. (A transaction that is executed on an uptick occurs at a higher price than the last preceding price, while a transaction that is executed on a downtick occurs at a lower price than the last preceding price.) Indeed, investors have remained totally unaware of the myriad controls over individual stock prices and the market as a whole accruing to specialists through their use of the short sale.

Lest my statement that the specialist is able to manipulate stock prices at will seem far-fetched, the SEC's Special Study

Report provides an illustration that documents this conclusion. Quoting Bill Meehan when he was the specialist in Ford, the Report provides us with an insider's view into a process in which specialists are able virtually to guarantee a profit for themselves in the course of a long bear market. Meehan shows us that he was able to do this by selling short and then lowering his stock's price to levels at which he then "covered" his short sales:

> Not that I am any student of charts, but I took a look at the Ford chart and it looked very dangerous to me. . . . I liquidated our whole position and went short and we have maintained a short position, actually in only three of our stocks, all the way through, practically, during this whole period. During the day, we have become long, but almost every night, we were short stock. [SSR, Part 2, page 113]

In order to understand the implications of what Meehan is saying, it is important to understand that when specialists rally stock prices, public buying is attracted. Conversely, when specialists drop the prices of their stock, the public on balance can be expected to sell. Thus Meehan, in the course of dropping the price of his stock in the market crash of 1962, accumulated an inventory of stock in the morning (in all probability most often at or near the market opening) from investors who, frightened by the decline that was taking place in the stock and fearful of a further decline, had entered their orders to sell. Thereafter, he was able to reduce his inventory by rallying stock prices—the rally attracting public demand in sufficient quantities to enable him not only to liquidate his trading account "during the day" but to "short stock" "almost every night" (afternoon—RN). As we see, his short sales were indispensable to taking down stock prices profitably in a bear market, in this case in what was one of the worst bear markets encountered by investors in more than a generation. Equally important for us to recognize is that this example documents the manner in which the short sale enables specialists to manipulate their stock prices up and down at will regardless of whether the market is a bull or a bear.

A *Business Week* article of December 4, 1971, stated that "if specialists' apparent monopoly looks like a license to steal, the specialists have an answer. 'If we make so much money,' they argue, 'why isn't everyone else trying to get into our business?'" When outsiders do investigate the possibility of this, they discover that it is probably easier to become a member of the British Royal Family.

Each of the specialist's privileges has a decisive influence on the destinies of investors; some offer him more opportunities for profit than others. Unknown to most investors, in addition to the profits from their trading accounts, specialists have what are called "long-term segregated investment accounts." Commenting briefly on these sources of specialist income, an article in *Business Week* of December 4, 1971, stated that the SEC's 1970 Institutional Investor Study had calculated that specialists make between 84 and 192 percent a year on their capital. The article stated, however, that the study had "ignored specialist investment accounts." The fact is that although the SEC has from time to time mentioned specialists' returns from their trading accounts, it has always consistently refused to provide any information concerning profits from a specialist's business or his investment accounts.

Observation of the specialist's activities reveals that once he has sold out his investment account and established a short position at his stock's high, his long-term objective is then to take stock prices down to wholesale price levels in order to cover his short sales and once again accumulate stock. The establishment of these accounts is, of course, the signal for a noticeable shift in the specialist's posture toward his stock's price trend. Once he accumulates or distributes his stock for his investment accounts, the manner and intent of his activities will be biased toward advancing or lowering his stock's price in order to maximize his personal profits.

Another feature of the investment account involves the manner in which the specialist links it with his trading account for both distribution and tax-planning purposes. The tax advantage the investment account offers is that it enables specialists to declare as long-term capital gains what are legitimately short-term capital gains. If, for example, he acquires a position in his investment account at his stock's low and advances his stock's price to its high in less than a six-month capital gains period, he can employ his investment account to turn what would otherwise be short-term gains into long-term gains. To do this he would liquidate whatever stock he has in his trading account at the high and then establish a major short position in that account. Then all he need do is wait until the six-month capital gains period has passed to qualify the accumulations in his investment account for long-term capital gains and deliver over those shares from the investment account to cover the short positions in his trading account. In this manner he can legally call his profits "long-term."

It was interesting for me to learn that this matter is of little concern to many investors. In fact, the comment of one was "So what? Everyone wants to save on taxes. Why shouldn't he be able to just like everyone else?" What my friend had failed to grasp was that the issues involved were far more important than whether or not specialists are allowed to enjoy the tax benefits of turning short-term gains into long-term gains. The issue, in fact, is whether or not millions of investors should be subjected to rhythmic market booms and busts so that specialists can establish their capital gains. It is also worth observing that if the matter were not of such an obvious and pressing nature, the specialist study group would not have so well presented the dark side of the issue (Special Study Report, Part 2, page 133):

> Purchases made on the Exchange for the purpose of segregation into *long term investment accounts* raise problems which go to the heart of the specialist system. The specialist

> is permitted to trade for his own account only when such trades affirmatively contribute to the maintenance of a fair and orderly market. . . . Where the specialist goes into the market with the intention of segregating the securities purchased and not with the purpose of creating a fair and orderly market, the trading is clearly contrary to the statutory and regulatory standards. Beyond this, the specialist with a long term position now has a stake in seeing that the securities rise in price—he has become an investor as well as a dealer. . . .
>
> A further problem arises when the specialist who maintains such long term accounts is required to sell stock to maintain a fair and orderly market and he has no stock in his specialist trading account. . . . [If] the six month period of the tax statute is almost over, the specialist may well be tempted to keep his stock in the long term account and neglect the needs of the market.

In reply, the NYSE maintained that specialists have a perfect right, like anyone else, to accumulate stock as investors and stated that "it believes that it is perfectly proper for the specialist unit to carry stock in a long term investment account. . . ." It terminated further discussions with the SEC on this matter with the statement that "further discussion of this question between the Exchange and the SEC has been deferred. . . ." This is the meaning of self-regulation.

It has been argued that great changes have occurred since the Special Study of 1963. In an article on page 10 in the June 1975 issue of *New York* magazine by Dan Dorfman, Arnold I. Minsky, who was a NYSE specialist for nine years and is now the head of his own consulting firm, offers some insight into this opinion:

> The Big Board is increasingly willing to let specialists bend the rules. . . . You've got increasingly flagrant situations

> . . . where if a specialist is long a stock [that is, he owns it] he simply raises the offering price, enabling him to make more money on his position. And if he is short a security, he drops the bid price more precipitously, enabling him to cover his short at a better profit. . . . Investors should be up in arms about the way many specialists are handling their securities. . . .

So too, one would imagine, should the SEC. For many years the SEC's methods of surveillance over the Exchange have been a source of mystery. When, for example, do SEC officials visit the Stock Exchange, and what checks do they maintain over the specialists' practices? These questions were answered for me in the course of a telephone conversation with an SEC official in March, 1975:

> Specialists are under the Exchange. We don't get too concerned with them. They're not directly regulated by the Commission. They all operate under self-regulation. They make their own rules—the Commission just o.k.'s them. Only if the Commission feels there is something not proper does it take exception. We check broker-dealers but we never go onto the Exchange to check out specialists.

Understanding this, we can begin to perceive why specialists are now being allowed to do quite openly what is still forbidden by the rules of their own Exchange. At present, for example, specialists are forbidden by Rule 113 from accepting directly from institutions any orders in their specialty stocks. Recently, however, institutions have been bypassing Rule 113 and their brokers and placing their orders directly with specialists. In an article in the May, 1975, issue of the *Institutional Investor*, page 33, entitled "Why Are Specialists Trying to Improve Their Image?" an important specialist stated that despite the existence of the rule, "113 is a dead issue."

Formerly, investment bankers and stockbrokers, by acting as their intermediaries, maintained the distance between specialists and institutions. Now that institutions are breaking these ties, specialists are faced with a situation in which they are pitted against each other in obtaining institutional business. The problem is further compounded for specialists by the inception of the new central market, which will present them with the prospect of increased competition for business from other Exchanges. Thus institutional traders have recently been faced with the curious spectacle of the Stock Exchange's usually arrogant, immovable high priests scurrying around Wall Street, soliciting business like common stockbrokers. In the article in the *Institutional Investor* one bank's head trader stated: "Since December we've had three of them over here, that's two more than we've seen in the previous three years." The Bank of America's trader also observed that specialists were revising earlier behavior patterns in the spirit of rapprochement: "We went for years without seeing specialists, but now we've seen two of them in just four weeks."

The article describing this new attitude of specialists toward institutional traders was sent to me by Senator Lee Metcalf. What we both found most interesting about the article was not so much the regulatory indifference to Rule 113 but rather the attitudes of institutions toward specialists' practices and what specialists revealed about their own activities.

The article pointed to the fact that the ruthless autonomy of the specialist is considered standard fare. According to the trader of one brokerage house, 50 to 75 percent of institutional traders consider the "majority of specialists . . . incompetent or dishonest."

Specialists are accustomed to the harsh opinions of institutional traders, and have regarded them like water off a duck's back. But now, specialists recognize that the indifference to criticism which has carried the day in the past will no longer be to their best advantage. Thus, in the same article, we have Donald Stott of the all-powerful specialist firm of Wagner, Stott (Xerox, Gulf Oil, International Telephone & Telegraph, etc.) yielding to an unusual degree of protocol. Observing that when an institutional customer is dissatisfied with an execution, Stott wants him to come and "talk it over." The solution he suggests is unique in the vexed craft of finance: "If I've done something and it's wrong, give me a chance to apologize."

The statement in the article that I found most intriguing, however, was the confession of a specialist who admitted in effect that he had sinned but would sin no more. He confessed that he had "learned" not to make institutional traders look bad by buying their stock from them at its low and then trying to "force the stock back up." Apparently he had been told that "if the stock moves back up the fund manager will come in and tell his trader, 'You dummy, you did it again. You sold at the low.'" Presumably this specialist symbolized the conscience of a community of insiders who had become fearful that, "if we make enough of those traders look bad, maybe they won't come back . . . and we need them back in."

Although my big block charts provide countless instances of specialists "forcing" stocks up (and down), I did not expect to see this practice so candidly revealed by a specialist. The fact is, the big blocks of institutional traders are still taken at a discount, and specialists still "force the stock up" either within the hour or the next day.

For as many years as specialists have been in business, investors have sought to obtain data on their incomes. Not surprisingly, the Exchange has refused to grant access to this information. It would have been absurd for specialists to surrender their income data voluntarily, since it has been through secrecy and the lack of regulation that they have been able to turn a humdrum job into a several-million-dollar-a-year job. Not only would this data reveal too much of the specialist's Sinbad-like voyage into paradise, but more importantly, when the years were examined in which he had made his fortunes, the figures would reveal the enormous profitability for him of a bear market. That is what is most important about the income data that form the core of the next chapter. Although they reveal only the tip of the iceberg, they reveal that tip with a historic and graphic clarity.

3

Specialist Income or Breathes There a Man with Heart So Tough Who Thinks $300 Million Ain't Enough?

Ney's Fourth Axiom: When we learn what a man is most anxious to hide, we also learn why he wants to hide it.

Self-regulation grants the specialist his power. It is the myths that surround him that sustain that power. Lacking the nourishment of fact about the specialist system, investors have been overfed and underprivileged by the media's fictions. Chief among these fictions is the belief, firmly embedded in investor consciousness, that the risks and financial losses suffered by specialists far outweigh those suffered by investors. This belief is fostered by the mercurial imaginations of financial columnists who (probably after receiving a call from the Stock Exchange News Bureau) bombard their readers with the idea that, in the course of a major bear market, specialists "have to sit there and take it." *Time* magazine, for example, carried this story in its August 10, 1970, issue:

> The well-publicized clobbering that Wall Street's professionals have taken during this year's slump has hit nobody more than the men who make the markets on the stock exchange floors—the specialists. Estimates of the losses absorbed by the 470 specialists on the New York and American stock exchanges run to tens of millions of dollars. That is not surprising, considering the seemingly thankless job that these insiders have. They are supposed to buy when most investors are selling and sell when most are buying.

The truth is deodorized even by the most well-intentioned financial writers. In a Washington *Post* column of May 4, 1970, Philip Greer described the visit to President Nixon of Bernie Lasker, one of the Exchange's most important specialists:

> Wall Street made a pilgrimage to Washington . . . trying to find somebody, anybody in the White House to listen to the tale of woe. . . .
>
> For emphasis, they only had to show off the battle scars in their checkbooks.

I had been trying since 1963 to obtain specific, documented information regarding specialist income, particularly the income from their investment accounts. In the course of a television debate with a financial writer in Chicago, I maintained that specialist firms in active Exchange stocks made millions of dollars each year. My comments were referred to as a "remarkable blend of ignorance, invention, and arbitrary assumption." I was certain, however, that specialists enjoyed an income commensurate with their power and its multiple and divergent purposes. My own long familiarity with their life-styles and the power of their financial resources lent credence to my opinion. I perhaps learned more about this subject, however, from the practical experience of an association with Ira Haupt, the head of a New York Stock Exchange specialist firm registered in Mobil Oil, Gillette, and many other stocks. As the financial consultant for his Beverly Hills office, I soon learned why the formulas of the Stock Exchange invest the *dolce vita* of the specialist with privileged insights into opportunities for profit.

I met Haupt in early 1962. My offices were in the same building as his brokerage firm. One morning, some time just before noon, a slightly portly, elegantly dressed gentleman was escorted into my office by an old friend, Bill Blatner. Blatner headed Mr. Haupt's operations in California. He introduced us, and we walked out onto the terrace of my office. I have always had a fondness for gardens, and I had filled the terrace with flowers and hanging baskets filled with plants of all kinds. The place was a refuge for me from the more fashionable but unfeeling aspects of the Beverly Hills business environment. I had arranged to have luncheon served on the terrace, and while the food was being prepared, drinks were served and we talked. I recall being enormously impressed by Haupt when he looked about and, in his quiet voice, as though speaking to no one in particular, said, "There is nothing in the whole world more worthwhile than the creation of something that is beautiful." "What about the creation of money?" I asked him. Very feelingly, he turned to me and with something like scorn in his voice said, "A distraction of the devil."

In the course of our luncheon he said he wanted me to consider becoming the investment consultant for his Beverly Hills office. He evinced the keenest possible interest in my approach to the market. When I had finished describing my methods of operation his only comment was "I think a relationship might be mutually advantageous." I told him I would like to think about it. We then discussed other things. We met again a month or so later at my place in New York, and I agreed to provide his office with purchase and sale recommendations. I was singularly impressed by the generosity of his retainer.

I had received wide recognition in *Time* magazine and other periodicals for having called the market crash of 1962, and there was no doubt in my mind that Haupt had retained my services more for the benefits my name might bring to his office than any belief he might have had in my insights into the stock market. The techniques I employed at the time were virtually the same as those of most market technicians. This meant they were a compound of flapdoodle and conventionality which served only to reaffirm the tenets of high risk propounded by the Stock Exchange and often confused with investment. It wasn't until late in 1963 that my researches revealed the Stock Exchange specialist as the heir to the American Dream of wealth, leisure, and total security. In the logical sequence of events it was after I had begun to describe the affluence of specialists that the conspicuous nature of our differences caused me to abandon my retainer with Mr. Haupt.

During the period of our relationship, however, I learned a great deal about the operations of the market from Haupt. Although he kept in touch with me personally, it was mostly through my close association with Bill Blatner that I discerned how pragmatic Haupt's approach to the market was. Everything about the man was, in demeanor and manner, traditional; yet the assumptions on which he based his investment decisions were those of an insider who operated on the basis of insider information.

It was my experience that while I had been retained to provide the customers of his brokerage firm with investment advice, as it turned out, the recommendations I gave them were generally based on suggestions that had been relayed to me by Haupt. I soon learned to confine my recommendations to his suggestions since this seemed to be his wish and since his ideas seemed to be more profitable than anything else I might have come up with on my own.

Apart from my conversations with him, on any number of occasions I was witness to telephone calls he made from New York to Bill Blatner which were often placed on Blatner's office intercom. The customers of Haupt's brokerage firm were thereby allowed to trade on the basis of the information he provided them as an insider. The facts of these occasions are best described by the man who was closest to Ira Haupt in affection and esteem—Bill Blatner.

Blatner was an old friend I will never forget. It was he who encouraged me to enter the investment business in 1961. Because of him my life is easier and more fulfilling. He died in 1972, still full of questions about people, life, and the investment business. For all his modesty and quietness of manner, he possessed a sense of identity that came largely from his position in the investment business and the high regard in which he was held by his contemporaries. Yet he was one of the most diffident and sensitive men I have ever known.

Bill had emphysema, contracted from a lifetime of cigarette smoking. Its corrosive physical force began to take its toll on him in the mid-sixties. Because my house was high on a hill overlooking Los Angeles and the air seemed better than almost any place else in the city, our doctor recommended that he spend his days at my home. For a time we thought it was improving his health. Our hopes were short-lived.

His life had been full of incident, mostly of conversations and experiences with people. We would talk about these on the terrace of my home. How well I recall sitting in the sun with him, listening to him speak in his low voice about his experiences of more than twenty-five years in the investment business. We would often reminisce about our first meetings in 1960. These took place in the Beverly Hills office of Bache & Company, where he was then resident manager.

When he discussed his relationship with Ira Haupt, I was unable to resist putting certain questions to him about the manner in which Haupt relayed investment recommendations to him. After he had answered some of these questions, I asked him if he would object to my taping our conversations on the chance that one day, through one of my books, his recollections might be of interest to investors. I told him I was particularly interested in any comments he had to make about the specialist system in general and his relationship with Ira Haupt in particular. He cut me short and said, "I could tell your readers stories that would make their hair stand on end."

I then began to record our conversations. It was apparent in the course of these talks that he had held Haupt in high esteem. In comparing Haupt to other specialists, Blatner maintained that "Mr. Haupt was a cut above anybody around." In the course of that same conversation about Haupt, he said: " . . . I feel an actual story here or there might give the public an idea of the odds that they are really fighting, and how bad the information is that is poured out by so-called brokerage firms, or wire houses, or retail firms, or whatever you want to call them. The particular situation I want to bring out is the one in the Amerada Oil Company. I'll start it this way by saying that when Ira Haupt opened his office on the West Coast . . . in 1962, I left Bache & Company to run the office for him. He put a great deal of money into it, and it was certainly the showplace of Beverly Hills. One of the things Ira wanted to do was to help the office out here. Mr. Haupt and I had a very warm feeling for each other, which also helped a great deal. As a result of this, in my office I had a direct phone to Mr. Haupt on the floor of the NYSE, where he was acting as specialist in his securities. He also had a couple of floor partners there with him, but he was the major person at his post and the one who made the decisions. At any given time he might place a call to me, stating that he liked the buying in a certain stock and wanted me to know it. This was always before real activity had appeared on the tape. Being a large office, we had many large trading accounts, which were made up of people who were there to speculate and trade securities on a risk basis. They were retired people, people in real estate, or people in oil who could stand short-term profits, taxwise, and this was really just another one of their investment businesses. Recommendations of securities were passed out to everybody who was in the office at the time via a speaker system. . . ."

"What would you say, for example, on the speaker system?" I asked.

"I would say that Mr. Haupt has just called and advised me that he likes the buying in XYZ stock, or Mr. Haupt may call me and say, 'There is important selling in XYZ stock.' That was it—the people who owned the stock might be interested in what was going on, or the people who did not own the stock might be interested in buying it; it's just that simple. As a result of the success of these calls, I was given discretionary power by a number of people as to the time to buy, or to sell a security if they had it. This was done because many times they were not available when these calls came. These were written powers of attorney and conformed to all security regulations. I did not think too much about this until I was in the New York office of Ira Haupt one day and one of Mr. Haupt's managing partners came up to me and said, 'Bill, I have noticed for the business that you are doing in certain securities that a group of people seem to take the same action at the same time and that they're always successful. I notice this is always done in quality stocks; we have checked and we know it is done by people who are in a position to do it; I'm not saying to you that there's anything that could be questioned about this, but I'm asking you how come you're always right? Where do you get your information?' And I said, 'Mr. Haupt calls me on the phone; it's just as simple as that.' He said, 'What do you mean, he calls you on the phone?' I said, 'He has a direct phone to me, and he calls me and tells me what he thinks; he just gives me his opinion; I pass on this opinion; you know, because you have approved the discretionary powers I have in certain accounts; there's no secret there; that's exactly what is done.' He looked at me and he said, 'Gee, I don't know, you certainly must be his favorite, because he doesn't do it with anybody else in the firm.' I said, 'That's something I don't know; I can just tell you how we do it.' Well, it seems that one day Ira called and stated that he liked the buying in Amerada. So we did our usual amount of business in that stock; it was selling at that time, as I recall, at around 55 to 60. After we had made our purchases, that afternoon Mr. Haupt, who had nothing to do with Amerada [as a specialist] as that was not one of his stocks, told me that he had received information of a large takeover by Amerada from another specialist with whom he had great rapport, great friendship, and a great deal of confidence."

"What year was this?"

"In 1963 . . .

"At the end of the first three or four days, we had probably a 6-, 7-point profit in Amerada. I received a call from Ira, who said, 'I know you have a nice profit; it is my opinion that you should not sell. You may see some denials by the company, by the president, but I would not sell. That is my advice to you; you may do what you want with it.' I said, 'Ira, that's fair.' Sure enough, the next day, there was an article in both *The New York Times* and *The Wall Street Journal*, in which the president of Amerada said he did not know why his stock was so active and so strong and that these rumors of a large find or a merger were completely unfounded. As a result of this statement during market hours, the stock turned down several points. People came to me who had bought the stock and said that they still had a nice profit and what was my advice? I said all I could say is from the information I had, these denials were not correct. Beyond that I can't tell you anything; the rest is up to you. A few people took their profit; most people stayed with it. The denials were forgotten by the next few days, and the stock again turned around and this time the stock got up to the high 90s."

"From what level was that?"

"That was from about the 73 to 75 level; it moved up to the high 90s, at which time another very strong denial was made, and this denial was made after the market had closed. Once again Mr. Haupt contacted me and said, 'Bill, as I told you the last time, my facts are still correct; it is going to take place in Amerada, and it is not too far in the offing. If people have stayed with it up till now, they have a great deal of profit to play with. It's my opinion that the stock should be held.' That was pretty much the end of that conversation. The next morning, as I recall, the stock opened down 4 or 5 points on a delayed opening, but before the day was over the stock had recovered most of its losses. . . . The situation turned out to be quite interesting and culminated in just a day or two over six months. But the merger was a fact, and Amerada had a value approximately 100 points above where we had started to buy it. I can only say that the people who stayed with it made a handsome profit; the people who got out of it on the way up made handsome profits; and the people who didn't buy it were sorry. The thing I'm trying to bring out here is that even though the top official and/or officials of a company come out and publicly deny things, the specialist in a stock is privy to information that is most confidential, most secret, and most inside."

The Amerada story is only one of many incidents that pointed to what Bill Blatner's and my own experiences had long before confirmed: that the specialist has unique opportunities to maximize profits for his own accounts and accounts in which he is indirectly interested.

However, although my researches strengthened my convictions about specialist profits, I had been unable until 1975 to obtain documentation that would provide my work with actual figures. Information that can improve the financial well-being of the average American consumer is almost impossible to come by. Certainly it is not possible without the commitment of a power source that, because of its links with government, is able to measure its achievements against those of the consumer's adversaries. It occurred to me to turn for help to Senator Lee Metcalf (D-Montana), who is a powerful consumer advocate.

Behind the activities of many legislators, there are often purely personal purposes that have nothing to do with the needs of those who elected them to office. That, however, is not the case with Senator Metcalf. As a former state Supreme Court justice and now a senator, he works conscientiously and anonymously on behalf of the commonweal. He has, for example, served the continuing struggle of consumers against the self-interest of public utilities. On February 26, I received the following:

SAM J. ERVIN, JR., N.C., CHAIRMAN
JOHN L. MCCLELLAN, ARK.
HENRY M. JACKSON, WASH.
EDMUND S. MUSKIE, MAINE
ABRAHAM RIBICOFF, CONN.
LEE METCALF, MONT.
JAMES B. ALLEN, ALA.
LAWTON CHILES, FLA.
SAM NUNN, GA.
WALTER D. HUDDLESTON, KY.
CHARLES H. PERCY, ILL.
JACOB K. JAVITS, N.Y.
EDWARD J. GURNEY, FLA.
WILLIAM B. SAXBE, OHIO
WILLIAM V. ROTH, JR., DEL.
BILL BROCK, TENN.

ROBERT BLAND SMITH, JR.
CHIEF COUNSEL AND STAFF DIRECTOR

SUBCOMMITTEE:
LEE METCALF, MONT., CHAIRMAN
JOHN L. MCCLELLAN, ARK.
EDMUND S. MUSKIE, MAINE
SAM NUNN, GA.
WALTER D. HUDDLESTON, KY.
WILLIAM B. SAXBE, OHIO
BILL BROCK, TENN.
CHARLES H. PERCY, ILL.
WILLIAM V. ROTH, JR., DEL.

VIC REINEMER, STAFF DIRECTOR
E. WINSLOW TURNER, CHIEF COUNSEL
161 RUSSELL BUILDING
(202) 225-1474

United States Senate
COMMITTEE ON
GOVERNMENT OPERATIONS
SUBCOMMITTEE ON BUDGETING, MANAGEMENT, AND EXPENDITURES
(PURSUANT TO SEC. 7, S. RES. 46, 93D CONGRESS)
WASHINGTON, D.C. 20510

26 February 1975

Mr. Richard Ney
10708 Stradella Court
Bel-Air, Los Angeles
California 90024

Dear Mr. Ney:

Enclosed is the material I received from the Securities and Exchange Commission in response to my request for information on Stock Exchange specialists' earnings.

I hope it proves helpful to you in writing your new book.

Best wishes.

Very truly yours,

Lee

Enclosures

SAM J. ERVIN, JR., N.C., CHAIRMAN

JOHN L. MCCLELLAN, ARK.
HENRY M. JACKSON, WASH.
EDMUND S. MUSKIE, MAINE
ABRAHAM RIBICOFF, CONN.
LEE METCALF, MONT.
JAMES B. ALLEN, ALA.
LAWTON CHILES, FLA.
SAM NUNN, GA.
WALTER D. HUDDLESTON, KY.

CHARLES H. PERCY, ILL.
JACOB K. JAVITS, N.Y.
EDWARD J. GURNEY, FLA.
WILLIAM B. SAXBE, OHIO
WILLIAM V. ROTH, JR., DEL.
BILL BROCK, TENN.

ROBERT BLAND SMITH, JR.
CHIEF COUNSEL AND STAFF DIRECTOR

SUBCOMMITTEE:
LEE METCALF, MONT., CHAIRMAN

JOHN L. MCCLELLAN, ARK.
EDMUND S. MUSKIE, MAINE
SAM NUNN, GA.
WALTER D. HUDDLESTON, KY.

WILLIAM B. SAXBE, OHIO
BILL BROCK, TENN.
CHARLES H. PERCY, ILL.
WILLIAM V. ROTH, JR., DEL.

VIC REINEMER, STAFF DIRECTOR
E. WINSLOW TURNER, CHIEF COUNSEL
161 RUSSELL BUILDING
(202) 225-1474

United States Senate

COMMITTEE ON
GOVERNMENT OPERATIONS
SUBCOMMITTEE ON BUDGETING, MANAGEMENT, AND EXPENDITURES
(PURSUANT TO SEC. 7, S. RES. 46, 93D CONGRESS)
WASHINGTON, D.C. 20510

10 February, 1975

Honorable Ray Garrett, Jr.
Chairman
Securities and Exchange Commission
Washington, D. C. 20549

Dear Mr. Chairman:

I would appreciate receiving information regarding Stock Exchange specialists' earnings. I am interested in data on the earnings, not only for their trading accounts, but also for their investment accounts.

Can you provide this information for me for the years 1970-74?

Very truly yours,

Lee Metcalf

SECURITIES AND EXCHANGE COMMISSION
WASHINGTON, D.C. 20549

OFFICE OF
THE CHAIRMAN

FEB 2 4 1975

Honorable Lee Metcalf
Chairman
Subcommittee on Budgeting,
Management and Expenditures
Committee on Government Operations
United States Senate
Washington, D. C. 20510

Dear Mr. Chairman:

This is in response to your letter dated February 10, 1975 in which you request information regarding stock exchange specialists' earnings for the years 1970-1974. Enclosed herewith are tables which contain income and expense information on specialists presently available to the Commission. Table 1 shows the income and expense data of New York Stock Exchange specialist firms not doing business with public customers for the years 1971-1973. At year-end 1973, there were 53 New York Stock Exchange member firms in this category. In addition, there were 28 specialist firms doing business with public customers in 1973 which are not shown in table 1 because their income from trading and investment accounts would include income from other activities not related to the specialist function.

Table 2 provides selected financial data for all American Stock Exchange specialist units. It should be noted that most of the American Stock Exchange specialist units are affiliated with New York Stock Exchange member firms.

Sincerely,

Ray Garrett, Jr.
Chairman

Enclosures

Note: Table 3–2 was not included, because we are concerned with the activities only of the specialists on the New York Stock Exchange.

TABLE 3–1
INCOME AND EXPENSE DATA
FOR NYSE SPECIALIST FIRMS
NOT DOING A PUBLIC BUSINESS

	1971		*1972*		*1973*	
Sources of Revenue	*Amount (millions)*	*Percent of Revenue*	*Amount (millions)*	*Percent of Revenue*	*Amount (millions)*	*Percent of Revenue*
Securities Commission Income						
Floor brokerage received	$ 45.5	42.8%	$42.7	44.6%	$37.6	66.5%
Other Securities Commission Income	.2	.2	1.0	1.0	3.5	6.2
Dealer Income	58.2	54.8	49.3	51.5	13.2	23.3
Dividends & Interest from Securities in Fire Investment Accounts	1.1	1.0	1.2	1.3	1.9	3.4
All other Income	1.3	1.2	1.4	1.5	.3	.6
Gross Revenue	$106.3	100.0%	$95.7	100.0%	$56.6	100.0%

Although I was delighted to have the one set of figures, I was disturbed that the Chairman of the SEC saw fit to supply the Senator only with information about specialists *not* doing business with the public. I had no idea there were such specialists. In any case, I wanted to have information involving the profits of specialists doing business with the public. I also saw fit to question the Chairman's assumption that the income data from specialist firms doing business with the public should not be included "because their income from trading and investment accounts would include income from other activities not related to the specialist function." I was certain it was impossible for specialists, whose only function (according to the Exchange) is to maintain a fair and orderly market, not to do business with the public in one way or another. Either through friendship or a reciprocal relationship with another specialist or investment banker, their investment and trading account profits *had* to be related to their functions as specialists. "Profits" is an ambiguous word and not an equivalent of "power," but profits in the financial establishment are always accompanied by power. Compelled to learn more about the whole matter, on March 7, 1975, I again imposed on Senator Metcalf's good will and time with another letter in which I said (in part):

> . . . Naturally I can't make any assumptions concerning the reasons why the Chairman decided not to provide the income statements of the specialists who deal with the public. It may be that he is being perfectly sincere. . . . I am perplexed, however, that he would not find it a simple matter to separate the sources of specialist income that are not directly attributable to his stock transactions for his trading and investment accounts. . . .
>
> It would be an enormous help and of much greater benefit to the public if at long last some information was provided that told us something about the profits of the 28 specialist units who conduct a public business.

> I would appreciate it therefore if I could impose on you one more time and ask you to request the Chairman to supply us with whatever information he has available concerning the income statements of these specialists. After all, what I am principally interested in is the annual income of these specialists from whatever source since it is apparent that if they derive income from their dealings with institutional bankers like Salomon Bros. by, for example, distributing their stock for them, their incomes are most certainly indirectly linked to their role as specialists dealing with the public. There are additional indirect ways of profiting from their position as specialists dealing with the public.

On March 15, I received a letter from Senator Metcalf, which I quote in part:

> I regret that the information supplied to me by the Securities and Exchange Commission was not wholly adequate for your needs. I have again written to Chairman Garrett to request that he provide me with the specific information on stock exchange specialists who conduct public business which you want. His reply will be forwarded to you.

Then on April 18, I received the following:

United States Senate

COMMITTEE ON
GOVERNMENT OPERATIONS
SUBCOMMITTEE ON REPORTS,
ACCOUNTING, AND MANAGEMENT
(PURSUANT TO S. RES. 111, 94TH CONGRESS)
WASHINGTON, D.C. 20510

18 April 1975

Mr. Richard Ney
10708 Stradella Court
Bel-Air
Los Angeles, California 90024

Dear Mr. Ney:

Enclosed is the reply I received from the Securities and Exchange Commission in response to my request for information concerning annual income statements of stock exchange specialists who conduct public business.

I hope the information proves to be helpful.

Best wishes.

Very truly yours,

Enclosure

[Mr. Ney has since changed his mailing address to Box H, Beverly Hills, California 90213.]

Along with his letter there was the following letter from Commissioner Philip Loomis of the SEC and the statement of specialist income:

SECURITIES AND EXCHANGE COMMISSION
WASHINGTON, D.C. 20549

OFFICE OF
THE COMMISSIONER

APR 1 1975

Honorable Lee Metcalf
Chairman
Subcommittee on Budgeting,
Management, and Expenditures
Committee on Government Operations
United States Senate
Washington, D. C. 20510

Dear Mr. Chairman:

In the absence of the Chairman and in response to your letter dated March 13, 1975 requesting annual income statement information for specialists who conduct business with public customers, I am enclosing information for NYSE specialist firms doing a public business for the years 1971-1973. Data for 1974 will not be available until August, 1975.

Sincerely yours,

Philip A. Loomis, Jr.
Commissioner

Enclosure

TABLE 3–2
INCOME AND EXPENSE DATA
FOR NYSE SPECIALIST FIRMS
DOING A PUBLIC BUSINESS

	1971		*1972*		*1973*	
Sources of Revenue	*Amount (millions)*	*Percent of Revenue*	*Amount (millions)*	*Percent of Revenue*	*Amount (millions)*	*Percent of Revenue*
Securities Commission Income						
Floor brokerage received	$ 28.6	10.5%	$ 30.8	10.4%	$ 21.3	16.9%
Other Securities Commission Income	130.9	48.0	152.1	51.1	75.3	60.0
Trading Income	46.2	16.9	43.8	14.7	9.4	7.5
Interest Income on Customers' Acct.	10.2	3.7	16.5	5.5	11.5	9.1
Underwriting Business	24.0	8.8	22.0	7.4	3.0	2.4
Sales of Investment Company Securities	1.2	0.5	3.2	1.1	1.2	0.9
Gain or Loss on Firm Investment[1]	15.8	5.8	11.7	3.9	(3.9)	(3.1)
All Other Income	15.8	5.8	17.5	5.9	8.0	6.3
Gross Revenue	$272.7	100.0%	$297.6	100.0%	$125.8	100.0%

[1]Of the 28 specialist firms which did business with public customers in 1973, six firms were not required to file income and expense information because their securities commission income was less than $10,000.

Source: X-17A-10 Reporst, Office of Economic Research, Securities and Exchange Commission.

Because of the inadequacy of the information made available by the SEC, the accuracy and completeness of one's assumptions are, necessarily, limited in scale. Nonetheless, the information provided by the foregoing income data offers us an opportunity to analyze and interpret evidence heretofore unavailable.

I have included the following chart of the Dow and the advance-decline line to give the reader a feeling for the period involved. Note that during the 1971–1974 period the overall market as evidenced by the advance-decline line was in a marked long-term downtrend. It is interesting to see that contrary to popular opinion a bear market enables specialists to rack up enormous profits. The Dow Jones during this period established a high in 1971, declined and then gradually climbed until the last quarter of 1972, when it closed the year with a sharp 2½-month rally. It then declined from the beginning of 1973 until the end of 1974. The divergent activity of the Dow provides us with the reasons why the income from the bear market years of 1971 and '72 was greater than the income from the bear market year of 1973.

Note the second row of figures marked "Other Securities Commission Income" in which the income in 1973 was approximately half that of 1971 and '72. The Dow rally highs of '71 and '72 account for the higher income in those years when specialists were able to obtain special fees and commissions from investment bankers who were unloading big blocks at that time. The year 1973 did not provide as large an income as usual from big block activity because it covered an intermediate phase in the market, the end of the decline not occurring until December, 1974.

Once again we can see the influence the Dow exerts over public thinking and how specialists and investment bankers are able to use this to their advantage. Another piece of evidence which supports this theory is the category marked "Underwriting Business." Income reached 24 and 22 million in 1971 and '72, but declined to 3 million in 1973. New issues, secondaries and

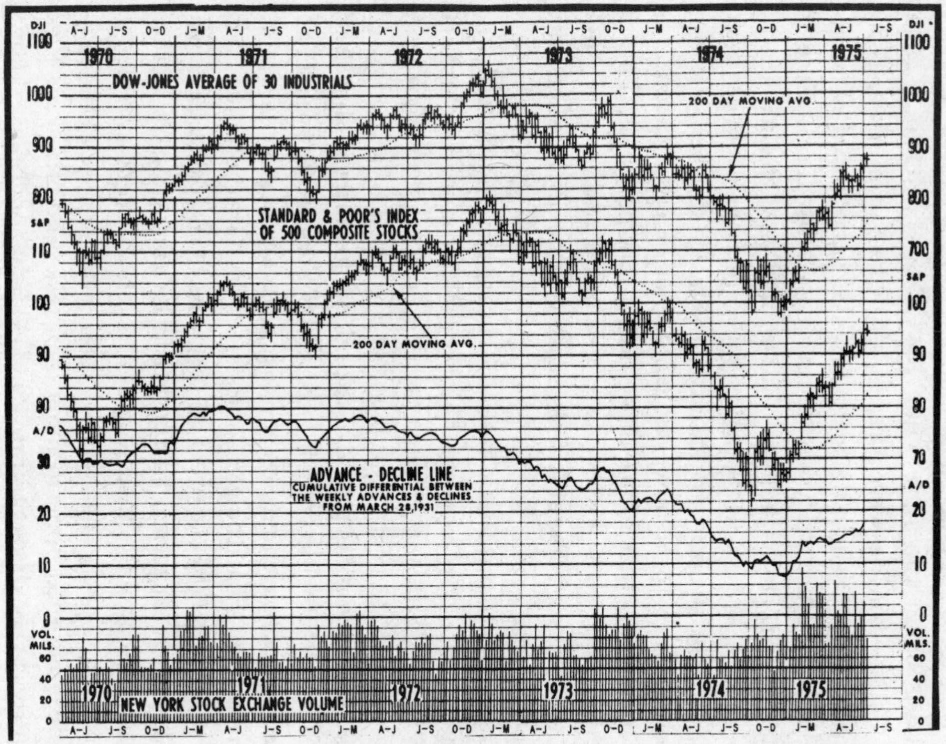
DOW-JONES AVERAGE OF 30 INDUSTRIALS
STANDARD & POOR'S INDEX OF 500 COMPOSITE STOCKS
200 DAY MOVING AVG.
200 DAY MOVING AVG.
ADVANCE - DECLINE LINE
CUMULATIVE DIFFERENTIAL BETWEEN THE WEEKLY ADVANCES & DECLINES FROM MARCH 28,1931
NEW YORK STOCK EXCHANGE VOLUME
1970
1971
1972
1973
1974
1975
DJI
S&P
A/D
VOL. MILS.

CHART 3–1

SOURCE: Trendline's Daily Basis Stock Charts

other distributions always fare better in the atmosphere provided by a rising Dow.

If we interpret "Firm Investment" to mean profits or losses from the firm's investment account, it is easy to see why the income is highest in 1971 while 1973 shows a deficit. Capital gains obtained in '71 were a result of the rise from May, 1970, to April, 1971, in which the overall market participated. The rise in 1972 was more selective (as evidenced by the decline in profits from 15 to 11 million) but a high *was* reached in the Dow, where heavy distributions for capital gains once again occurred. The majority of the investments established in terms of short sales in 1973, however, would not be covered until the 1974 bottom in order to maximize their profit potential. Thus it is conceivable that losses were established in 1973 while enormous profits from these short sales were not established until the end of 1974.

A footnote tells us that 6 specialist firms were not included in the figures for 1973 "because their securities commission income was less than $10,000." Hence the data for that year represents the income for 22 firms. Is it possible that these 6 firms showed unusually large profits in one of the other categories in that year, the disclosure of which might have raised a few eyebrows? Half-truths are the Exchange's escape hatch, its secret passageway to nondisclosure. Had their incomes been less in the other categories as reported by the other 22 specialist firms, past experience would seem to suggest that the Stock Exchange News Bureau would most certainly have seized on such an event in order to publicize it. Special handouts would have stressed the risks specialists assumed in performing their tasks and "the scars they had in their checkbooks to prove it." Alas, we will never know. Like the queens of a burlesque emporium, their figures are tantalizingly suggested and then, just as one expects total revelation, relentlessly withdrawn.

It is worth pointing out that unless there has been a change in the list of specialist firms doing business in listed stocks traded on the NYSE, my own count reveals that there are more than 75 specialist firms doing "business with the public." It would be interesting to know what the Chairman's definition of "doing business with the public" is. Moreover, if the income of the 28 listed here (and it would be nice to have their names) is acknowledged as being at (a minimum of) $297 million in 1972, what, it would be fair to ask, would the additional income amount to if the other 50-odd specialist firms were included?

It should be recognized, moreover, that despite the magnitude of the profits realized by the 28 specialist firms represented here, these figures are woefully inadequate. For unlike the data presented for specialists doing a "nonpublic" business, which includes information on the *income* from their investment accounts, the income from, not to mention the profit data for, specialists' personal (as distinct from their firm's) investment accounts is purposefully excluded from the information provided for specialists doing a public business. In addition, since the fringes are often brighter than the center, it would be important to know (1) what specialist profits are from the many accounts in which they have a direct and indirect interest; (2) what the profits are of their wives, daughters, sons, other relatives, and partners; (3) what profits are from investments in the accounts of other specialists; and (4) what profits are from secret omnibus* and foreign-based trading accounts.

Although specialists' financial credentials and self-regulated license are much to the point, they are minor compared to those for whom the specialist serves as flunkey. Thus while the specialist is important, we must not delude ourselves into ignoring his significance as doorman to those who come and go as they choose on the floor of the Exchange. I am, of course, referring to

*Omnibus accounts are accounts that are kept with another brokerage firm or a bank which allow the specialist to facilitate trading for himself under the bank's or brokerage firm's name.

the specialists' bankers. It would be interesting to learn the incomes they derive from their trading and investment accounts.

Another service these income figures provide is a rare public view of the regulatory attitude toward the Stock Exchange specialist. One can better understand why a job as commissioner of the SEC is, ultimately, so deeply appreciated and rewarded when one considers the doctrinal soundness of the Commission's hands-off policy concerning specialist practices. In view of these income figures from the SEC, one can only wonder about the present Chairman when, in an address before the Securities Industry Association meeting in Boca Raton (December 4, 1973), he stated that "those in the securities industry are entitled to bemoan the fact that almost all of them have had a rotten year financially." Using language to strafe reason, the Chairman had to be aware that while he was providing the industry's stockbrokers with a slap and a tickle, there were specialist firms that had incomes of millions of dollars that year.

What I find genuinely remarkable about the general ideas that lie at the bottom of the Commission's correspondence about either the Stock Exchange or the specialist system is that they appear to be not only ineffective but purposeless. Perhaps this is because, as John Kenneth Galbraith mentions in his *Economics and the Public Purpose:*

> Public regulatory bodies, it has long been observed, tend to become the captives of the firms that ostensibly they regulate. This is because the rewards of cooperation between the technostructure and the regulatory agencies normally outweigh those of conflict.

In the present instance the Commission's unwillingness to provide the data requested can be viewed as simple obedience to what they know would be the wishes of the Exchange. Thus, despite the ethical doctrine and obligations of the Commission, it remains fundamentally unconcerned with the investor's right to information.

The Commission's refusal to provide information on the profits of the specialists' investment accounts lingered in my mind. It was obviously reluctant to supply this information since its absence spared the Commission from the possibility of having to reconcile the specialists' cash flow with a working democracy's "auction market." Yet the income statements shine out to remind us that lying beneath the surface there are mysteries worthy of investigation. Thus while partial figures on the incomes of 28 specialist firms conjure up an image of robber barons, the important questions these figures raise leave one with the inescapable impression that as one rabbit is being pulled out of the hat, a dozen more are being kept carefully hidden.

Aware of Senator Metcalf's enormous interest and enterprise in this matter, I sent him a letter in which I discussed my convictions about the SEC's correspondence with him. It seemed to me that the adequacy and availability of the information provided by the Commission could be improved. I wondered too whether their management of information was meant to serve investors or the Stock Exchange. In a few days time I received a letter from the Senator with the following enclosure:

ABRAHAM RIBICOFF, CONN.

JOHN L. MC CLELLAN, ARK.
HENRY M. JACKSON, WASH.
EDMUND S. MUSKIE, MAINE
LEE METCALF, MONT.
JAMES B. ALLEN, ALA.
LAWTON CHILES, FLA.
SAM NUNN, GA.
JOHN GLENN, OHIO

CHARLES H. PERCY, ILL.
JACOB K. JAVITS, N.Y.
WILLIAM V. ROTH, JR., DEL.
BILL BROCK, TENN.
LOWELL P. WEICKER, JR., CONN.

RICHARD A. WEGMAN
CHIEF COUNSEL AND STAFF DIRECTOR

JOHN L. MC CLELLAN, ARK.
EDMUND S. MUSKIE, MAINE
SAM NUNN, GA.
JOHN GLENN, OHIO

BROCK, TENN.
CHARLES H. PERCY, ILL.
LOWELL P. WEICKER, JR., CONN.

VIC REINEMER, STAFF DIRECTOR
E. WINSLOW TURNER, CHIEF COUNSEL
161 RUSSELL BUILDING
(202) 224-1474

United States Senate

COMMITTEE ON
GOVERNMENT OPERATIONS
SUBCOMMITTEE ON REPORTS,
ACCOUNTING, AND MANAGEMENT
(PURSUANT TO S. RES. 111, 94TH CONGRESS)
WASHINGTON, D.C. 20510

23 May, 1975

Honorable Ray Garrett, Jr.
Chairman
Securities and Exchange Commission
Washington, D. C. 20549

Dear Mr. Chairman:

The information which Commissioner Loomis provided me regarding specialists who conduct business with public customers was informative and is appreciated. I commend the Securities and Exchange Commission for helping illuminate one of the more important aspects of stock trading.

I would appreciate your commission's response to the enclosed questions regarding specialists. Also could you provide me with the Commission's definition -- or the definition used by the Exchange -- of a specialist firm doing a public business, as opposed to a specialist firm not doing a public business.

Very truly yours,

ORIGINAL SIGNED BY
LEE METCALF

Enclosure

Concerning firms not doing a public business

1. Is there some profitable reason why so many more specialist firms are on the floor and *not* doing business with the public (53) compared to those who do business with the public (28)?
2. If not, why are most specialist firms not doing business with the public when the income data shows it is more profitable to do business with the public?
3. Since the Exchange maintains that the function of a specialist is to maintain "a fair and orderly market," what is the function of those specialists who do not deal with the public?
4. Does not this group enjoy a unique competitive advantage over the public when dealing for their investment accounts?
5. Why are only the "dividends & interest from securities in firm investment accounts" listed and not the profits from their investment accounts? Capitalizing $1.9 million at 3% would suggest their profits from this source would be in excess of $50 million.
6. What is the breakdown for "all other income"?
7. Re "interest income on customers' accounts": To what kind of customers do these firms grant credit since they do not do business with the public?
8. What are the specifics of their underwriting activities?
9. Are they also investment bankers? Do they associate their activities with investment bankers, and if so, in what capacity?
10. What services do they perform in order to receive floor brokerage income since they are not doing business with the public?
11. Do these specialists obtain their "dealer income" trading with the public?
12. How do they derive "dealer income" if they don't do business with the public?

13. Why did the number of specialist firms not doing a public business decrease from 63 in 1971 to 53 in 1972?

Concerning firms doing a public business

1. Why are their investment accounts not shown?
2. Why are their dividends and interest from their investment accounts not shown as is the case with specialists not doing business with the public?
3. "Other securities commission income" in 1973 is listed as $75.3 million, which is less than half of what it was in 1972. Yet daily volume on the NYSE in 1973 was much more than half what it was in 1972. What then is it that causes the great difference in these figures?
4. What is "firm investment"?
5. Under what category are the profits listed for their omnibus accounts?
6. Is any provision made for an accounting of the profits made by members of their families or other accounts in which they may have a direct or indirect interest?
7. Does their granting credit to their customers in any way restrict their capital requirements as specialists? Could they not keep larger trading accounts and, therefore, not have to short so much stock if they did not use their capital to finance customer loans?
8. Who are their customers?
9. Would not such customers obtain a competitive advantage over the public?
10. Can the income statements of their customers be made available?
11. Do these specialists use LIFO or FIFO inventory accounting?
12. What are the specifics of the losses supposedly established in 1973 on "firm investment"?
13. Could this be stock which was taken into inventory in the course of the November–December decline in the market and then subsequently sold at a profit in 1974?

14. Are the investment account profits and profits from the short sales established at the October–November 1973 market high included in this statement?
15. What were the profits established for investment accounts and short sales for that period?
16. In what ways can a specialist firm *not* doing business with the public work with specialist firms doing business with the public?

May I also have whatever data are available on the income (profits as well as dividends and interest) from specialist investment and omnibus accounts as well as a breakdown of the income obtained from trading in the stocks of other specialists? Do purchases and sales made in specialist investment accounts include stocks which are handled by other specialists?

On June 9, 1975, I received another letter from Senator Metcalf. It contained a reply from the SEC:

SECURITIES AND EXCHANGE COMMISSION
WASHINGTON, D.C. 20549

OFFICE OF THE CHAIRMAN

JUN 6 1975

Honorable Lee Metcalf
United States Senate
Washington, D.C. 20510

Dear Senator Metcalf:

This will acknowledge your letter, dated May 23, 1975, concerning specialist activity.

In order to furnish you with a prompt and complete response to your inquiry, I have referred your letter to Mr. Lee A. Pickard, and have asked him to prepare a report on this matter. You may expect to hear from me further as soon as I have received Mr. Pickard's report.

Sincerely,

Ray Garrett, Jr.
Chairman

I wondered whether the reply ultimately forthcoming from the SEC would be, in fact, provided by the SEC or by the NYSE.

On June 10, 1975, Senator Metcalf announced on the floor of the Senate that he would begin conducting hearings on information management by independent regulatory agencies on Tuesday, June 24, and Wednesday, June 25. The purpose of the hearings would be

> to study and investigate the collection, tabulation, use, evaluation, and dissemination of information filed with the regulatory agencies by companies subject to Federal reporting requirements.
>
> We shall seek the answers to two central questions:
>
> How good is the data upon which Government regulatory decisions are based?
>
> How can its accuracy, adequacy, timeliness and availability be improved?

Metcalf's hearings will extend into the fall. The goals of most such investigations are generally an exercise in evasion. From everything I know about Metcalf, his hearings will be an exercise in confrontation.

4

Las Vegas East or Heads I Win; Tails You Lose

Ney's Fifth Axiom: It is not public demand that creates rising prices but rising prices that create public demand.

To know your adversary, you must know his customs; to understand the influence that specialists exercise over the market, you must be able to identify the practices they employ to rig stock prices. In this chapter the reader will be shown that the interdependence of such underlying functions as specialist short selling, of public supply and demand, of volume as it interacts with price, along with the Dow industrial average and the role of the media, is the foundation for the specialist's ability to consistently maximize his profits. The reader must understand these practices and processes if he is to analyze actual market events at a level of critical awareness that enables him to maximize his own profits.

Recognizing that investors must be provided simple solutions for complex investment problems, the Exchange has conditioned them to respond to the surface appearance of price action. If specialists want investors to buy stock, they simply raise stock prices sharply. This creates demand. If they want to cause massive selling, they drop stock prices precipitously. It is merely a problem in engineering. The significant function and underlying objective of such price action is, of course, to serve the specialists' inventory needs. In the course of a rally, therefore, specialists supply public demand by unloading their inventories and then selling short. By precipitating a decline, specialists are able to use the ensuing public selling to cover their short sales and to accumulate stock for their trading and/or investment accounts.

Since specialists can predict the behavior of the public when they raise or lower stock prices, they have only to decide how they wish investors to behave. How they wish investors to behave will depend on the disposition of their inventory and whether they wish to advance stock prices to dispose of inventory or lower stock prices in order to accumulate inventory. It might be easier for the investor to envision this process if he places it in the context of a merchant:

1. Once the specialist has accumulated an inventory in a

stock in which he is registered at wholesale, his objective will be to rally prices to retail in order to divest himself of this inventory.

2. Having sold this stock at retail, he will want to lower stock prices to wholesale in order to reaccumulate a new inventory of this stock.

It should be made clear that there is no specific price in any stock that can be consistently called wholesale or retail. A price of 80 in Eastman Kodak, for example, would be wholesale if the specialist buys stock at that level with the intention to sell at 90; 80, on the other hand, could be retail on another occasion if the specialist shorts stock at 80, then drops the price to 70. Obviously, the specialist's prime objective is simply to sell any given block of stock at a higher price than that at which it was bought.

It is important to note that in lowering stock prices from retail to wholesale, the specialist's profit incentives insist he must not carry down to wholesale price levels the stock he must buy from investors at what are still retail price levels. In order to observe this requirement, therefore, once he drops stock prices, causing public selling, he must rally prices until he can divest himself of that inventory before continuing to lower levels. Thus we see that when the specialist's long-term objective is to lower stock prices to wholesale levels, the techniques he will employ will favor a course of action that enables him to conduct a continuing series of declines followed by advances.

He will tend to avoid the straight-line decline, which could precipitate heavy selling, thereby causing him to acquire an inventory that he would be able to dispose of only in the course of what might have to be a long-term, rather than a short-term, rally. Thus, in the course of a routine decline of 100 to 200 points in the Dow, as specialists trend stock prices lower, they will generally advance prices as often as they drop them, the difference being that the amounts of the declines will be, on balance, greater than the advances. Naturally, when the specialist wishes to conduct a major rally, he will either conduct a long period of accumulation at a low critical price level or he will employ a sharp straight-line decline as he rushes toward a bottom. It is in the fear engendered by a sharp drop that he accumulates the largest amount of stock possible in the shortest time because of the "panic selling" that always results when the market drops 100 or more points in four or five days.

As we mentioned earlier (and at length in *The Wall Street Gang*), whether it is a move toward wholesale or retail, the short sale enables specialists to determine the short-, intermediate-, and long-term price objectives of their stocks. Utilizing the short sale, specialists in active stocks like General Motors, Eastman Kodak, or General Electric, for example, can halt the advance or decline of their stock at whatever price they wish.

The specialist employs his short sale in the context of the following process:

1. His objective is to accumulate stock at wholesale and then rally stock prices.
2. By rallying stock prices he stimulates public demand for his stock. The larger the price advance, the greater the demand he stimulates. (More often than not, this demand will occur the day following the advance.)
3. Once public demand has enabled him to dispose of his inventory at retail price levels, in order to supply additional demand he then sells short—at what are oftentimes even higher retail price levels.
4. Since the profitability of his short sales depends on a subsequent decline in his stock, he will tend to limit the extent of any additional advance beyond the price levels at which he sold short. For practical purposes it can be said that once he begins to sell short he will try to limit his short selling (depending on the price of the stock) to within a two- to five-point range. Once he halts his stock's advance, demand soon thereafter begins to dry up.
5. When this happens, the specialist is in a position to begin the movement of his stock's price toward wholesale price levels.
6. As his stock declines from its high, he may encounter

heavy public selling. He can then use his short position to absorb that selling by short covering.

We must reconcile ourselves to the fact (and learn how to exploit it) that the specialist is able to control both advances and declines through the medium of his short selling.

Nothing reveals the specialist's inventory objectives more conclusively than the manner in which price is used to influence volume. Most investors take no account of the implications of different volume characteristics that exist in one stock or between one stock and another. To the average investor the price of a stock is all that matters. To the specialist, however, the function of price is the intercourse it has with volume. A stock's volume characteristics, therefore, are the means by which the investor may determine that a change is taking place or about to take place in that stock or in the internal character of the market. The higher the specialist advances the price of, say, a stock like Eastman Kodak, from 60 to 90 in the course of a rally, for example, the greater will be the demand, or volume, that this specialist will be able to produce for his stock. If the specialist raises the price substantially, he will also expect to increase volume materially. Once again we come to a conclusion fundamentally different from that now held by investors—i.e., *it is not demand that causes rising stock prices but rising stock prices that cause demand.* It is the demand that results from rising prices that enables the specialist to unload the greatest portion of his inventory at the most profitable price levels. The exact reverse would, of course, hold true in the course of a decline from 90 to 60 in a stock like Eastman Kodak. The specialist would be able to accumulate the greatest amount of stock as his price declined to the 60 level.

During those rare moments when investors do think quantitatively about the rise and fall of prices, their beliefs are, naturally, opposite to what is actually the case. Hence they consider it ominous when stock prices decline on heavy volume and assume the decline is temporary when it is on light volume. What the investor must recognize is that rather than foreshadowing lower prices, heavy selling *ultimately* causes prices to advance. When specialists trigger heavy public selling they of course are buying. Since they will not wish to carry this stock to lower price levels, thereby incurring a loss, they will advance stock prices to unload this inventory at a profit. *It is only when they are able to decline on light volume that they can afford to carry the decline to lower price levels.* If, for instance, the specialist in Eastman Kodak is in the process of dropping his stock from 90 to 80 and incurs heavy selling as he reaches 84, he will be obliged to rally prices back up to 88 or higher to divest himself of this inventory. Having done this, he can then proceed back down through that same territory to the accompaniment of lighter selling—lower volume.

Thus it is that the specialist's objective is to raise or lower prices on light volume until he reaches the price objective at which he wishes to see heavy volume. It is for this reason that the appearance of big blocks consistently defines the short-, intermediate-, and long-term reversal points in stock prices. If, for example, the specialist wishes to lower prices on light volume but instead incurs heavy selling at, say, the halfway point toward his downside price objective, that volume will manifest itself as big blocks, at which point he will invariably reverse his direction in order to rally his price to unload that inventory. When he does this, big blocks again define the upper limits of the price level at which he will once again reverse the trend in order to resume the decline. Big blocks at the tops and bottoms of all moves become larger and more frequent depending on the duration and precipitousness of the move.*

*Unfortunately the ticker tape is the only means by which an individual can obtain up-to-the minute big-block information. This, however, is essential only for the most active trader. Once he has become proficient at interpreting big-block activity on the ticker tape, there will be nothing that can more dramatically engage his attention than the revelations provided by the tape.

The Francis Emory Fitch Company, 80 Broad Street, New York, New York, 10004, also publishes all stock transactions for the NYSE and AMEX, but the sheets arrive by mail two or three days after each trading day and are quite expensive. They are,

As the reader advances his knowledge of the specialist, he will observe that in the course of a major rally or decline, volume will increase as stocks move toward or just through what I refer to as their "critical numbers." Big-block activity is localized around prices like 20, 30, 40, 50, 60 because of the way exponentials of 10 are charged in the investor's mind with subconscious associations.* Man's ten fingers have exercised a tremendous influence over him. For example, ten is used as the base of our numbers system. Many different languages including the Semitic, Mongolian, Indo-European, and most primitive cultures employ different words to represent numbers up to ten; beyond ten they all employ some compounding principle until they get to one hundred. This is referred to as the "decimal system." The upshot of its existence is that men tend to think of numerical progression in patterns of 10—i.e., 10, 20, 30, 40, 50, etc.

There is also another classic way of looking at numbers. It is called the "vigesimal system" and employs a base of 20. The people of many countries, the United States included, who employ the decimal system also employ the vigesimal system. Thus we will say "a score of men" for 20 or "two score years" for 40; the Gettysburg Address begins with "Fourscore and seven years ago our fathers . . ." The French also use 20; the French word for 80 is "quatre-vingt" (4 × 20).

The point of this is that the investor's perception of his environment and his response to it are quite often ruled by a compulsion to conform his activities to sets of numbers in terms of the manner in which the decimal system or the vigesimal system has come to influence him. In short, it is precisely for this reason that specialists have learned that there is a certain predict-

---

however, timely enough for both the intermediate- and long-term investor. Although there is no question that a ticker or the Fitch sheets greatly add to the investor's accuracy in the marketplace, he can still do fairly well on the basis of the total volume figures published daily for all stocks on the NYSE and AMEX in his newspaper's financial section.

*See *The Wall Street Gang*, Chapter 9.

able pattern investors follow in buying and selling stock and that this pattern is based on the legacy of what I refer to as the "numbers theory." The evidence of this, as I previously mentioned, is the striking volume of patterns that tend to occur at the multiples of 10. Thus specialists tend to base the manner in which they manipulate their stock prices on the most ordinary of plots—i.e., that if a stock is dropped from, say, 70 to 60, of the investors who sell that stock during the decline, a greater percentage will sell near the 60 level than anywhere between 70 and 60.

Investors naturally have no idea that the reason the impulse to sell at 60 is much stronger than at 65 is that they are doing the bidding of an instinct that is older than the pyramids. Nor do they realize that the misfortunes surrounding their investment decisions are greatly caused by the consistency with which specialists are able to exploit the manner in which investors' number instincts cause them to act. For example, a specialist will drop his stock's price to a critical number, acquire the increasing amount of shares that are sold to him as he approaches this price level, and then, having cleaned out his book down to the critical number (30, 40, 50, etc.), he will launch a rally that oftentimes carries the stock to just under or just above another critical level (60, 70, 80, etc.). Whether he stops just under or just above the critical level depends on the amount of buy or sell orders he sees on his book just beyond the critical number and what his objective is at the time.

A study of the following charts can provide the investor with valuable insights into some of the ways specialists use critical numbers. Charts 1, 2, and 3 show how they are able to accumulate stock by cleaning their books of stop loss orders when they penetrate important critical numbers; Charts 4, 5, and 6 show how they are able to prevent public selling by halting their stocks' advance just under a critical number; and Charts 7, 8, and 9 show how they are able to trigger buying when a stock makes a breakout above a critical number.

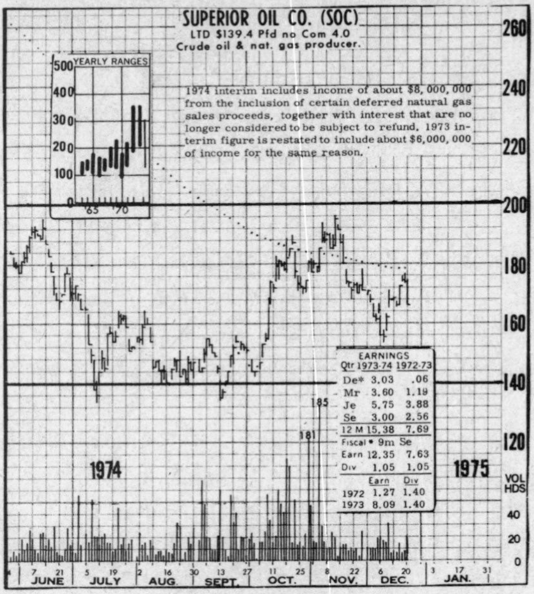
SUPERIOR OIL CO. (SOC)
LTD $139.4 Pfd no Com 4.0
Crude oil & nat. gas producer.
1974 interim includes income of about $8,000,000 from the inclusion of certain deferred natural gas sales proceeds, together with interest that are no longer considered to be subject to refund. 1973 interim figure is restated to include about $6,000,000 of income for the same reason.
YEARLY RANGES
EARNINGS
Qtr 1973-74 1972-73
De* 3.03 .06
Mr 3.60 1.19
Je 5.75 3.88
Se 3.00 2.56
12 M 15.38 7.69
Fiscal • 9m Se
Earn 12.35 7.63
Div 1.05 1.05
Earn Div
1972 1.27 1.40
1973 8.09 1.40
1974
1975
VOL HDS
JUNE JULY AUG. SEPT. OCT. NOV. DEC. JAN.

CHART 4–1

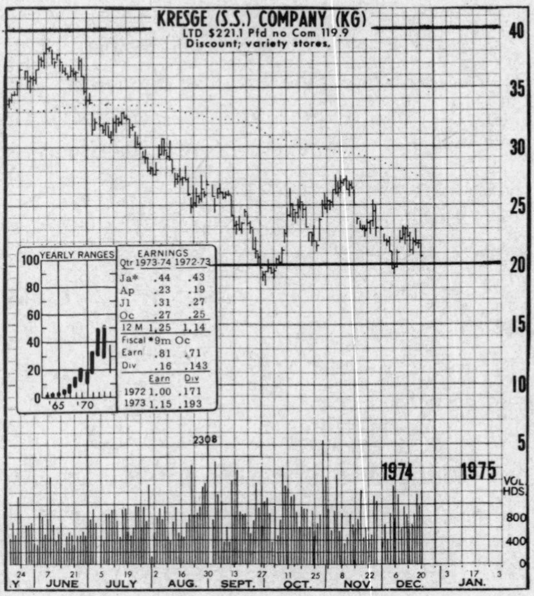
KRESGE (S.S.) COMPANY (KG)
LTD $221.1 Pfd no Com 119.9
Discount; variety stores.
YEARLY RANGES
EARNINGS
Qtr 1973-74 1972-73
Ja* .44 .43
Ap .23 .19
Jl .31 .27
Oc .27 .25
12 M 1.25 1.14
Fiscal *9m Oc
Earn .81 .71
Div .16 .143
Earn Div
1972 1.00 .171
1973 1.15 .193
2308
1974
1975
VOL HDS
JUNE JULY AUG. SEPT. OCT. NOV. DEC. JAN.

CHART 4–2

SOURCE: Trendline's Daily Basis Stock Charts

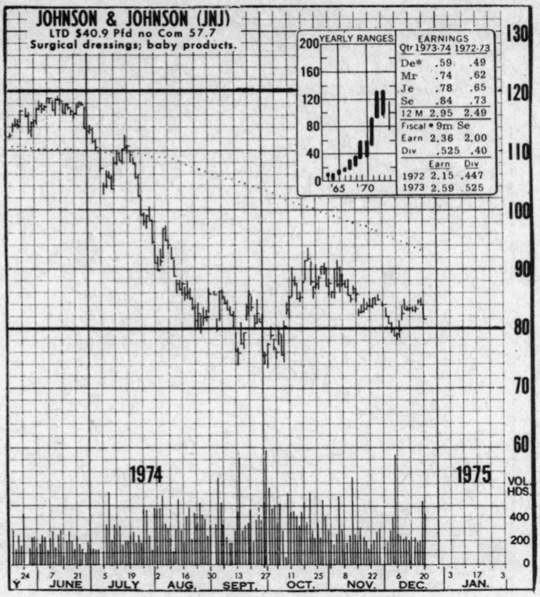
JOHNSON & JOHNSON (JNJ)
LTD $40.9 Pfd no Com 57.7
Surgical dressings; baby products.
YEARLY RANGES
EARNINGS
Qtr 1973-74 1972-73
De* .59 .49
Mr .74 .62
Je .78 .65
Se .84 .73
12 M 2.95 2.49
Fiscal • 9m Se
Earn 2.36 2.00
Div .525 .40
Earn Div
1972 2.15 .447
1973 2.59 .525
1974
1975
VOL. HDS.
JUNE JULY AUG. SEPT. OCT. NOV. DEC. JAN.

CHART 4–3

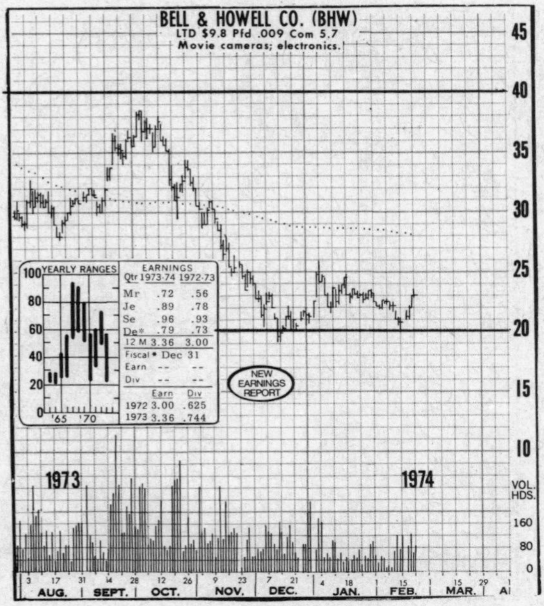
BELL & HOWELL CO. (BHW)
LTD $9.8 Pfd .009 Com 5.7
Movie cameras; electronics.
YEARLY RANGES
EARNINGS
Qtr 1973-74 1972-73
Mr .72 .56
Je .89 .78
Se .96 .93
De* .79 .73
12 M 3.36 3.00
Fiscal • Dec 31
Earn -- --
Div -- --
Earn Div
1972 3.00 .625
1973 3.36 .744
NEW EARNINGS REPORT
1973
1974
VOL. HDS.
AUG. SEPT. OCT. NOV. DEC. JAN. FEB. MAR.

CHART 4–4

SOURCE: Trendline's Daily Basis Stock Charts

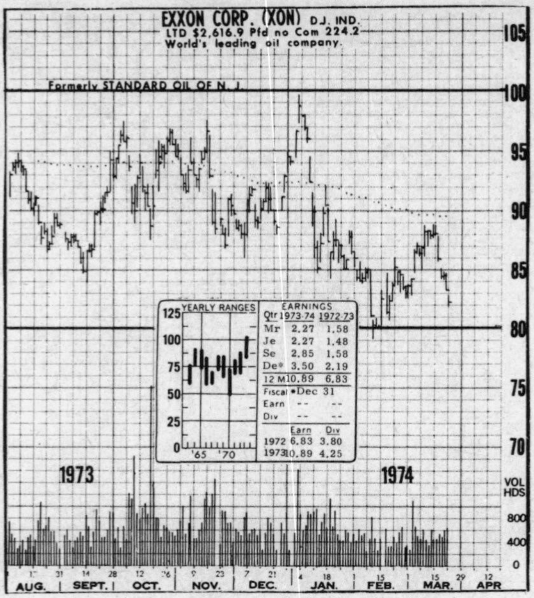

EXXON CORP. (XON) DJ. IND.
LTD $2,616.9 Pfd no Com 224.2
World's leading oil company.
Formerly STANDARD OIL OF N. J.
YEARLY RANGES
EARNINGS
1973
1974
AUG.
SEPT.
OCT.
NOV.
DEC.
JAN.
FEB.
MAR.
APR

CHART 4–5

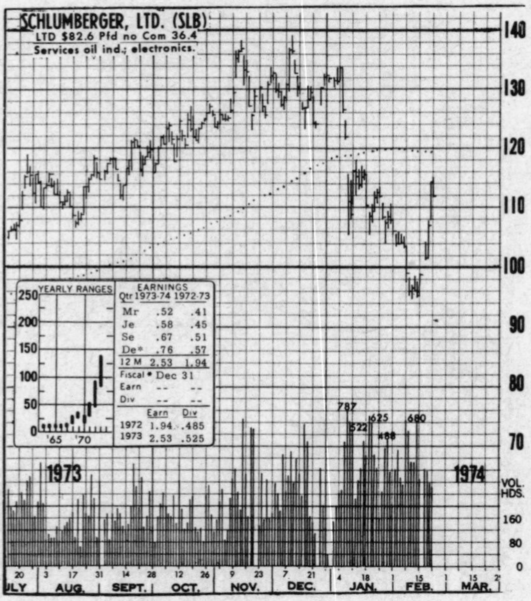

SCHLUMBERGER, LTD. (SLB)
LTD $82.6 Pfd no Com 36.4
Services oil ind.; electronics.
YEARLY RANGES
EARNINGS
1973
1974
JULY
AUG.
SEPT.
OCT.
NOV.
DEC.
JAN.
FEB.
MAR.

CHART 4–6

SOURCE: Trendline's Daily Basis Stock Charts

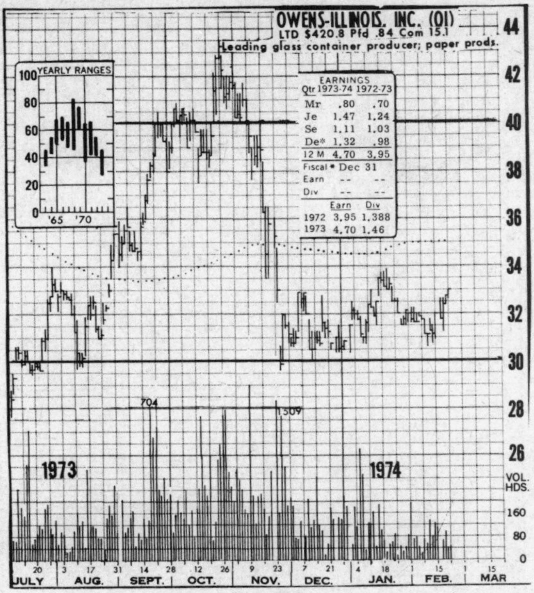
OWENS-ILLINOIS, INC. (OI)
LTD $420.8 Pfd .84 Com 15.1
Leading glass container producer; paper prods.
YEARLY RANGES
EARNINGS
Qtr 1973-74 1972-73
Mr .80 .70
Je 1.47 1.24
Se 1.11 1.03
De* 1.32 .98
12 M 4.70 3.95
Fiscal * Dec 31
Earn Div
1972 3.95 1.388
1973 4.70 1.46
1973
1974
704
1509
VOL. HDS.
JULY AUG. SEPT. OCT. NOV. DEC. JAN. FEB. MAR

CHART 4–7

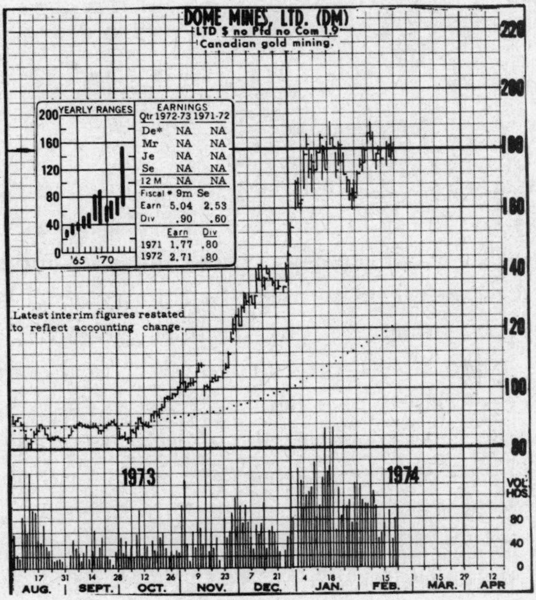
DOME MINES, LTD. (DM)
LTD $ no Pfd no Com 1.9
Canadian gold mining.
YEARLY RANGES
EARNINGS
Qtr 1972-73 1971-72
De* NA NA
Mr NA NA
Je NA NA
Se NA NA
12 M NA NA
Fiscal * 9m Se
Earn 5.04 2.53
Div .90 .60
Earn Div
1971 1.77 .80
1972 2.71 .80
Latest interim figures restated to reflect accounting change.
1973
1974
VOL. HDS.
AUG. SEPT. OCT. NOV. DEC. JAN. FEB. MAR. APR

CHART 4–8

SOURCE: Trendline's Daily Basis Stock Charts

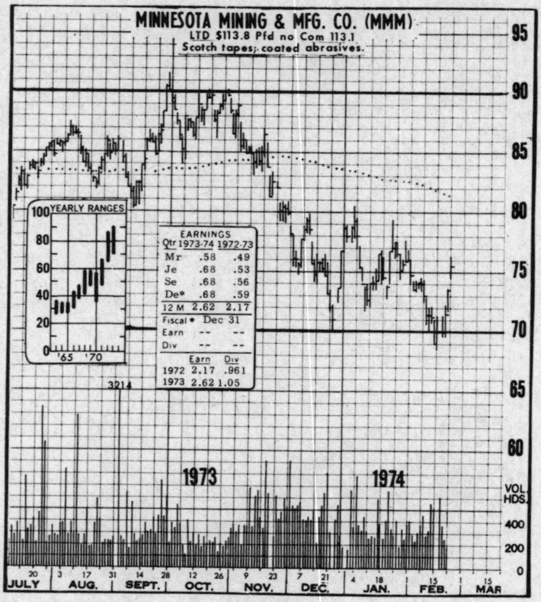
MINNESOTA MINING & MFG. CO. (MMM)
LTD $113.8 Pfd no Com 113.1
Scotch tapes; coated abrasives.
YEARLY RANGES
EARNINGS
Qtr 1973-74 1972-73
Mr .58 .49
Je .68 .53
Se .68 .56
De* .68 .59
12 M 2.62 2.17
Fiscal • Dec 31
Earn Div
1972 2.17 .961
1973 2.62 1.05
1973
1974
VOL. HDS.
JULY AUG. SEPT. OCT. NOV. DEC. JAN. FEB. MAR

CHART 4–9
SOURCE: Trendline's Daily Basis Stock Charts

In later chapters, we will have occasion to see these processes in operation as important Dow stocks decline and are accumulated at critical price levels and as they advance and are distributed at critical price levels. Gradually the reader will learn how, in the course of a major rally or decline, specialists move price like a pendulum back and forth across the critical numbers until, because of the action of price, the action of volume either subsides or increases dramatically, thereby moving the market into areas of new definition—from bear to bull or bull to bear.

In defining the instruments employed by specialists to achieve their ends, we should not overlook the distortions of reality created by the Dow Jones industrial average. Employing daily announcements about this average, the media bullies investors into mass movements in and out of the market. When I entered the securities business, I assumed I understood the manner in which the DJIA was utilized to express the health of the market. I assumed it was an index that consisted of a group of 30 stocks, the sum of whose advances and declines, when they were plotted at the end of every day, every week, or every month, gave the investor a fairly accurate picture of what was happening in the market. Several years passed before I realized that the assumption was misleading. I understood more clearly the function of the Dow and its importance to the Stock Exchange's processes when, after a sharp advance of more than 100 points in the Dow, I observed that of the 30 stocks in this average, 6 were down, only 5 had advanced more than 6 to 7 points, and in this group, only one had advanced more than 7 points. Yet listening to the conversations of others, many of whom were wealthy investors, one might have assumed that their blue chips had risen 20 or 30 points.

To understand the function of the Dow, the investor must look at it from the point of view of the Exchange insider who is constantly mindful of his duty to indoctrinate investors into ways of analyzing events and taking actions which are dependable for the achievement of the specialist's merchandising objectives. From the specialist's point of view an index like the Dow brings it all together, since it has the ability to create herd enthusiasm on the one hand or panic on the other. It is the perfect tool for creating emotional rather than logical reactions. Although a 100-point rally in the Dow may mean very little in terms of the individual stocks in this index (it represents an average gain of 5 points in each of the 30 Dow stocks), the advance of 100 points creates a grip on the investor's emotions that distorts his thinking regarding the function of the rally. The Exchange discovered long ago that because investors assume that an important move in the Dow corresponds to an important move in all stocks, like the dogs responding to Pavlov's bell they can be easily persuaded to leap into action when this index dramatically advances or declines. To counteract this the investor should keep in mind that while most stocks tend to rise and fall with the movements of the Dow, a 15-point rally in the Dow will often correspond to an advance of less than 50 cents per share in the NYSE Composite.

The knowledge that "the market" does, however, move "in sympathy" with the Dow can be of great use to the investor. In future chapters the reader's attention will be directed to an analysis of the market on the logic implicit in the merchandising practices of the twenty-two specialists who control the thirty stocks in the Dow industrial average. As the reader examines their habit patterns he will see that it is virtually impossible for the investor to solve the problems of timing until he learns to differentiate and describe the movements *not* of the Dow but of the individual stocks that comprise the Dow. In so doing he will come to appreciate how Dow specialists work together as a group, exercising their power through consensus, harmonizing their movement like so many musical instruments to produce the market's full orchestration.

Like the musicians in an orchestra, the specialists who conduct the movements of each of the Dow stocks work on behalf of their own interests while at the same time working for the fulfillment of the objectives of the system as a whole. This could well mean that while Du Pont is advancing to compensate for the decline in other stocks, some specialists in the Dow would, so to speak, be sitting with their hands in their laps until their moment came to perform. And although the specialist in General Motors may have solved his inventory problems on the upside at the top of a rally by establishing a major short position that will carry him profitably to lower price levels, if necessary he will at the market's opening raise the price of his stock, as will other Dow specialists, in order to help other Dow and non-Dow specialists divest themselves of their inventories.

Thus the specialists in four or more Dow stocks may move to within two to three points of their highs, where they will wait until the prices of other Dow and non-Dow stocks have also moved within striking distance of their highs. Then at what is obviously a prearranged signal, most specialists will simultaneously launch their stocks toward their highs. This will then bring in the crescendo of investor demand that enables specialists to establish major short sales before dropping stock prices. In order to rationalize such an advance in the public mind and to provide it with the semblance of legitimacy, this event can be timed to coincide with an economic or political announcement investors will assume has major bullish implications for the overall market.

It is only by grasping the ideas implicit in *pattern recognition* that the investor can begin to understand the direction in which specialists intend to move their stocks in order to assure the fulfillment of the goals of the unit as a whole. At the same time, only pattern recognition provides our educated intuitions with an understanding of the goals of the unit as revealed by the simultaneous interplay of price and volume in each of the thirty Dow stocks. It is this interplay that translates itself into recognizable patterns or mosaics that tell us what the specialist is planning and what his stock's future pattern can be expected to look like. This information cannot be gathered from watching the Dow, since the Dow does not prescribe the movement of the thirty stocks; rather, it is the thirty stocks that prescribe the movement of the Dow.

The Stock Exchange is able to command because the information provided investors by the media invests it with the apparatus of control. More from ignorance on their part than from a realization of the clear and conscious intent on the part of their publishers, most of the writers who prepare an analysis of daily market action do so from material prepared for them by Stock Exchange sources and relayed to them through the various wire services. This information is of great practical utility to the Exchange, for it is well structured and integrated into the investor's emotional life. The material that is most effective in the formation of investor opinion is always furthest from reality. In consequence the public is persuaded to believe that the market advanced because of a high short interest or a lowering of interest rates. On the other hand they will become encouraged to believe it declined because of an increase in the wholesale index or because of "profit-taking by investors." It is therefore not surprising that investors always look for solutions that do not correspond to reality.

Investors are easy marks for the seeming logic of half-truths and judgments. Thus it is a simple matter for the Exchange to move them in directions contrary to those in which investors would like to go. By the same token the media's unexamined premises lead investors to conclusions that are at a great distance from what is in fact occurring on the floor of the Stock Exchange. The only news that's fit to print is the official proclamations of the Stock Exchange or the semiofficial comments (what "brokers say") of its surrogates. Thus do the media grant the Stock Exchange establishment "squatter's rights" over the expression of opinion.

Although it is not possible for the investor to escape from the Exchange's daily propaganda barrage, he can learn to avoid its consequences by questioning the premises and the value judgments that even the most thoughtful investors accept at face value.

The elements I have discussed in this chapter will begin to come together for the reader as he is brought into contact with the actualities of market events. At that point, he will begin to understand how the specialist structures his game plan and how his practices interlock and interact. His reasoning and learning will grow, it is hoped, along with his interest as the sources of the specialist's power to control price and volume become apparent.

If the proposal that we should try to beat the specialist at his own game seems impossibly ambitious, the counterproposal that we should simply abandon the field to him is even more absurd. For the fact is, effective information about the specialist and his merchandising practices can have highly constructive consequences. Investors can continue to shift the blame for their losses on their stockbrokers for all that they've done or left undone, or they can stop worrying about what is being done *to* them in order to learn what there is they can do for themselves. Heady possibilities will open up once they come to understand the game play of the stock market's principal croupiers.

5

The Gift of Grab or The End of the Decline – The Beginning of Crisis

Ney's Sixth Axiom: Every decline provides the investor with a chance to learn that changes in the market are due not to outer events but to inner conditions.

The economy was in a steep slide. The sense of economic crisis so persistently headlined by the financial press had taken hold. The whole country was growing restless. The mood of weariness and woe besetting the average investor in early October 1974 reflected the collective mood of most Americans toward the economy and the unconvincing pretensions of those in charge of its direction. Like mice on a treadmill, the public was coming to recognize that the more it labored to advance itself, the more hopeless its situation became. If experience was teaching Americans anything, it was that, from one administration to the next, their destinies were controlled by the concerted efforts of an undisguised pack of knuckleheads and scoundrels—all of them out to add to their income by sticking it to the taxpayer.

The swindled and despairing consumer was trying to cope with the problems created by a new administration whose taxing, subsidy, energy, and welfare policies were a standing subversion to the needs of the poor and the economic survival of the middle class. The accumulating incompetence of this administration, like the one that had preceded it, could be attributed to the fact that the nation's present heads of state consisted of a former football coach, Wall Street stockbrokers, analysts, lobbyists, and a representative of, among other things, the eastern financial establishment's most important bank and the world's largest oil company. All of them had been selected for their jobs by the football coach, who had himself been appointed by his good friend, a head of government who was an acknowledged criminal. Each of them in his own way was now adding to the crisis caused by the increasing collisions of the economy with the great body of problems created by earlier administrations.

If the investor was more uneasy than almost any other still somewhat solvent group it was because his mood was also the by-product of the most recent in a long series of declining stock prices. Indeed, his one consolation was that he had been assured by the interacting comments of the media and his stockbroker that neither he nor anyone else was directly responsible for the stock losses he had suffered. These, he was told, were caused by the mysterious and always unpredictable dynamics of the market. Traditionally, stock prices are defined in relation to the most ambiguous of all financial phenomena, economic conditions. Since the economy was being clobbered, the ideological rationale existed for the Exchange to lower stock prices. It was easier for investors to accept the difficulties of insolvency if they believed that their value judgments and the hypotheses that determined their approach to the market were not at issue.

The doubts that had been raised about the future of the economy seemed to center chiefly around the obstinate unwillingness of Americans to uphold the principles of conspicuous consumption. Wholly indifferent to the consequences of thrift and prudence, government economists were suggesting consumers had fallen down on the job. Visions of affluence and an ever-expanding economy are coefficients of indulgence, not abstinence. Spending, *not* saving, is required if the corporate complex is to work off inventories and rebuild cash balances. The American desire to possess and consume was failing to keep pace with the needs of the American Dream and industry's logarithmically spiraling productive capacity. The consequences of this failure to observe the truth of contemporary economic realities had been:

1. Cutbacks in production
2. An increase in personal bankruptcies and business failures
3. Collapse of the automobile industry
4. A drop in corporate earnings
5. Millions of unemployed young workers and unskilled blacks who further diminished major sources of consumer purchasing power, thereby further reducing the demand for goods

A degree of intelligence was needed in government, where intelligence is always a measurable luxury, to perceive that it was government's policy of raising and maintaining prices *above* a certain level for consumer products in key industries which was the primary energy of inflation and unemployment. Instead of ordering business to slow down and cut back, government had given it a whump on the tail and told it to speed up. Consumer markets were drying up at an alarming rate, but because the braying chuckleheads in government were linked ideologically and financially to big business, government, in order to sustain the GNP myth, was supporting rate and price increases to enable big business to maintain its growth rates. Minimal taxes for big business compared with high tax rates for the lower- and middle-income classes accelerated income inequality. The poor were growing poorer and the rich were growing richer and plowing more and more of their capital into new enterprise, plant, and equipment, which necessitated further consumption by the public. Not only were consumer markets drying up, but credit limits were becoming exhausted. The masses had long ago overborrowed against future income. Capitalism had been forced out of business. The alchemy of the system was destroying the goose that laid the golden egg. Because the consumer market was being forced to the wall, General Motors was no longer competing with Chrysler but with the shoe store and the meat and vegetable counters of the local supermarket.

In addition to the doubts raised by conditions that caused investors to wonder where the economy was headed, there were the problems raised by the bear market that had been launched in April 1971. The duration of the decline had surprised everyone, including myself. I had not thought it would take specialists more than four years to work stock prices to long-term wholesale levels.

We could take it for granted that for all the investors who had come and gone in the course of the past four years, there were many more where they had come from who would soon prove to be just as expendable. Many had gone by the board in the course of the rallies that specialists had launched during the long period of decline. Most of these rallies had been conducted at ever lower price levels. By inviting the public to buy stock at the top of every rally, specialists were able to divest themselves of their inventories and then establish short sales that allowed them to absorb public selling as prices were lowered. Eventually it would once again become practicable and profitable for them to conduct a long-term (six months or more) bull raid on the market.

At the end of the first week in October 1974, investors were trying to cope with the latest decline in the Dow—a drop of more than 200 points in less than two months. Looking at the following chart of the DJIA, it was apparent why investors were confused. While they had been persuaded to magnify the importance of earnings, Chart 5–1 reflects the fact that, while the earnings curve advanced, stock prices declined. On October 3 the Dow index dropped below the 600 level. Judging from the letters coming to my office, most investors didn't know whether the penetration was a signal to buy or to sell.

By analyzing the decline in terms of specialist strategy, the course of action investors should have taken becomes clear. Studying Charts 5–2 and 5–3, we note that several days before the August decline began, the Dow advanced approximately 8 points (August 5) on comparatively light volume. The next day the Dow advanced approximately 13 points, and volume increased to 15.8 million shares. This was in keeping with our axiom that "it is not demand for stock that creates rising stock prices but rising stock prices that create demand." It is significant that upon this occasion many specialists employed the opportunity provided by increased demand to supply that demand by selling short 789,240 shares of stock. An almost 24-point advance in the Dow on the seventh then served to increase volume to 16 million shares on the eighth. On that occasion the Dow reached an intraday high of 803, and specialists again conducted short-selling operations (780,420 shares). Once the goal of rising prices had been met, a new goal emerged that was to take stock prices lower so as to maximize the profit potentials of the heavy short selling on the sixth and eighth. Having established their short sales at these highs, specialist short sales then, as always, fell off appreciably as stock prices began to decline.

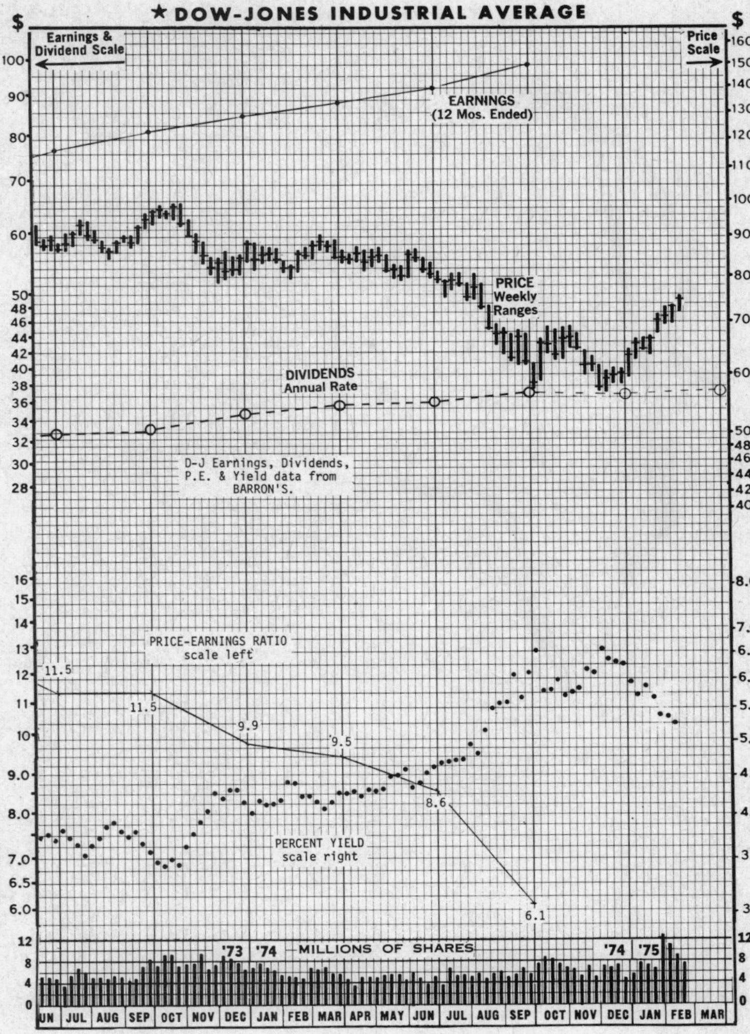
★ DOW-JONES INDUSTRIAL AVERAGE
Earnings & Dividend Scale
Price Scale
EARNINGS (12 Mos. Ended)
PRICE Weekly Ranges
DIVIDENDS Annual Rate
D-J Earnings, Dividends, P.E. & Yield data from BARRON'S.
PRICE-EARNINGS RATIO scale left
PERCENT YIELD scale right
MILLIONS OF SHARES
'73
'74
'74
'75
JUN
JUL
AUG
SEP
OCT
NOV
DEC
JAN
FEB
MAR
APR
MAY
JUN
JUL
AUG
SEP
OCT
NOV
DEC
JAN
FEB
MAR

CHART 5–1
SOURCE: Securities Research

CHART 5–2
ROUND-LOT SHARE VOLUME ON
THE NEW YORK STOCK EXCHANGE
(IN SHARES AND WARRANTS)

August, 1974

			Share Volume of Specialists (Except for the Odd-Lot Account) in Stocks in Which They are Registered		*Other Member Share Volume Initiated on the Floor*		*Other Member Share Volume Initiated off the Floor*	
			Sales		*Sales*		*Sales*	
Date	*Day*	*Dow/NYSE Vol.*	*Total*	*Short*	*Total*	*Short*	*Total*	*Short*
1	Thursday	751.10/11.47	1,450,420	309,040	104,700	17,600	920,347	160,400
2	Friday	752.58/10.11	1,249,570	294,300	69,900	8,600	795,609	211,200
5	Monday	760.40/11.23	1,663,680	354,260	114,200	17,100	819,935	178,100
6	Tuesday	773.78/15.77	2,871,280	789,240	211,000	42,900	1,397,573	380,000
7	Wednesday	797.56/13.38	2,217,940	509,060	176,400	45,600	1,174,576	357,830
8	Thursday	784.89/16.06	2,919,630	780,420	262,600	97,000	1,480,904	336,970
9	Friday	777.30/10.16	1,520,250	384,810	86,000	21,300	830,562	183,230
12	Monday	767.29/ 7.78	1,160,920	290,240	58,600	23,300	663.626	172,400
13	Tuesday	756.41/10.14	1,194,500	286,920	48,453	16,800	738,700	114,850

14	Wednesday	740.54/11.75	1,284,130	252,610	69,100	9,800	893,798	89,280
15	Thursday	737.88/11.13	1,456,660	340,540	76,100	13,700	880,609	177,800
16	Friday	731.54/10.51	1,354,470	341,370	67,500	9,700	707,398	114,200
19	Monday	721.84/11.67	1,392,640	322,040	67,700	12,000	743,780	135,000
20	Tuesday	726.85/13.82	1,751,710	445,190	104,300	10,100	921,791	113,640
21	Wednesday	711.59/11.65	1,590,970	383,120	123,700	9,300	774.534	102,800
22	Thursday	704.63/15.69	1,995,630	391,780	100,200	13,000	1,151,344	260,900
23	Friday	686.80/13.59	1,598,760	355,930	96,600	9,000	892,082	200,700
26	Monday	688.13/14.63	2,118,040	502,180	144,100	16,400	985,199	178,820
27	Tuesday	671.54/12.97	1,662,870	345,700	147,600	10,400	880,199	126,490
28	Wednesday	666.61/16.67	1,808,820	379,850	121,000	15,700	906.440	173,600
29	Thursday	656.84/13.69	1,737,540	258,100	81,000	8,600	839,551	148,640
30	Friday	678.58/16.23	2,600,720	561.220	123,400	30,400	1,108,431	315,070

Source: Statistical Bulletin, published by the SEC.

DOW JONES INDUSTRIALS

	VOL. (TH SH)	CLOSE
8 1	1024.3	751.10
2	1035.3	752.58
5	862.0	760.40
6	1417.3	773.78
7	1097.6	797.56
8	1539.4	784.99
9	973.4	777.30
12	806.2	767.29
13	823.3	756.41
14	1041.5	740.54
15	1015.7	737.88
16	881.7	731.54
19	1001.3	721.84
20	1164.2	726.85
21	1078.2	711.59
22	1438.5	704.63
23	1226.4	686.80
26	1417.5	688.13
27	1060.6	671.54
28	1277.4	666.61
29	1140.8	656.84
30	1190.7	678.58
9 2	HOLIDAY	
3	1085.9	663.33
4	1478.2	648.00
5	1264.0	670.76
6	1262.6	677.88
9	811.5	662.94
10	899.7	658.17
11	969.4	654.72
12	1197.3	641.74
13	1338.4	627.19
16	1804.6	639.78
17	1195.8	648.78
18	932.0	651.91
19	1388.4	674.05
20	1389.9	670.76
23	1078.0	663.72
24	887.7	654.10
25	1655.5	649.95
26	1008.6	637.98
27	1084.1	621.95
30	1409.0	607.87

CHART 5–3

SOURCE: ISL Daily Stock Price Index, published by Standard & Poor's

At market highs, specialists account for approximately 75 percent of all short selling, other Exchange members about 15 percent, and the public about 10 percent. What the investor must do is learn how to recognize specialist short selling. Once he is able to identify its signs, he can use it as a decisive signal that warns him of impending danger. Dow volume is one of the most important means of identifying specialist short selling. When in the ordinary course of business the daily volume in this index of 30 stocks exceeds 1.4 million shares, the investor should be on the lookout for a short-term reversal in the Dow average and the overall market. As stocks move to an important high or low, one can expect to see Dow volume reach between 1.8 to 2.5 or more million shares for three or more days before a reversal occurs. Thus when stocks are in transit from short- or intermediate-term lows to their highs, it is a general rule that when the daily Dow volume exceeds 1.4 million shares it can be assumed Dow specialists have liquidated or are in the process of liquidating their trading account inventories and are selling short to supply demand. Note, therefore, on Chart 5–3 that on August 8, as the Dow established an intraday high at the 803 level, that the volume of the Dow was 1,539,400 shares.

As previously mentioned, volume figures are the most important clue to specialist intent. Specialist control over volume is a highly creative exercise in the psychological management of the investment community's thinking as a whole. The specialist's merchandising strategies are organized to minimize public selling during a decline and, therefore, the amount of inventory that they must absorb, place on their shelves, and carry with them as they lower stock prices toward wholesale levels. Just how well specialists solved their immediate goal of low volume as they manipulated stock prices down from the August 8 high can be seen from a glance at the opposite chart. Volume was limited to 11-, 12-, and 13-million-share days. What this comparatively low volume indicates is that the public had been subtly and silently persuaded *not* to sell stock they would have sold had they thought for a moment that prices were headed lower.

This is always a very difficult trick to pull off. It is done by rallying stock prices from time to time, and rallying the investor's hopes so that, although the evidence of declining stock prices is right there before his eyes, he will flatly refuse to believe the evidence of his senses. It is this mastery over investor psychology that allows specialists to dominate the investment process. Intensely aware of the conditioning power of price, specialists are able to invade the investor's intellect and to distort the investor's perception of reality so that his formalized response to continually lower stock prices will be to do nothing except watch them decline still further.

It was as though, in the course of the August–September decline, investors had suddenly discovered they were on a burning ship. But because the investor has a strong belief in salvation, he does not abandon ship as soon as a fire is discovered. He first persuades himself that the fire will somehow go out, that "things will get better." As with most gamblers his unconscious belief is always that, by some magic, a miracle will take place.

If the investor asked who or what had started the blaze and was to learn it was another passenger who had deliberately set fire to his mattress, he would assume the arsonist was a madman. What is totally alien to the understanding of most investors is that Exchange insiders are able to derive benefits from a crashing stock market and that in order to enjoy these benefits, stock values must go down.

Although by early October, specialists were not facing the conditions that would have been attendant on a series of 30-million-share days on the downside, they had probably exhausted their short sales at the end of a two-month decline and inventoried a large accumulation of stock. These accumulations increased as they moved into the first week in October. We are also able to observe a volume buildup in Dow stocks as they move down to or through critical price levels. Much of the selling that came into the market that week could be attributed to the sudden momentum given the drop in stock prices during the weeks of September 23 and 30, when the Dow declined almost 39 and 37 points respectively. The interesting fact is that while the overall volume for the New York Stock Exchange was comparatively low in the course of this last week's decline, it was comparatively high for Dow stocks. This could be attributed to the increase in volume as stocks like General Electric, Du Pont,

Sears, and Procter & Gamble moved toward or through critical price levels.

On Monday, September 30, a large increase in volume could be seen in General Electric as it declined to 31¼ (108,700), in General Motors as it declined to 35⅝ (118,500), in American Telephone as it declined to 41 (112,200), and in U.S. Steel as it declined under 40 to 38½ (121,800). Without doubt, the volume in individual Dow stocks was the most substantial evidence that a rally *had* to take place and *would* take place over the very near term. On that Monday, Dow volume reached 1.4 million, increased to 1.8 Tuesday, 1.1 Wednesday, 1.7 Thursday, and 1.6 Friday. No alibi about unemployment figures, inflation, or anything else could alter the documented historical fact that specialists were covering their short sales and adding to inventory.

The following excerpts from my diary will help provide the reader with my thought processes on that occasion and the reasons I concluded that a rally was in the offing.

Tuesday, October 1, 1974
Dow –3.05/604.82 Dow Vol. 1,804,600 NYSE Vol. 16,890,000
The pressure building up for a rally becomes more evident with the passage of each day. . . . The inventory buildup in AT&T must be critical. This specialist unit conducted transactions (on the floor) for 419,500 shares today with a valuation of approximately $16.7 million. What we may have to see is Eastman Kodak move under its critical price level of 60 and General Motors under 30 before a rally gets seriously underway.

It was possible on the following day to advance further toward a definition of specialist intent. While I was aware of the psychic shock that would be created by a penetration of the psychologically important 600 level in the Dow, I was far more interested in the interior activity of the stocks in the Dow. Very few investors sensed that it was because Dow stocks were penetrating or about to penetrate their critical price levels that the index itself would penetrate the 600 level. It was highly unlikely that General Motors at 35 would initiate an important rally at a point midway between two critical price levels. If it was ultimately to move to the 30 level, therefore, the rest of the market would also be moving lower. There was no doubt we were about to enter a market that would lend itself at least to trading profits. Whether it would be suitable for long-term investment purposes I was not yet certain.

Wednesday, October 2, 1974
Dow –3.29/601.53 Dow Vol. 1,115,900 NYSE Vol. 12,230,000
Of more than passing interest is the holding pattern established by today's events. Like squadrons of bombers that hover over an aircraft carrier until the entire force is airborne and ready to move together toward the target, Dow stocks will move to and then away from their launching areas until all the important Dow stocks have assembled. Having moved through the 40 level last week down to 35¼ yesterday, General Motors closed today at 35¾. Telephone also maintained its price level on relatively high volume, closing at 40⅜ on 167,400 shares. Texaco at 20⅝, Standard Oil of California at 21, Procter & Gamble at 69¾, and American Brands at 29¼ also moved toward the starting gate in preparation for the rally. Of interest is that daily volume figures in Dow stocks are still not large enough to warrant a long-term rally.

Also worthy of note: Exxon moved under the critical 60 level last week and dropped another 2⅛ points today to 56¼ (on 52,100 shares). The accumulation patterns in this stock indicate that it most assuredly will soon advance to at least 69 on the basis of my theory of numbers.

Describing the causes of today's decline, *The New York Times* financial writers reported that it was due to "concern over the inflationary spiral . . . the unsettled world situation . . . a lack of favorable economic news and . . . increasing margin calls." The *Times* has provided a classic solution for a declining stock market—do not send out margin calls.

I was aware by Thursday's close that we had reached a point in the market's history in which the specialist would clarify his plans for the future. On Friday he would either precipitate a flood tide of public selling as he dropped stock prices toward the 500 level in order to accumulate additional inventory, or he would rally stock prices in order to unload inventory he had already accumulated. In the former instance, if he dropped prices further it would enable him to ultimately launch a long-term rally. If, on the other hand, he advanced stock prices, the rally would be short-term in nature.

Thursday, October 3, 1974
Dow −13.92/587.61 Dow Vol. 1,718,900 NYSE Vol. 13,150,000
Today's decline carried the Dow sharply under the 600 level. After about 10 trading days of consistent decline (from 674), it is apparent specialists are taking enormous quantities of stock into inventory that *must* result in a bull raid on the market. What makes this day's events so intriguing is that we have arrived at a point where certain combinations of market events could lead to two distinct and opposite courses of action.

If there is a sharp advance tomorrow, it will indicate that specialists wish to use the weekend interest to build up the kind of optimism which would propel investors into the market on Monday morning. Under such circumstances the rally would be very short-term in nature. For one thing, specialists would never afford investors the opportunity to buy at the bottom of an advance with such a clear-cut signal.

On the other hand, if there is a further sharp decline tomorrow—say of 25 points—it will indicate specialists intend to go for broke beginning Monday. The Stock Exchange would thrive on the panic buildup in investor emotions that would occur over the weekend. If that happened a frightened public could be expected to enter their sell orders for the Monday opening. Another 25-point decline on Monday would bring the Dow down to the 540 level. This would panic even more investors so that the Tuesday opening would reflect the will of those whose only thought would be to get out of the market. Granted the decline could continue for another day or two, carrying the Dow under the 500 level, it is also possible that after a sharp morning drop on Tuesday, specialists could rally the market at midsession with a large enough inventory to warrant a major bull raid. That being the case, it would be foolhardy to postpone commitment in an attempt to catch the exact bottom. I would, therefore, move my clientele into the market at the Tuesday morning opening. Many of them have been waiting in cash instruments for as long as 3½ years for this event to take place.

Tomorrow, then, will tell us whether we are to have a short-term rally or the beginnings of a major long-term advance in stock prices.

Had I been a trader I would have entered my order to buy one of the more volatile Dow stocks fifteen minutes before the close on Friday. That is because the Dow declined only three points on Friday. This indicated that specialists were set for a short- rather than a long-term rally and would be more likely to advance immediately rather than decline further for additional accumulations.

Friday, October 4, 1974
Dow –3.05/584.56 Dow Vol. 1,630,400 NYSE Vol. 15,910,000
The Dow closed at 584.56, down only 3.05 for the day. Obviously, specialists are not yet interested in conducting a long-term bull raid on the market. . . . The significance of today's action, therefore, is not only that we should have a rally next week, possibly beginning Monday, but that if specialists are not interested in launching next week's rally from what could easily have been the 540 level or lower, it could mean they want to do it sometime in the future from a point that could possibly be even lower—perhaps near or under 500. . . . President Ford will deliver his economic address next Tuesday at 4:00 P.M., right after the market's close. This also fits in with my assumption that we can anticipate a sharp but very short rally. From past experience one can suppose that the timing of Ford's announcement, like Nixon's on Sunday, August 15, 1971, will enable specialists to suck the public into the market in large numbers. . . . Characteristically *The New York Times* is advising its readers that yesterday's 13.92 decline was caused by "high interest rates, inflation, and oil problems." What, I wondered, would the *Times* say when the market rallied next week?

Throughout the book I've tried to make the point that the use of the Dow average as an indicator is a source of investor error; that it is the movements of the stocks that comprise the Dow that are important. Nonetheless, both in my narrative and in my diary entries, I refer to the Dow index figures. I do this because the movements of this average have in one sense tremendous significance since they point to an illusion that has enormous psychological impact on investors. For this reason when I discuss the penetration of the "600 level" or a move to the "500 level" it is because such movements enable specialists to predict the behavior of the average investor.

Insofar as market actualities are concerned it is obvious that the Dow may decline under 600 on one occasion and that stocks like Eastman Kodak, Du Pont and Procter & Gamble may approximate lows on this occasion, while the next time this average declines to that same level, these same stocks may be much lower or much higher. Thus the reasons the Dow might decline under 600 at one time could conceivably have little to do with the reasons it approximated the same price level on another occasion.

In determining a sound buying opportunity, what is important is that the evidence of specialist accumulations indicates preparations for an advance of significant proportions and—most important of all—an elimination of the risk factor. Thus it is conceivable that one may be able to acquire a better portfolio of some of the best stocks with the least risk when the Dow is at 600 than when it is at 500. The investor must remember that it's better to acquire 50 shares of an $80 stock in an environment in which the downside risks are limited than 100 shares of $40 stock in a market that might see that stock declining to $15.

In the present instance most investors were reeling from the specialist's roundhouse blows and had no idea that a happy footnote was about to be added to the market's present unhappy chapter. From some of the calls coming to my office, however, I was pleased to note that there were some nimble-footed tyros for whom the decline under the psychological 600 level in the Dow had acted as a challenge and spur to fresh improvisations. I would have liked to be able to tell them that if they could be lightning quick in their in-and-out trading, the price and volume characteristics of stocks like Eastman Kodak and Procter & Gamble left little doubt that there was a splendid opportunity for profits in these situations. For a number of reasons, I refrained from offering this advice. For one thing, it is dangerous to give anyone trading advice unless you are familiar with their financial and psychological backgrounds. Another equally valid reason few of my callers ever take into account is that as a registered investment adviser it is not ethical or in the best interests of my firm's own clientele to offer specific investment advice to others.

I did think it fitting to point out that although the market might be about to provide traders with a sharp rally, when trading is deliberately adopted as a way of life, the ending for most traders is unhappiness. For it is invariably the case that while there are some traders who can tell when to buy, these same individuals are unable to overcome the pressures that are calculated to keep them from selling. Thus, while they recognize that there is no profit without risk, they have little understanding of where the profits leave off and the perils begin. Unless the investor knows, or can learn, when to sell, the pains engendered by a rally can greatly outweigh its advantages.

6

Baiting the Hook or Keeping Up with the Dow Joneses

Ney's Seventh Axiom: He who sells and runs away will live to buy another day . . . tra la.

The reason the industry fastens the public's attention on economic fundamentals is that they cause the investor to plot a curve for buying at the top of a rally and selling at the bottom. The financial myths created by our institutions and cherished by most investors are merely instruments for their defeat. In the final analysis there is no question but that investors would have a much higher standard of living now had it not been for the financial myths they learn in school—and devour each day in their newspapers' financial pages.

That certainly was the problem investors faced in early October 1974. The instruments of communication were occupied chiefly with the revitalizing of myths for the efficient and legal confiscation of the investor's savings. Thinking they were absorbing financial ideas that would promote a more abundant life, investors were being conditioned to leap into the market at the forthcoming rally high.

This was borne out by events beginning on Monday, October 7, when the rally was launched with a 23-point advance in the Dow. In the course of that week (October 7–11) the Dow advanced from 584.56 to 658.17. The public had once again responded to the manner in which specialists had raised the prices of their shares, thereby enabling insiders to unload inventory and sell short.

In the previous chapter I commented that the explanation for the increase in volume during the week ending October 4 could be attributed to specialist short covering which overlapped with specialist accumulations. It is fundamental to an understanding of the specialist's merchandising practices that ordinary familiar things, such as an increase in volume, may be a consequence of different forms of specialist activity. Thus far I have asked the reader to accept the conclusion that different forms of specialist activity (short selling, short covering, and accumulation) are revealed by the same content—volume. Now, examining the following figures for specialist and member short selling, we see that specialists and members minimized their short-selling activi-

CHART 6–1
ROUND-LOT SHARE
VOLUME ON THE NEW YORK STOCK EXCHANGE
(IN SHARES AND WARRANTS)

October, 1974

			Share Volume of Specialists (Except for the Odd-Lot Account) in Stocks in Which They Are Registered		*Other Member Share Volume Initiated on the Floor*		*Other Member Share Volume Initiated off the Floor*	
			Sales		*Sales*		*Sales*	
Date	*Day*	*Dow/NYSE Vol.*	*Total*	*Short*	*Total*	*Short*	*Total*	*Short*
1	Tuesday	604.82/16.89	2,110,500	531,930	157,600	15,200	1,305,173	242,100
2	Wednesday	601.53/12.23	1,691,370	411,560	172,300	33,300	1,191,590	225,350
3	Thursday	587.61/13.15	1,451,590	301,830	105,500	11,200	1,252,765	205,120
4	Friday	584.56/15.91	2,000,020	478,130	136,000	24,500	1,617,648	313,710
7	Monday	607.56/15.00	2,371,810	625,830	154,500	32,100	1,379,081	307,700
8	Tuesday	602.63/15.46	2,222,360	683,700	184,800	70,800	1,555,660	431,510
9	Wednesday	631.02/18.82	2,868,750	917,220	183,000	50,500	1,974,497	536,130
10	Thursday	648.08/26.36	4,636,960	1,962,960	401,100	232,300	2,772,930	860,370
11	Friday	658.17/20.09	2,914,230	1,242,960	163,300	66,300	1,937,436	630,680
14	Monday	673.50/19.77	2,924,590	1,257,760	256,200	172,800	1,728,359	544,350

15	Tuesday	658.40/17.39	2,336,220	917,530	172,800	119,300	1,410,120	429,450
16	Wednesday	642.29/14.79	1,883,590	691,140	100,000	46,800	1,213,657	283,200
17	Thursday	651.44/14.47	2,067,850	691,730	78,900	24,400	1,429,255	407,400
18	Friday	654.88/14.50	2,388,650	952,150	109,100	66,000	1,313,262	397,330
21	Monday	669.82/14.50	1,836,420	670,910	96,800	52,100	1,359,957	477,350
22	Tuesday	662.86/18.93	2,600,100	901,560	186,800	107,300	2,019,452	528,800
23	Wednesday	645.03/14.20	1,845,280	513,030	117,100	44,900	1,142,212	185,050
24	Thursday	636.26/14.91	1,941,740	489,230	116,300	25,400	1,141,059	213,600
25	Friday	636.19/12.65	1,915,150	601,640	137,600	51,300	1,165,751	285,240
28	Monday	633.84/10.54	1,362,070	407,380	88,100	33,500	806,512	198,500
29	Tuesday	659.34/15.61	2,313,440	761,490	143,600	56,300	1,522,130	505,720
30	Wednesday	673.03/20.13	2,911,370	1,123,070	196,600	98,600	1,804,622	526,800
31	Thursday	665.52/18.84	2,468,740	897.050	159,300	76,500	1,462,758	421,600

Source: Statistical Bulletin, published by the SEC.

ties during the first four days of October and established major short positions as stocks moved to their highs on the tenth, eleventh, and fourteenth.

For the first four days of October, when the market was at its lows, specialist short-selling totaled 1,723,450 shares. Note the drop in specialist short-selling when the Dow penetrated the 600 level on Thursday the third. Now observe that for the three-day period of Thursday, October 10, Friday, October 11, and Monday, October 14, when stock prices advanced to their highs, specialist short-selling totaled 4,463,680. What the relatively low amounts of specialist and member short-selling from October 1 through 4 indicate is that insiders were, on balance, covering their short sales and accumulating stock in anticipation of the rally they would launch the week beginning October 7.

It is also interesting to observe the minimal amount of short selling by other members (insiders) on the floor during the first four-day period. Compare these figures with the 232,300 sold short by them on Thursday, October 10. Public demand for stock on the tenth (on daily volume of 26,360,000 shares) was precipitated by the 28.32 gain registered by the Dow on Wednesday (the day after Ford's speech on the nation's economy). Thus we see once again that it was Wednesday's increase in prices that caused the increase in demand on Thursday which enabled specialists and other members to dispose of inventory and maximize their short sales.

In studying these figures it should be recognized that a special SEC loophole has, knowingly, struck a valiant blow for financial inequality by allowing specialists and other insiders not only to sell short on downticks but not to record their short sales as such. Thus it is that the actual figures for specialist short sales are not really available. It is therefore impossible for the investor to establish their full extent. Nonetheless, the figures presented here are important, since they point the direction of specialist intent and thereby enable us to validate our assumptions concerning the methodical and consistent manner in which specialists neutralize the economic force of public demand.

Thus we see that the specialist's ability to predict the future is based on the power granted him by the short sale to shape the future. The ability to sell short at a top in response to public demand and then to cover the short sales in response to public selling allows the specialist to create a situation that, in the stock market, would seem at first glance to be manifestly impossible—i.e., one in which it would be possible, for practical purposes, to eliminate uncertainty.

From the following diary entry we are able to gain insight into another method whereby the specialist's shift of emphasis from a market advance to a market decline directs the investor's attention away from a market condition in which the specialist is, for a moment, vulnerable to purchases by the public at the very time he is attempting to stimulate public selling. Thus instead of making a decision that would enable him to trade profitably in the market, the trader is focused on the seeming unpredictability of the environment. At the moment when the specialist's confrontation with public competition is most intense, the specialist pits the trader against what *seems* to be the forces of gravity. Not for a moment does the trader recognize that the forces of gravity are capable of reversal at the specialist's pleasure—and will be reversed once the trader's loss of confidence causes him to question the validity of his decision to buy stock.

Tuesday, October 8, 1974
Dow –4.93/602.63 Dow Vol. 1,404,300 NYSE Vol. 15,460,000
Today's decline of 4.93 is evidence of the specialist's professional skill as a practiced hand of the shell game. Yesterday's sudden advance of 23 points enabled specialists to sneak prices up without undue public participation. Today's decline took the wind out of the investor's sails, causing him to remain out of the market at what has to be the beginning of a sharp, although short, rally. That was its function. Just as prices began to sneak up, the Exchange focused the trader's attention on the empty shell and he bought it.

Ford's address delivered at the market's close provided investors with armfuls of smoke. His approach to the issues of inflation and spiraling unemployment and his exhortations to practice thrift were so disappointing to those who had hoped for something concrete that if we had a legitimate auction market it would now crash. Instead, specialists will probably raise the Dow like a rocket—or should I say like a guillotine.

The specialist's power is vividly illustrated in the way he is able to break the investor's spirit one day and then, to serve his purposes, generate new faith the next. The nature of these routine triumphs is examined in the next entry.

Wednesday, October 9, 1974
Dow +28.39/631.02 Dow Vol. 1,486,400 NYSE Vol. 18,820,000
Sharply rising prices today tell us the Exchange wants sharply rising demand tomorrow. For the artifice of yesterday's decline there is the deceptive dialectic today of a 6¼-point advance in Kodak, a 4⅛-point advance in Procter & Gamble, and the 2- to 3-point gain registered in such stocks as Alcoa, Allied Chemical, General Electric, International Paper, Sears, Union Carbide, U.S. Steel, and Exxon.

It is in the very nature of a rally like today's that shadow outweighs substance. Much of the buying that came in toward the close was due to the fears of those who had sold short and who were now rushing to cover their previously established short positions.

The same blindness that caused one group to flee from the market today will cause another to stampede into it tomorrow. Thus do clerks, teachers, widows, and a bewildered middle-income class provide the bread, butter, and filling to the specialist's late afternoon sandwich.

Few practices are more secret than the specialist's highly sophisticated trick of raising stock prices one day in order to stimulate demand the next. Thus I was certain that because of Wednesday's 28-point advance, investors would be falling all over each other on Thursday in their efforts to buy stock.

Thursday, October 10, 1974
Dow +17.06/648.08 Dow Vol. 2,218,400 NYSE Vol. 26,360,000
Following on the heels of yesterday's fast run-up prices, there were big opening blocks this morning in major Dow stocks. Du Pont opened at 105½ on 20,000 shares, up 4 points. General Electric opened at 36⅞ on 15,500 shares, up ½ point; it then moved up to the 39 level. Procter &

Gamble opened at 71¾ on 19,000 shares, up 3⅞. And so it went. As stocks like General Motors and General Electric were dropped from their highs, the advance in other stocks in the Dow that opened up on important gaps masked their decline. It is because the pattern obtained by the decline of some Dow stocks and the advance of others is not reflected in the movements of the Dow that the Exchange is able to use this index as an instrument of deception to suck the public into the market at the very time its principal stocks may already have turned down. As the last stocks to open joined in the decline, the Dow Industrials dropped from +22 to +12. In order to unload more inventory and establish additional short sales, the Dow was once again raised. Shortly thereafter it was back to +24 on 18,300,000 shares. Volume once more provides the key to the market's future. Insiders were selling their stock to outsiders. When this process has been completed *there is only one direction in which the market can move. As always, volume, not price, is the principal guarantor of the market's direction.*

Speculating in the market is a game that's rough on morale. This morning was an exception. Traders were slapping each other on the back and happily swapping trade talk in the local Bache office as the Dow posted a 20-point gain during the first hour. When the figures for specialist short selling are published for today, I would not be at all surprised to see that their short sales are in excess of 2 million shares.

There is a canny wisdom in the way in which the specialist creates a confrontation with the market's innocents. Too late, the latter discover they were unequal to the encounter and that the hands of their invisible adversary have them by the throat.

Thus, with infinite subtlety, the specialist advances his plot line one step further by showing the investor that what he feels he is unable to gain in the market because of his lack of skill he can gain because of the existence of good luck. By raising prices high enough the specialist easily persuades the investor to forget the bad luck he had in the past.

Friday, October 11, 1974
Dow +10.09/658.17 Dow Vol. 1,804,500 NYSE Vol. 20,090,000
My survey of the scene leaves no doubt in my mind that the market has been set up for a decline that will probably begin next week. For one

thing, once the public has been sucked into the market in large numbers, generally speaking, the terminal point of that rally is, pricewise, not far distant. Of course one can never know exactly how high specialists will want to raise prices in order to hypodermic demand. One thing is certain, they are a practical breed and under no circumstances would they advance prices to a point at which the mass of investors would be allowed to find themselves in a position where they could establish a handsome profit. If I am correct and the rally does peak out under the 700 level, the Dow will have risen approximately 100 points from its bottom. This would average out to a 5-point advance in each of the Dow stocks. Since only a few Dow stocks account for most of an advance in a bear market, it is probable that the mass of investors, finding themselves with only small profits, would tend to hold on through this rally and ride it all the way down to sell at new lows.

One has only to consider the increase in volume of the 30 Dow stocks (2.2 million yesterday, 1.8 million today) to recognize that among the 22 specialists who control the "dirty thirty," a number of them have, in all probability, already committed themselves to the short side of the market. This is borne out by the fact that the volume on rising prices in Kodak (114,100 shares), General Motors (103,600 shares), and Texaco (100,500 shares) indicates that the specialists in these stocks have established the conditions that will enable them to drop their prices profitably in order to clear the territory below of inventory.

It is also unlikely that specialists had liquidated the inventory they accumulated in the course of the August to early October decline. Although there is a Stock Exchange rule stipulating that a specialist cannot be long and short in his trading account at the same time, specialists have different accounts that allow them to evade the rule. Thus it is logical that specialists would maintain their large accumulations of inventory in both investment and omnibus accounts, while for purposes of the rule, they could have established short sales only in their trading accounts.

The nature of the present rally raises another point. If specialists are ever to invade the territory profitably that is just above or under the 500 level in the Dow, as I believe is quite possible, they have yet to establish the kind of short positions that would enable them to do this. Thus while demand was heavy yesterday and today and will, in all probability, be as great on Monday, it is apparent that the demand forthcoming in the course of the present rally will be inadequate to fully service the specialist system's needs. This being so, it would seem logical to assume that, as is often the case, specialists will have to conduct another and more important rally if they are to service their short-sale needs.

One question that might be asked at this point is, Why don't specialists simply raise prices from the current level to create further demand in order to accomplish their goals? In attempting to answer this question it might prove helpful to list some of the factors we know to be operating at this point in time. Thus as we have previously stated:

1. The public was sucked into the rally two or three days after it was launched. Thus the present rally is generally short-term in nature and soon to end.
2. Specialists probably have large inventories from the August–October decline.
3. Specialists have established new short sales, but not enough for a severe decline.

From this set of conditions, we can draw the following deductions:

1. The amount of short sales established will not allow prices to decline much lower than the October 3 low.
2. The decline will be on light volume.
3. It will be necessary to establish another short-term rally (6 months or less) of greater dimensions.

Looking backward and using history as our guide, we are able to gain insight into the possible reason specialists have arrived at this particular strategy. We know that the seasonal need of investors to sell for tax purposes is soon to come. Typically, we can expect specialists to drop prices before these sales take place and then, once they have, to rally in order to unload this inventory at higher prices.

On the morning of October 11, I appeared on the NBC-TV *Today* show. I pointed out that, in disagreement with the financial media, I did *not* believe the rally then underway was the beginning of a bull market. In reply to a question by Barbara Walters concerning the extent of the rally, I stated, "I expect to see the decline begin next week." As the program came to an end she turned to me and asked, "In view of what you've said should begin to take place in the market next week, do you have any final word of advice for investors?" I replied, "He who sells and runs away will live to buy another day . . . tra la!"

The following Monday was the beginning of what I assumed would be the end of the rally. To understand the stock market one must understand that Monday rarely means what it says and that those who invest on a Monday because of the promise provided by rising prices on Friday are optimists, not empiricists. The policy makers of the specialist system know this. The Friday, October 11, 10-point gain in the Dow was a case in point. Because of Friday's gain, a leap in morale over the weekend interval would inevitably be followed by the commitment of many investors on the following Monday.

Monday, October 14, 1974
Dow +15.33/673.50 Dow Vol. 2,005,500 NYSE Vol. 19,770,000
Final comments about today's market:

1. Dow volume is 2,005,500 shares. The meaning of this is that specialists are signaling that the rally has probably reached its high for the present and that they have completed the establishment of their first set of short sales.
2. The configuration of major Dow stocks at today's close suggests specialists established the high at the intraday peak of 689.30. Had specialists been interested in moving the Dow higher tomorrow, they would not have backed off so much from the highs established in major Dow stocks.
    a. The difference between Friday's high in Du Pont (108) and today's high (116¼) is 8¼ points with a close at 113 (on only 5,400 shares).
    b. Kodak advanced 4½ points to 78½ and then closed at 76.
    c. General Motors and General Electric advanced close to their critical number 40 (38½ and 38 respectively) and then declined.
3. If, indeed, today did provide us with the rally high, then although the advance to the high required only four days, the decline back down will probably be protracted over a period of at least several weeks. For although the short sales established today were large in number, they would still not have provided specialists with a large enough inventory of short sales to make it possible for them to absorb the selling that would take place were they to attempt a sharp decline from present levels.

Public demand for stock on the tenth through the fourteenth was a portent of the crisis to come. Simply by presenting investors with a pattern of rising prices packaged for their palates, specialists persuaded them to assume the direction of stock prices was up when, in fact, the conditions that actually characterized the downtrend were still in existence. The consequences of investor action were, therefore, painfully predictable.

On the morning of Tuesday the fifteenth, I appeared on the ABC-TV morning show from 7:15 to 7:45 EST. "Take all the time you want to get your message out," Don Segal, the producer, told me. "We called the Stock Exchange and tried to get a specialist to go on with you. There were no takers. Most of them didn't even call us back."

With Monday's 2-million-plus volume in the Dow, I assumed it was a safe bet that the market would be down sharply Tuesday. Hence as soon as possible after the program began, I stated, "The market should start down today." One person calling in had difficulty understanding why I had stated that Stock Exchange insiders had been heavy sellers in Monday's market. I pointed out that the Exchange was a supersupermarket that operated exactly the same as Macy's Department Store with one difference. When Macy's wants to create demand for its merchandise, it conducts a sale by *lowering* prices. When the merchants on the New York Stock Exchange want to conduct a sale, they attract customers by *raising* prices. It occurred to me that the investor's misfortunes could be attributed to his vain attempts to acquire bargains in the course of one or another of the many sales conducted by the Stock Exchange. That afternoon the Dow closed −15 points. By Wednesday it was down 16 points.

7

Whatever Goes Up...
or
Apes Living in Trees Are the Real Swingers: They Know When to Let Go

Ney's Eighth Axiom: The pain comes later. It's called hindsight.

Having completed my business in New York, I flew to Palm Beach. Although the transition is always to an area of less concentrated activity, I find it an amiable setting of clean air, beautiful ocean, and warm friendships. Even though most of its inhabitants have accumulated great wealth, they nonetheless share with most Americans the same naïve investment habits. During dinner at their homes the conversation inevitably turns to the market. I am always astonished to observe the willingness with which these otherwise intelligent individuals commit millions of dollars into the market on the basis of the superficial information they obtain from their brokers, friends, or the financial pages. They are perfectly content to work within the traditional mold. They will attach great importance to newspaper headlines such as "Analysts Say a New Bull Market Has Begun." Not for a moment does it occur to them that the story that carries the quote was probably written by a newsman who would be quite frank to admit that because of his inability to understand the workings of the market, he was accustomed to simply refurbishing the handouts from the wire services.

It is only natural that investors should want to know what is happening in the market, but for their own sake they should learn not to believe any absurdity merely because it was said by a Wall Street stockbroker or banker and quoted in *The New York Times* or *The Wall Street Journal.* One of the most popular myths is that the lowering of interest rates causes the market to rally.

The fact is the rise and fall of interest rates serves as a convenient ploy to rationalize the movement of stock prices. Once the relationship between the Stock Exchange and the eastern banking establishment is identified, it becomes apparent that the critical task of these institutions is to employ whatever strategies are required for competing successfully against the public sector—the area upon which they mutually depend for the growth of their relationship and their incomes. That is not to say that the relationship is overly complicated. It isn't. The fact is, many major banks have specialists in their stocks on the floor of the Exchange with whom they do business. Each knows how and when investment accounts are accumulated and the manner in which these accounts are connected with an enterprise contrary to the interest of investors. When Exchange specialists require credit to finance either their investment accounts or their short sales, these banks stand ready to supply it.

In order to make matters easier for themselves, specialists have devised a rule that allows them to borrow money from their bankers on "terms that are mutually satisfactory." Since the banks' fortunes are closely linked with the specialists', such loans are made on the basis of a common interest. As most bankers know, the policies of the Fed are determined not so much by the chairman of the Fed as by the directors of the Federal Reserve Bank of New York. There are three classes of directors who oversee the workings of this bank: Class A, Class B, and Class C. The Class A directors are the bank's policy makers. The three Class A directors of the Federal Reserve Bank of New York are the chairman of a little bank in Passaic, New Jersey; the president of a little bank in Saratoga Springs, New York; and David Rockefeller, chairman of the Board of Chase Manhattan Bank.

It is difficult for the average individual to appreciate that the Federal Reserve system serves as one of the chief apologists for the Stock Exchange establishment. The basic operations of an institution like the Fed, its relationships with other institutions such as banks, corporations, the Stock Exchange, and government, are accepted as being inexplicable but constructive.

The irrational movements of stock prices are also made to appear rational to the public. It is not at all surprising that, in order to make its practices palatable, the Exchange has created a highly functional body of myths to support the concept of an auction market that operates according to the laws of supply and demand. This not only is simple for the public to understand, but it enables the Exchange to command a continuing series of headlines.

Since the heads of the Stock Exchange establishment are also the heads of the eastern banking establishment, it is a simple matter for them to determine when to raise and lower rates. The timing of either is never by chance. Since billions of dollars are involved, anachronistic scruples about the economic implications of high interest rates are willingly sacrificed to serve a rationale that justifies sharply rising or falling stock prices. Thus by utilizing a formula in which stock prices advance as interest rates are lowered, the actual objective underlying advancing stock prices, which is to create demand for stock, is disguised. In the uninformed public mind, the event conforms to economic criteria. Thus the public is easily persuaded to buy when interest rates decline and to think about selling when they begin to rise.

Once insiders accumulate a large inventory of stock, merely by lowering interest rates, they can justify a bull market in stock prices. It was for this reason that in June, July, and August 1970, when I was appearing on TV and radio to promote *The Wall Street Jungle*, I found it a simple matter to forecast that interest rates would be coming down in November and December 1970 (as indeed they did). I knew that, by that time, stock prices would have risen to a point where specialists would be preparing to distribute investment accounts in which they were "directly and indirectly interested." The ritual of lower interest rates would then pull the public into the market. As it happened, this was also true of the October 1974 rally.

For my part, there was little doubt that the logic underlying the October rally had again run into the stone wall of specialist short selling on October 14 and that the two-day decline of the fifteenth and sixteenth substantiated this. The dangers of the specialists' calling are such, however, that unless the declines that follow on the heels of a rally are carefully managed, the public's faith in the validity of the "bull market" can falter. This can then precipitate too much selling too soon, thereby causing specialists to rally stock prices again. Such was not the case with the two-day decline of the fifteenth and sixteenth. A technique that is consistently in vogue with Dow specialists was employed to prevent too devitalizing an influence on investors. Thus the two-day decline was followed by a sharp rally (October 17, +9.15; October 18, +3.44; October 21, +14.94), which provided investors with the catharsis that always occurs with rising prices.

Through careful press agentry, the market's buoyant future continued to be proclaimed and promoted. In commenting on the advance, *The New York Times*, on October 19, upheld the establishment's current myth:

> Sparked by a reduction in the prime rate by two major banks early in the session, the stock market managed to maintain most of its gains and finished higher in heavier trading.

By Tuesday, October 22, specialists had rallied stock prices to an intraday high of 680.07. No sooner was the high established than they once again dropped stock prices. This decline lasted from October 22 to October 28. By the twenty-eighth the Dow had declined to an intraday low of 624.06. Then on the twenty-ninth, after again dropping stock prices and cleaning out their books, specialists rallied prices (approximately 25 points).

During the last quarter of 1974, I began discussing the specialist's habit patterns in the course of different radio interviews conducted by telephone from my office. I tried to make my listeners understand why the Stock Exchange was referred to as a private club. I explained how insiders, particularly specialists, operate as members of a closed group with a code of conduct and ethics all their own. I stated that because they deal in big money they are highly organized.

I had been discussing these matters with Dick Clayton of radio station WCAU in Philadelphia. I contended that in order to achieve unanimity of purpose, specialists are in the habit of discussing their objectives *before* the commencement of trading. This makes sense, I said, since they are dealing in hundreds of millions of dollars each day and could subject themselves to heavy losses if their efforts were not perfectly coordinated. I then told him that I could tell his audience how the majority of stocks would open on the morning of my next broadcast (October 24), and whether the Dow would be up or down, merely by observing the prices of the first three or four Dow stocks as they opened. At that time I also gave him the names of twenty of the Exchange's most important specialists and suggested he try to obtain one of them to debate with me. The plan was for me to talk from California and the specialist to debate with me via telephone from New York.

Clayton's program began at 10:00 A.M. sharp. Thus on October 24, as the market opened and stock prices began to move across my ticker tape, I quoted the first three stock prices and stated that the Dow would be down.* Esmark opened at 25¾, down ½; U.S. Steel opened at 38, down 1; and Johns-Manville opened at 15½, down ⅛. I then stated that these three transactions led me to expect declines in the opening prices of stocks like General Motors and General Electric. A few minutes later, corroborating my statement that there is a kind of understanding among Dow specialists as to how prices will open, General Motors, General Electric, and many other Dow stocks opened on the downside. I asked Clayton if he had made any effort to get a New York Stock Exchange specialist to debate with me. He told me he had tried for several days to persuade one of the specialists I'd listed to go on with me but had failed in his effort.

The subtle balance between the forces of supply and demand is inoperative only because the specialist's thumb is always on the scales. I have already mentioned the specialist's book. The Special Study Report of the SEC stated (Part 2, pages 77 and 166):

> In executing his brokerage functions the specialist has a powerful tool, available to him only, giving him insight into the possible course of the market . . . [his] exclusive knowl-

*I should point out that 30 of the 40 stocks quoted by this particular ticker tape are Dow stocks.

> edge of the orders on the book and the known sources of supply and demand available to him through the book give him a definite trading advantage over other market participants. . . .

It is my opinion that once the investor determines that he wishes to sell his stock, he should enter his order with his stockbroker *after the close of the market* to sell this stock (at the market) at the following morning's opening. By avoiding placing a limit order on the specialist's book, the investor can, in this fashion, limit his risk.

The October rally is a case in point. With an understandable loss of perspective, investors entered stop loss orders (orders to sell if the price should decline to a certain level or below) on the assumption that their orders would protect them from the hazards of a falling market. Thus when specialists purposefully dropped their stock prices, they were able to clean out (purchase stock from investors) these stop loss orders and then, after rallying prices, establish profits for themselves by selling this stock at higher prices. A secondary benefit accruing to the specialist from this maneuver was, of course, that it enabled him to conduct his next decline through the same area on lower volume.

This, then, was the experience of investors who saw their stop loss orders executed as stock prices were dropped toward the October 28 low. That specialists were then again able to rally stock prices back up to the intraday high of 681 by Wednesday the thirtieth pretty much sums up the profit potentials of the specialist's book when it is combined with the remarkable gifts of insight made possible by self-regulation.

The press of course played its role to perfection on this occasion. On October 29, commenting on the previous day's decline of 2.35 in the Dow, *The Wall Street Journal* issued the following disclaimer for the failure of lower interest rates to rally the market:

> Unfavorable earnings of auto and related companies overpowered the positive effects of eroding interest rates. . . .

(What, one wonders, was the depressant cited by the *Journal* to account for the decline in the price of General Motors from the 90 level in April 1971, when earnings were rising from $2.00 to more than $8.50 a share by the third quarter of 1973?)

Showing the manner in which interest rates or indeed anything can provide a rich and fertile compost for the PR experts of the Stock Exchange, we have *The New York Times* comments on October 30 on the previous day's 25-point advance in the Dow:

> Spurred by a continuing decline in short term interest rates, the stock market ignored some bearish news yesterday and registered its biggest gain in almost three weeks.

And from the Washington *Post* of October 30:

> The stock market, aided by hopes for oil price reductions and prospects for a coal industry contract settlement, staged its best rally in nearly three weeks today in fairly active trading on the New York Stock Exchange.

Where an alibi is concerned, you pays your money and you takes your choice.

When more suitable rationalizations are lacking, the media will often quote someone who suggests that the market possesses characteristics capable of complex levels of consciousness. Thus, from the Washington *Post* of October 31, 1974:

> There was no specific news event to spark this rally. "The market was doing its own thing," said one observer. "It opened quietly, looked around, then took off."

Largely because of the advance of 25.50 points on October 29, volume swelled to 20.2 million on the thirtieth. Prices were again dropped for the next three trading days and then, on November 5 and 6, advanced to establish the rally's final intraday high at 692.82. The Dow closed at 669.12, off 5.63 points for the day. NYSE volume was 23.9 million shares. The Dow volume was 1,871,400 shares.

My diary excerpts for November 5 and 6 suggest how difficult it is for the investor to formulate investment policy on the basis of the information provided by the media.

Tuesday, November 5, 1974
Dow +17.52/674.75 Dow Vol. 1,225,000 NYSE Vol. 15,960,000
Despite the fact that "the market" supposedly finds its inspiration from economic events, the circumstances that are said to cause it to decline one day are, more often than not, ignored as the market advances the following day. Investors are told that the market declined yesterday because of the coal strike. Today Dow specialists advanced prices. What do the media say under these circumstances? On November 6 the Los Angeles *Times* ran the following headline:

STOCKS POST BEST CLOSE IN 2 MONTHS: DOW LEAPS 17.52

and then accounted for the rally by suggesting that

> . . . investors were shrugging off much in the immediate news of the day—including the evidently heightened prospect of a coal strike. . . .

The Los Angeles *Times* and the Washington *Post* are published in different cities. Thus, while the Los Angeles *Times* suggested that the market advanced *despite* the threat of a coal strike, the Washington *Post* told its readers that, in effect, the market went up *because* of the coal strike:

> A belief on Wall Street that a threatened nationwide coal strike would be short helped push prices sharply higher today in fairly active trading on the New York Stock Exchange.

Excerpts from the entry of November 6 are also included, because I believe they place the investor in the context of the price action that exists at a rally high.

Wednesday, November 6, 1974
Dow −5.63/669.12 Dow Vol. 1,871,400 NYSE Vol. 23,930,000
Commanded by yesterday's sharp rally in the Dow, investors obediently charged into the market today. Specialist short selling absorbed the force of their demand when it was at its strongest—during the first hour. General Motors moved to 36¼ from yesterday's close at 35⅜—and the rest of the market played follow the leader.

When stock prices are breaking from stock market or rally highs, the Exchange often exhibits a certain mechanical clumsiness. Either its specialists drop stock prices sharply at the opening, announce a delayed opening or a halt in trading, or there is a late tape. Oftentimes, with pagan innocence, the Exchange will announce a breakdown of its equipment, after which prices are discovered to be markedly lower. Investors in IBM are not unfamiliar with the experience. During the first hour, stock prices were up more than 15 points—on high volume. Not long afterward, after IBM had begun to decline, a late tape carried the information that IBM had "sold" 500 shares at 200. The next transaction was for 196. This is typical in a down market. Quotations are quite often provided only when prices have already moved lower. A late tape is an excellent device for this purpose.

The price action of Dow stocks once again showed us why we must look to the tricky changes of pace in individual Dow stocks rather than to the movements of the Dow average to see what is taking place. For example the intraday highs in Dow stocks like Du Pont at 112¾ on 83,600 shares, General Motors at 36¼ on 137,500 shares, and Eastman Kodak at 77½ on 93,500 shares all were under the (short-selling) highs of October 14 (DD 116¼, GM 38, EK 78½). One thing this shows us is that although the Dow average had established a higher rally high on November 6 than on October 14, this was not due to the action of the stocks that had been major contributors to the rally high of October 14. To understand this is to define the predicament in which thousands of investors found themselves who, in their innocence, rushed into the market and bought these stocks on the fourteenth of October. Then, having watched them drop in price since that date, they waited for them to recover, hoping only to be able to sell them at the prices at which they were purchased. Many of them were probably even foolish enough to enter limit orders to sell with their brokers which were then entered in the specialist's book, thereby enabling him to discern their intent.

The evening television news reported that it was the threat of the coal strike that had caused the collapse in stock prices—but neglected to say that the Dow advanced the first hour to enable specialists to establish additional inventories of short sales. *The New York Times,* on the other hand, pointed to the first hour's advance and then described the events which it cited as the cause of the later decline:

> The stock market finished mixed in the heaviest trading in almost a month yesterday as profit taking and bearish economic news eroded strong earlier gains. . . .
>
> The negative news included a brief by the Justice Department calling for the restructuring of International Business Machines to allow more companies to enter the computer field and the announcement by the General Electric Company that it was laying off 11,200 workers at its major appliance plant in Louisville because of the slowdown in the housing market. . . .
>
> Another late depressing factor was the Securities and Exchange Commission's announcement that it would not object to the Big Board's proposed 8 per cent increase in fixed commission rates applying to orders between $5,000 and $300,000. This would make it more expensive for investors to deal in the market.
>
> Another depressant was fear that a strike in the coal industry seemed inevitable. . . .

In the land of the pushers and the pushed, *The New York Times* is firmly on the side of the pushers. The *Times* comments on November 7 made no mention that the bulk of the "profit taking" at a market high is by specialists. Nor were any brokers quoted to the effect that the market "looked like it could be topping out." It is only at the bottom that the financial page turns bearish.

Most investors failed to recognize the change in trend. Nor were they aware that since October 14, the rally had been like a chicken running around the barnyard with its head cut off. Granted it had leaped quite high from time to time, ultimately it recognized the sanctions of the axe. Such is the lesson for all those who fail to understand that a rally can seem to be possessed of life long after the life has left it.

But having beheaded a capon, specialists would soon replace it with a turkey.

8

Pressing the Down Button or The Customer Is Always Wrong

Ney's Ninth Axiom: What nobody wants everybody gets.

The Exchange is always able to trap investors into buying stock by raising prices. The question, however, is, How much demand can be brought forth by how large an advance during a particular period of time with its particular economic background. It naturally follows that if specialists are able to discover that a certain amount of demand is present at a certain period in time, then they know it can be tapped again provided it's within the same approximate time frame. Thus in the broadest sense, one of the principal functions of the October rally, as I saw it then, was to enable specialists to reconnoiter the environment, to examine investor attitudes, investor response to the stimulus of rising prices, the onset of seasonal tax selling factors and the manner in which a first rally high could be employed as an overall organizational base from which to launch a second rally.

The restraints that a faltering economy and a long-drawn-out bear market might have imposed on the will of investors had been investigated and the authority of rising prices to create demand was again affirmed. Thus as the market turned down in November, it was apparent that a second rally would enable specialists to profitably dispose of the stock in January that they acquired from tax sellers in December. A rally for this purpose was S.O.P.

Price, as always, was employed as an investigative tool. Much as a Geiger counter is used to locate radioactivity, price is used by specialists to locate volume. Because of its distortions of perspective, investors fail to recognize the dangers to which their attitudes toward price subject them. In the present instance the October rally provided specialists with an insight into the perplexing question of investor demand.

Volume is the investor's window onto the floor of the Stock Exchange. Properly utilized, it brings the investor face to face with the specialist's attitude toward his inventory—whether he wants to dispose of it or add to it and, therefore, raise or lower his price. The problem is that investors have not been trained to examine the movements of volume as an indicator of change.

Instead they believe that high volume in the course of a rally is proof of the "market's underlying strength." *In fact the very opposite is true.* Volume is either a manifestation of specialist accumulation when it is on the downside or an indication of specialist distribution when it occurs on the upside.

Since specialist short-selling is an aspect of specialist distribution, an understanding of the volume of specialist short-selling is fundamental to an understanding of the specialist's intent toward his processes of decline. The only assurance the investor can have that a limitation has been placed on the market's downward processes is that a decline is generally directly proportionate to the specialist's inventory of short sales. In other words, how severe a decline will be in a stock depends on the extent of the specialist's short sales and how well he conserves them.

Although specialist short-selling at the October high had been significant, it was not of the proportions that would allow a plunge under the 500 level. As I indicated earlier, it was quite logical to assume that specialists might ultimately wish to take stock prices under this important psychological price level. A realistic appraisal of the specialists' short-sale requirements for such an event would insist they husband their short sales very carefully in anticipation of heavy public selling as they again went under 600. This was the case when the declines got under way in the drop from the October–November 1973 highs. Thus the basic foundation for a 200-point decline having been laid at that time, it was maintained intact until prices moved toward their lows. In the present case, however, I did not believe that the remaining inventory of short sales could support a drop much lower than the October lows. If my analysis was correct, it would mean specialists intended to launch a decline to lower levels from still higher levels—in other words, at the end of another, more dramatic rally. Regrettably, a second rally would significantly increase the number of investors who would become enmeshed by the market as the rally moved toward its high.

If during the present decline, my technical indicators signaled that insiders were accumulating their investment accounts, I would move my clients into the market. Under these conditions I would be virtually certain of obtaining long-term capital gains in a minimum risk environment. By the same token, if I had to wait until the end of the next rally for this event, I would commit then. Professionally it made very little difference to me what course of action specialists chose. I was happy enough to stand on the sidelines and patiently wait for low-risk long-term investment opportunities.

Rallying stock prices almost immediately after they have begun to decline is an institutionalized system for unloading the first batch of stop loss orders that are accumulated by specialists from their books. Thus the 5.63 decline of November 6 after the Dow had established an intraday rally high that morning was followed by an advance of 2.81 on the seventh. In case it might seem as though a 2.81 advance in the Dow is insignificant, it should be pointed out that the investor whose attention is focused exclusively on the Dow tends to obtain a false picture. What is important here is that in the course of such an advance, although Dow stocks may end the day with a sum total of only +2.81, inventory distributions can and do occur in the course of intraday highs which are significantly above closing prices. Thus on the seventh we find that Eastman Kodak had advanced 2½ points from the previous day's close, Du Pont almost 4 points, and Procter & Gamble 2⅝ points. Specialists in these and other stocks were then able to resume their downtrends on Friday, November 8, with a decline of 4.77.

The scale of organization inherent in a decline—any decline—imposes on specialists in highly active stocks functions that demand their most scrupulous attention. The conflict of opposing interests between insiders and outsiders must be carefully disguised so as to not cause a breakdown in the game plan that would result in an avalanche of selling by outsiders. The events of November 11 to 13 provide the reader with another instance in which the price action of these three days can be seen to advance the progression of the decline while at the same time giving the impression of "underlying strength in the market."

Monday, November 11, 1974
Dow +5.48/672.64 Dow Vol. 895,900 NYSE Vol. 13,220,000
Competent observers of the market should have been warned of high risk on the downside when they saw that after the first hour's decline on downside volume of only 2.88 million shares the market rallied. That, as much as anything else, was something on which a shrewd trader could have capitalized, since such a rally after a decline on light volume suggested strongly that the market would soon resume its downtrend.

An early morning decline enables specialists to clean out their books of stop loss orders and to absorb any additional selling. Then in the course of a rally, they are able to unload this stock at higher prices. This maneuver enables specialists to make the best use of their short sales by covering them at lower price levels. By first dropping stock prices and then rallying them, they avoid the necessity of having to use their short sales to absorb the public's sell orders at the morning's lows. Today's 5-point rally, therefore, enabled specialists to conserve their short-sale inventories.

Of interest: Volume in General Motors dropped from 120,500 Friday (5-day average was 118,500 shares) to 78,000 today. While it closed only ⅛ lower (at 34⅛), it established an intraday low of 33⅝. Obviously this specialist is bringing daily volume in this stock down to manageable proportions; within the next day or so we can expect to see GM decline further in price.

Knowing that taste must be created, especially in the face of a declining market, on November 12 the Los Angeles *Times* financial page headlined the following information about the market of the eleventh:

MARKET OVERCOMES NEGATIVE
NEWS DJ MANAGES TO GAIN 5

This was followed with the encouraging news that

> The stock market drifted upstream Monday against a flow of adverse developments from the start of a national coal strike to persistent recession worries. . . .

Comments found in *The Wall Street Journal* were also in keeping with this tradition:

> "There have been all kinds of provocations to send the market down, but none seems to be taking hold," said Leslie M. Pollack, senior vice president of Shearson Hayden Stone, Inc. Besides the coal strike, he added, other recent depressants have included the rise in unemployment to 6% and the threat of another war in the Middle East.
>
> A strong offset to these negatives, however, has been the continuing easing of short-term interest rates, brokers said. . . .

Tuesday, November 12, 1974
Dow −13.46/659.18 Dow Vol. 1,035,000 NYSE Vol. 15,040,000
The volume in General Motors declined to 69,200 shares—even as the price declined ½ point to 33⅝, yesterday's intraday low. Volume should rise in GM tomorrow, however, as the stock continues its decline. This should then prompt a rally in the stock and the market either tomorrow or the next day. Volume should also increase in the overall market because of today's 13-point decline.

The Wall Street Journal scenario for the 13.46 decline of November 12:

> Growing concern over the coal stoppage took hold of an uncertain stock market yesterday afternoon and tipped it into a steep and broad retreat. . . .
>
> Another factor that troubled investors, brokers also said, was the British budget message's statement carried by wire services about mid-session. . . .

Wednesday, November 13, 1974
Dow .00/659.18 Dow Vol. 1,316,800 NYSE Vol. 16,040,000

Today's events bring the following into sharp focus:

1. Because the Dow did not register a significant decline, most investors will assume that the threat to the market posed by the coal strike is over.
2. An early morning decline enabled specialists to clean out their books of stop loss orders. Having done this, it was a simple matter to then rally stock prices in order to liquidate at higher prices the inventories acquired during the first hour. This was notably evident in General Motors. As anticipated, volume almost doubled in this stock from yesterday (from 69,200 to 136,800). Having closed at 33⅝ yesterday, General Motors opened on 12,700 shares at 33¼, declined to 33 on big blocks, and then rallied to close at 34¾. It was as simple for the specialist as playing with a yo-yo.
3. It is now probable that GM's specialist will soon attack the 30–32 level. As GM moves toward 30, volume should increase dramatically.
4. The Dow closing unchanged masks the fact that almost twice as many stocks declined today as advanced and that this, as much as anything, signals the kind of deterioration now taking place in the overall market.

The market declined further on Monday, November 18. By this time, the public had been so conditioned to believe declines were of a temporary nature that although the Dow lost 22.09 points, suffering its biggest loss in more than ten months, volume was light. General Motors opened at 32½—down ¾ from the Friday close on a block of 20,000 shares. By the close, it had been dropped 1 point to 31½ on 161,600 shares. American Telephone & Telegraph declined 1½ points to 46 on 105,900 shares. Of particular interest was that General Motors was now close to its lows, while Telephone had only begun to retreat from its high. Obviously they were moving toward a rendezvous at lower price levels. The specialist in GM would arrive there first, while the specialist in T would have to hurry things along in order to catch up.

The Dow declined 10.95 on the nineteenth, and on the twentieth it declined 4.46, with Telephone remaining unchanged at 45⅝. It was not until Thursday, November 21, that the specialist in Telephone made his move. Confronted by the possibility of heavy selling if he lowered his price in routine fashion, he took the only course that made any sense.

Thursday, November 21, 1974
Dow −1.02/608.57 Dow Vol. 1,869,900 NYSE Vol. 13,820,000
There are certain individuals who, by long training, are singularly equipped to dominate others. Among these I would include specialists, the Sanhedrin of the Stock Exchange. The great central theme of their spiritual dust bowl is always to augment their vested interests. This they do superbly and rarely better than today when the specialist in Telephone opened his stock at 42½, three points lower than the previous close, and closed it at 42⅝ on a volume of 870,300. Another occasion on which this kind of price action occurred was when John F. Kennedy was assassinated on November 22, 1963. (See *The Wall Street Jungle,* Chapter 12.*)

Had he wished, the specialist in Telephone could have supported the price of his stock ⅛ or ¼ of a point under yesterday's closing price. But why should he? Because he had sold his stock short, a headlined Justice Department antitrust suit which was old, old news gave him all the excuse he needed to drop the price of Telephone three points to the 42½ level. If you don't mind a little blood, there's nothing like a meat cleaver.

The investor is able to learn how to gauge the specialist, anticipate his intent and his movements from only two things—the worm of his price and its shadow, volume. Although the specialist is the only one who knows what his plans are, what he is going to do, and when he is going to do it, the investor does

*Having established a major short position at the 138 price level, he dropped Telephone on November 22, 1963, to 130, where he conducted major short-covering operations and accumulated a large inventory of stock. At the resumption of trading on November 26, he opened the stock at 140, supplying 11,000 shares at the opening from his own inventory. Since he was employing a FIFO method of accounting, with this transaction alone he was establishing an additional profit for his long-term investment account of $110,000 (investment accounts were accumulated at the 100 level in October, 1962).

know *what* he did, when he did it, and quite often, what it means he must do in the future because of what he has done in the past. The investor has one advantage over the specialist. The specialist can't hide from him. He is, therefore, vulnerable. At the right time, all the investor need do is walk up to the specialist's crap table and place his bet. The specialist has to cover it.

In the present instance, working on the assumption (according to a major polling service) that the general level of intelligence among Americans has been arrested at a point somewhere between the twelve- and thirteen-year-old level, specialists had, as the following figures attest, defied all rational analysis by repeating in November the formula they had employed in the August–October decline for dropping stock prices on the lowest possible volume.

Note in Chart 8–1 the manner in which accumulations in Dow stocks increased as the decline approached its bottom. This was particularly noticeable on Tuesday the twenty-sixth and Wednesday the twenty-seventh when, although overall volume on these two days was 13.6 and 14.8 million shares, the Dow volume was 1.5 million shares on both days. This was a definite signal that accumulations were building up that would ultimately require a rally.

On November 25, General Motors declined to an intraday low of 30⅛ on only 100,000 shares. Obviously, more public selling would be induced prior to a rally. Equally obviously, the specialist in General Motors would have to go under 30 to get it. The volume in Kodak had not reached 100,000 shares on any day since it penetrated the 70 level. This suggested to me that Kodak (and therefore the Dow as a whole) would be moving lower until higher volume entered the picture.

On November 26, major reversal volume entered General Electric as the stock dropped to an intraday low of 34 on 349,000 shares. This specialist's efforts will probably now be bent on slowly sneaking his stock up 10 or more points and then, in the course of a sharp overall rally, unloading everything. In view of

DOW JONES INDUSTRIALS

	VOL (TH SH)	CLOSE
11 1	1268.9	665.28
4	966.3	657.23
5	1225.1	674.75
6	1871.4	669.12
7	1320.6	671.93
8	1187.9	667.16
11	895.9	672.64
12	1035.0	659.18
13	1316.8	659.18
14	1021.6	658.40
15	966.9	647.61
18	1386.7	624.92
19	1483.1	614.05
20	1089.9	609.59
21	1869.9	608.57
22	1224.5	615.30
25	1064.9	611.94
26	1507.6	617.26
27	1517.4	619.29
28	HOLIDAY	
29	815.8	618.66

CHART 8–1

SOURCE: ISL Daily Stock Price Index, published by Standard & Poor's

the accumulations on the twenty-sixth, it is possible he may rally to just under the critical 50 price level to unload this inventory. General Motors, having touched 30 on only 117,100 shares, still indicates that the decline should continue until there is bigger buildup in inventory.

By the end of the week, it was apparent that important Dow specialists were still without the inventories that would make a rally highly profitable. As might be expected, just as the Dow invariably terminates a major rally in a euphoric upward explosion of stock prices, thereby causing investors to feel outside of things unless they move inside the market, so during the week of December 2, the investors' homemade vision of the market was confined to a pessimistic view of a sharply dropping Dow, which caused many to sell. This naturally enabled specialists to accumulate. On Monday, December 2, the Dow was down 15.64, on Tuesday −6.41; on Wednesday the possibility of a more constructive relationship was introduced between the investor and the market's unknown forces when the Dow advanced 3.29. For that reason, the investor's disappointment was all the greater when the last two days of the week produced declines of 11.58

and 9.46, carrying the Dow to 577.60 on Friday the sixth. By week end, General Motors had dropped under 30, a critical price level, to the 28 level on high volume (see Appendix, page 422). On Friday, Eastman Kodak had dropped under its critical 60 level (to 59⅛) on 120,500 shares. As it happened, Friday's close also established the Dow's bottom.

In seeking to perpetuate the power of the Exchange establishment, the media are, of course, bullish at the market's highs and bearish at its lows. Providing relief and false sunshine as counterpoints to declining stock prices, the media remain bullish until stock prices move within two weeks or so of their bottoms. Then, with all the force that their gifts of immediacy and a free press grant them, the media manufacture despair. Once again, therefore, as the Dow moved toward its December low, the media hastened to express a bearish view of the market's events.

The investor's attitudes were, in consequence, molded without his conscious awareness. In order to help the reader visualize more easily the subtle tyranny of this indoctrination process, I have provided the following list of excerpts from the media for the time span under consideration.

On November 26, the Dow advanced 5.32. Yet according to *The Wall Street Journal* of November 27:

> Brokers said worry about how deep the recession will cut continues to limit investor aggressiveness. Treasury Secretary William Simon said yesterday the U.S. may be facing its longest economic setback since World War II and budget officers said the nation's budget deficit could grow to more than 17 billion in the current fiscal year.

Then according to a vice president of Morgan Stanley:

> Portfolio managers who had planned to buy stocks when interest rates came down are stepping back because of nervousness about the recession. . . .

On November 27 the Dow advanced 2.03. According to *The Wall Street Journal* of November 28, good news concerning a trade surplus was "overshadowed somewhat by the announcement that the government's composite index . . . fell last month for the third month in a row." On Friday, November 29, the Dow was up 1.08. *The Wall Street Journal* commented that (at the top of the column):

> Investor's psychology is being colored—and darkly—by the realities of the deepening recession. . . . People are really accentuating the negative (according to the vice president of a St. Louis bank). What's disturbing is the rapidity with which things have deteriorated. . . . There's almost complete unanimity that we're in for a serious recession. . . . Besides the slowdown, the other negative factors facing the market . . . [are] the high price of oil with the accompanying mass flow of petrodollars that poses a threat to the stability of the international banking institutions. . . . [and] an added blow to an already bruised psychology is the Justice Department's antitrust action against American Telephone. . . .

A partner in a brokerage firm is quoted:

> The recession will be more severe than previous World War II slowdowns.

On December 2 the Dow was down 15.64. According to *The Wall Street Journal* of December 3:

> "A dismal economic outlook continued to depress the stock market yesterday," according to the analyst of a brokerage firm. "A concentration of bad economic news has caused investors to sit back and wait for the time being."

On December 3 the Dow was down 6.41. According to *The Wall Street Journal* of December 4:

> "There are so many outside negatives that there isn't any reason to buy stocks at this point," according to a vice president and director of technical research at Hornblower & Weeks-Hemphill, Noyes.

On December 4 the Dow was up 2.03. According to *The Wall Street Journal* of December 5:

> "Even though the coal agreement yesterday seemed headed for approval, institutions continued to take a guarded approach," according to a vice president of Merrill Lynch. He added, "The institutions feel comfortable with their large cash positions because they want to wait and see how vulnerable the market will be to the dire recession news coming in."

The rest of the column was in the same vein. On December 5 the Dow dropped 11.58. According to *The Wall Street Journal* of December 6:

> "The recession is biting harder than many people expected and stock market participants are giving up hope that the October lows will hold," according to the director of investments of a brokerage firm. He also added that "the failure of the coal strike settlement to rally the market and the inability of the decline in short term interest rates to stir buying surprised many. . . ."

The limitations imposed on investor thinking by such comments cause many investors to throw up their hands in despair and run from the market as fast as they can. This in itself might not have been so bad were it not for the fact that less than a month after the Dow had moved away from its December lows the media would be back at their old stand, seeding the investor's mind with their graffiti, encouraging him once again to buy at a new high.

For the present, however, it was apparent specialists were busily occupied with the tangible consequences of public selling. The question I had to decide was whether they were accumulating for long- or short-term goals. The evolution of the decline in General Motors and Kodak had seen both these bellwether Dow stocks penetrating critically important price levels (GM 30, EK 60). Yet, these penetrations had been to the accompaniment of only moderately high volume. Although it was eminently possible that Dow specialists would advance from present levels, they could just as well send shock waves through the investment community by dropping their stocks sharply enough to carry this index through the emotionally charged 500 level. Were this to happen, investor panic could easily enable specialists to accumulate investment accounts at much lower price levels.

As an investor, my vision of the future was highly speculative. It was a simple matter, however, for me to project myself into the past and to imagine how I would have zeroed in on the events transpiring in Dow stocks had I still been *trading* in the market. In the present instance, a penetration of critical price levels in Dow stocks left no doubt that short covering was functioning as an important preliminary to the technology of accumulation. The image provided by the increase in volume that had occurred in General Motors and Kodak when they declined to 29 and 59 was bullish.

As a trader, therefore, I would by now be shooting for results. In a world dominated by the croupier-specialist, I would have placed my bets alongside his. In so doing, I would have had to accept the fact that he might still carry the Dow under the psychologically important 500 level and that investors might become so panicked it might cause massive dumping. I also knew that if this happened, specialists would exploit public selling by dropping stock prices still further. But, past experience would also have suggested the specialist would first carry stock prices back above critically important price levels before dropping them further. I would, therefore, have gambled on my ability to leap out of the market before he again dropped stock prices. Thus, had I been advising traders in the market, I would have told them to buy, but only with the recognition that they were doing it with the acceptance of high risk.

As an investment adviser, however, a much more rigid set of principles distinguishes my present approach. As an investor, I look at the market, as well as life, differently. My approach to the market focuses on preservation of capital and the low risk factors I *insist* on seeing before I commit clients into the market.

In the present instance, the decline under critically important price levels in Dow stocks could, once again, prove to be no different from similar declines at higher price levels. While volume had moved over the 100,000 range in these stocks, it did not yet suggest major accumulation. There are markets that offer investors the opportunity for gain with minimum risk; there are also markets that offer the investor opportunity for gain that is attendant only on the acceptance of high risk. I believed the present market to be of this latter kind. The risks were too great, just as the risks of crap-shooting are too great, whether the crap-shooter makes two, or twenty-two, straight passes. That he may win is beside the point and does not alter the fact that he placed after-tax dollars at high risk in order to win.

This, then, from my point of view, was a time to remain beyond the reach of the entrenched, complex power of the specialist; to wait until the *end* of the present rally when, after the violence of what I expected to take place had been exhausted, there would be time enough to commit—in a minimum risk environment.

9

Psychological Warfare or How to Employ One Stock as a Standard for Appraising the Movements of All Stocks

Ney's Tenth Axiom: To understand what you do, you must only do what you understand.

Never before in the entire history of the stock market had the Exchange employed the philosophy of the shell game to greater perfection than in the explosive rally launched by its specialists during the first quarter of 1975. The only way such an event can be placed in perspective is to look at it against the background movements of individual stocks. Although I have discussed this principle in broad outline and provided examples of the manner in which the interaction of individual Dow stocks provides insight into the future movements of the Dow index as a whole, I have not yet shown how analysis of the price action of a single Dow stock can often perform the same function. The dimensions of the January rally allow me to show dramatically how the pricing practices of a single specialist unit in a highly active stock reveal a strategy employed by most specialists in the course of a market rally.

Few specialists enjoy the same degree of power and prestige as the specialist in General Motors. As much as anyone else on the floor, he is aware of the power granted him by self-regulation to dominate his merchandising processes. Nowhere is this more apparent than at his stock's tops and bottoms. Liberated from the restrictions that regulation might impose, he is free, for example, to drop his price from a high or to raise it from a bottom on large gaps, thereby leaving unexecuted the hundreds of thousands of shares that might have been entered on his books.

The investor must learn to recognize the psychological implications involved in such movements of price if he is to fulfill his investment goals. The best way to understand how this specialist conducts his operations is to imagine how *you* would operate if no limitations were placed on your activities. Finding yourself at the 62 price level and knowing your objective is to move as vertically as possible to the 50 level, with possibly a million or more shares on your book that you would have to take into inventory as you moved down to and penetrated the 60 level, what would you do? Borrow 60 million dollars? Resign? Why? These are alternatives you would have to consider only if you had to observe the rules of an auction market. You don't. With that in mind, let us examine just such a situation.

Because his stock is one of the most active, the specialist in General Motors is able to dominate its price structure and his customers as though he were the lord of some feudal compound. Thus if the stock is at 62⅝ (as it was on November 9, 1973; see Chart 9–1) and he wants to avoid as much selling by the public as possible, it should surprise no one that at the opening on the following day of trading he drops his stock's price 4⅛ points to 58½. Since his power is a creation of our present political structure, he is under no compulsion to concern himself with what investors may think of this action. They have been condi-

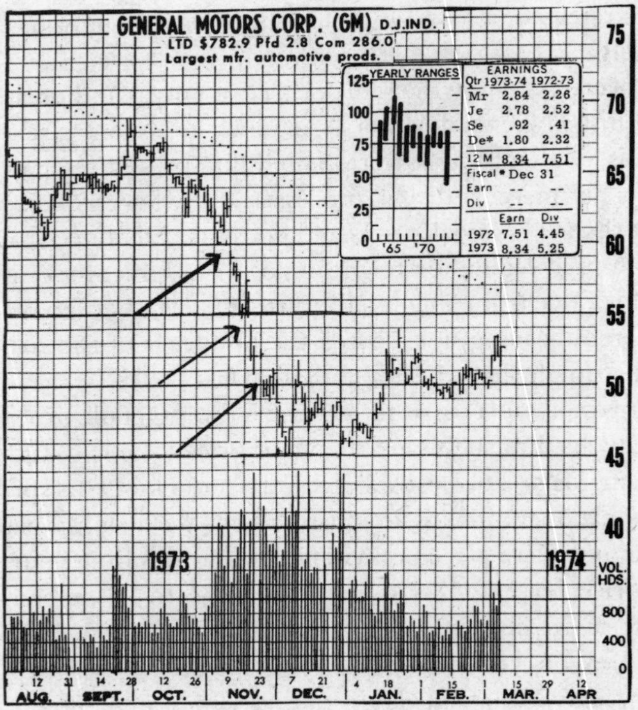
GENERAL MOTORS CORP. (GM) D.J.IND.
LTD $782.9 Pfd 2.8 Com 286.0
Largest mfr. automotive prods.
YEARLY RANGES
125
100
75
50
25
0
'65 '70
EARNINGS
Qtr 1973-74 1972-73
Mr 2.84 2.26
Je 2.78 2.52
Se .92 .41
De* 1.80 2.32
12 M 8.34 7.51
Fiscal * Dec 31
Earn -- --
Div -- --
Earn Div
1972 7.51 4.45
1973 8.34 5.25
75
70
65
60
55
50
45
40
1973
1974
VOL. HDS.
800
400
0
AUG. SEPT. OCT. NOV. DEC. JAN. FEB. MAR. APR

CHART 9–1

SOURCE: Trendline's Daily Basis Stock Charts

tioned to accept such openings as a necessary adjunct to his function as a specialist. Moreover, investors are unaware that when they place their orders on the specialist's book, they are merely showing him where the loot is buried. Under the circumstances it is not surprising that he should, when it suits him, dig them up or, when these orders act as obstacles, pass them by. In the present instance the investor, thinking he was "limiting his loss" if GM penetrated the 60 level, placed a limit order on the specialist's book to sell once GM reached 59¾. Checking with his broker during the day, he learned the stock was at 59. He assumed his GM had been sold, only to learn the stock opened at 58½ and that his order had not been executed.

As the stock moved down through the 55 and 50 levels, additional investors who had entered limit orders to sell were also left on the book as the specialist passed through these levels on gaps. In Chart 9–1, I have marked with an arrow the instances in which, adopting the slogan "caveat emptor," the specialist dropped the price he was willing to pay on the trade.

This manipulation provides us with another insight into the bag of tricks the specialist employs in order to effect sizable alterations in his merchandising processes. In the present instance the meaning of a drop in price on a large gap at the end of a rally is an indication that the stock's price is headed lower. What the specialist is telling us when he leapfrogs an important price level like 60, 50, or 40 is that he is anxious to skip the accumulations of inventory at specific price levels that would then oblige him to conduct an important rally in his stock. But more than that, he is employing working principles that subtly coerce investor thought and conduct to enable him to accumulate his investment inventories at price levels that will probably be at least 10 points lower. If, for example, he had wished to conduct an important rally at the 60 level, he would have dropped his price just under 60 in routine trading. In this way he would have cleaned his book of an enormous accumulation of sell orders and then, having placed that stock in inventory, proceeded to sell it as he moved to a rally high. If on the other hand, his intent is to proceed lower, the limit orders on his book inform him that the most effective way of avoiding an inventory is to halt trading and then open his stock under the bulk of his limit orders. When his intent is to advance his stock's price, he can employ the same techniques to avoid selling to investors who entered their limit orders to buy. (See Chart 9–2. I have indicated with the letter "A" a dramatic instance in which this strategy was employed. The reader can study the chart in order to observe other instances.)

Specialists also employ this leapfrogging strategy at tops and bottoms in order to condition unwary investors. It should therefore be studied as a tool for discerning specialist intent. Looking at Chart 9–2, point B, and the manner in which the specialist in GM shot his stock's price up to and down from its highs, we might ask how the impact of such price movements condition investor consciousness.

As an adjunct to rising prices, there are always the phantoms of fear and hope. But for whom is a jump in price a cause of fear and for whom does it represent hope? In one case, the rising price is a prophetic warning to short sellers that the invisible sources of power may cause still higher prices to follow. Of necessity these investors become emotionally involved in the dramatic conflict of the stock's potentials. Unaware that this kind of price rise invariably signals the end of the stock's rally, they throw in their orders "to cover" at the very moment the stock's specialist has decided to reverse the trend. In all probability the specialist in GM is selling short to them as they "cover" at a loss.

And what of the investor who hopes to profit from rising stock prices? Must not the direction of his vision insist that he is being offered an opportunity to "get in on" a good thing? Thus although the hope of the one investor seems to be the very opposite of the fear of the other, is not hope the invisible side of fear? Will not the sudden upward thrust of stock prices serve as a

CHART 9–2

SOURCE: Trendline's Daily Basis Stock Charts

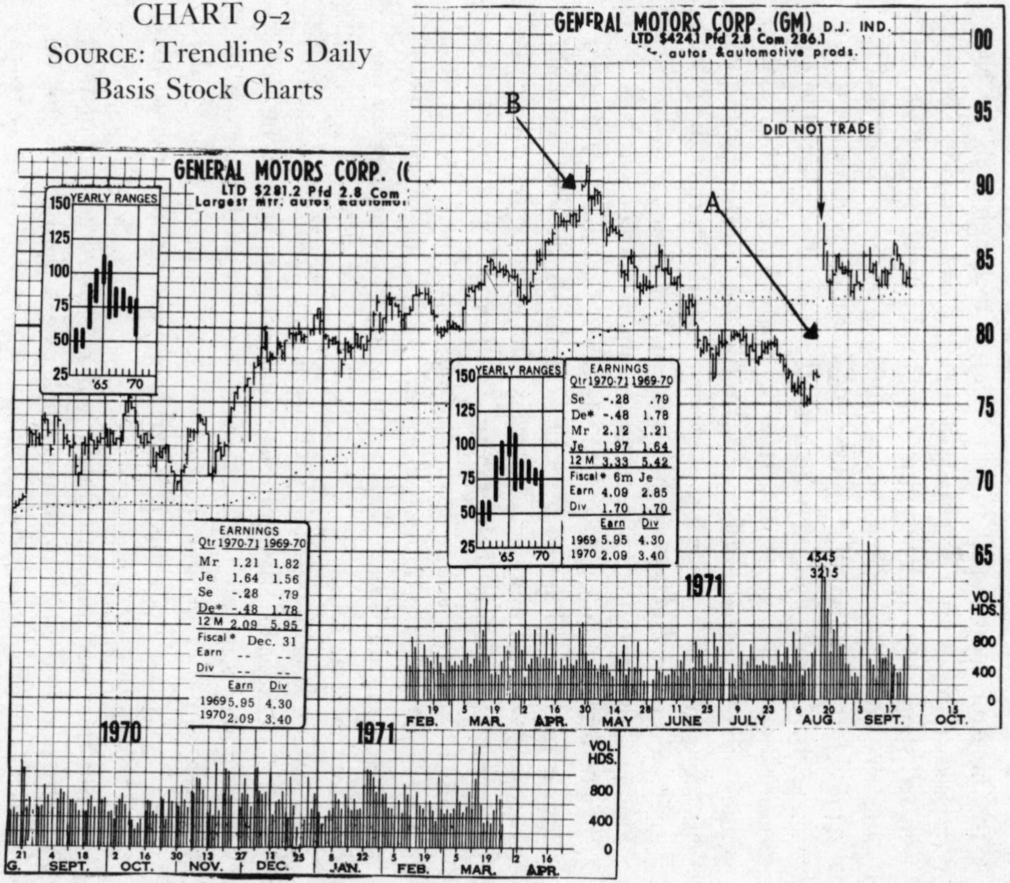
GENERAL MOTORS CORP. (GM) D.J. IND.
LTD $424.1 Pfd 2.8 Com 286.1
autos &automotive prods.
B
A
DID NOT TRADE
GENERAL MOTORS CORP.
LTD $281.2 Pfd 2.8 Com
YEARLY RANGES
EARNINGS
Qtr 1970-71 1969-70
Se -.28 .79
De* -.48 1.78
Mr 2.12 1.21
Je 1.97 1.64
12 M 3.33 5.42
Fiscal* 6m Je
Earn 4.09 2.85
Div 1.70 1.70
Earn Div
1969 5.95 4.30
1970 2.09 3.40
Mr 1.21 1.82
Je 1.64 1.56
Se -.28 .79
De* -.48 1.78
12 M 2.09 5.95
Fiscal* Dec. 31
1970
1971
4545
3215
VOL. HDS.
FEB. MAR. APR. MAY JUNE JULY AUG. SEPT. OCT.
SEPT. OCT. NOV. DEC. JAN. FEB. MAR. APR.

warning that unless the investor acts immediately he will miss the opportunity to participate in rising prices?

Then, as the price of GM falls precipitously from its highs, the investor who hoped to sell short at the high feels he has missed an important percentage decline and so he may decide *not* to sell short. Investors who just bought the stock at its high see the very ground on which they stand being cut away from them. Many in this group will therefore sell, but most will decide that, since the information on which they should have based their actions was vitiated by the time it reached them, their only alternative is to wait until once again the stock moves back up to its high and they are given the chance to sell the stock at the price they paid for it. Such price drops, when they occur, usually continue for two or more points for two or more consecutive days.

The reverse holds true at GM's bottom. Investors are allowed ample time to sell as the price of GM slowly declines. Around the image of declining prices there is a language of despair that is as great as anything in literature. Confronted by a world that offers no quarter, suffering daily pangs of anguish, the investor is plagued by a profound sense of unease. Ultimately he is pushed over the brink by a sudden drop of the stock to its bottom, and he sells.

Looking at each of the GM charts in this chapter, we see that once the specialist has completed his accumulations, he does what comes naturally. He deters (1) buying at the bottom by investors and (2) new and old short sellers from covering their short sales. He does this by sharply advancing the price of his stock from the bottom.

But there are long intervals when stocks are neither *at* their highs nor at their lows, when stock prices are merely moving *toward* their highs or lows. Looking at Chart 9–2 for the 1970–71 period, we can see from the price pattern in GM that it appears to be moving in a slow but never-ending curve toward new highs.

How would you, were you the specialist in GM, proceed were

you intent on distributing millions of shares of stock (working for a fee with investment bankers on behalf of their institutional clients)? Granted you would do all in your power *not* to erect barriers to investor interest, how would you go about creating the conditions that would cause overly cautious investors finally to commit into your stock? Is it not reasonable to suppose that most investors will respond in only one way when the account of a stock's slow but steady rise on the financial page also includes the information that, with the passage of each day, it is establishing new highs? It is a simple matter to see how the investor comes to regard the advance in GM in much the same fashion as a trout might view the dizzying implications of a large worm dangled in front of its nose day after day.

No other institution in our society could draw men into its net as the stock market does when prices are rising. The investor is rare, indeed, who can resist the pressure to buy occasioned by anything so ritualistic as the opportunity to do what he thinks everyone else is doing—making money in the market. Inevitably, staring day after day at the stock page for inspiration, the investor is driven to desperation in trying to accept the proposition that he's better off with his money in the bank. Ultimately, whether it be at the end of one, two, three, or four months, the probability is, if he has ever entertained the notion of being an investor, he will rationalize his motives and spell out his greed by purchasing 100 or more shares of stock. Thus we see that what the slow but steady advance in the price of GM accomplished was the creation of an enormous willingness on the part of countless thousands of investors to believe that the vision of rising prices was never-ending.

During this period, Dow stocks provide us with an excellent illustration of the manner in which they work together as a team. An examination of the volume in excess of 1.4 million shares a day in the DJIA stocks for the January–April 1971 period reveals that as the Dow was rising, the market's foundations were being eroded by distribution. As one stock group after another moved down from its high, it was replaced by another, so that the Dow continued to advance to new highs almost to the end of April.

General Motors established its high on April 29, 1971, at 91⅛, GE on the same date at 124⅜; Eastman Kodak after a 4⅜-point gain on the twenty-seventh established its high on the twenty-eighth at 86¼. Du Pont, however, established its high on April 20 at 149¼. By the twenty-ninth Du Pont was down to 145½, but the decline in this and other Dow stocks was then masked by the advances in General Motors, Eastman Kodak, United Aircraft (now United Technologies), and particularly by Procter & Gamble, which continued its climb through January 1973.

Throughout the market in December 1974 (and through the first half of 1975) the Exchange establishment paid strict attention to form. Its dominating nature was strongly paternal. It was the Exchange's idiom of thought and speech, the money man's shrewd, hard-hitting assumptions and assertions that cause selling at the bottom and buying at rally highs that provided the environment's PR. Inevitably, everything went off according to a formula that had its roots in the fundamental myths of the establishment.

Not surprisingly, particularly at this time in the market's history, the specialist in General Motors found himself flourishing. Life on the floor of the Exchange had taught him that his greatest profits are to be found where everyone thinks alike, for it is only in such an environment that no one thinks very much.

The manner in which the specialist in GM pursues his ends as a unit in the specialist system is, in microcosm, a reflection of the macrocosm. Although the system cannot be said to prescribe his pricing policies, in seeking his own goals he is pursuing ends that both reflect and support the behavior patterns of the group as a whole. If we turn to an analysis of the manner in which this specialist seeks to gain his ends, we can discover how other specialists tend to behave under similar circumstances.

With no restraints on his power and no concern but to pass

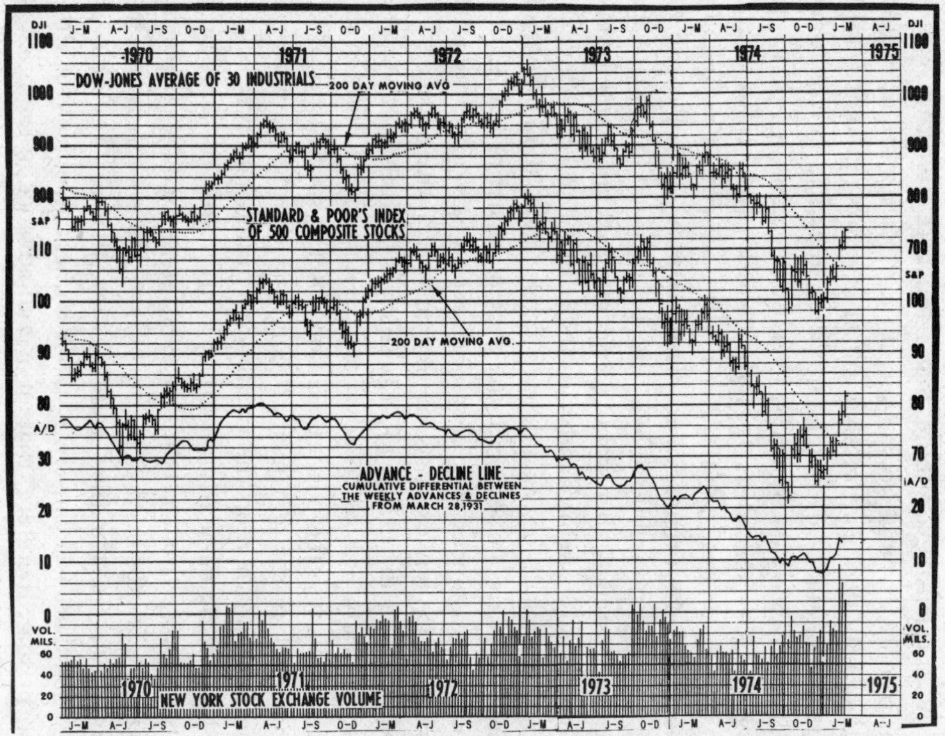
DOW-JONES AVERAGE OF 30 INDUSTRIALS
200 DAY MOVING AVG
STANDARD & POOR'S INDEX OF 500 COMPOSITE STOCKS
200 DAY MOVING AVG.
ADVANCE - DECLINE LINE
CUMULATIVE DIFFERENTIAL BETWEEN THE WEEKLY ADVANCES & DECLINES FROM MARCH 28,1931
NEW YORK STOCK EXCHANGE VOLUME
1970
1971
1972
1973
1974
1975
DJI
S&P
A/D
VOL. MILS.

CHART 9–3

SOURCE: Trendline's Daily Basis Stock Charts

rapidly and profitably into the future, it is the specialist in General Motors who showed us that he had officially launched the December rally. His accumulations of stock were seriously underway at the 29–30 level during the first week in December. For this specialist everything that happened after that was a means to only one end: to so control the close texture of events that the easily deranged mechanism of investor thinking would postpone the bulk of its buying until his stock had moved to its rally highs. Motivated by investor tax-selling considerations, he and other Dow specialists kept their stock prices close to the early December level for the remainder of the month. Wholly responsive to the impulses and circumstances that give rise to public buying and public selling, the specialist in GM was aware of the circumstances that would cause investors not to sell for tax purposes. Had he significantly advanced GM's price during the December period, he would have caused untold numbers of investors to postpone selling in the hope of higher prices. Under certain circumstances this course of action is not without its advantages. If, however, as in this instance, the specialist is aware that he will be able to dispose of all his inventory in the course of a rally, it is to his advantage to maximize selling in the present. This was the posture assumed by the specialist in GM.

Dow stock prices remained at their lows during the whole of December, and then on the twenty-fourth (having dropped the Dow 8.04 to 589.64 on Monday the twenty-third), the last day in which investors could establish losses for tax selling purposes, the Dow was advanced 8.76 on only 9,580,000 shares. This advance reflected a unified point of view that can be achieved only when there is a consensus about immediate objectives. It is not surprising, therefore, that an overall advance in the price of Dow (and other) stocks shortly thereafter coincided with an advance in the price of GM.

The impulse of all specialists is to avoid the hazards of competition, to exploit demand by thwarting it and supply by capitalizing on it or avoiding it. Because their power is total, specialists like those in GM enjoy the advantages of a virtually riskless environment in which the continuity of their arbitrary power allows them to profit with equal ease whether stock prices are declining or advancing.

Recognizing the manner in which specialists in important Dow stocks serve their own ends as well as the ongoing enterprise of the market as a whole, the reader is able to see that the strategies employed by the specialist in GM in handling his stock are also expressive of the strategies employed by other specialists. In the following chapter we will move forward to an examination of the manner in which these principles were applied in early January and then culminated in the sharp advance in the Dow beginning the last week of January.

10

The Media Hotfoot or First You Plan a Rally—Then You Organize Ignorance

Ney's Eleventh Axiom: A man must learn to avoid losing what he has today before thinking of what he hopes to get tomorrow.

The organization of a rally depends on the organization of opinion. For good reason, investors were nervous about the market in early January 1975. Their hopes having been raised in the past and then left unfulfilled, these investors now distrusted the market and were reluctant to commit their savings into another rally.

Adding to their problems, as stock prices began to rise, the financial pages blurred the edges of reality by emphasizing the opinions of experts who maintained that the prospect of a serious depression was an important obstacle to the existence of rising stock prices. The information the investor obtains from his financial page always strikes him where his emotions are. It causes him to act during a state of euphoria, in which he either purchases or holds on to stock, or to act during a state of despair, in which he either sells or stays out of the market. What investors do not understand is that these effects are, all too often, intended. The information has been engineered to cause him to take one or another particular course of action. In the present instance a few excerpts suffice to show the reader the manner in which the investor is persuaded to remain out of the market until stock prices have moved to a level at which the Exchange wishes to trigger him into the market.

On January 2, 1975, the very day it was announced that Chrysler had closed additional auto and truck plants and that the government reported that new claims for unemployment benefits had reached 667,800 in the week before Christmas, the Dow was up 15.80. The wire services saw fit to characterize this advance with a debilitating "but":

> The stock market, continuing its New Year's Eve rally, climbed sharply and broadly higher today, *but* in only moderately active trading. . . .

That day, General Motors was up 1⅛.

On January 3, First National City Bank raised its prime rate

¼ percent to 10.25 percent, gold prices dropped in Europe, and it was announced that auto output in 1974 was off 24 percent from 1973. The Dow advanced 2.50, and GM responded to the auto industry's bad news by advancing 1¾ points.

On Tuesday, January 14, commenting on the previous day's decline of 4.61, *The Wall Street Journal* had this to say:

> Analysts weren't surprised by the late pullback yesterday because they said that after its recent sharp climb the market was extremely "overbought."

On Thursday, January 16, after a gain of 4.69 on the fifteenth, *The Wall Street Journal* quoted the vice president of a major brokerage firm:

> "People have been listening to the preliminaries as well as to the [President's] actual state of the union speech and have taken a sideline stance waiting to see what the institutional reaction would be."

He added that after the market's recent climb

> "It was overbought and some downward reaction was to be expected."

On Friday, January 17, commenting on the previous day's gain of 2.35, the Los Angeles *Times* stated:

> Stock prices showed little change Thursday. . . . "Investors want to see what Congress will do with the President's proposals to increase energy prices and cut taxes," said one analyst. . . .

On Wednesday, January 22, *The New York Times* commented on the previous day's advance of 2.82:

> Until the administration's proposals for coping with the recession, inflation and the nation's energy problems are taken up by Congress and specific legislation takes shape, market observers are not looking for very decisive day-to-day trading patterns.

It then quoted the investment adviser for seven mutual funds:

> "There are really more questions than answers at this point."

To the accompanying orchestration of the media's platitudes, by Friday, January 24, the Dow had inconspicuously advanced another 22 points to 666.61. This was approximately 97 points from the December low. Ordinary investors, bewildered by the market at all times, were now more bewildered than ever. Having been provided all the popular, plausible, and *prima facie* reasons for the market to go down, they were pessimistic about the circumstances (whatever they were) that were responsible for causing it to go up. They were reassured, however, by the constant reminders from their financial page that even the media's professional analysts had reconciled themselves to the existence of paradoxes not resolvable to common sense. Under such circumstances, investors found themselves confused and unimpressed by the advance. With the philosophic detachment of spectators observing a mugging in Central Park, they were reluctant to become involved.

But, giving investors what they wanted to see most was the best way to make them unhappy—if they weren't also able to profit from seeing it. In my journal entry for January 24, I meditated on the root causes of investor discontent:

Friday, January 24, 1975
Dow +9.85/666.61 Dow Vol. 1,819,400 NYSE Vol. 20,670,000
Is a new crisis looming up? With today's advance the Dow has gained

almost 100 points from its December low and is now running neck and neck with the October rally highs. Kodak has declined sharply from Wednesday's high of 68—and on heavy volume. Yesterday's decline to 67 on 140,000 shares was slightly in excess of the volume on September 18, 1973, when the price dropped from 133¼ to close at 129½ on 133,500 shares. The following day, this joined other Dow stocks in what was the beginning of the September rally. Today's decline in Kodak to an intraday low of 63¼ (close at 65⅛) on 125,500 shares would seem to complete the picture. If anything else was needed to make me suspect that the Kodak specialist is recoiling for a sharp jump in price, there is the *Journal's* bleak report today on Kodak's prospects. These are invariably the known preliminaries to known ends.

Meanwhile, the investor is peering into the market's dark mirror in the hopes of discerning its destiny. He wishes he were in the market, but because he is timid and anxious to escape from anything that might be painful, he is skeptical. Yet it would take very little to cause him to change his mind. Any kind of economic announcement from Ford like a wage-price freeze would do the trick.

On Wednesday the twenty-second, Eastman Kodak had advanced from 63⅞ to 68 on light volume. On Thursday it declined to 67 on 140,000 shares, and on Friday, to an intraday low of 63¼, closing at 65⅛ on 125,500 shares. It was obvious something was in the wind. Moreover, on Friday, *The Wall Street Journal* had carried a major story on Kodak in its "Heard on the Street" column, a column that exercises an autonomy over investor thinking second only to its "Abreast of the Market" column. On Friday, one trading day before Eastman Kodak launched its rally (with a gain of 4⅛ points on Monday), this space was devoted entirely to a discussion of negative fundamental factors relating to this stock. Needless to say, investors are conditioned to assume that fundamentals relating to earnings are the primary determinants of all change in a stock's price structure. There can be no question, therefore, that this article had a profound impact on investor thinking—and on stockbrokers who immediately communicated its contents to their customers. It began with a major headline:

KODAK STOCK SEESAWS AS PICTURE GETS FUZZIER;
MANY ANALYSTS SEE PROFIT DOWN AGAIN IN 1975

> The chancy environment for consumer goods that accompanies a recession is causing some investors to think their stocks are shuttlecocks. When the company involved is Eastman Kodak, with heavy exposure to foreign consumer moods, too, the impression is magnified. . . .
>
> What's happening is that the 1975 picture, as seen by Wall Street analysts, is getting fuzzier and fuzzier, largely because of the deteriorating climate for foreign earnings but also because of increased concern over the company's sensitivity to the domestic economic cycle. Nearly 40% of Kodak's sales and about 25% of profit are accounted for by its international operations.
>
> One consequence is that Wall Street earnings estimates for 1975 have begun to stretch over a wider range, and several currently contemplate that Kodak could have its second consecutive year of declining earnings. . . .

The *Journal* has never received the critical acclaim its distinctions merit. Its secret is the extreme simplicity of its articles and their timing. Not surprisingly, a great many investors read this article and sold their Kodak. They saw the stock drop to an intraday low of 63¼ that day and then close at 65⅛. On Monday the gloomy opinions surrounding its earnings no longer appeared to have any currency, for again the stock advanced to close at 69¼. Thereafter, the most striking characteristic of this stock was its ability to lead the rally *despite* its unfortunate earnings prospects.

Obviously, the timing of the article had great utility. It served the internal necessities of the Kodak specialist by providing him with a rationale for dropping his price and cleaning out his book. It also helped cause greater selling in the stock, which could be depended upon to add to this specialist's future income, a fact that, from his viewpoint, made any other consideration seem absurdly unnecessary.

I had by this time come to feel strongly about the possible appearance of the unexpected. Long before, I had learned that this is the way major market rallies always begin and end. All the same, I had no thought that the Exchange was about to pull a rabbit out of its bag of tricks once again.

11

Shock Treatment or IBM Drops the Other Shoe

Ney's Twelfth Axiom: There are few patient investors who do not soon weary of their patience.

As it happened, after the close of the market Friday, January 24, 1975, investors were informed that a Federal Appeals court had reversed a 1973 trial court finding that IBM had engaged in predatory pricing and other antitrust violations. The appeals court had also overturned a $259.5-million damage award to Telex. According to the Stock Exchange News Bureau, financial circles in New York were greatly agitated and exhilarated by this unforeseen event.

Few investors realize that the market is always full of causes and effects for which the Exchange is the chief "cause." Although the IBM announcement might have been unforeseen by investors, it wasn't by insiders. It was apparent from the price action of Eastman Kodak and a number of other stocks that many specialists had dropped their stock prices and cleaned out their books early in the week in anticipation of the price rises they would conduct subsequent to this announcement.

My own attitude toward the court's decision was of a piece with my attitude toward the financial establishment. Established power is tenacious of its privileges and recognizes that to prevent change in the ways and in the conditions of doing business, it must be able to exercise control over the processes (and therefore the men) that are always at work beneath the surfaces of government. There was no question in my mind that, impressive as was the court decision against IBM, requiring the multimillion-dollar award to Telex, it would be practical to assume that ways would be found to avoid the payment of damages of such magnitude. It was certain that a reversal of the first court's decision would be effected on appeal and that the timing of this decision would be dramatically employed to rationalize a major advance in the price of IBM. This in turn would provide a seemingly coherent rationale for an overall rally in stock prices. Indeed, I suggested as much in *The Wall Street Gang:*

> The fluctuations in the price levels of IBM, for instance, are seen to be characteristic of a stock that is destined for a

> dramatic penetration of the important 300 level. It is quite obvious in fact that IBM is being set up like a clay pigeon for the shot that will knock it off its perch. What then remains is merely the pretext that will provide the specialist in IBM with a seemingly legitimate rationale for taking it down (to the 260 level) and once having acquired an enormous inventory, the pretext that will allow him again to raise stock prices in order to liquidate that inventory. *In this instance since the courts were used to alibi a decline, it is reasonable to suppose the courts will be used to alibi a rally.*

One had only to wait for IBM to drop the other shoe. In the absence of a favorable court decision, an earnings announcement or an overall statement of U.S. economic policy by the President would have served equally well.

On Monday, February 16, 1971, the day after Nixon's wage-price announcement, it was claimed by the Exchange that because of an influx of buy orders, the opening in General Motors would have to be delayed until Tuesday. The consequences of this decision are obvious. Not only would public demand be enormous because of the Exchange propaganda surrounding the interest in General Motors, but the opening on Tuesday served as a double-barreled blast that precipitated a significant increase in demand when General Motors opened approximately 10 points higher. It was not surprising, therefore, that the same strategy should be employed on this occasion and that it should be claimed that an excess of buy orders prevented IBM from opening on Monday, January 27, 1975. On Tuesday, when the stock opened 25 points higher—the same amount, incidentally, that it advanced subsequent to Nixon's August 16 announcement—stockbrokers across the country could well assume an "I told you so" stance with their customers. It was a simple matter, therefore, to persuade those who had been hesitant about committing on Monday to commit on Tuesday, when the market's "underlying strength" was linked to the "new attitude" of the courts toward big business.

It can be said that the leap of +26.05 that occurred in the Dow industrial averages on Monday, January 27, was promoted by the effective combination of financial folklore and specialist techniques, and that the chief aspect of these techniques was the strategy of rising prices. Observing the price and volume figures for Dow stocks (Appendix, pages 461–463) for the week beginning January 27, it becomes apparent that price gains of 5 points in Du Pont, 4⅛ in Eastman Kodak, 3¾ points in Procter & Gamble, etc., all of which added up to a gain of 26 points in the Dow, were certain to throw both the public and even most professionals into a buying panic. Like a new style in dress that suddenly becomes the current fashion, such an event holds the buying public everywhere under its spell. No law can compel such unhesitating compliance as that caused by a sharp rise in the Dow which investors attribute to an important economic event. My own expectation, based on the past performance of such rallies, was that the rally would probably not begin to roll over until Dow stocks reached critical price levels. Little did I realize at the time that these critical price levels would coincide with the launching of a major underwriting of American Telephone & Telegraph stock, and indeed, it was only because Dow stocks continued to be advanced by their specialists that the credentials of a bull market were certified, thereby making it possible to sustain public interest in the purchase of this stock. Furthermore, the high volume of 32.2 million shares showed that the Stock Exchange had a good thing going and that the on-balance movement of Dow stock prices would not decline so long as volume remained high.

The Exchange rules with a high hand. It almost always establishes its capricious reign of fear and hope over the market toward the end of a rally by first causing stock prices to decline. These declines are conducted strictly in order to frighten investors into selling stock, which specialists are then able to resell at higher prices. In the present instance, after approximately two weeks of decline, the Dow advanced sharply. Its rise was loudly heralded as a new bull market. This inspired enough conviction to cause the masses to swarm into the market like pirates after treasure, thus relieving specialists of the stock they had acquired on the decline in addition to enabling them to sell short large quantities of stock. But inevitably the disparity between form and content, between hope and realization, makes itself quite apparent. In the case of the September 1973 rally in the market, it took four weeks for the DJIA to begin to decline—although many Dow stocks had initiated their declines long before then. Once again I would point out to the reader that the Dow is merely a stage piece that masks the movements not only of the overall market but of the individual stocks in the Dow.

In the following chart, the letter "A" points to the declines that usually occur in the course of sharp rallies in stock prices. The reader can discover other instances for himself. The effect of such declines is as vivid as their appearance. They serve to reveal that such rallies tend to have at their center hidden formulas which the investor can depend on for guidance. Certainly if the investor is trading in such a rally, he should learn to anticipate such declines so that his sense of security is not undermined by them. A glance at the volume figures in each instance also shows the efficient manner in which the strategy of a sharply rising Dow average fulfills the Exchange's objective of pulling the public into the market. What it comes to, then, is that the success of the Exchange's efforts depends on its ability to persuade investors to construe the market's fundamental realities so that they accept the market's risks when they should not and do not accept them when they should. Not surprisingly, therefore, while most traders had avoided the market like the plague when stock prices were at their December lows, the universal direction of their attitudes was toward commitment by the last week in January just as stocks came under the first wave of insider distributions. Stripping away façade, we see that the rules of conduct that caused investors to buy into the rally are like little knives with which the Exchange ultimately chops up investors into digestible little portions.

Tuesday, January 28, 1975
Dow +2.11/694.77 Dow Vol. 2,929,600 NYSE Vol. 31,760,000

If the events of the past two days prove anything, it is that while everyone is agreed on the benefits of prudence, they are unable to agree as to the means of putting it into effect. Many investors are probably mortgaging their homes, borrowing from their banks and on their insurance policies, in addition to going on margin in order to participate in this rally. This is an inevitable corollary to every major rally and is always subsequently borne out by the figures reflecting the increase in public borrowing from commercial banks and savings and loan institutions as well as borrowing on margin from Stock Exchange member firms. Figures also bear out the fact that the sum total of such borrowings is now well in excess of 10 billion dollars. It's an old story.

Yet the investor's decision to invest at this time is not a consequence of enlarged human thought and understanding. Instead, he has responded to the graffiti of the financial page. In these times, it is more difficult than ever for the individual to employ good judgment when he is faced with the intolerable visage of inflation and loss of income unless he somehow adds to his savings. Driven to the wall by fear and anxiety, however rash his belief that the appearance of a rising stock average offers the promise of security, how can he be expected to know that he is enmeshed in illusion and false rhetoric; that he is being driven by economic compulsions and temptations which, inevitably, will be turned against him?

Yet to make money in the market, the investor must face this challenge. He must understand why in almost every instance his losses are usually generated and sustained by the very ideas and beliefs that propel him into a rally like the one now underway. For most investors it all began with a telephone call from their broker, who then read them excerpts from his morning's *Wall Street Journal:*

IBM RULING IGNITES MARKET AS DOW ROCKETS 26.05 ON RECORD TURNOVER

This was followed by the comments of those who are looked upon as insiders:

> A favorable court ruling for International Business Machines ignited a stock market explosion yesterday. . . .
>
> "The market was ready to give birth and it did," commented Leslie M. Pollack, senior vice president of Shearson Hayden Stone, Inc. It had been "forming a base for a couple of months," he asserted, and the IBM news was enough to pull

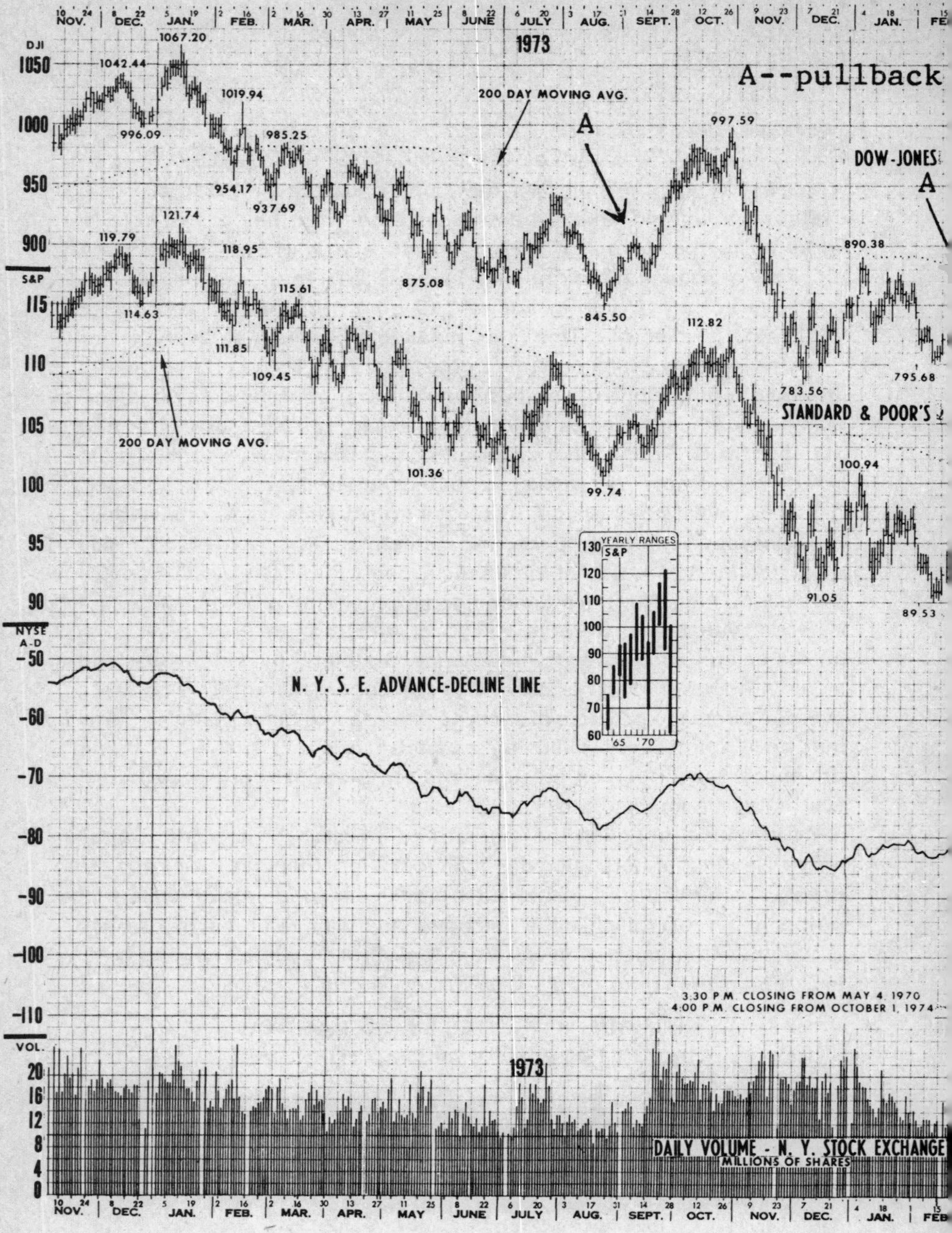
1973
A--pullback
DJI
200 DAY MOVING AVG.
A
DOW-JONES
A
S&P
STANDARD & POOR'S
200 DAY MOVING AVG.
YEARLY RANGES S&P
NYSE A-D
N. Y. S. E. ADVANCE-DECLINE LINE
3:30 P.M. CLOSING FROM MAY 4, 1970
4:00 P.M. CLOSING FROM OCTOBER 1, 1974
VOL.
DAILY VOLUME - N. Y. STOCK EXCHANGE
MILLIONS OF SHARES

CHART 11–1

SOURCE: Trendline's Daily Basis Stock Charts

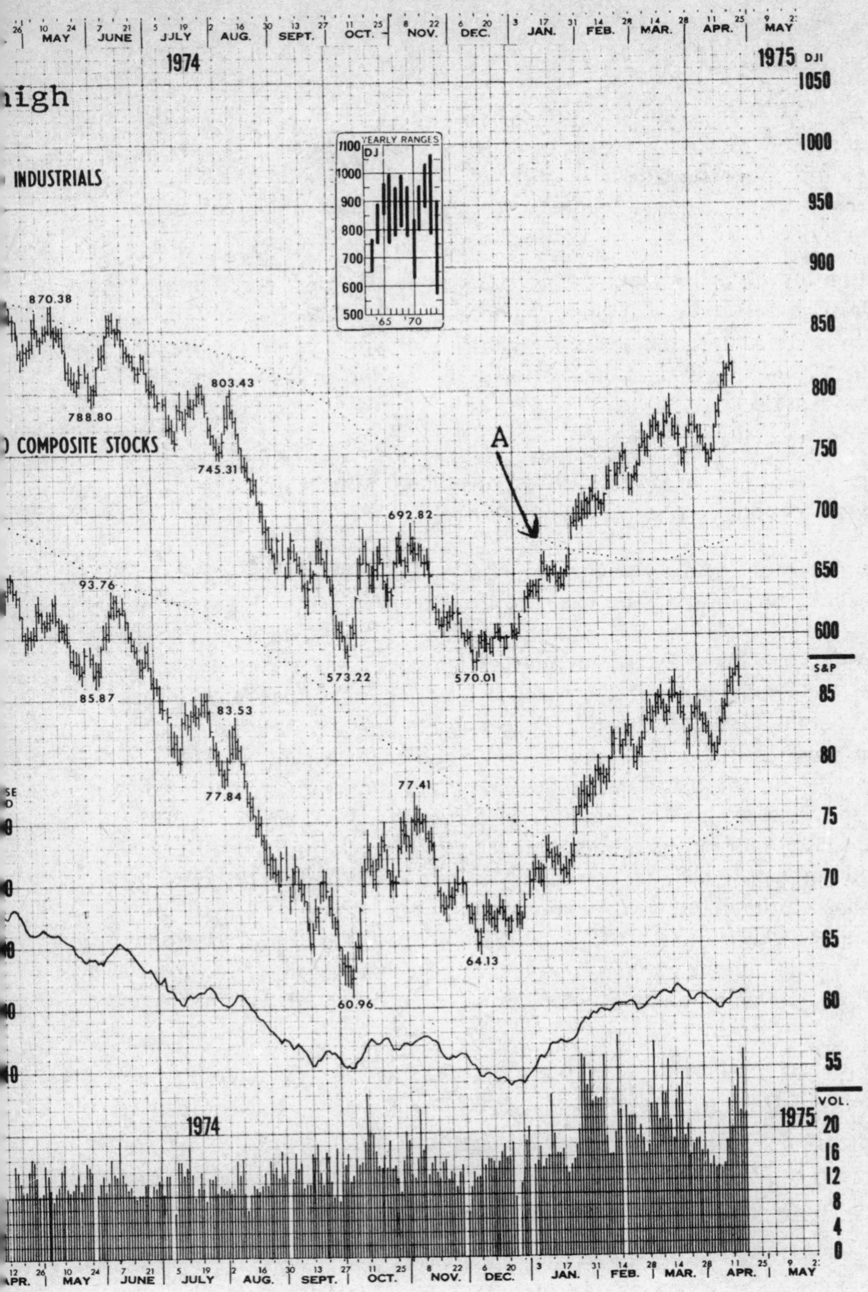

high
INDUSTRIALS
COMPOSITE STOCKS
1974
1975
DJI
S&P
VOL.
YEARLY RANGES
DJ
870.38
788.80
803.43
745.31
692.82
573.22
570.01
93.76
85.87
83.53
77.84
77.41
64.13
60.96
A
APR.
MAY
JUNE
JULY
AUG.
SEPT.
OCT.
NOV.
DEC.
JAN.
FEB.
MAR.

> some of the "nervous money" from the sidelines. Eldon A. Grimm, vice president of Birr, Wilson & Co., said the IBM decision "showed that the big, big companies mayn't be as vulnerable as many suspected."
>
> Setting the stage for the "bandwagon syndrome," said Larry Wachtel, Bache & Co. vice president, was the recent decline in short term interest rates. "Institutional funds were moving from the dead area of the money market to the equity market," he asserted. . . .
>
> A "buying panic" developed, said Newton D. Zinder, vice president of E.F. Hutton & Co., because "a lot of institutions were caught with big cash positions."

The press imparted a sense of tremendous authority and inevitability to the events surrounding the opening in IBM. Thus when the stock did open at 188, the investor identified the leap in its price as a warrant of the ideal workings of an auction market. Nowhere else is there a system so perfectly in accord with the compulsions of human nature. Whereas the Christian-Judaic tradition offers man only the promise of a posthumous reward and a philosophy that enables him (on occasion) to accept life's inevitable anguish, the Exchange shows the investor how, by some strange alchemy, his deep and ingrained longings for material and bodily fulfillment can be satisfied here and now.

In the face of this childlike hope, it is not surprising that the investor fails to ask himself today where the stock he is buying is coming from—or whether the specialist in IBM could have opened his stock yesterday had he not known he could more profitably initiate the investor into his primitive culture by delaying that opening until today.

By the week ending January 31, the Dow had advanced 37.08 points to 703.69, and the image of the Exchange's golden calf had been raised high on the media's tall pedestal. Yet there were signs of contrast between the image and the actuality that could not be concealed.

As mentioned earlier, the study of today's market is an ambiguous pursuit for many investors primarily because of their failure to analyze its movements in terms of the 30 stocks in the Dow average instead of the Dow average itself. The Dow is not intended to aid in the understanding of an institutional process in which it functions to mask the intent of insiders who exercise financial power. The fact is, these insiders were, even then, acquiring their power over investors principally because investors had failed to understand that their desire to buy stock was occasioned not by the movements of the Exchange's 1,500-odd common stocks but by the movements of a few stocks in the Dow. Moreover, along with other stocks, Dow stocks like American Brands, American Can, American Telephone & Telegraph, Anaconda, Chrysler, Esmark, General Foods, Johns Manville, Sears, Standard Oil of California, and Texaco had come under heavy distribution, and their advances stopped dead in their tracks.* Although a clear majority of Dow stocks were still laboring to impress the stamp of a bull market on the investment community, there was absolutely no doubt in my mind that heavy distributions of stock were being conducted in many other stocks as well as the previously mentioned Dow stocks. It was clear that insider selling had begun to dominate the market's processes; that the Exchange, having awakened investor demand, was now responding to it; that having regulated choice and brought it into existence, it had, by virtue of its short selling, already begun to deny its fulfillment.

In the present instance, the insider and the outsider were intent on an exchange of values. It was the insider who developed and inculcated in the outsider the desire to make the exchange possible, in the course of which the outsider receives what (he thinks) he wants, which is stock, and the insider receives what he wants, which is cash.

On the face of things, it is a seemingly simple transaction in which each individual obtains what he wants and bargained for from the other. Because the nature of the transaction presents the appearance of a fair exchange, the investor is unaware that the ultimate consequence of this exchange is the immediate

*See Chapter 15, Charts 15–2 through 15–31.

establishment of the investor's potential vulnerability to declining stock prices, a threat not faced by the insider who sold him his stock. In fact, what the exchange of values between the insider and the outsider had done in the present instance was to place the available instruments of coercion in the hands of the insider. A crisis was in the making, and the public wasn't remotely aware of it.

The credentials of the present rally, with all its aggressive overtones, had been vehemently certified as bullish by some of the country's most eminent market analysts and economists. None of them seemed at all unwilling to express his thoughts about the market even though they all acknowledged that they find the market difficult to analyze rationally. Nonetheless, their views are considered important by investors, and so they are sought out. John Maynard Keynes, himself an economist, was aware of this when he maintained, "the ideas of economists and political philosophers, both when they are right and when they are wrong, are more powerful than is commonly understood. Indeed, the world is ruled by little else."

The networks provided live broadcasts right off the floor of the Stock Exchange. These broadcasts were then updated in the network commercials of major brokerage firms. Stockbrokers, professional economists, and professors of finance were rounded up for various television programs. In a festive mood, these gentlemen voiced their opinions on what they termed a new bull market. "The market was looking for direction through most of January. It found it last week," was the view of one economist.

The most damaging aspect of the rhetoric of such economists is that it creates a sense of urgency among investors to commit into the market. Their conversation revealed that the world of the Stock Exchange was alien to them. They pointed to the 37 points chalked up that week by the DJIA. Never considering that there might be a reality that exists beyond their understanding, they asserted that the movement of stock prices was a reflection of the impenetrable forces of supply-demand operating within an equally impenetrable market mechanism. Although they admitted their ignorance of just how it was done, they were satisfied that the inward faculties and powers built into the market possessed a consciousness and intelligence that now presaged a revival of economic growth in the country by midyear or the third quarter. The market, according to them, was "discounting" this event.

They attributed the market's movements to changes within the economy, instead of attributing changes within the economy to the market's movements. They maintained that "our present system requires periodic slumps to restore profits and discipline labor." They failed to recognize how seriously the technology of consumption is impaired when approximately twice every decade in excess of $400 billion in investor stockholdings is lost because of a failure to "discipline" members of the Stock Exchange establishment, or that the fate of the American economy is indivisible from the fate of the stock market. Yet it was for this reason that, gauging the consequences of the coming bear market, I stated in the course of an interview in 1970 that "we're really in for it. . . . There will be an increase in bankruptcies; there will be continued high unemployment . . . and if you think this seems far-fetched, wait another five years and see what happens to this country" (Seattle *Times*, December 10, 1970).

Economic stability can endure in capitalist economies but not in coexistence with the Exchange establishment's machinery of transaction. The consciousness underlying the forces needed to sustain the Exchange's economic processes reflects a submission to political and economic patterns that are in marked contrast to those sanctioned by "capitalism." That the Exchange has survived so long despite the consequences caused by its technology is, in its own way, a great if not bizarre achievement.

12

The Short Shell Game or The Time Bomb at the Heart of the Market

Ney's Thirteenth Axiom: The test of freedom is in how much of it is granted some so that they may limit the freedom of others.

The January 1975 short-sale figures (published by the SEC in April) confirmed that my assumptions were on target concerning the manner in which the Exchange was preparing the blueprint for a major decline. The existence of these January short sales is symptomatic of the general order of events. The myth of the Exchange as a keystone of capitalist enterprise has a strong appeal for many Americans. Never before did it stand out as a myth that has ravaged investors as it did when these figures were published and their implications grasped.

Earnings, however excellent, can never compete for a position, in the hierarchy of values, comparable to that of the specialist's short sales. These sales absorb the market totally as they are employed by insiders in the continuing fulfillment of their downside objectives. Whereas the investor is forever seeking answers to the market's riddle, using an indicator like the Dow average, here before him is the one indicator that harnesses in a single tight rein all the market's countless relationships and activities.

Looking at these figures, one can see immediately the manner in which specialists placed their interests above those of the community—and never more so than in the last week of January 1975, when their short sales proclaimed their intention, to conduct once again, sooner or later, a circus that would put the investor, as clown, in the center ring.

Although it is not my intention to overly concern myself with the ethics of insider short-selling, it should be clear that in a national community of heightened economic interdependence a large range of critical economic issues are raised by the magnitude of insider short-selling. As I pointed out in an earlier chapter, the SEC makes no attempt to regulate the practices of Stock Exchange specialists. In consequence the investor must strive to place limits on the coercive authority of the specialist's short sale.

Most individuals are not at home with ambiguity. A thing is expected to be what it is and not also something else quite

CHART 12–1
ROUND-LOT SHARE VOLUME ON
THE NEW YORK STOCK EXCHANGE
(IN SHARES AND WARRANTS)

January, 1975

			Share Volume of Specialists (Except for the Odd-Lot Account) in Stocks in Which They are Registered		*Other Member Share Volume Initiated on the Floor*		*Other Member Share Volume Initiated off the Floor*	
			Sales		*Sales*		*Sales*	
Date	*Day*	*Dow/NYSE Vol.*	*Total*	*Short*	*Total*	*Short*	*Total*	*Short*
1	Wednesday	EXCHANGE HOLIDAY						
2	Thursday	632.04/14.80	3,119,220	659,360	382,530	29,000	1,683,427	267,100
3	Friday	634.54/15.27	2,639,870	679,470	229,100	40,200	1,570,036	267,970
6	Monday	637.20/17.55	2,758,080	819,230	293,800	122,800	1,745,264	331,000
7	Tuesday	641.19/14.33	2,005,740	570,710	158,700	58,300	1,532,881	341,510
8	Wednesday	635.40/15.60	1,958,950	665,950	195,300	89,600	1,612,385	321,710
9	Thursday	645.26/16.34	1,984,860	574,940	121,100	30,500	1,783,193	364,600
10	Friday	658.79/25.89	3,671,100	1,264,380	282,600	126,100	2,513,747	511,900
13	Monday	654.18/19.78	2,715,300	907,510	249,500	161,800	1,744,641	365,550

14	Tuesday	648.70/16.61	1,853,640	619,120	152,900	74,200	1,545,530	365,050
15	Wednesday	653.39/16.58	1,989,050	656,070	150,000	37,200	1,623,019	405,200
16	Thursday	655.74/17.11	2,151,800	618,470	244,800	89,500	1,694,012	336,150
17	Friday	644.63/14.26	1,722,190	455,700	144,850	77,100	1,221,927	179,800
20	Monday	647.45/13.45	1,544,000	448,640	67,000	17,200	1,196,062	335,800
21	Tuesday	641.90/14.78	1,861,200	567,030	243,200	71,900	1,604,563	337,100
22	Wednesday	652.61/15.33	1,847,870	463,430	118,800	27,500	1,296,987	277,900
23	Thursday	656.76/17.96	2,424,490	762,310	255,300	65,500	2,060,057	504,700
24	Friday	666.61/20.67	2,405,240	688,070	114,700	32,000	2,100,791	473,490
27	Monday	692.66/32.13	4,281,950	1,566,180	360,100	223,900	2,790,513	656,400
28	Tuesday	694.77/31.76	4,527,690	1,967,550	406,700	263,000	3,065,902	759,300
29	Wednesday	705.96/27.41	3,441,850	1,435,070	245,300	155,000	2,620,254	671,050
30	Thursday	696.42/29.74	3,762,410	1,675,570	340,650	253,200	2,713,722	464,300
31	Friday	703.69/24.64	3,031,180	1,053,820	165,100	91,000	2,575,639	602,600

Source: Statistical Bulletin, published by the SEC.

different. To understand fully the phantasmic qualities of the short sale and the genesis of its power, the investor must understand the manner in which he is trapped between regulation and its myth because of the ability of Wall Street to turn the SEC into the handmaiden of the Stock Exchange. As the reader gains insight into the formation of the first Securities and Exchange Commission prototype, he will recognize the manner in which the Commission's programmed myths and polite conventions (including occasional investigations of the Exchange at the request of Congress) sustain the existence of the short sale.

Of all the regulatory commissions now in existence, the nature of the SEC's jurisdiction over the wealth-creating organs of the financial establishment places this regulatory body at the top of Washington's pyramid of power. Because of the implications of the financial establishment's far-reaching economic role in the nation's destiny, it would be impossible to overestimate the magnitude of the SEC's importance as a political agency. Indeed the SEC, of all the government's agencies, is the only government body that is in a position to resist the dominance of the financial establishment.

When it was formed, the Commission was fully aware of the self-interest of the insiders it was supposed to regulate. Considering the nature of its task and the powers it was granted in order to perform this task, there was every reason to assume that, with men at the helm like Ferdinand Pecora, formerly chief counsel of the Senate Banking and Currency Committee and chief investigator into Stock Exchange insider practices, and Judge Robert Healy, formerly a trustbuster with the Federal Trade Commission, the SEC would observe its responsibilities with impartiality and equality. Its commissioners appeared to be men of integrity, courage, and wisdom.

Aware of the divergence of interests and goals between Exchange insiders and investors and the consequences this divergence engendered, one would think there might have been a consensus within the SEC as to the measures that had to be instituted, particularly concerning the regulation of specialists and their short selling. Indeed, the investigations conducted by Ferdinand Pecora had been chiefly responsible for the passage of the Securities and Exchange Act of 1934. But the repertory of human nature is such that the Commission did not strike at the myth of Exchange authority; it enthroned it. The motivations of succeeding commissioners and chairmen were set by the first chairman. With the passage of the years the myths surrounding the Exchange and the investment business hardened into tradition. Thus it is symbolic of the pathology of what, for want of a more appropriate term, we can call self-interest that the evolution of the SEC produced the devolution of the investor.

An idea so inconsistent with the intent underlying the thrust of the securities laws of 1933 and 1934 could be sustained only by a mythology that was a compound of hypocrisy and contradiction. For that, a man was needed within the SEC who previously had demonstrated his willingness to destroy rather than affirm investor well-being. The securities industry knew just the man the President should appoint for the job. Experience in the securities industry was the ingredient needed to bypass regulation.

Unfortunately it was not the character of the Pecoras, the Healys, or the other SEC commissioners that determined the bias of the Commission toward the Exchange but the habit patterns of the man who became its first chairman, Joseph Kennedy. President Franklin Roosevelt had taken a very commonplace, old-fashioned, ambitious Irish politician, one-time stockbroker and shrewd and ruthless manipulator of stocks, men, and women, and placed him at the helm of the SEC. Instead of an individual who was noble, honest, and courageous, Roosevelt had appointed a man who, four months earlier, had been cited by Pecora as a stock swindler. It would have been impossible for Roosevelt to choose a more grasping mammal or one more avid for power. According to Richard J. Whalen, in his excellent book *The Founding Father*, Kennedy "had the sense to recognize the opportunity offered by the SEC. While the Secretary of the Treasury *symbolized* power and prestige, here, in the new SEC, was the *real* power." There is no question but that once the appointment was made, the man who sat in the White House had less influence on the financial well-being of the nation than the chairman he had appointed to the SEC!

The work habits of a man influence his character. You cannot change this character by giving him a title, placing him in a position of trust, and hoping that the title will transform his outlook on his environment and so change his character—leastways not in Kennedy's case. He had started out in the investment business in 1919 as a humble stockbroker in the Boston branch of Hayden Stone & Company. He remained with this company for five years as manager and learned all he needed to know about the business of stock manipulation. In 1924 he left for New York, where he opened an office and had a sign painted on his door: JOSEPH P. KENNEDY—BANKER. Soon thereafter he established his reputation as one of Wall Street's most unscrupulous stock manipulators.

As chairman of the SEC, he enjoyed his job as policeman of the securities industry. "You know," he is quoted, "when I took this job I told the boss [Roosevelt] that I didn't want to tie myself down or take on work that would be more than temporary, but I must admit, I do get a kick out of it." His appointment had been severely criticized. John T. Flynn, writing in *The New Republic*, was thunderstruck: "It is impossible," he said. "It could not happen." The owner of Scripps-Howard, publisher Roy Howard, protested personally to Roosevelt. When Roosevelt was adamant, Howard ran an editorial denouncing the appointment. Roosevelt was indebted to Kennedy for his support during the election, and this was his way of repaying his debt.

The demand for action produced the supply. Kennedy launched an all-out attack across the country against the promoters of new issues or phony oil stocks and others who presumed they could poach in the Stock Exchange's preserve. Yet between these forays and the questionable practices of Stock Exchange members, there was a wide and tragic gap.

One realized with a painful start that Kennedy's efforts everywhere else were meant to hide the fact that, not only was he responsible to the interests of his friends and former associates on the floor of the Stock Exchange, but he argued and fought for the right of the Stock Exchange hierarchy to organize and express its own interests. In his way Kennedy had employed that rare sleight of hand that conjured an image of purpose and regulatory enterprise without ever disturbing the manipulations that were always in the process of unfolding on the floor of the Stock Exchange. In fact the structured counterpoint of his active silence toward investment bankers and Exchange specialists underscored the special care he took not to turn them into objects of public scrutiny.

Sensing that the wave of the future would support the proposition that self-interest precedes public interest, Kennedy sought to ride it by showing his friends on Wall Street he was not altogether footloose in a void. He invited Wall Street's leading luminaries down to Washington. Totally uninhibited, a man who was now secure of his position, he escorted them into his office singly and in small groups—the heads of the major investment banking firms and the officials of the Stock Exchange along with its most important specialists and floor traders. It was an occasion on which Kennedy was very careful to say what was expected, having been even more careful not to do what was needed. Each of them shrewdly planned his little homespun haymakers; then all of them together masterminded a blueprint for the future. Not surprisingly, they were enchanted with Kennedy as the new chairman. One thing was certain, he was not out to break new ground. According to Whalen, Kennedy "set out to allay the fears of Wall Street. . . . They were pleasantly surprised by their important role in the new scheme of things. Exuding sweet reasonableness, Chairman Kennedy asked merely that they accept the SEC's rules and act as their own policemen." And, according to *The New York Times* (August 14, 1934), Kennedy was quoted as saying: "In a large measure we would have the exchanges do their own policing. They are in much better shape to do this than to have the government send in a staff." The relationship between the Stock Exchange and Kennedy was best summarized by the then president of the Stock Exchange, Richard Whitney. Commenting on Kennedy's efforts, he referred to them as "sane and sound." (Whitney was later sent to Sing Sing for multimillion-dollar fraud.)

Just how well Kennedy managed to load the dice in favor of the Stock Exchange has escaped most of his admirers' attention. Even as eminent an authority on the period and the Kennedy family as Arthur Schlesinger, Jr., has written: "As chairman [of the SEC], Kennedy moved cautiously but firmly . . . though his gestures were conciliatory he did nothing to diminish the Commission's authority. . . . Kennedy, whose objective had been to secure the adoption of new trading rules and to restore the capital market, now resigned. . . . Kennedy's contribution had been substantial. He had achieved the acceptance of SEC without sacrifice of principle, and he had given its administrative operators invaluable momentum. . . ."

Aiming at a rigid objectivity, Schlesinger fell into the trap of most historians who write about the flora and fauna of the securities industry. Unaware it was the floor of the Stock Exchange that was in need of policing far more than the boiler-room tactics of stockbrokers, Schlesinger, it is conceivable, might have assumed Kennedy was doing a good job by virtue of the quantity of court actions for fraud leveled at the industry's small fry. Moreover, it is understandable that he might applaud Kennedy's efforts unaware that he had served as apologist and spokesman for the Stock Exchange. The truth of the matter, however, was that Kennedy was indeed the voice and executor of self-regulation.

With respect to the regulation of the specialist's use of the short sale, one's awareness of Kennedy's omissions becomes even more acute. Certainly he was conscious of the original intent of the Exchange Act regarding the short sale. He was also aware of the lobbying efforts that had been employed by Wall Street to torpedo any attempt to restrict the use of the short sale. It was no secret that when the teeth were being introduced into the Securities and Exchange Act, the highly solvent and substantial image of Richard Whitney led his platoon of anxious Wall Streeters and corporation executives into battle against the Act. In short order, because Congress is a human as well as a legislative institution, the teeth were summarily extracted one by one. Everything that had been created was eliminated that might conform with the investor's concept of the market as a place where fair play was observed. Never-never land was to remain the wasteland. Instead of prescribing its own statutory restrictions, the Act empowered the Commission, at its own discretion, to establish the Exchange's regulatory guidelines. It was up to the Commission, therefore, to decide whether the Exchange would be forced into a recognition of the investor's rights. As Richard Whelan phrased it, "Plainly the SEC would be what the first commissioners made of it."

In the give-and-take of the legislative hearings, Whitney was able, successfully, to oppose segregation of the functions of specialists, floor traders, and stockbrokers; moreover, specialists and other Exchange members would continue to trade for their own accounts. In the elaborate battle of wills over the highly combustible provisions governing the specialist's use of the short sale, Whitney packed the hearing rooms with his supporters. None of the Act's provisions came under as heavy attack as those governing the short sale. Sam Rayburn called it "the most powerful lobby ever organized against any bill which ever came up in Congress" (footnote, *The Founding Father*, page 138.) Needless to say, by the time Wall Street's Ivy Leaguers and their lawyers left town, the role of the short sale was reaffirmed as the Stock Exchange's most important tactical weapon. Whitney had seen to it that its provisions had been altered so that instead of placing restrictions on short selling, it made short selling subject solely to the regulatory power of the Commission. In other words, subject to the old, inborn compulsions of Joseph P. Kennedy.

Given the premises of the short sale and its sequence of cause and effect, there can be no question concerning the origin of investor crisis. Aware of these facts Kennedy prepared for battle—not, however, on behalf of the investor but on the side of the Exchange's short-selling specialists.

Nothing is more important to an understanding of the course of the stock market which ensued than comprehending Joseph Kennedy's decision to protect the power of the Stock Exchange and the myth of regulation by *granting the Exchange sole jurisdiction and control over the formulation of rules and usages governing the short sale.* The major booms and busts that followed have their historical roots in the concrete realities of Kennedy's decision to abandon his regulatory responsibilities by handing the rule-making authority over the short sale to the very people whose violent use of the device the Exchange Act had sought to outlaw. For practical purposes, it drained regulation of its active principle. In effect, Kennedy told Wall Street to do as they liked without risk of intervention from the Commission. Thus did he feather his Wall Street nest for all the years to come.

The short-sale rule finally adopted by the Exchange required that "a member shall not effect a sale which would demoralize the market. . . . Accordingly the 1935 rule introduced by the Exchange prohibited the short sale of a security at a price below the last sale price. . . ." This is commonly known as the "uptick" rule. The Exchange then saw to it that there were specialist exemptions to the rule.

Having provided the solution to the Exchange's major dilemma, Kennedy, the master of transition from nonregulation to self-regulation, resigned from the Commission. In an article published at that time, John Flynn stated: "The law as it now stands forbids and requires so little that we may truthfully say there is no body of laws yet governing the securities markets."* Plainly, what had promised to be an exciting experiment in reclaiming the American securities markets for Americans fizzled out.

The crisis caused by a sharp drop in the market in the autumn of 1937 and the conflicting claims of Stock Exchange specialists and investors provoked bitter divisions within the SEC, with the result that an investigation of the Stock Exchange was launched by the Commission. It was concluded that there was not the slightest doubt that specialist short-selling had contributed to the force of the decline and that the Exchange rule governing short selling left investors in a highly vulnerable position. Accordingly, a new set of short-selling rules, designed to correct some of the limitations of the 1935 provision, were formulated and went into effect in February 1938.

The months following the passage of the new short-selling regulations were a period of estrangement for the Exchange. Deprived of a license to employ to the full the mastered intimacy of their craft, specialists saw their short selling fall by more than 50 percent. Then, once again, the deep kinship existing between the Exchange and the SEC surfaced.

Exchange officials traveled to Washington and were made comfortable at the Commission's headquarters. Polishing their words as carefully as a jeweler his lenses, they made it clear how much income and control over stock prices they lost by virtue of the SEC's modification of the short-sale rule. In March 1939, therefore, the Commission succumbed. Responding to the political realities of Stock Exchange influence and the fact that a man's future is often his greatest temptation, the Commission promulgated what is now the main posture of the short-sale rule (10a-1[a]). Whereas the old rule had prohibited all short selling at the

*For a fully documented report on Flynn's comments, see *The Wall Street Jungle*, pages 227–30.

last long-sale price, the new rule permitted specialists to sell short at such prices if that price was higher than the last different price (the zero-plus tick).

More than forty years have passed since the formation of the SEC, and the more the rules governing short sales have seemed to change, the more they have remained the same. In the final analysis, we see that the investigations conducted to resolve the problems caused by specialist short-selling have been great theatrical events, sideshow acts in the great arena of American history played out by senators, congressmen, regulators, and Exchange insiders for the benefit of an audience of 33 million investors.

Yet the fact is that these investigations have had, in one sense, enormously constructive consequences. Their findings have provided investors with irrefutable documentation concerning the consequences of specialist short-selling. For example, this was accomplished by the Special Study Report of 1963 when it described what happens to stock prices once specialists have established their short sales. More than this, the Special Study described how specialists are actually able legally to circumvent the supposed intent of existing rules to protect investors from specialist short-selling.

Concerning the effectiveness of the uptick rule, for example, the Special Study Report had this to say (Part 2, page 289):

> *Ample illustrations have been brought to light* of the fact that plus or zero plus ticks may be commonplace during sharply declining markets.

Discussing specialist short-selling during the course of the market decline of 1962, the Special Study pointed out that specialist short-selling is minimal as stock prices advance from their lows. There is not the slightest question that specialist short sales *increase* as the market moves to its highs. This is because one group of specialists after another raises its stock prices to their highs and then sells short. We see this happening in the course of the rally that began in January. The Special Study Report (Part 2, page 257) stated that specialists and other members

> . . . increase their proportion of all short selling as an advance in stock prices progresses. . . . The reverse is true during declines.

In other words, as the decline "progresses," there is less and less short selling by specialists until finally, at the bottom, there is, on balance, short covering.

To compound the investor's problems, he is persuaded that as long as he owns blue chips he need not be apprehensive about declines of these stocks. Little does he know that the most popular stocks for specialist short-selling are the so-called blue chip "market leaders," or current "trading favorites." In fact, it is because these stocks are such trading favorites that, by virtue of his short-selling and short-covering operations, the specialist has the power to rule a trading process that, at first glance, might seem to rule him. Obviously the SEC is aware of this condition, since its study group commented that (Part 2, page 101):

> This emerging picture of a substantial volume of short selling in prominent stocks during intervals of price weakness indicates the inadequacy of current rules to cope with the harmful effect of short selling. . . .

One of the problems with the Special Study is that the members of its study group assumed that the function of the existing rules governing short selling was

> to prevent the use of short selling . . . to accelerate a declining trend. . . .

The study group seemed unaware that these rules had initially been carefully formulated by the Exchange for the benefit of its specialist system and that it was for this reason that they were totally ineffective. Despite this omission the group saw through the limitations in the existing rules. In their findings they

> concluded that [specialist] short sales may contribute importantly to accelerating the trend of a falling market.

Unfortunately the exemptions from the short-sale rule granted specialists have not been explained to the public in the published material of the Stock Exchange or the SEC. In the course of my researches, I discovered that the Exchange, working in close harmony with the SEC, has managed for practical purposes to tear the old rule to shreds. Here is how a specialist can now effect a short sale that is exempt from the restrictions of the short-sale rule: If the specialist owns the stock to be sold (for example, in his investment account) and intends to deliver that stock "as soon as possible" but "without undue inconvenience or expense," then the sale of that stock can be considered by him as a long sale not subject to the short-sale rule, "and the sale may be effected on a minus tick" without being marked as a short sale.*

Thus in the present instance, if the specialist accumulated his investment accounts during the month of December, for example, but wants to drop the price of his stock before the six-month long-term capital gains period has been completed, the SEC's short-sale exemption now allows him to use his short sale to establish a long-term capital gain. For example, having established his investment account in December he can sell short on downticks at or near his stock's highs in March and again in April and then, having dropped his price 25 percent or more from its high by early June, still deliver over his investment account to his trading account and establish his long-term capital gains on

*These are direct quotes from a letter to me written by the SEC's Division of Market Regulation.

the basis of the prices at which he sold short in March and April.

We can further clarify the manner in which specialists can use the exemption from the uptick rule during the rally that began in January, 1975. As a specialist establishes a rally high in his stock and can see orders placed on his book *under* the present market price by investors who told themselves they didn't want "to chase" the stock, the specialist can drop his price in order to execute these transactions by selling short to them when he is long-stock in an investment or omnibus account which he can subsequently deliver over to his trading account to cover his short sales.

What is also of great importance is that the specialist is exempted from the short-sale rule that requires that the trade be marked a short sale. Thus the short-sale figures supplied by the Exchange to the SEC which the SEC then publishes in its Statistical Bulletin is misleading information. It in no way reflects what, in the course of the rally that began in January, undoubtedly represented a preponderance of the specialist's activities as a dealer for himself. The investor, however, can begin to guess what the nature of his problem must be like when he examines the accounts of specialist short selling for the month of February. Looking at these figures, it is fair to say they represent the tip of the iceberg as far as specialist short sales are concerned.

With the rise in short sales to the range of 1.9 million shares a day, it is conceivable the investor might suppose that specific stocks on these particular days might lend themselves very well to a short sale. For example, looking at the Dow stocks that had high volume and that had big-block transactions at their highs on February 13, I noted that Chrysler had a block of 18,900 shares at 11, General Motors a block of 18,700 at 37½, and Eastman Kodak a block of 18,000 shares at 85¾. One might suppose that under these circumstances the evidence of big blocks suggested that these stocks were ready for reversal. Indeed, under routine

CHART 12–2
ROUND-LOT SHARE VOLUME ON THE NEW YORK STOCK EXCHANGE (IN SHARES AND WARRANTS)

February, 1975

			Share Volume of Specialists (Except for the Odd-Lot Account) in Stocks in Which They are Registered		*Other Member Share Volume Initiated on the Floor*		*Other Member Share Volume Initiated off the Floor*	
			Sales		*Sales*		*Sales*	
Date	*Day*	*Dow/NYSE Vol.*	*Total*	*Short*	*Total*	*Short*	*Total*	*Short*
3	Monday	711.44/25.40	3,236,040	1,271,690	309,500	219,300	2,630,844	637,900
4	Tuesday	708.09/25.04	3,095,370	1,254,110	287,000	155,300	2,221,951	448,300
5	Wednesday	717.85/25.83	3,187,320	1,235,550	231,420	133,500	2,790,891	662,800
6	Thursday	714.17/32.02	4,148,890	1,840,910	296,500	180,700	2,862,087	589,100
7	Friday	711.91/20.06	2,186,450	739,360	119,100	40,600	1,430,616	319,250
10	Monday	708.39/16.12	2,101,300	773,710	184,600	105,500	1,312,796	288,200
11	Tuesday	707.60/16.47	1,906,470	665,190	167,800	54,300	1,313,346	201,600
12	Wednesday	715.03/19.79	2,476,390	772,910	244,000	92,700	1,947,986	340,200
13	Thursday	726.92/35.16	4,623,440	1,952,500	394,100	234,100	2,760,264	619,920
14	Friday	734.20/23.29	3,006,050	1,314,740	130,200	67,200	1,892,589	365,200

17	Monday	EXCHANGE HOLIDAY						
18	Tuesday	731.30/23.99	2,962,130	1,191,470	220,000	117,000	1,855,370	479,600
19	Wednesday	736.39/22.19	2,470,090	813,560	172,900	93,900	1,868,070	407,160
20	Thursday	745.38/22.26	2,653,110	960,400	114,900	48,100	1,869,818	419,100
21	Friday	749.77/24.44	2,907,450	1,030,920	139,500	54,600	2,052,392	471,650
24	Monday	736.94/19.15	2,315,070	785,390	145,300	55,900	1,547,441	278,650
25	Tuesday	719.18/20.91	2,159,930	647,510	135,200	51,100	1,669,916	231,600
26	Wednesday	728.10/18.79	2,549,780	665,710	181,400	21,600	1,488,853	267,660
27	Thursday	731.15/16.43	2,323,100	699,040	179,500	61,100	1,610,681	280,500
28	Friday	739.05/17.56	2,229,890	731,970	144,600	49,500	1,771,304	324,500

Source: Statistical Bulletin, published by the SEC.

trading circumstances, this might have been true. However, in the course of a rally that has been triggered by a major announcement such as the IBM court decision in the present instance or the Nixon announcement on August 15, 1971, of his new wage-price policies, blocks in the 18,000-share range are not by themselves indicative of a reversal. One of the major clues the prudent investor should look for is that provided by General Motors. Has the stock at the end of a sharp advance in prace proceeded to advance two or more points over at least a two-day trading period? As we pointed out earlier, the signal for a reversal in General Motors (and oftentimes the overall market) is characterized by this culminating advance in the price of this stock. On the day in question, General Motors advanced only ¾ of a point and, the day before that, a full point on what was still not heavy (193,000 shares) volume. As for Eastman Kodak, we know from our numbers theory and the past performance of this stock that it tends to reverse its trend at or near a critical price leve, not midway between two critical price levels (i.e., 80 and 90).

It is my opinion, therefore, that investor short selling should not be conducted until a major turning point has been approximated in these and other Dow stocks and the trend has been reversed. It is possible to make a tentative assessment that such an event has occurred when:

1. major highs appear to have been established at or slightly above critical price levels in the Dow stocks that have been leading the rally and the stocks close *down* a point or so from their highs;
2. these highs have been to the accompaniment of significant volume in the overall market;
3. other Dow stocks closed a point or so lower than their intraday highs;
4. one or more big blocks have appeared at or near the high of the stock you wish to sell short, suggesting major short selling by its specialist; and
5. the media and the public are exceptionally bullish.

Any attempt to establish a successful short sale before these elements are present could conceivably cause the trader to attempt to beat against the tide. Thus, while it is always possible that one might establish a successful short sale in a stock like American Can in mid-February or mid-March and then with patience see it pay off, there will be ten others that look good on paper but prove to be premature. The wiser course of action is always to wait until either the Dow has reversed itself or the stock itself has completed a major reversal pattern. An examination of most stocks will show that although specialist short selling will stop them in their tracks, their prices tend to move sideways or only slightly down until the stocks leading the rally have reversed and the overall trend is once again down.

Thus we see that although specialist short sales shape the trend of the market, they do not always do so immediately. Instead, these short sales are often inventoried and held on the shelf until such time as the trend is down. In the meantime, looking with an eye into the future, specialists in these stocks will employ their time to good advantage by adding to their short sales.

Correlating the following chart of the Dow with the February short-sale figures, we see that specialists continued to maintain their overall short sales above the 4-million-share-a-week level as specialists established the February high in the Dow.

From this standpoint, chances are that traders who sold short in the month of January would have had to submit to the necessity of waiting several months—even if they chose a good candidate for a short-sale—before their stocks began to decline. The probability is that if they sold short under these conditions, the mental strain to which they will have subjected themselves will cause them to be traumatized by the slightest advance in stock prices. This then brings us to the principal theoretical objection to short selling by anyone except the most experienced professional. The focus of the inexperienced short seller will become as narrowed as though it were confined by blinders. A continuing stream of remorse and anxiety will flourish like

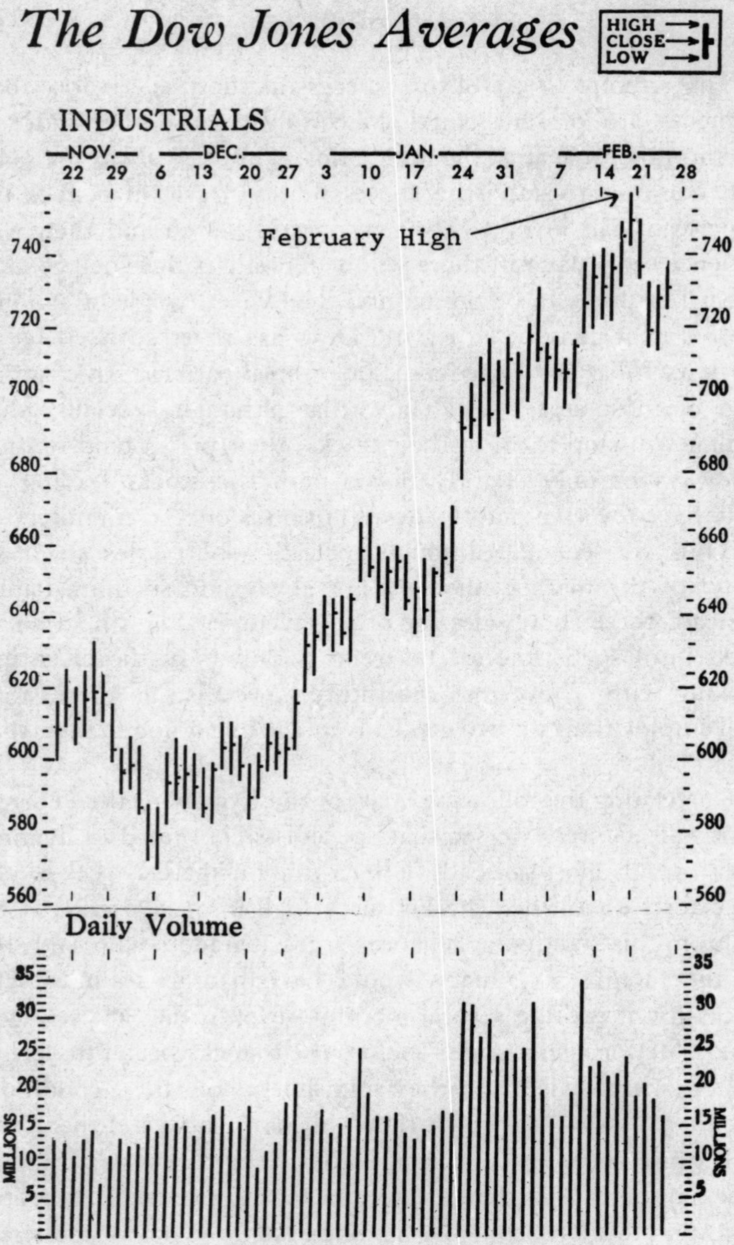
The Dow Jones Averages
HIGH
CLOSE
LOW
INDUSTRIALS
NOV.
DEC.
JAN.
FEB.
22
29
6
13
20
27
3
10
17
24
31
7
14
21
28
February High
740
720
700
680
660
640
620
600
580
560
Daily Volume
35
30
25
20
15
10
5
MILLIONS

CHART 12–3

SOURCE: *The Wall Street Journal*, February 28, 1975

mushrooms in the damp. Unable to cope, his psyche having been pushed and shoved about by the specialist's price movements, the investor will think only of escape. Under these circumstances he will most likely resolve his problem by telling his broker to "cover at the market."

I recall a former client who called me in late 1972. He asked me to sell short for him. He was a very well-known minister whom I had assumed would be the last person in danger of placing himself in a position where he would allow himself to view the market in greed's unrealistic light. I asked him to be patient, to wait until I could commit him safely into the market on the long side. He was adamant. "Please, Mr. Ney," he pleaded, "just tell me one stock to sell short." I reminded him that he was a minister and that I expected him to be able to devote himself to more spiritual activities during this period in the market. But he was desperate and I relented. The conversation took place on a Friday. I told him to call me back on Monday, when I would give him the name of a stock to sell short.

When he called on Monday I warned him that before I gave him the name of the stock, I knew no matter how right I was in my choice that he would be subjecting himself to a nerve-racking experience, that he would sweat. He assured me he had no such concerns. I made one additional stipulation: He was not to call asking if he should "cover his short." The stock, I said, could fluctuate within a trading range before it declined but I definitely saw it declining. I told him that I would call him to cover only when I felt it had touched an important bottom. He agreed to these conditions, and I told him to sell General Motors short. The price was then approximately 78.

Shortly thereafter, the stock dropped to approximately 73 and he called, asking if he should cover. I reminded him that I was not going to trade the stock for him. General Motors subsequently advanced to the 80 level, and I received another call. "I'm sorry to bother you, but I'm losing a lot of money. Shall I cover?" I again reminded him of our earlier conversations and advised him that he was experiencing the anxieties he was so certain he was immune to. I told him that the rally was routine and that the stock was destined to resume its decline once the specialist had unloaded his inventories. The stock then moved sideways, longer, indeed, than I had expected. This was a price action that collided with the yearnings of the human mechanism. It caused sleepless nights that were ultimately an invitation to surrender. The stock, however, subsequently dropped under 70. I was still not ready to recommend a covering transaction, since I anticipated a further decline to at least 59.

Shortly thereafter, I received a curt letter from him, dismissing me as his investment adviser. His abruptness of tone suggested that, in a burst of self-confidence, he was about to try it on his own. I was familiar with the scenario. All I could do was thank him for his letter and wish him well. I wondered whether he had held onto his short or whether he had become frightened and covered. I never did learn.

At the end of a year, I had a midnight telephone call from him. "Do you know who this is, Mr. Ney?" He said he was in a terrible psychological state because of the losses he had sustained in the market. I suggested that he lacked the "spiritual" equipment for the market and that he should stick to preaching. He said he would like to do that if I would take him back as a client. I agreed, until he said, "You can handle half, and I will trade the other half." I thanked him, declined his offer, and went back to sleep.

Almost another year passed and I had a final call from him. "Mr. Ney, they're calling me for more margin. What shall I do?" I told him it was my policy to never, under any circumstances, use margin. He said that it was his broker's fault; that his broker hated all my ideas; and that his broker had recommended margin and he'd listened to him. Now he wanted to know whether or not he should answer the margin call for more money. I told him that while I couldn't advise him since he wasn't a client, I *could* tell him my clients were still in cash. "Do you mean you've remained in cash all this time?" he asked. I told him that was exactly what I meant. He was silent a moment and then asked, "Can you tell me anything that might help me?" I told him I didn't see how anything I might say could help him now.

It would seem that the history of most investors is one of deliberate forgetting. They are incapable of seeing that it is their thought processes that are accomplices to their self-destruction.

Looking at the bait of rising stock prices, investors walk into the trap that has been prepared for them. They have no idea how fast stock prices can drop once the trap is sprung and the active direction of the trend is downward. Nor are they aware that the specialist's continuing use of the short sale as stock prices decline creates an irreversible situation, since the specialist's short sale is the ultimate policy-maker and the determinant of trend. Buying into a rally in the presence of heavy specialist short-selling is the resource of investors who have never properly understood the investment environment. Theirs is the kind of behavior one must avoid if one is to survive in the market.

The investor must see clearly that the error that has always been committed by him is that he has been unconscious of the way the specialist's short sale provides the subtext for the Exchange's economic drama and that he and other investors have failed to see that it is actually their demand that calls the specialist's short sale into existence. Unaware of this, they look upon the current demand for stock as a reflection of "the market's underlying strength." They have failed to recognize that their demand has created and moved into position the Exchange's juggernauts of transition and crisis. The reader must learn to rise above the emotional impress of the conventional thinking and responses of other investors by evolving a procedure that will enable him to act in a way that is not a response programmed or contrived by the Stock Exchange. The best way for him to do this is to practice one-upmanship on the specialist. The investor must employ his imagination to move through the specialist's looking glass to see himself as he is seen by the specialist. To do this, he must imagine himself a specialist and then project what his attitudes and behavior patterns would be toward investors. Employing this kind of rear-view mirror gazing, the investor can then more readily begin to recognize specialist short-selling for what it is; and to understand what his own response would be to a great influx of public demand. The very first thing that then happens, of course, is that the investor sees quite clearly that were he in the specialist's position, he too would employ the opportunity to maximize profits by acquiring an investment account of short sales. This then would also be *his* ultimate response, as a specialist, to public demand.

The power of recognition is the investor's best tactical weapon. It is the prelude to confrontation, a confrontation that can take one of two forms: Either the trader can sell short when the price and volume action of Dow stocks like General Motors, Eastman Kodak, and Du Pont indicate major short selling has taken place in them at an intermediate or rally high, or the investor can totally withdraw from the battle that specialists are about to launch against him. In this latter case, the investor must then move himself to the sidelines until after stock prices decline and he sees evidence of massive specialist short-covering at critical wholesale price levels. (This was typified by the kind of price action we saw in General Motors in December 1974.) The investor can then return to the battle, prepared to plunge into the action that is about to begin. At that time, the trader who sold short would be profitably covering his short sales and accumulating stock.

13

Muddle Crass Traditions or First You Gotta Beat the Dog Ma

Ney's Fourteenth Axiom: You can discover what the specialist wants you to do by observing what he wants you to want.

I don't believe I am being too free in my predictions of events to come when I say that most of the soul searching that will be done by investors in the third and fourth quarters of 1975 will be caused by their ignorance of specialist short-selling in the first and second quarters of 1975. By mid-February fully half of the Dow stocks had been stopped dead in their tracks by massive specialist short-selling (see Chapter 16, Charts 15–2 through 15–31).

By the week ending Feburary 21 it was apparent that many traders were being subjected to sharp shake-outs that were making it difficult to establish consistent gains. My diary entry for February 21 suggests one of the forces that restricted the trader's profits.

Friday, February 21, 1975
Dow +4.39/749.77 Dow Vol. 2,224,500 NYSE Vol. 24,440,000
In my conversations with traders who call seeking advice, it is apparent that most of them misunderstand the nature of the processes now under way in the market. Although the Dow appears to be making enormous gains, the fact is that since the rally took off at the end of January (launching traders into the market), the price reversals of many stocks were almost as sharp on the downside during February as on the upside in late January.

This is upsetting to those accustomed to assessing the market in terms of the Dow. Having committed into active stocks that they expect to see make broad fluctuations within a trading range, they are either frightened into selling because of an unexpectedly sharp drop in price, or the fluctuations in stock prices barely allow them to cover commission costs. Thus while many of them quite prudently may have entered sell orders in GM today, as the stock advanced to 39 on high volume—a 1⅝-point gain—it is unlikely they will be allowed to enjoy much in the way of profits if they sold this stock short.

Since GM tends to move in five-point spreads, it is unlikely it will drop any lower than 35 at this time. Further, in view of the volume figures (211,200), this specialist's move to 39 today is obviously indicative of only the *very beginnings* of distribution. To move the enormous inventory of stock off his shelves that he has gathered there, he will have to advance not only to 40 but probably beyond that. How much beyond one can't be certain.

One thing traders should always consider is that at an important stock's arrival at the critical 40 (60, 80, etc.) level, there will probably be as much or more selling as buying by traders who bought the stock at lower price levels and held on to it expecting a move to 40. Thus if the specialist is to unload the shares he has to absorb at a profit, it is common sense to assume he will subsequently advance his stock *at least* to 41 and probably closer to 45.

Another reason the present market has begun to take its toll on the trader's spirit is that all too many stocks have stopped advancing. This is something else traders don't understand. IBM is typical of many important stocks (like American Can, American Home Products, American Telephone & Telegraph, Texaco, and Xerox). Having crashed against the barrier of specialist short selling, they are now merely moving sideways, despite endless gabble about a bull market. It is hard for the trader to understand that the target has shifted and that investor demand is now being aimed at a new group of stocks; that specialists rotate the privilege of short selling among themselves and their different stocks. Thus, once specialists have maximized their short sales in one group of stocks, pricewise these stocks become comparatively immobile. Then, since hope, if it is to be activated, must have a focus, the prices of other stocks are raised, and public demand for these stocks then enables their specialists to sell them short. Once that's completed, most of the stocks in this group will then join the first group, and the target is again shifted to still another set of stocks. As this group advances, the first two groups then move sideways, and all this time specialists are selling short more and more stock. And so it goes, until the catalyst of specialist short selling has totally permeated the market. At that point, the two or three Dow stocks that have been raising the investor's temperature as they raised the Dow can be expected to turn down. It may take another month, two months, or more, but when it happens, *as* it happens, the market's gladiators can be expected to hold onto their stocks as the market's Caesars subject them to a ruthless onslaught of declining stock prices.

Although, as I mentioned earlier, it is not my practice to dispense specific investment advice to individuals who call or write, I was happy to have had a call from an investor in Minnesota. His reason for calling was practical: he wanted to know the value of two books he was reading on the stock market.

In particular he wondered what my opinion was on an aspect of market theory on which the authors of these two books held totally contradictory opinions. Both of the authors were financial journalists. One was a former financial columnist for *The New York Times*, and the other had been a financial writer for the Los Angeles *Times* whom I'd known and for whom I had a warm regard. As it happened, he'd also been a "stringer" for *The New York Times* and had been responsible for a mild quake on Wall Street when, in 1965, he sent in a major story on my work and my attitude toward the specialist system. The *Times* printed the story on the front page of its financial section. (I was later told the financial editor "caught hell" for running it.)

Now it seemed my friend had written a handbook for investment clubs in which he vehemently opposed the use of stop loss orders, whereas the former *Times* financial columnist seemed committed to the stop loss order. My caller said that the members of his investment club were divided on the matter and would welcome my opinion. I asked him if he knew what a specialist was. He said that he did, that he had just finished reading my first book, *The Wall Street Jungle*. I then asked him what he would do if he were a specialist who intended to conduct a sharp rally in his stock and who also had a large quantity of stop loss orders on his book. He said he didn't know, but he understood immediately when I told him the specialist would, of course, drop the price of his stock, pick up the stop loss orders at the lower price, and then unload them for a profit at the rally high.

My caller then asked me what I thought of buying stocks as they established new highs. This was one of the guides to action recommended by the ex–*New York Times* columnist. I replied that this has always seemed to me to be one of the surest ways to ruin. I told him that buying stocks as they break out to new highs can be a profitable way of approaching the market at an early or even the middle stage of a rally. Ultimately the stock will establish a new high, in the course of which the specialist will unload all the shares he owns and then having sold short whatever additional stock is needed to supply public demand, he will drop the price of the stock. It could well be at this point that he launches the stock on a long-term decline. This is the reason I think the advice to buy a stock as it establishes new highs can be very dangerous. I was well aware, however, that the same ingenious advice was routinely dispensed by many market professionals and that this book had been one of the most widely read books on investing for more than a decade. Its ideas are interesting, if only because they are so typical of the opinions held by most stockbrokers, analysts, and investment counselors. Curiously enough, we are warned in the foreword that the book contains the ideas of many "professional advisers" and that the wisdom of fully fifty "authorities" has been included. It occurred to me that it would be useful for the average investor to have a list of some of the more commonly held opinions on what constitutes a successful approach to investing in the market, compared with my own views. I have already discussed two favorites: the stop loss order and the concept of purchasing stocks when they make new highs. Following are a number of additional comparisons of my own principles with traditional investment concepts:

1. TRADITIONAL VIEW: At times of recession one should buy "defensive" issues, including bonds. Defensive issues are, among others, utilities, foods, tobaccos, food chain stores.

NEY VIEW: In times of recession common stocks can advance more dramatically than in more prosperous economic periods. This is because the tendency of the public is to assume that stock prices advance only to the accompaniment of good earnings announcements. Specialists capitalize on this myth by advancing stock prices when conditions are at their worst and dropping stock prices when conditions are booming. As for buying defensive stocks: the *only* stocks that should be bought are (a) those that give evidence of specialist accumulation and (b) those that serve to limit the investor's risks because of active institutional participation.

As for investing in bonds, I do not commit client's funds into them. I consider them high risk for the simple reasons that bond prices are even more manipulated by insiders than stock prices, trades are not visible on a tape, and information concerning the transactions of insiders is nonexistent. Bonds are an indispensable method of corporate financing which provides the investment banking industry with enormous sources of income. If these profits are to continue, the industry must condition investors to believe that their portfolios should at times include a large percentage of these issues. Naturally, it is in the interest of Exchange insiders to spread the propaganda that a move out of common stocks into bonds as a "defensive measure" during periods of recession is advisable, because investors then sell their common stocks to these insiders at the very time stock prices can be expected to soon advance. Their chief advantage to an investment adviser is that tradition allows him to stick half of a multimillion dollar portfolio into bonds, thereby cutting in half his work load and his exposure to criticism. He is "safe" when he loses money in bonds since, like everyone else, he acted in what is termed a "defensive" manner.

2. TRADITIONAL VIEW: There are times when it is safer to trade than invest.

NEY VIEW: If the investment environment does not appear conducive to commitment for long-term capital gains under minimum risk circumstances, then one should properly remain out of the market and in cash instruments such as commercial paper and C.D.s. Although trading on the basis of short-term rallies can occasionally be profitable, the risks, in my opinion, are too high and the rewards too small to be acceptable.

3. TRADITIONAL VIEW: Economic developments affect public opinion, which affects stock prices.

NEY VIEW: The stock market is an internal operation. Economic developments do not, therefore, *cause* stock prices to move one way or the other. They can be used to rationalize stock price movements or to exploit investor psychology. In the final analysis, however, although economic conditions do not influence the market, the market does have an enormous impact on economic conditions.

4. TRADITIONAL VIEW: The Federal Reserve controls booms and busts through control of the money supply and interest rates, which in turn affect the market.

NEY VIEW: The Federal Reserve system is an instrument of the Stock Exchange establishment. Thus, when a major rally or bull market is underway, the Fed can be expected to create conditions that cause interest rates to decline. When stock prices are ready to or begin to decline, the Fed will institute conditions that again cause interest rates to rise.

By lowering interest rates the Fed and the banks cause the public to move out of cash instruments and into stocks as stock prices move to their highs. Since the public has been conditioned to believe that lower interest rates cause an advance in stock prices, the Exchange has a ready alibi to hand to the media for rising stock prices. When interest rates are raised to higher levels as stock prices move to their lows, the public is persuaded to sell their stocks and move into cash instruments—thereby not only enabling insiders to accumulate more shares but preventing these investors from profiting from the advance in stock prices when it occurs. By the same token, the increase in interest rates also provides the Exchange with the alibi it needs to legitimatize falling stock prices.

5. TRADITIONAL VIEW: Play a trend and get out when it seems to be stopping.

NEY VIEW: A stock's price trend will *always* seem to stop at one time or another as it proceeds towards its highs. That is because specialists will attempt to shake investors out of stocks before advancing them to their highs. The only time to "get out" is on the appearance of major short selling by specialists.

6. TRADITIONAL VIEW: Cut your losses, let your profits run.

NEY VIEW: Follow this bit of market folklore and, on the one hand, you may well be cutting your loss just before a major rally, while on the other hand, by letting your profits run, you are assuming you can determine when your profits are about to become losses. The fact is, specialists will always drop prices before a major rally so that you could well be "cutting a loss" just before it turns into a gain. The time to sell, whether you have established a profit or a loss, is when, after an advance in stock prices, you have evidence of big-block specialist selling.

7. TRADITIONAL VIEW: On tape watching: Expanding volume on a rising market is bullish. Expanding volume on a falling market is bearish. Declining volume on a rising market is bearish. Declining volume on a falling market is bullish.

NEY VIEW: Expanding volume on rising stock prices is bearish, since it indicates increasing insider distribution, which tends to maximize itself as stock prices near their highs. Expanding volume on falling stock prices is bullish, since it indicates that specialists are accumulating increasing quantities of stock which they will wish to dispose of at higher price levels. Declining volume on rising prices is bullish, since it indicates specialists are managing to advance stock prices covertly without attracting public attention. This is a strategy employed by specialists when they have accumulated large inventories of stock at a low price which they wish to dispose of at much higher levels. An advance on low volume, therefore, allows them to retain the bulk of their inventory in order to dispose of it at optimum price levels. Declining volume on falling prices is bearish, since it indicates that specialists will continue to lower stock prices until their inventory accumulations necessitate a rally.

8. TRADITIONAL VIEW: Big blocks on upticks are bullish.

NEY VIEW: Big blocks on upticks are bearish, since they indicate that insiders are distributing inventory and are or soon will be selling short. On the other hand, big blocks on downticks are bullish, since they indicate insiders are accumulating stock that they will soon want to sell at higher price levels.

9. TRADITIONAL VIEW: A high short interest is bullish.

NEY VIEW: Short selling is an activity that makes declines in the market profitable to specialists, *not* investors. Most investors are persuaded by the media, however, to believe that investors are responsible for a high short interest. It is then suggested that since they must inevitably "cover" their short sales, this will cause a sharp advance. Hence investors are led to believe that a high short interest is bullish and a low short interest is bearish. The fact is, however, that specialists *only* sell short when they intend to drop stock prices. Since 85 percent of all short selling is by Stock Exchange specialists and other members, a high short interest is a sign that the market is doomed.

The Wall Street Journal of February 24, 1975, provides us with an example of the manner in which this myth is perpetuated:

BIG BOARD SHORT INTEREST RISE TO RECORD IN FEBRUARY 14TH MONTH; INCREASE ALSO SET HIGH

This was then followed with a statement to the effect that "short interest on the New York Stock Exchange rocketed to a record 25,121,419 shares in the month ending February 14." This should have surpised no one in view of the figures released by the *Journal* that day on its back page to the effect that specialist short-selling for the week ending February 14 was 5,547,050 shares. Furthermore, on Tuesday, February 18, the last page of the *Journal* had included the information that for the week ending February 7, specialist short-selling had amounted to 6,341,620 shares. The week before that (January 31) specialist short sales were reported in the *Journal* as having totaled a record 7,689,620 shares.

What is surprising is that the *Journal*'s editors saw nothing inconsistent in the statistics it had been providing on specialists' short sales and the suggestion that the record short interest was due to public short-selling. According to the *Journal*'s weekly figures, specialist short-selling accounted for 22,507,340 shares, or 90 percent of the total of 25,121,419 shares sold short for the month ending February 14. Yet the *Journal* points its finger away from the specialist and levels it at the market's poor wretch—the investor:

> Wall Street analysts said emerging short interest on the Big Board reflected some investors' skepticism that the current market rally would continue. . . .

In the course of another month, from the February high to the March high, the Dow had advanced less than 40 points; yet most investors were being made to believe they were intimately involved in the beginnings of a long-term bull market. Following is how I viewed the matter in my diary entry.

Tuesday, March 18, 1975

Dow −7.12/779.41   Dow Vol. 2,249,200   NYSE Vol. 29,180,000

The momentum of public demand underlying a rally can be maintained only when it is made to seem as though stock prices are proceeding from one exceptional marvel to another. For this reason, investors are being subjected to an exhausting succession of puff pieces whose intent is to assure them that if they have not already committed into the market, then most certainly they must have shut their eyes to the fact that it offers the investor the prospect of a bountiful paradise. Today's headline from *The Wall Street Journal* is charged with this meaning:

INDUSTRIALS STEAMROLL AHEAD TO ADD 13.06 POINTS; TRADING STAYS HEAVY

Since the end of January, the editors of the *Journal* have been shutting their eyes to the implications of daily high volume. Despite this heavy trading, between the intermediate highs of February 21 (749.77) and yesterday's high (786.53), the fact is, the Dow has advanced only 37 points! Undoubtedly the Dow will move higher. It will be interesting to observe which of the investor's particular fears the *Journal* will then seek to anesthetize.

Because it would be repetitious to treat the problems presented investors by the rally launched into high gear at the end of January 1975 in terms of a run down of each day's activities,

I will discuss it in terms of its evolutionary stages and their significance. Like a theatrical production, it has been created for the public but with this difference: Its crude effects and violence are sustained by the participation of the audience.

Since mid-March, 1975, investors have been subjected to two sharp shake-outs leading to the formation of what traditional chartists refer to as a rising head and shoulders pattern. What this meant, in the view of most of the market's technicians, was that the market was ready for a sharp decline once the neckline of the head and shoulders pattern was penetrated.

It had seemed to me at the time that this analysis of the market was too pat and too conformist, and too likely therefore to be exploited by the Exchange for all it was worth. With that in mind, it had seemed eminently logical to me that the Exchange would confound technicians and traders by conducting a sharp rally. The practical rewards of this maneuver were obvious. For one thing, such a rally in the Dow would bring in a whole new round of investor demand. This would enable specialists to conduct another splurge of short selling before dropping stock prices. The other point that had to be considered was that, had specialists dropped stock prices according to formula, from the 742 level beginning on April 8, they would undoubtedly have subjected themselves to heavy selling.

My diary entry of April 16 is concerned not only with the rally that in fact did take place as I had anticipated, but with what I now fully expected to see take place in the market over the near term.

Wednesday, April 16, 1975
Dow +0.63/815.71 Dow Vol. 2,043,900 NYSE Vol. 22,970,000
Exchange insiders are quick to exploit any change in attitude toward the market by the mass of investors. Their short-term plans are always in a state of flux. Let investors assume the market is going up, and the Exchange will take it down. Let them think it is going down, and the Exchange will take it up—which is just what it has done for the past six

trading days. Its movement of stock prices chronicles a world far removed from the perspective of Newton's apple.

Thus, from 742 on April 7, the Dow now stands at approximately 816 (some 20-odd points higher than the March high). After the preceding period of nervous uncertainty caused by the decline to 742, the present upswing in the Dow caused another round of heavy demand for stock. The rational conduct of investor thinking has now merged into a belief that stock prices will continue to advance. I can think of nothing, therefore, that would better serve the Exchange's interests than to exploit bullish sentiment further by beginning to drop stock prices sometime next week. The high volume of the past few days offers more than a hint of the specialist short selling that has been taking place. The logic of these short sales has yet to be heard from. To what extent, I wonder, will they be utilized to bombard the market?

As it happened, the April high was established the following day. Specialists feasted. The Dow advanced from 815.71 to an intraday high of 835.18 and closed at 819.46 on a near record turnover of 32.6 million shares. The major section of *The Wall Street Journal*'s "Abreast of the Market" column was devoted to the bullish forecasts of the Dreyfus Corporation's oft-quoted and now-more-than-ever bullish vice president. In his opinion, "all of the market's fears the past 2½ weeks have been allayed."

That was Thursday. A 32-million-share turnover under ordinary circumstances would have represented reversal volume. I therefore anticipated something in the nature of a plus or minus one or two points on Friday. When, instead, the Dow dropped 11 points, it was apparent that my grasp on the future of the Dow, at least over the short term, was something less than a stranglehold. Obviously, if the Exchange intended to conduct a decline, it would have to be on light volume. Equally obviously, an 11-point decline on Friday would cause investors to experience something akin to simple panic over the weekend, which the Exchange could only counteract by rallying stock prices on Monday either to unload inventory or to *prevent* heavy selling. What the Friday decline meant, therefore, was that specialists were in the process of acquiring stock by cleaning out their books in anticipation of a further advance in stock prices.

It was probable that the Dow was being set up to go higher over the short term. But why? All the profit incentives seemed to exist on the downside for specialists. They were sodden with short sales. What incentive was there, then, that could serve to immobilize, at least for the time being, these authentic barometers of change?

14

Another Burnt Offering or Ma Bell Gives the Investor a Punch on the Nose

Ney's Fifteenth Axiom: Investment banking is everything you ever wanted to get away with.

I spent a week in Palm Beach. One morning, in the course of reading *The New York Times*, I began to uncover the forces that would influence the subsequent course of action of the stock Exchange.

On Monday, April 21, as I had anticipated, the Exchange forestalled the possibility of heavy selling that would have occurred had they dropped prices after Friday's decline of 11.03 points. Instead, it opened the Dow virtually unchanged and then slowly raised prices. At the close, the Dow was up 7.43. On Tuesday and Wednesday, it was down 1.72 and 11.66. On Thursday and Friday, the Dow was up 1.17 and 8.14. Thus, the week ended with the Dow advancing approximately 3.50 points on an average volume of 22 million shares a day.

On Friday morning, April 25, I read *The New York Times*' financial page and grasped the fundamental motives underscoring the reason why stock prices had been kept up and why they would be headed higher through mid-May. The *Times*' financial columnist had done a piece on the merits of the AT&T warrants.* He began by pointing out that

> . . . in three weeks, American Telephone warrants to purchase 31.3 million Telephone shares at $52 each are due to expire and with AT&T stock at 48½, it is widely believed that the warrants will be worthless . . .
>
> To make the warrants valuable, American Telephone stock must be worth in excess of $52 a share at the expiration date, with every penny of value above $52 a penny to the good for the warrant holders. . . .

Overlooked, of course, was the fact that the specialist in Telephone had, on many occasions in the past, demonstrated his ability to raise or lower the price of his stock 8–10 points at a

*Warrants are options to buy a stated number of shares of stock at a pre-determined price during a specified period of time. This privilege, popularly considered a favor to stockholders, generally has much less value than is supposed by investors.

moment's notice. Moving it from $48 to $52 would be child's play for him.

Only one other thing would be needed to persuade investors to buy Telephone (or *any* stock) before the warrants expired, and that was the existence of a market that gave them the conviction they were witnessing the continuation of a rally in an important bull market. Rising prices and only rising prices aroused the will to buy. They objectified one's emotions, yearnings, aspirations. They insisted on action. *Hence, as we learned earlier,* "*It is not demand that creates rising prices but rising prices that create demand.*" Thus, whether it concerns the overall distribution of hundreds of millions of shares or, as in the case of the Telephone offering, 31 million shares, the Exchange is aware that such a distribution of stock could not be performed by an advance in Telephone alone, but only if specialists in Dow stocks advanced their stock prices in unison with the specialists in Telephone. Under these circumstances, the Exchange is able to construct a mosaic of ideas which causes investors to equate today's rising prices with tomorrow's rising profits.

In the meantime, of course, the oversimplified but seemingly plausible interpretations of the media had investors firmly convinced that economic conditions were improving and that a future of ever lower interest rates presaged an ever higher market. Typical was an article published on April 18 on *The Wall Street Journal's* front page suggesting that the rally was due to a perfectly normal anticipation of good times ahead.

> FOLLOWING THE SCRIPT
> GAIN IN SHARE PRICES
> IN MIDST OF RECESSION
> ADHERES TO PATTERN. . . .
>
> Business is near the pit of the worst slump since the 1930s—and the stock market is soaring. . . .
>
> As peculiar as it all may appear at first glance, the situation is eminently normal. Share prices invariably do rise sharply

> toward the end of a period of declining economic activity. And economists generally are convinced that the latest such period is about to end, or has in fact ended. . . .

However, the reader will notice that *with the onset of a major decline, interest rates will be cited as a causal factor not only for the decline in stock prices, but quite probably for worsening economic conditions.*

Logically, the life expectancy of the current rally could now be pegged at May 15—the day the warrants expired. The fact is, I hadn't given the existence of the warrants more than a passing thought in more than five years. I now recalled that they had been issued in 1970 in order to "sweeten" the sale of some debentures that AT&T's investment bankers suggested might otherwise be *difficult* to unload on the public. Under these circumstances, the use of warrants is an investment banker's technique for persuading investors to purchase an underwriting in the hope that some time in the future an advance in the stock's price might enable them to buy at $50 what was then selling for $100 a share. What is inevitable about such devices is that the investor can always be expected to leap at the chance to "get something for nothing."

Obviously, the article and its quality of assurance and inevitability was meant to serve as a puff piece created out of urgent necessity. It reflected an obscure process of reasoning, concluding that

> It is reasonable to expect the brokerage community to support American Telephone as a sound investment in a period of considerable concern about the future . . . many brokers have been impressed with the business-like quality of the current AT&T management team and the company's ability to dramatize its case before various rate making agencies. . . . Clearly, as already suggested, brokers can recommend AT&T in good conscience. . . .

As the reader has learned by now, when it comes to the investment business, "conscience" has little to do with it.

The article then went on to say that Telephone's investment bankers, Morgan Stanley, were standing by "to handle the mechanics of the exercise just in case American Telephone comes to life and bounds the $52 barrier." For a few moments, the column produced the eerie sensation that I'd read it in the same space years earlier. Then I recalled that what I had read was not an article on AT&T, but a PR piece on Penn Central in January, 1970, that helped the Butcher brokerage firm of Philadelphia unload the stock at the 30 level, long after the Stock Exchange's most important insiders had pulled out of this situation.

I called my office in Los Angeles to check out the details of the offering and learned that if Telephone ever got within shouting distance of $52, brokers would be receiving a commission of $150 on 100 shares paid by AT&T, instead of the usual $84 for buying or selling a similar amount of stock.

Monday and Tuesday of the following week (April 28 and 29), the Dow dropped 1.80 and 6.96 points. Much more significant than the almost 9 points of decline was what it portended. Having reached a high on April 17 of 106¼, Eastman Kodak had now dropped under 100 to 99⅞ and closed at 100⅛ on Monday, April 28, on 103,800 shares. On Tuesday it dropped to 97⅝ and closed at 98½ on 168,000 shares. It almost didn't matter what other Dow stocks did. This was one of the two Dow stocks (the other being Du Pont) that had been contributing most to the rally. If it was to continue to lead the market to a rally high, then it seemed logical that this specialist would want to gather in as much stock as possible (by cleaning out his book) under 100 which he would then be able to sell for a handsome profit at prices increasingly higher than 100. Since the specialist in Kodak is also the specialist in Du Pont, I looked to see if he would take advantage of the investors in Du Pont who'd placed their orders to sell on a drop under 120. Sure enough, on Tuesday, the twenty-ninth, he also dropped the price of Du Pont to 119⅜. The following day, April 30, taking their cue from the movements of these two stocks, many Dow stocks were advanced (see Appendix, April 30) 2 and 3 points. Du Pont and Kodak advanced 6⅝ and 6 points, respectively, with the average itself registering a gain of 18.30 points.

Specialists advanced Dow stocks again on Thursday and Friday, the first and second of May, the average posting gains of 9.78 and 17.52. Volume on Friday reached 25 million shares. The catalogue of similarities with other sharp advances in price was too striking to be ignored. Advancing their stocks more than a point, specialists in stocks like General Motors, Sears, Union Carbide, General Electric, and Exxon closed at their highs (or, as in the case of General Electric and Exxon, within ⅛ and ¼ of their highs). Meanwhile, Telephone had advanced to 49⅝ on Thursday and 50⅛ on Friday on increasingly high volume. That was all it took to start the gossip mills rolling. In defiance of all reason, in less than two days, it had become a commonplace of boardroom scuttlebutt that Telephone would be well above 52 by May 15. Heavy trading in the warrants made it clear that as far as investors were concerned this kind of talk was like spreading molasses in front of flies.

After Friday's advance of 17.52, it was inevitable that investors' hopes would build over Saturday and Sunday. By Monday morning, May 5, they were vulnerable to the slightest rise in stock prices—or suggestion. Few traders could have resisted their brokers' solicitation to buy stock when *The Wall Street Journal's* lead comment was quoted to them: "the economic decline is near its end." This was followed by the opening statement in "Abreast of the Market" that: "Money managers keep looking for a correction and the stock market just as persistently keeps ignoring expectations for such a pullback." In the same column, the senior vice president of the Hartford National Bank and Trust Company's Investment Department then provided investors with a list of his favorite industry groups and a recommendation that "growth oriented portfolios should have a maximum of 80 percent in stocks . . ." The vice president of Drexel Burnham, who supervises $800 million in mutual funds, then told us, "We think the rally this year has been justified and our portfolios are approaching a fully invested position . . . we see the economy turning up fairly sharply by the fourth quarter this year. . . ."

The Dow's gain of 7.12 that day only served to reinforce the investor's expectations about the future. *By now the reader is aware that once investors have been conditioned to expect one thing, the specialist soon hands them another.* Thus, Monday's first hour volume of 5.5 million shares and the daily total of 22.4 million shares left no doubt that specialists had been selling short massive quantities of stock. This was confirmed by Dow volume of 1.8 million shares. *Moreover, as the reader has learned, a movement in the price of General Motors oftentimes opens the doors of perception wider than anything else.* The fact that on the fifth this specialist advanced his stock *only* 3/8 of a point to 45¼ and closed it unchanged at 44⅞ on *high volume* (148,300 shares) suggests that once again, having added to his short position at the day's high (the fifth big block of the day in GM was for 33,200 shares at 45, followed by another block for 5,000 at 45), he was prompted to lead the way for other Dow specialists one day before the battle plan called for them to take stock prices down. Finally, since the Dow had advanced more than 45 points in three trading days, I didn't expect Dow specialists to continue to advance it until the fifteenth—another nine trading days away. A shakeout was, therefore, logical. My diary entry of Tuesday, May 6, deals with that event:

Tuesday, May 6, 1975
Dow −20.89 834.71| Dow Vol. 1,996,100 NYSE Vol. 25,410,000
Investors might not be so quick to throw up their hands in dismay at the 20-point decline if they understood that the mosaic of Dow stock volume patterns represented by a Dow volume of 2 million shares

suggests vitality rather than weakness; that the specialists in these stocks have begun and, in many instances, probably completed short covering operations (for their trading accounts only) and are now ready to advance their prices. As we have seen (in November, 1974), as the Dow moves toward an important high, it is not at all surprising to observe the market advancing sharply for three or four days and then plunging sharply for one or two, with the moves becoming shorter and the hope and the fear of investors coming closer together.

Many now fear a continuation of the decline. Specialists will count on this. Thus we can expect at least a sharp decline at the opening and possibly through the morning. However, after short covering in the A.M., I would not be surprised to see the market start up again before the close—if not tomorrow, then certainly Thursday. Today's deviation from what investors expected is a prime characteristic of specialists' merchandising strategy and can only be understood in terms of the misdirection of attention it causes which, in this case, enables specialists to accumulate stock prior to a further advance.

Today's decline of 1¼ points in General Motors to 43⅝, in line with the broad overtones of the rest of the market, should not, therefore, have caused any concern. Quite the contrary, the volume indications on the drop were eminently bullish. Telephone declined ½ point today to 50⅛ on very heavy volume (157,800 shares), suggesting that it has higher to go (this decline on heavy volume also being bullish).

On Monday, May 5, the day before the decline, the *Journal* had sounded a note of tremendous optimism in the future economic outlook. But on Wednesday, May 7, the boom forecasts of yesterday were forgotten in the slump talk of today:

> One factor that helped fuel the pullback "was George Meany's prediction that the nation's unemployment rate will increase to about 11.5%. . . ."
>
> Other depressants mentioned by analysts were uncertainty over the ability of investors to absorb the stampede of corporate borrowers into the debt market, a 26% slump in new car sales last month, and a statement (by the Chairman of U.S. Steel) that steel industry profits in the second quarter "won't be as good." Some hesitation was also attrib-

> uted to waiting for President Ford's news conference last night.

For the remainder of the week, the Dow advanced 1.72 on Wednesday, 4.06 on Thursday, and 9.63 on Friday. Friday's advance prior to the weekend was of signal importance. Its spell served to dismiss Tuesday's collapse as an aberration. On Wednesday, the Dow's bellwether stock, General Motors, advanced ⅞ to 44½ on only 80,200 shares—a bullish sign—and on Thursday to 45 on only 98,500 shares—another bullish omen. On Friday it declined ⅛ to 44⅞ on 89,000 shares. GM's specialist was now marking time. But the price action of the Dow on Friday had ended the week with a rainbow in the investor's sky.

I'd always considered La Branche, the specialist in Telephone, to be one of the market's more controversial specialists. In the past, raising or dropping his stock on large gaps, he had used his book like the tight net of a master fisherman, exhibiting an overt disdain for discretion. Now he seemed to be behaving as a man of almost clerical principles. On Wednesday, May 7, he had advanced his stock ⅜ to 50½ on 131,600 shares. Thursday he advanced it to 51⅛ on 146,100 shares, and on Friday to 51⅜ on 93,900 shares.

Then on Saturday, May 10, *The New York Times* ran still another article on the Telephone warrants. It emphasized for the investor the subsurface values inherent in Telephone. Brokers were quoted as saying that

> In an era of reduced dividends and omissions—even General Motors and Du Pont have cut dividends—AT&T is a standout for income seekers . . .

Naturally, there was no discussion of the appalling performance of the stock since 1963, despite steadily rising earnings. Instead, the *Times*' columnist seemed as naïve about Telephone as any market innocent:

> Those who counted the issue dead just weeks ago failed to reckon with a generally stronger market and, equally important, an underwriting team led by Morgan Stanley & Co. . . .

He did give us some insights, however, into why the issue was not dead:

> Morgan Stanley is to get a single-shot fee of $100,000 plus 8 cents a warrant exercised. If all are exercised through the Morgan Stanley group, Morgan Stanley would get $2.48 million through the warrants. Morgan Stanley would also receive 5 cents for each share sold by the dealer group . . . that . . . [could] mean an additional $1.55 million for Morgan Stanley. . . .

Naturally, no mention was made anywhere that the specialist in Telephone was the one man who had all the answers to Telephone—who, in fact, had many of them right there in his book. He had it in his power not only to create but to anticipate every whim of the public. What happened would merely be a question of how best he could maximize his profits. Perhaps he would relate his operations to the Morgan Stanley play, perhaps he wouldn't. My bet was he would. Avoiding cross purposes always increased everyone's profits. Although it was supposedly against the rules for specialists to show their books to the investment bankers involved in underwritings in stocks in which they were registered, the SEC Staff Report on the conduct of members of the American Stock Exchange revealed that investment bankers were able to get a good peek at the specialist's book when they wanted to size up the problems they faced in the launching of an offering. One official of the AMEX testified that "the proper procedure" on both the American and New York Stock exchanges concerning offerings

> is for the underwriter to obtain the necessary information from an Exchange official . . . However, it appears that the Exchange government has failed to provide a clear written

statement as to what its officials recognize as proper procedure and that in practice there have been significant departures from such approved procedures.

Wickliffe Shreve, senior partner of Hayden, Stone & Co., has testified that it was his practice, with regard to secondaries on both the American and New York Stock Exchanges to inquire of the specialist directly, a day or more prior to the date of the offering, as to the aggregate bids on the book between the market price and the estimated offering price.

It was likely, therefore that, in view of the existing profit potentials for everyone involved, not only would the specialist in Telephone see to it that the price of Telephone advanced to the 52 level, but he would also see that it stayed in that vicinity. If Telephone moved much higher than 52, holders of the warrants would have no incentive to deal with Morgan Stanley. Instead they would simply make direct conversions. Another reason was that holders of the warrants could sell the stock short if it rose to a higher price and then make an immediate profit by covering their short sale by exercising the warrants at $52 a share.

Although the specialist was not about to allow holders of the warrants to profit from selling short above the 52 level, he certainly exercised his prerogatives to sell short for himself. In

300	51	7/8	12.40
5000	52		12.43
100	52		12.43
5000	51	7/8	12.43
3000	52		12.46
2500	52		12.46
5000	52		12.46
100	51	7/8	12.46
500	52		12.47
100	51	7/8	12.49
1000	51	7/8	12.50
500	51	7/8	12.50
1000	51	7/8	12.54
200	52		12.54
1000	51	7/8	12.55
100	51	7/8	12.55
400	51	7/8	12.57

CHART 14–1

SOURCE: Stock Sales on the New York Stock Exchange, published by Francis Emory Fitch, Inc.

the following excerpt from the Fitch Sheets of May 13, the reader will note the manner in which the specialist in Telephone executed at 52 what were undoubtedly short sales for accounts in which he was directly or indirectly interested.

On Tuesday, May 13, another major article on the AT&T warrants on the first page of *The New York Times*' financial section helped Morgan Stanley and the specialist in Telephone to profit in their operations. The article indicated that "a number of stockholders have moved to exercise their warrants to buy the stock at $52 a share even though the price hovers a fraction below the critical level." This, it was pointed out, "can prove advantageous since the stockholder does not pay a brokerage commission upon exercising the warrants."

When trading halted at 4:00 P.M. Tuesday afternoon, 729,000 shares of Telephone had traded. The specialist in Telephone and the Morgan Stanley outfit had good reason to be confident of themselves. The fact that they had merchandised almost $38 million of stock was proof they could sell anything.

During the last hour of trading, the Dow reached an intraday high of 857.87. It then dropped. Investors, however, were cheered by the close at 850.13, up 2.66 for the day. The advance in GM to 46⅛, a gain of 1¼ points on 160,400 shares, was a bearish indication signaling the fact that this stock had begun an important move that would probably culminate at least one to two points higher—and that this high would probably be established on the fifteenth, the day the Telephone offering would be completed. This would be totally according to formula for the specialist in GM.

Most investors were unaware of the price-pegging operations that were launched on the thirteenth by Morgan Stanley at 51⅞. Pegging the price of Telephone at 51⅞ would enable Wall Street insiders to pull off what, in the final analysis, might be considered a legalized shell game.* Because Telephone was

*The following is the dissent of Judge Healy, a former SEC Commissioner from an SEC rule "permitting . . . the pegging, fixing or stabilizing of security prices on stock exchanges . . ." (SEC release No. 2446, 1940). His opinion was that ". . . pegging,

going across the tape at 51⅞, most investors assumed that it had been demand for the stock that had pushed the price to that level. It is highly probable that many investors who bought the stock would not have done so had they known the price had been "pegged" at that level.

On Wednesday, May 14, in a continuing effort to accelerate interest in the AT&T offering, *The New York Times* carried still another article on Telephone with a picture on its front page showing a senior partner of Morgan Stanley and his associates hard at work on the offering at "a special distribution center . . . set up to handle traffic in AT&T warrants and new common shares." What, in fact, the *Times* had provided was a picture of how a group of men, with the help of mass communication and advanced technology, were seeking to organize investor attitudes.

When asked the number of shares it had sold on Tuesday, Morgan Stanley refused to disclose this information. What it did disclose, however, was of far more importance. For the first time, investors learned that the price of Telephone had been pegged at 51⅞:

> . . . the investment banking firm did confirm that it had entered a stabilizing bid at 51⅞ for the purchase of Telephone stock in conjunction with its lay off, that is, Morgan Stanley indicated it stood ready to buy at that price any Telephone stock offered. "It would take a battleship to budge that bid," one Wall Streeter noted.

"Stabilizing," as the reader now knows, is a euphemism for price fixing. The last paragraph of the May 14 article indicated that the movement of the price of Telephone had produced an effect of jingling coins in the Morgan Stanley boardroom:

---

fixing or stabilizing the price of a security . . . permits an interference with the free forces of supply and demand and thereby tolerates the creation of a price mirage and the distortion of the price which would be set by the market if it were to function without artificial support."

> At 12:45 P.M., Telephone common, after holding up at 51⅞, moved up to 52. "Hey, hey," murmured a Morgan Stanley partner in approval.

What, in fact, it signified was that the specialist in Telephone had just sold short at the stock's high.

The bullish press releases on May 14 concerning Telephone and the market in general were abetted by the price action of Dow stocks like Du Pont and Eastman Kodak, both of which established their highs that day (133⅜ and 120). There were also big gains in General Electric, Sears, Procter & Gamble, Bethlehem Steel, U.S. Steel, and Union Carbide.

Wednesday, the fourteenth, was also a big day in Telephone. 1,503,100 shares went across the tape, all of them at 51⅞. General Motors advanced from the previous day's close of 46⅛ to 47⅝ on 206,700 shares. This was a bearish signal. The Dow closed at 858.73, a gain of 8.60 for the day. It reaffirmed the investor's confidence in the future of the market. As my diary entry for Thursday the fifteenth suggests, this euphoria was short-lived.

Thursday, May 15, 1975
Dow −9.93 848.80/ Dow. Vol. 2,514,500 NYSE Vol. 27,690,000
It was announced on the tape during the morning trading hours that the Telephone warrants would expire at noon. By then, the Dow had reached an intraday high of 868.51. First hour volume was on the upside with 7,360,000 shares traded. After the announcement on the tape, the Dow began to decline. By noon, it posted a gain of less than one point. Morgan Stanley was then officially able to collect its base fee of $100,000 from AT&T (this was in addition to being guaranteed against any losses they might suffer). They also were paid 8¢ for each warrant exercised, and 5¢ for each share of common stock sold by the dealer group. As was later reported, approximately 3.1 million warrants were converted into $52 a share common stock, which, if my arithmetic is right, would have meant an additional $403,000. Morgan Stanley's visible profits, therefore, totaled a fast half million. If Morgan Stanley fared well, however, the public was not as fortunate. For the rest of the afternoon—till 3:00 P.M.—the Dow was off less than a point. By the

close, however, the window dressing had been removed and the Dow had dropped more than 9 points. By this means, the Exchange had contained public selling until the final hour.

Not surprisingly, the processes surrounding today's events place additional restrictions on the future course of the market. For example, after reading the piece in *The New York Times* on April 25, which reminded me of the expiration of the Telephone warrants, I predicted that the market would remain in a rallying phase until the warrants expired on the fifteenth. I also thought at the time we might be witnessing the high point in the market on the fifteenth. Now, however, I see that because of today's price action, downside volume in many stocks is such that specialists must ultimately move prices higher in order to unload the heavy inventories they will be accumulating as they begin to clear out the territory under present price levels. For example, having reached an intraday high of 48⅛, General Motors declined today on heavy volume (139,300). In all likelihood, this specialist will advance his price higher than 48⅛ to liquidate the stock he acquired at the 48 level. He will almost certainly have to since many investors tend to buy stocks like GM only on breakouts *above* previously established highs.

Telephone opened on May 16 at 10:47 A.M. at 50½ on 22,500 shares. Curiously, the amount of the decline exactly eliminated the amount of the discount given dealers who participated in the underwriting. For obvious reasons, severe criticism was leveled at the manner in which the distribution had been handled. Many investors threatened lawsuits. According to the manager of a Harris Upham branch office, Harris Upham reduced the cost of the Telephone purchased by its customers to $50.75. This was obviously done in order to maintain good customer relations and, quite possibly, to prevent a repeat of the unpleasantness experienced by the firm in the Bertha Hecht case.* At that time, new precedents were established for the investment industry, the courts having decided *against* Harris Upham on behalf of one of its customers.

I received a number of phone calls on the sixteenth complaining about the price pegging in Telephone. One was from a broker in

*See The Wall Street Gang, Chapter 12.

Mississippi who threatened to sue the Stock Exchange, the investment bankers, and the specialist.

Another broker with whom I do business called. He referred to "the Telephone affair" as "the greatest ripoff in Stock Exchange history. . . . It was a real sucker game if you analyze what happened here." He also pointed out that those who subscribed to the stock on the "lay off" were not allowed to sell it until the 29th of May. I pointed out to him I thought it absurd for anyone to buy the stock with this limitation since, undoubtedly, it would be down considerably in price by May 29. Obviously, if the price was not allowed to drop below 51⅞ and didn't budge above 51⅞—if, in other words, the existing specialist incentives prohibited him from raising the price above the floor that supported it—once that floor was removed, the price had to drop.

If I received numerous complaints about Telephone, I was sure that the SEC was deluged. Apparently it had anticipated this for on the sixteenth, it was announced in *The New York Times:*

SEC STARTS AN ENQUIRY
AS PHONE OFFERING ENDS

Then, in an attempt to misdirect public attention from the area that warranted the sharpest critical focus, investors were told:

> The Securities and Exchange Commission launched a broad investigation yesterday into foreign dealings in American Telephone & Telegraph Company shares almost simultaneously with the close of the biggest stock offering in Wall Street history . . .

The final paragraph gave the nature of and reasons for the SEC's investigations:

> The SEC, meanwhile, began looking at reports that foreign dealers had bought large chunks of AT&T stock directly from Morgan Stanley and then sold the stock back to Morgan Stanley at a higher price.

In other words, the SEC wasn't really concerned with what happened to the public in the course of this offering but merely that Morgan Stanley may have suffered a shakedown from some of its foreign associates.

It was not until the nineteenth that the *Journal* acknowledged the fact that circumstances surrounding the offering hadn't been entirely kosher:

> AT&T FINANCING RAISES $161.2 MILLION;
> POSSIBLE TRADING IRREGULARITIES STUDIED
>
> . . . the possibility that the price of AT&T common might have been artificially inflated prior to the warrants' expiration is being investigated by the Securities and Exchange Commission, sources at the government agency disclosed. Although no hard evidence has been unearthed, the commission staff in Washington and the New York regional office are beginning to reconstruct the heavy trading in AT&T common and warrants over the past three or four weeks.

Again it seemed that the SEC was only interested in protecting Morgan Stanley—not the public:

> . . . the SEC is investigating reports that some dealers who earlier took stock from Morgan Stanley at $50.50 turned around and resold it to the firm for $51.875 instead of reselling it to the public. . . . There isn't any indication that Morgan Stanley knowingly participated in any wrongdoing. . . .

One can always observe the manner in which the SEC acknowledges the status of the specialist by the way it keeps his name out of the news. In all likelihood, what had, in fact, taken place was a product of specialist manipulation for the maximization of profits. Specialists know that if demand for stock is to be adequate to serve their purposes, price must first be raised. In this way an environment can be created in which the continuing influx of demand for stock makes it possible for them to distribute and sell short. In this case, the rise in the price of Dow stocks was also intended to support the efforts of the specialist in Telephone.

Observing the manipulations performed by Dow specialists preceding and during the Telephone offering provides us with a perfect illustration of the independent yet interdependent nature of specialist units. In helping their fellow specialists it is customary for them to also help themselves. Thus, as the specialists in Eastman Kodak, Du Pont, and General Motors raised their stocks' prices in order to assist in launching the "lay off" in Telephone, their juggling act can be seen to have been a source of major profit to themselves as well as the specialists in Telephone.

The investor's status in the investment industry is at the bottom of the pecking order. As the consumer, he is meant to be consumed. As such, he can expect help from no one, least of all government or the SEC. The Telephone offering is a case in point. No one in government sought to prevent the charade, nor did anyone in the media warn the investor against it. Indeed, the press labored mightily to reinforce the Exchange's control over investors by writing articles which served as PR releases. Obviously the individual must learn to fend for himself. Major market events such as the Telephone offering provide investors with exceptional opportunities for adding to their skills. An analysis of the circumstances surrounding the Telephone warrants offers the reader a number of important object lessons:

1. Investors should look upon favorable news articles concerning such offerings as danger signals.
2. Investors should be aware that when offerings occur after a rise in price, or in the course of a major rally, that insiders are anxious to unload before a decline.
3. Additional warning signals for investors are the incentive bonus paid to stockbrokers along with the special carrot that allows investors to buy the stock "net, no commission."
4. It is always important to watch the price action in General Mortors. In the present instance, GM provided the in-

> vestor with another opportunity to observe the fact that an advance in the price of this stock on heavy volume is bearish—for the market as a whole.

If one is an investor, he will, of course, want to stay as far away as possible from such ventures as the Telephone offering. His objective being to preserve his capital, he will ignore the propaganda that impairs clear thinking and wait for the opportunities that are certain to come when he can commit his capital at low risk.

Assuming, however, that he is a trader and that he is fully versed in the objectives underlying the specialist's practices, once he is made aware of an event like the offering in Telephone, he will seek to profit from his knowledge of how such ventures are manipulated. In the present instance, being certain that human nature as it exists on the floor of the Exchange will always behave according to irresistible laws, the trader would have committed himself on April 29 to the stocks that had been principally responsible for the sharp rise in the Dow when they dropped under their critical levels on high volume (Du Pont under 120, and Kodak under 100). The probability would exist that he could make good gains were he then to sell out his holdings in these stocks at the opening on May 15 and reverse his position by going short in the same stocks. (On April 29, Eastman Kodak closed at 98½ and opened at 109¼ on May 15. Du Pont closed at 119⅞ on April 29 and opened at 133 on May 15.)

One can trade on the knowledge that the Exchange operates according to the principle "the best way to control history is to shape it yourself." This, it goes without saying, should also be the motto of all investors and traders.

15

When to Buy and Sell (With and Without the Use of Charts) or The Buyer Needs a Hundred Eyes, the Seller Only One

Ney's Sixteenth Axiom: The market is always there for those with cash.

By now the reader is surely aware that most investors are ruined in the market because of their failure to recognize the causes of the market's trends are due to a succession of concrete and particular events, all of which are linked to one another through the specialist as today is linked to yesterday and tomorrow. Isolated, the various activities of the specialist may make no sense whatever. Yet systematic knowledge of the market's historical trends reveals that while the specialist will be profoundly influenced by what happens in the present, what happens in the present or over the short term will also be profoundly affected by and runs parallel, so to speak, with his longer-term inventory objectives. In other words, if he establishes a downtrend from a high today, he will begin to precipitate public selling tomorrow. The inventory he acquires in the course of this first decline from a high then becomes a permanent element of the rallies which must follow and which he conducts in order to unload his inventory. *One can make the following generalization about these rallies: that the insider selling and short selling occurring at the rally highs have a specific relationship to the forthcoming declines from the rally highs.*

Insider selling and short selling are not, however, the only determinants of the extent of a decline. *The relationship between public selling and its impact on specialist inventories also determines the extent of a decline from a rally high* and the plan of action that will be taken by specialists to unload this inventory.

Thus, in order to estimate the existing potentials for a decline, one must estimate the amount of public selling that may have occurred at a high and in the course of the subsequent decline from that high. To do this, one must consider the price at which the high occurred and the volume figures in the course of the decline. If the rally high occurred at a critical number like 40, 60, or 80 (or slightly above), there will have been heavy public selling. High volume on a decline also indicates public selling—and public selling in the course of a decline is bullish, since it indicates heavy specialist buying—i.e., accumulations of inventory.

Insider and public selling at the high and subsequent public selling, then, are the salient events the investor should single out when he considers the selling that took place as Dow stocks declined from approximately 870 on May 15 to 810 by the end of May. As is often the case when the Dow moves down from a high, investors were told "the market is consolidating its recent gains." In my opinion, however, the decline took place in response to the pressures and profit potentials of massive specialist short selling at the May 15 high. Because of the selling and short selling that was *also* conducted by the public during the week of May 12 and in the course of the decline from the May 15 high, specialists were subjected to the pressures of inventory accumulation. This made it highly probable that the extent of the decline would be limited in order to limit the further influx of major public selling at that time.

Further, while it is probable that many specialists had already laid away massive inventories of short sales by May 15, it is also quite possible that many specialists had a number of stocks in which they had not yet established an adequate inventory of short sales in order to enable them to profitably lower stock prices. Just as specialists will raise and then drop the stock prices of one industry group after another so that public demand for stock can be most effectively directed toward solving the specialist's (and his institutional clients') distribution problems, so too will specialists tend to select among themselves the stocks they will rotate for short-selling purposes. Thus the short sales of one group of stocks will be consummated at one high, another group at another high, and so on.

In the following Dow chart, the reader can see for himself what took place—i.e., three rallies subsequent to the decline from the May 15 high were required for specialists to dispose of inventory and establish their short sales.

The excerpt from my diary entry of July 15 is concerned with the balancing processes that come into full play as the specialist, having advanced to one high and then declining, adapts to the

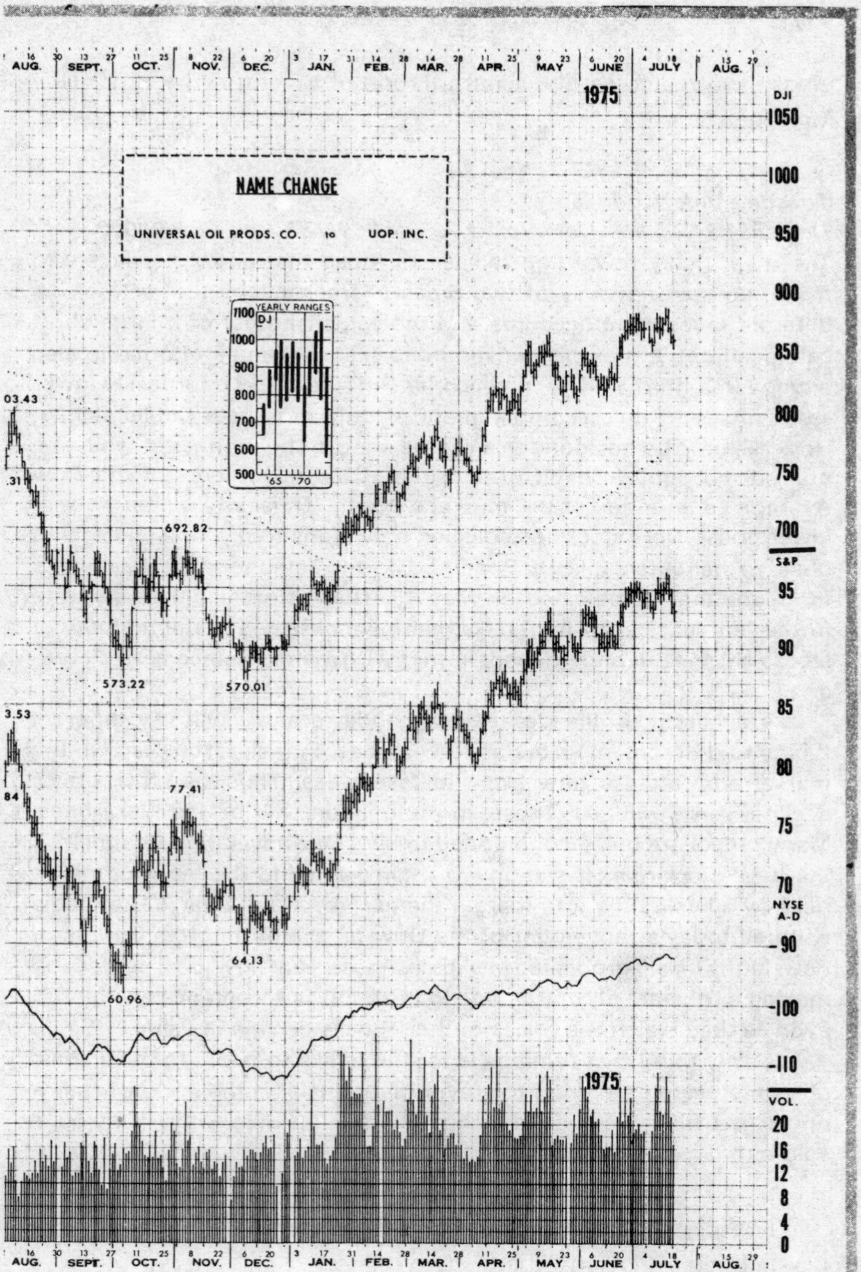
NAME CHANGE
UNIVERSAL OIL PRODS. CO. to UOP. INC.
YEARLY RANGES
DJ
1975
DJI
S&P
NYSE A-D
VOL.
692.82
573.22
570.01
77.41
60.96
64.13
AUG. SEPT. OCT. NOV. DEC. JAN. FEB. MAR. APR. MAY JUNE JULY AUG.

CHART 15–1
SOURCE: Trendline's Daily Basis Stock Charts

pressures created by the accumulation of inventory by establishing a new high.

Tuesday, July 15, 1975
Dow 881.81/+5.95 Dow Vol. 1,793,800 NYSE Vol. 28,340,000
The most richly rewarding rallies are those that allow specialists to make the best not only of two types of transactions (the sale of his different investment accounts and the establishment of a large short sale position), but by his consummate skill in the use of price to also engage in a third activity in which he can freely and effortlessly lower stock prices to the accompaniment of only moderate public selling. How skillfully he has done this can be seen in the manner in which he utilized the public's habit of consulting the movements of the Dow Average as an index of the market's health. Thus, while a number of lower priced Dow stocks established new highs today, it is possible to observe that others (like Du Pont, Kodak, and Telephone) declined from the highs they established on May 15. These circumstances serve to further emphasize the high risks that have obtained in the majority of stocks since April and, indeed, in many Dow stocks since early February.

Like all declines, the decline from today's highs will say different things to different investors as to what has, in fact, taken place in the market and what is now likely to take place. Thus, as stock prices decline, some will sell. These, in my opinion, will be the lucky ones. Many others are being conditioned to buy. One adviser on Channel 22, the local stock-market station, was compounding the investor's high risks by advising them to margin themselves "to the hilt." The media will hail today's movement of the Dow as establishing an important new high. In all probability its bullishness can now be counted on making a substantial contribution to the public's acceptance of high risk even as they watch the prices of their stocks decline in value.

The only thing that remains is for the banks to begin to once again raise interest rates in order to provide a rationale for the decline in stock prices that will have been launched. By then insiders will already have sold out.

The following letter sent to clients on the same day was in the perspective set by my diary entry:

RICHARD NEY & ASSOCIATES
INCORPORATED
INVESTMENT COUNSELLORS
Box H
Beverly Hills, California 90213

Dow: 881.81 July 15, 1975

To All Clients: Investment Policy: CASH

Although the price of the Dow Index has advanced slightly higher than the 860 level established in April, we have been witnessing a steady intensification in the hold of hope on the investor's imagination as major liquidations of stock are carried out at each rally high. In short, what continues to force today's investors to follow yesterday's investors into the market is the drama provided by lower priced Dow stocks as they have advanced to compensate for the declines or absence of further upside movement in higher priced Dow stocks since April.

These changes in the format of Dow stock prices correspond, of course, to stages of market history—the preparations launched in April to turn the market around slowly prior to sharply dropping stock prices. That stock prices can be expected to tumble very sharply, there is not the slightest doubt in my mind. The manner in which stocks have been distributed possesses all the characteristics that insist on such a decline. Such declines, when they occur, can run their full course in a matter of two months or less. Certainly no more dangerous situation could face the investor in today's market. Under existing conditions, his capital is at high risk.*

Actually, what happened was that after the first heavy wave of specialist short selling in January–February, the advance of a

*Stock prices began to decline the following day, July 16.

great many Dow stocks was halted. Small wonder that these stocks either declined or moved sideways until April (or, in some instances, much later), when stocks like Kodak and Du Pont began to move sideways and down. At that time many of the stocks that had been stopped by short selling in January–February took up the slack by advancing, thereby causing the Dow to register a new high in July. By examining the following charts of the thirty Dow stocks, the investor can see not only this rotation of price movement, but also what happened to the prices of those stocks when they were hit by specialist short selling beginning in late January through mid-February, and at the highs of each month thereafter.

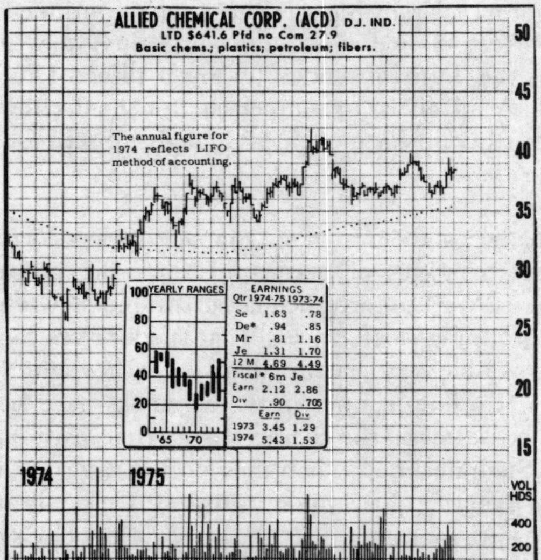
ALLIED CHEMICAL CORP. (ACD) D.J. IND.
LTD $641.6 Pfd no Com 27.9
Basic chems.; plastics; petroleum; fibers.
The annual figure for 1974 reflects LIFO method of accounting.
YEARLY RANGES
EARNINGS
Qtr 1974-75 1973-74
Se 1.63 .78
De* .94 .85
Mr .81 1.16
Je 1.31 1.70
12 M 4.69 4.49
Fiscal * 6m Je
Earn 2.12 2.86
Div .90 .705
Earn Div
1973 3.45 1.29
1974 5.43 1.53
'65 '70
1974
1975
VOL HDS.
DEC. JAN. FEB. MAR. APR. MAY JUNE JULY

CHART 15–2

The specialist in Allied Chemical launched major distributions beginning in early February. He subsequently established short sales at the May high and then began to lower stock prices by employing a series of declines and rallies.

SOURCE: Trendline's Daily Basis Stock Charts

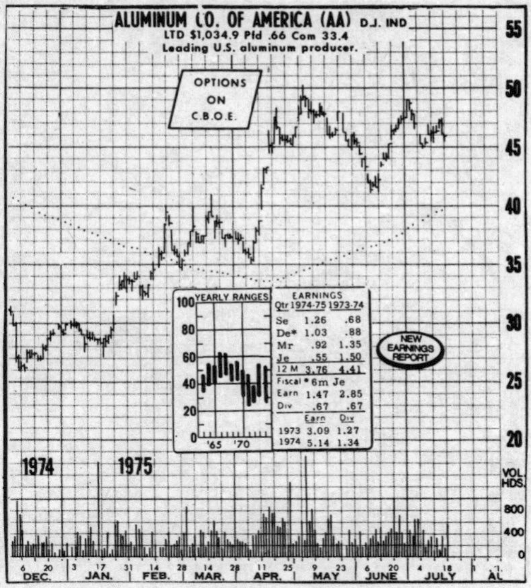

ALUMINUM CO. OF AMERICA (AA) D.J. IND
LTD $1,034.9 Pfd .66 Com 33.4
Leading U.S. aluminum producer.
OPTIONS ON C.B.O.E.
YEARLY RANGES
EARNINGS
Qtr 1974-75 1973-74
Se 1.26 .68
De* 1.03 .88
Mr .92 1.35
Je .55 1.50
12 M 3.76 4.41
Fiscal * 6m Je
Earn 1.47 2.85
Div .67 .67
Earn Div
1973 3.09 1.27
1974 5.14 1.34
NEW EARNINGS REPORT
1974
1975
VOL. HDS.
DEC. JAN. FEB. MAR. APR. MAY JUNE JULY

CHART 15–3

Having attracted investor attention with a sharp 10-point advance in early April, this specialist then began to distribute stock at the 45 to 50 level. Having established his short position in May at the 50 level, he initiated a preliminary decline down to the 41 level in order to clean out the stock on his books. Once he has unloaded this inventory, he will then be ready to lower the price of Alcoa on light volume.

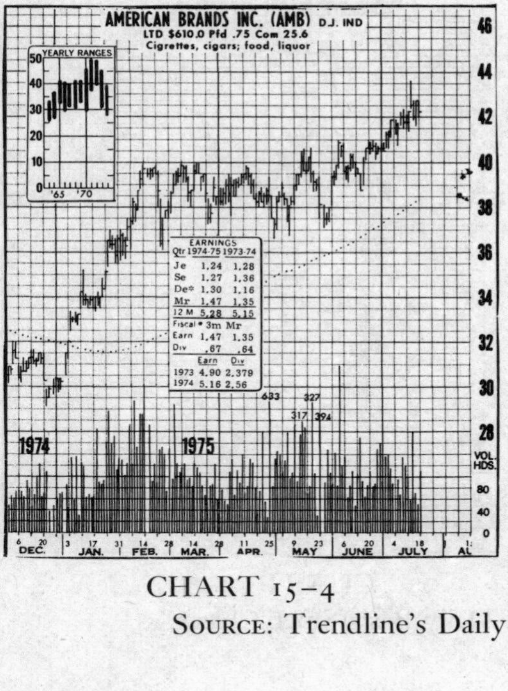

AMERICAN BRANDS INC. (AMB) D.J. IND
LTD $610.0 Pfd .75 Com 25.6
Cigrettes, cigars; food, liquor
YEARLY RANGES
EARNINGS
Qtr 1974-75 1973-74
Je 1.24 1.28
Se 1.27 1.36
De* 1.30 1.16
Mr 1.47 1.35
12 M 5.28 5.15
Fiscal * 3m Mr
Earn 1.47 1.35
Div .67 .64
Earn Div
1973 4.90 2.379
1974 5.16 2.56
1974
1975
VOL. HDS.
DEC. JAN. FEB. MAR. APR. MAY JUNE JULY

CHART 15–4

Because of specialist selling at the July 15 high, it is probable that investors who bought American Brands at the end of January and early February when the media suddenly proclaimed the existence of a new bull market) may find some difficulty in establishing long-term capital gains.

SOURCE: Trendline's Daily Basis Stock Charts

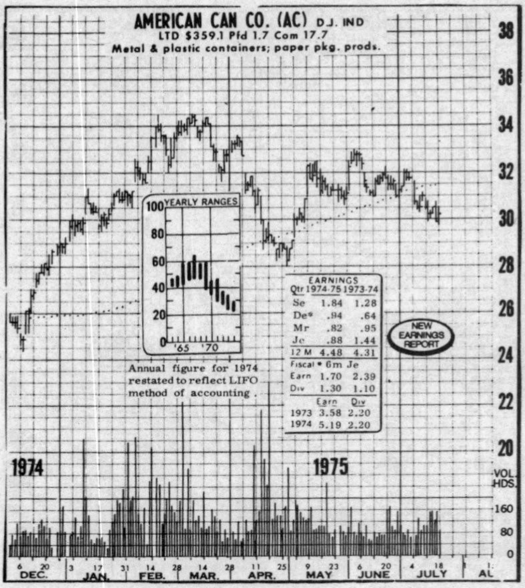
AMERICAN CAN CO. (AC) D.J. IND
LTD $359.1 Pfd 1.7 Com 17.7
Metal & plastic containers; paper pkg. prods.
YEARLY RANGES
Annual figure for 1974 restated to reflect LIFO method of accounting.
EARNINGS
Qtr 1974-75 1973-74
Se 1.84 1.28
De* .94 .64
Mr .82 .95
Je .88 1.44
12 M 4.48 4.31
Fiscal * 6m Je
Earn 1.70 2.39
Div 1.30 1.10
Earn Div
1973 3.58 2.20
1974 5.19 2.20
NEW EARNINGS REPORT
1974
1975
VOL. HDS.
DEC. JAN. FEB. MAR. APR. MAY JUNE JULY

Those who invested in American Can in late January and early February will also find it difficult to establish capital gains in July and August.

CHART 15–5

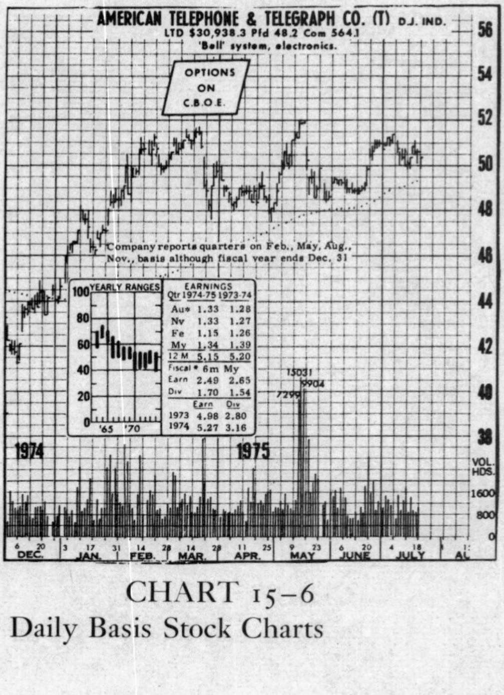
AMERICAN TELEPHONE & TELEGRAPH CO. (T) D.J. IND.
LTD $30,938.3 Pfd 48.2 Com 564.1
'Bell' system, electronics.
OPTIONS ON C.B.O.E.
Company reports quarters on Feb., May, Aug., Nov., basis although fiscal year ends Dec. 31
YEARLY RANGES
EARNINGS
Qtr 1974-75 1973-74
Au* 1.33 1.28
Nv 1.33 1.27
Fe 1.15 1.26
My 1.34 1.39
12 M 5.15 5.20
Fiscal * 6m My
Earn 2.49 2.65
Div 1.70 1.54
Earn Div
1973 4.98 2.80
1974 5.27 3.16
15031
9904
7299
1974
1975
VOL. HDS.
DEC. JAN. FEB. MAR. APR. MAY JUNE JULY

Note the manner in which this specialist avoids the accumulation of a major inventory by dropping price on important gaps from a rally high.

CHART 15–6

SOURCE: Trendline's Daily Basis Stock Charts

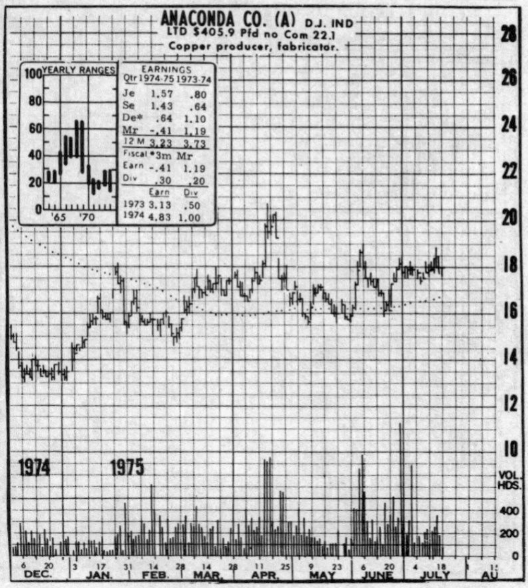
ANACONDA CO. (A) D.J. IND
LTD $405.9 Pfd no Com 22.1
Copper producer, fabricator.
YEARLY RANGES
EARNINGS
Qtr 1974-75 1973-74
Je 1.57 .80
Se 1.43 .64
De* .64 1.10
Mr -.41 1.19
12 M 3.23 3.73
Fiscal * 3m Mr
Earn -.41 1.19
Div .30 .20
Earn Div
1973 3.13 .50
1974 4.83 1.00
'65 '70
1974
1975
VOL. HDS.
DEC. JAN. FEB. MAR. APR. MAY JUNE JULY

CHART 15–7

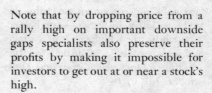

Note that by dropping price from a rally high on important downside gaps specialists also preserve their profits by making it impossible for investors to get out at or near a stock's high.

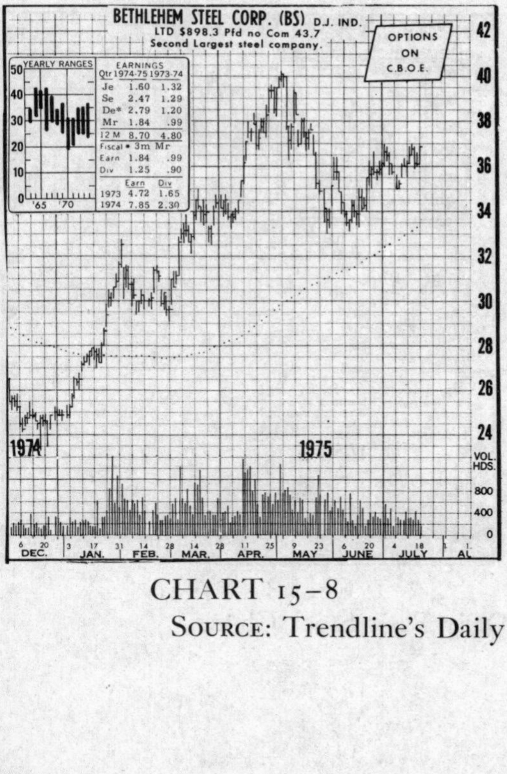
BETHLEHEM STEEL CORP. (BS) D.J. IND.
LTD $898.3 Pfd no Com 43.7
Second Largest steel company.
OPTIONS ON C.B.O.E.
YEARLY RANGES
EARNINGS
Qtr 1974-75 1973-74
Je 1.60 1.32
Se 2.47 1.29
De* 2.79 1.20
Mr 1.84 .99
12 M 8.70 4.80
Fiscal * 3m Mr
Earn 1.84 .99
Div 1.25 .90
Earn Div
1973 4.72 1.65
1974 7.85 2.30
'65 '70
1974
1975
VOL. HDS.
DEC. JAN. FEB. MAR. APR. MAY JUNE JULY

CHART 15–8

Those who bought Bethlehem Steel in February and March and are holding it through July and August in the hope of a sizable long-term capital gain may end up just barely covering their commission costs.

SOURCE: Trendline's Daily Basis Stock Charts

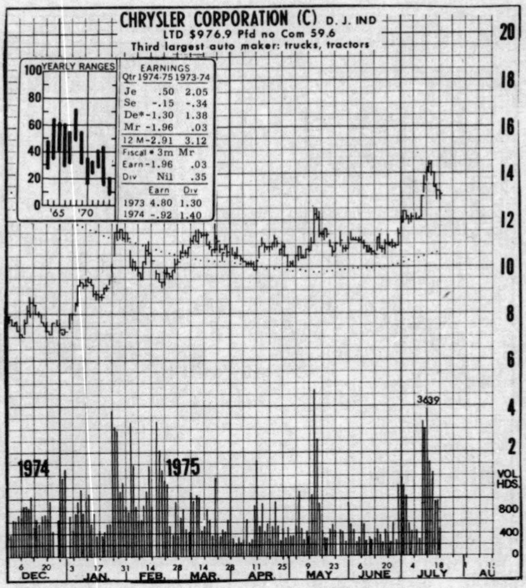
CHRYSLER CORPORATION (C) D. J. IND
LTD $976.9 Pfd no Com 59.6
Third largest auto maker: trucks, tractors
YEARLY RANGES
EARNINGS
Qtr 1974-75 1973-74
Je .50 2.05
Se -.15 -.34
De* -1.30 1.38
Mr -1.96 .03
12 M -2.91 3.12
Fiscal • 3m Mr
Earn -1.96 .03
Div Nil .35
Earn Div
1973 4.80 1.30
1974 -.92 1.40
1974
1975
3639
VOL HDS.
DEC. JAN. FEB. MAR. APR. MAY JUNE JULY AU

Interestingly enough, the timing of the advance in the price of Chrysler not only enabled this specialist to unload at the 14 level just before a bad earnings announcement gave him the alibi to lower his price—but helped contribute to a higher Dow average by compensating, a little, for the decline taking place in other Dow stocks.

CHART 15–9

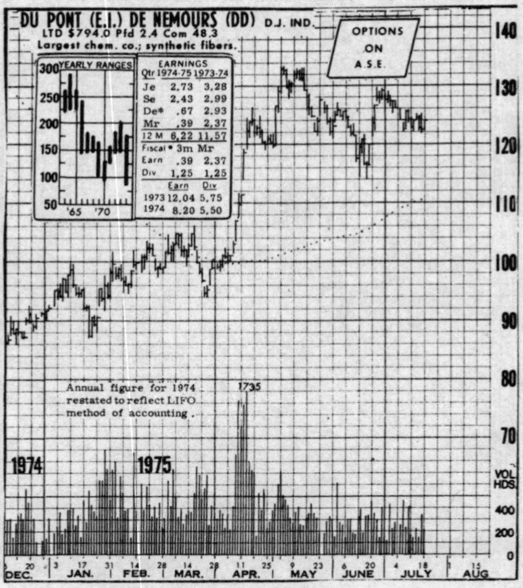
DU PONT (E.I.) DE NEMOURS (DD) D.J. IND.
LTD $794.0 Pfd 2.4 Com 48.3
Largest chem. co.; synthetic fibers.
OPTIONS ON A.S.E.
YEARLY RANGES
EARNINGS
Qtr 1974-75 1973-74
Je 2.73 3.28
Se 2.43 2.99
De* .67 2.93
Mr .39 2.37
12 M 6.22 11.57
Fiscal • 3m Mr
Earn .39 2.37
Div 1.25 1.25
Earn Div
1973 12.04 5.75
1974 8.20 5.50
Annual figure for 1974 restated to reflect LIFO method of accounting.
1735
1974
1975
VOL HDS.
DEC. JAN. FEB. MAR. APR. MAY JUNE JULY AUG.

The volume figures in Du Pont show us how the specialist immediately maximized investor demand for his stock with a 20-point advance in April. He was then able to distribute stock and establish short sales in his trading and investment accounts at the 120–133 price levels. The rise in this stock also helped in the distribution of other stocks, since the gain in Du Pont added dramatically to the gain in the DJIA, the principal focus of investor attention.

CHART 15–10

SOURCE: Trendline's Daily Basis Stock Charts

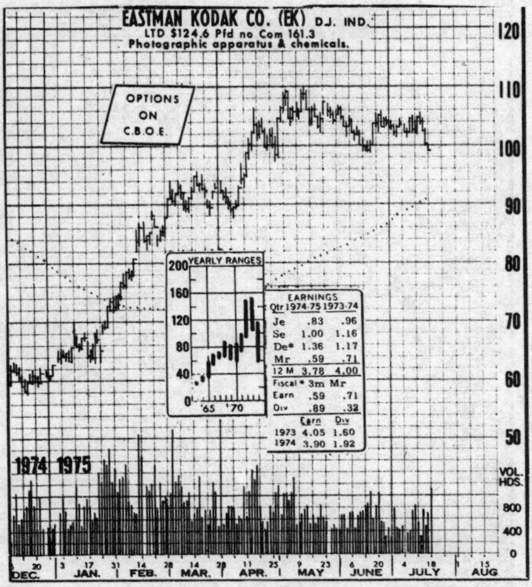

EASTMAN KODAK CO. (EK) D.J. IND.
LTD $124.6 Pfd no Com 161.3
Photographic apparatus & chemicals.
OPTIONS ON C.B.O.E.
YEARLY RANGES
EARNINGS
Qtr 1974-75 1973-74
Je .83 .96
Se 1.00 1.16
De* 1.36 1.17
Mr .59 .71
12 M 3.78 4.00
Fiscal * 3m Mr
Earn .59 .71
Div .89 .32
Earn Div
1973 4.05 1.60
1974 3.90 1.92
1974 1975
VOL. HDS.
DEC. JAN. FEB. MAR. APR. MAY JUNE JULY AUG.

CHART 15–11

Since the specialist in Du Pont is also the specialist in Eastman Kodak, it is not surprising that the price movements and chart patterns of Kodak are quite similar to the price movements and chart patterns of Du Pont. Note how the chart shows us that in all probability the specialist saw more public selling than buying above the critical 110 level in early May. Except for just testing the 110 level on an intraday high, therefore, this specialist by remaining under 110 avoided the necessity of accumulating inventory at a time when he was attempting to maximize short sales.

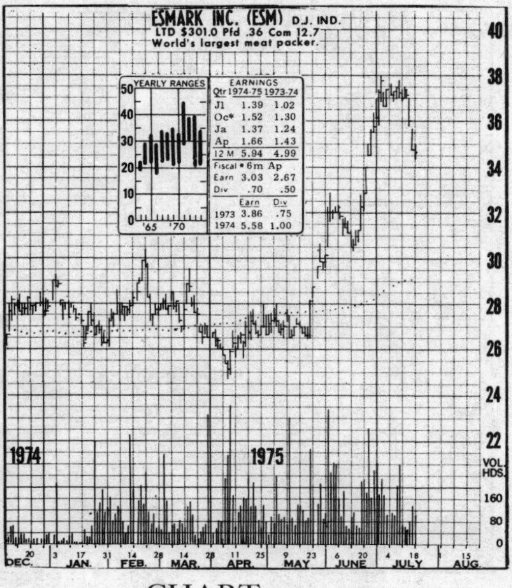

ESMARK INC. (ESM) D.J. IND.
LTD $301.0 Pfd .36 Com 12.7
World's largest meat packer.
YEARLY RANGES
EARNINGS
Qtr 1974-75 1973-74
Jl 1.39 1.02
Oc* 1.52 1.30
Ja 1.37 1.24
Ap 1.66 1.43
12 M 5.94 4.99
Fiscal * 6m Ap
Earn 3.03 2.67
Div .70 .50
Earn Div
1973 3.86 .75
1974 5.58 1.00
1974
1975
VOL. HDS.
DEC. JAN. FEB. MAR. APR. MAY JUNE JULY AUG.

Here again we see how, once the specialist has sharply raised prices to attract demand, he must, equally sharply, drop them if he is to preserve his profits.

CHART 15–12

SOURCE: Trendline's Daily Basis Stock Charts

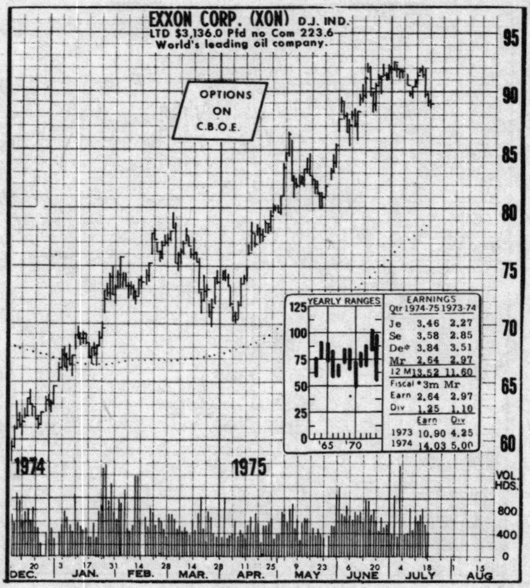
EXXON CORP. (XON) D.J. IND.
LTD $3,136.0 Pfd no Com 223.6
World's leading oil company.
OPTIONS ON C.B.O.E.
YEARLY RANGES
EARNINGS
Qtr 1974-75 1973-74
Je 3.46 2.27
Se 3.58 2.85
De* 3.84 3.51
Mr 2.64 2.97
12 M 13.52 11.60
Fiscal * 3m Mr
Earn 2.64 2.97
Div 1.25 1.10
Earn Div
1973 10.90 4.25
1974 14.03 5.00
1974
1975
VOL HDS.
DEC. JAN. FEB. MAR. APR. MAY JUNE JULY AUG

CHART 15–13

The problems involved in lowering the price of a $90 stock like Exxon, which is widely held by institutions, are a great deal more complicated than those in a stock like Esmark at $38. This specialist must be very careful not to precipitate major selling at the 85–90 level if his objective is to drop his price significantly lower.

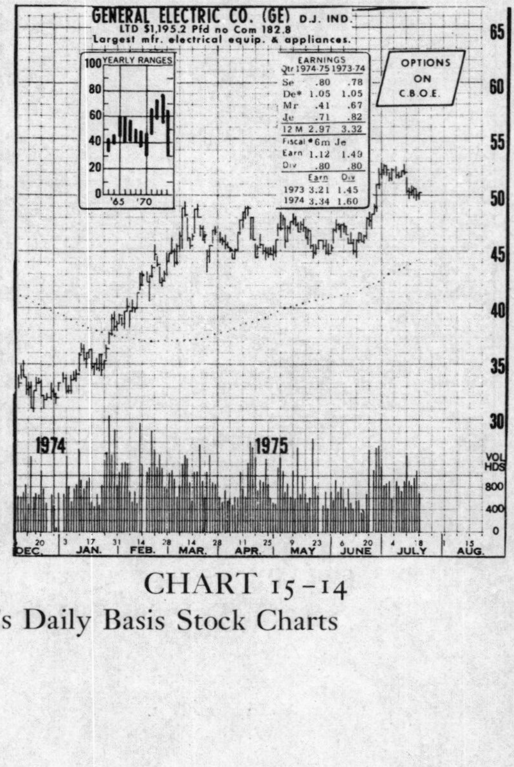
GENERAL ELECTRIC CO. (GE) D.J. IND.
LTD $1,195.2 Pfd no Com 182.8
Largest mfr. electrical equip. & appliances.
YEARLY RANGES
EARNINGS
Qtr 1974-75 1973-74
Se .80 .78
De* 1.05 1.05
Mr .41 .67
Je .71 .82
12 M 2.97 3.32
Fiscal * 6m Je
Earn 1.12 1.49
Div .80 .80
Earn Div
1973 3.21 1.45
1974 3.34 1.60
OPTIONS ON C.B.O.E.
1974
1975
VOL HDS
DEC. JAN. FEB. MAR. APR. MAY JUNE JULY AUG.

CHART 15–14

Not all stocks can move to their highs at once. Investor demand would be inadequate to allow for maximum distribution of stock and the establishment of short sales. Hence, specialists in many stocks, like GE, waited until July to maximize their short sales. This also added a plus factor to the Dow Average as other stocks in this index moved down from their highs.

SOURCE: Trendline's Daily Basis Stock Charts

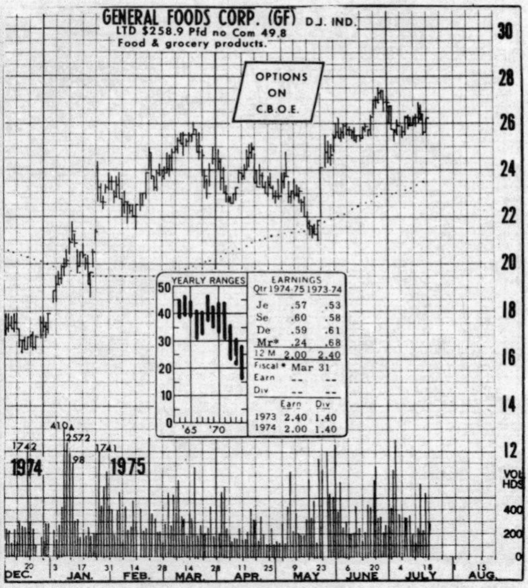
GENERAL FOODS CORP. (GF) D.J. IND.
LTD $258.9 Pfd no Com 49.8
Food & grocery products.
OPTIONS ON C.B.O.E.
YEARLY RANGES
EARNINGS
Qtr 1974-75 1973-74
Je .57 .53
Se .60 .58
De .59 .61
Mr* .24 .68
12 M 2.00 2.40
Fiscal * Mar 31
Earn -- --
Div -- --
Earn Div
1973 2.40 1.40
1974 2.00 1.40
'65 '70
1974
1975
VOL HDS
DEC. JAN. FEB. MAR. APR. MAY JUNE JULY AUG.

CHART 15–15

Once the specialist has lured investors into his trap with sharply rising stock prices, he rarely changes his tactics. Thus, once he decides to lower stock prices, he can be expected to yank the carpet out from under them. It is quite possible, therefore, that this stock will drop faster on the down side than it rose on the up side.

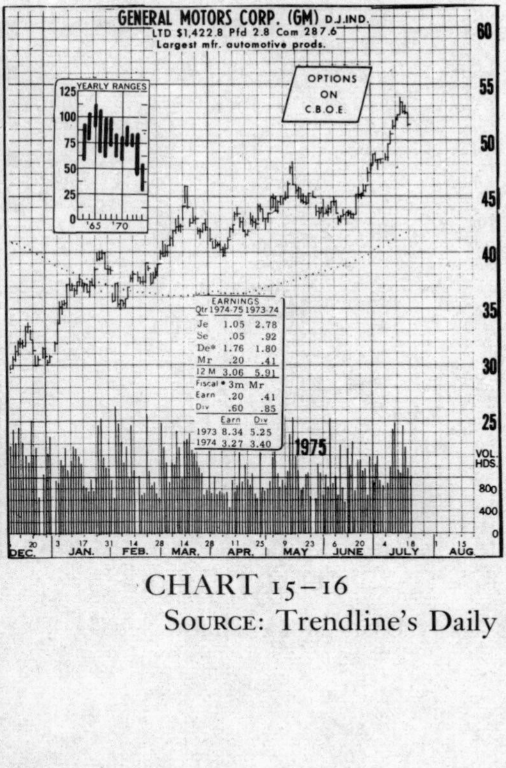
GENERAL MOTORS CORP. (GM) D.J.IND.
LTD $1,422.8 Pfd 2.8 Com 287.6
Largest mfr. automotive prods.
OPTIONS ON C.B.O.E.
YEARLY RANGES
'65 '70
EARNINGS
Qtr 1974-75 1973-74
Je 1.05 2.78
Se .05 .92
De* 1.76 1.80
Mr .20 .41
12 M 3.06 5.91
Fiscal * 3m Mr
Earn .20 .41
Div .60 .85
Earn Div
1973 8.34 5.25
1974 3.27 3.40
1975
VOL. HDS.
DEC. JAN. FEB. MAR. APR. MAY JUNE JULY AUG.

CHART 15–16

SOURCE: Trendline's Daily Basis Stock Charts

The advance conducted by the specialist in General Motors from late June to the July high was a carefully calculated plan where GM provided rear-guard action that served to mask the major retreat that had already been launched in most stocks.

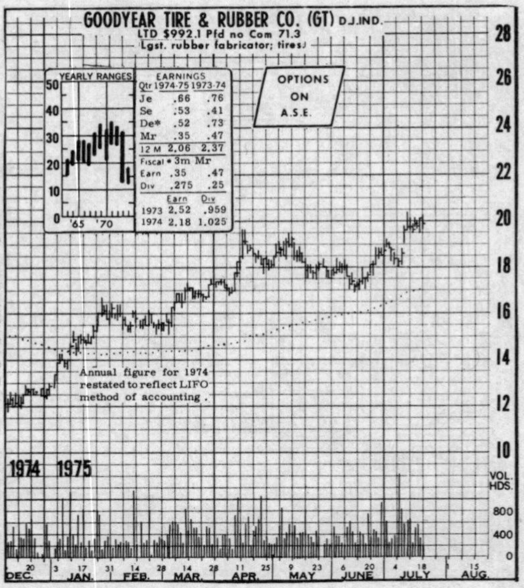
GOODYEAR TIRE & RUBBER CO. (GT) D.J.IND.
LTD $992.1 Pfd no Com 71.3
Lgst. rubber fabricator; tires
YEARLY RANGES
EARNINGS
OPTIONS ON A.S.E.
Annual figure for 1974 restated to reflect LIFO method of accounting.
1974 1975
VOL. HDS.
DEC. JAN. FEB. MAR. APR. MAY JUNE JULY AUG.

Note that it is the sharp leap in price in this stock from 18 to 20 in July that enabled the specialist to sell short to those who, frightened by this advance, now sought to cover their short sales.

CHART 15–17

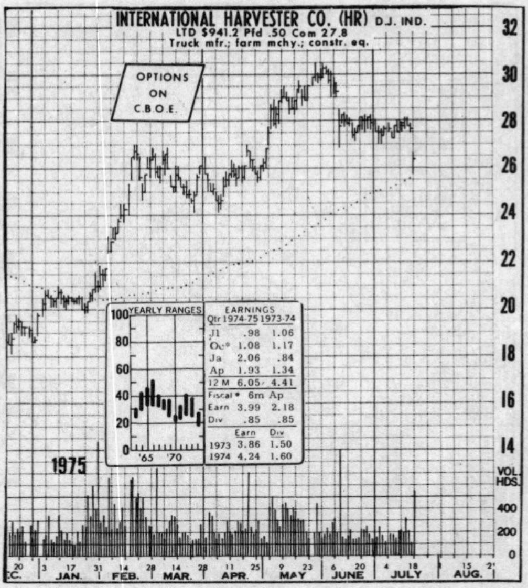
INTERNATIONAL HARVESTER CO. (HR) D.J. IND.
LTD $941.2 Pfd .50 Com 27.8
Truck mfr.; farm mchy.; constr. eq.
OPTIONS ON C.B.O.E.
YEARLY RANGES
EARNINGS
1975
VOL. HDS.
JAN. FEB. MAR. APR. MAY JUNE JULY AUG.

Once specialists have exhausted demand at one price level, as was the case with the specialist in International Harvestor (at the 26 level), they must raise prices, to a still higher level in order to revitalize the investor interest that will enable them to distribute their stock and establish short sales.

CHART 15–18

SOURCE: Trendline's Daily Basis Stock Charts

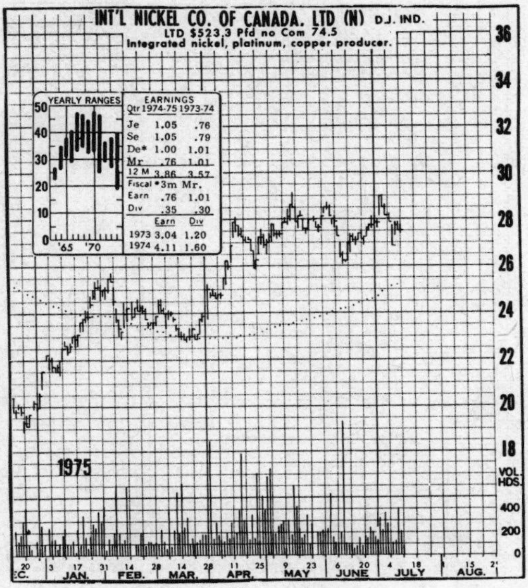
INT'L NICKEL CO. OF CANADA. LTD (N) D.J. IND.
LTD $523.3 Pfd no Com 74.5
Integrated nickel, platinum, copper producer.
YEARLY RANGES
EARNINGS
1975
VOL HDS.
JAN.
FEB.
MAR.
APR.
MAY
JUNE
JULY
AUG.

CHART 15–19

Having acquired a large inventory at the 26 level in the second week in June, it appeared as though the specialist had divested himself of his inventory by the time he reached the 29 level in the first week in July. He was then able to drop his price on considerably lower volume.

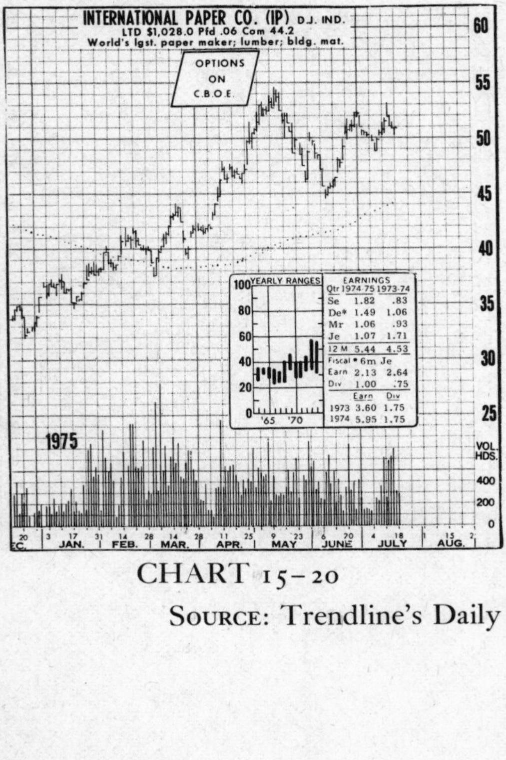
INTERNATIONAL PAPER CO. (IP) D.J. IND.
LTD $1,028.0 Pfd .06 Com 44.2
World's lgst. paper maker; lumber; bldg. mat.
OPTIONS ON C.B.O.E.
YEARLY RANGES
EARNINGS
1975
VOL HDS.
JAN.
FEB.
MAR.
APR.
MAY
JUNE
JULY
AUG.

CHART 15–20

Heavy public selling in this stock at the end of May and in early June caused this stock to advance thereafter.

SOURCE: Trendline's Daily Basis Stock Charts

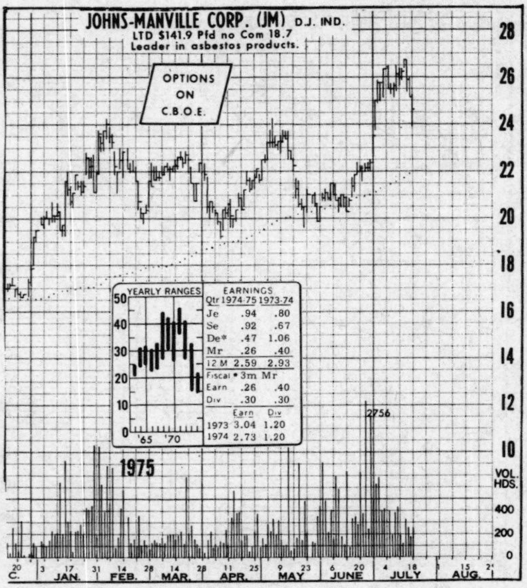
JOHNS-MANVILLE CORP. (JM) D.J. IND.
LTD $141.9 Pfd no Com 18.7
Leader in asbestos products.
OPTIONS ON C.B.O.E.
YEARLY RANGES
EARNINGS
Qtr 1974-75 1973-74
Je .94 .80
Se .92 .67
De* .47 1.06
Mr .26 .40
12 M 2.59 2.93
Fiscal • 3m Mr
Earn .26 .40
Div .30 .30
Earn Div
1973 3.04 1.20
1974 2.73 1.20
'65 '70
1975
2756
VOL. HDS.
JAN. FEB. MAR. APR. MAY JUNE JULY AUG.

Specialist short selling in this stock in late January, early February, and May created an environment in which a 4-point decline from 24 to 20 enabled this specialist to maximize profits. In this same sense, the sharp advance in price to the July high is like raising a guillotine.

CHART 15–21

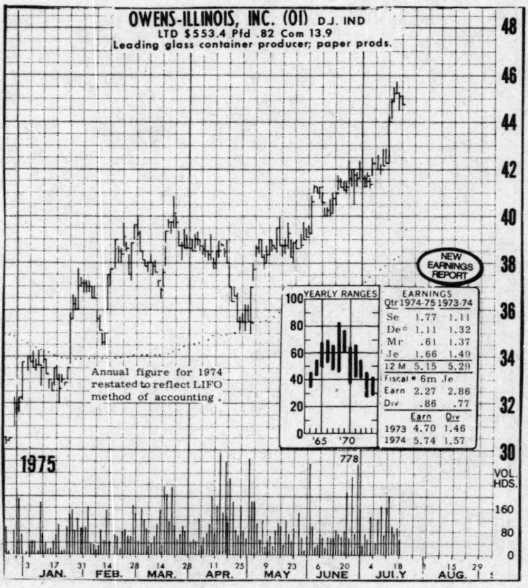
OWENS-ILLINOIS, INC. (OI) D.J. IND
LTD $553.4 Pfd .82 Com 13.9
Leading glass container producer; paper prods.
NEW EARNINGS REPORT
YEARLY RANGES
EARNINGS
Qtr 1974-75 1973-74
Se 1.77 1.11
De* 1.11 1.32
Mr .61 1.37
Je 1.66 1.49
12 M 5.15 5.29
Fiscal • 6m Je
Earn 2.27 2.86
Div .86 .77
Earn Div
1973 4.70 1.46
1974 5.74 1.57
'65 '70
Annual figure for 1974 restated to reflect LIFO method of accounting.
1975
778
VOL. HDS.
JAN. FEB. MAR. APR. MAY JUNE JULY AUG.

At one time or another in the course of a major rally, each Dow stock will add something to the Dow's gain. Having been held in reserve from January through April, the specialist in this stock beginning in May made a contribution of 8 points to the excitement surrounding a rising Dow.

CHART 15–22

SOURCE: Trendline's Daily Basis Stock Charts

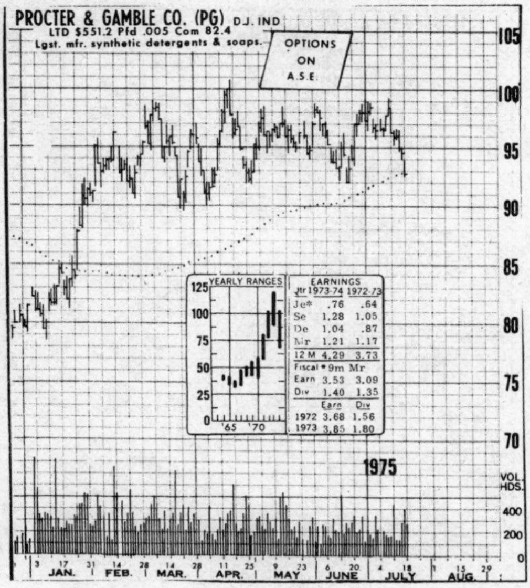
PROCTER & GAMBLE CO. (PG) D.J. IND
LTD $551.2 Pfd .005 Com 82.4
Lgst. mfr. synthetic detergents & soaps.
OPTIONS ON A.S.E.
YEARLY RANGES
EARNINGS
1975
VOL. HDS.
JAN. FEB. MAR. APR. MAY JUNE JULY AUG.

CHART 15–23

The specialist in this stock is prudent as well as patient. Note, therefore, that he has already conducted more than a dozen rallies above the 90 level and that the course of the subsequent declines has invariably been on increasingly lower volume. When finally he moves down from 90 to lower price levels there will be only a minimum of selling in this stock. His careful conditioning will have caused investors to expect still another sharp rally. By the time they see things as they are most of them will decide it has become too late to sell.

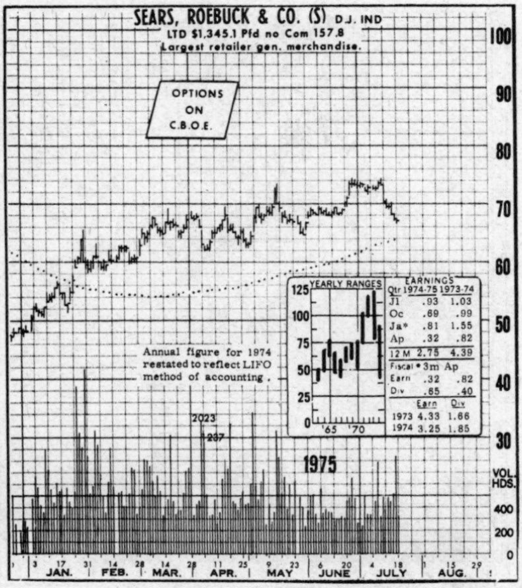
SEARS, ROEBUCK & CO. (S) D.J. IND
LTD $1,345.1 Pfd no Com 157.8
Largest retailer gen. merchandise.
OPTIONS ON C.B.O.E.
Annual figure for 1974 restated to reflect LIFO method of accounting.
YEARLY RANGES
EARNINGS
1975
VOL. HDS.
JAN. FEB. MAR. APR. MAY JUNE JULY AUG.

CHART 15–24

The gains this specialist established over a six-month span from the end of January to the middle of July can be wiped out in less than one month's time.

SOURCE: Trendline's Daily Basis Stock Charts

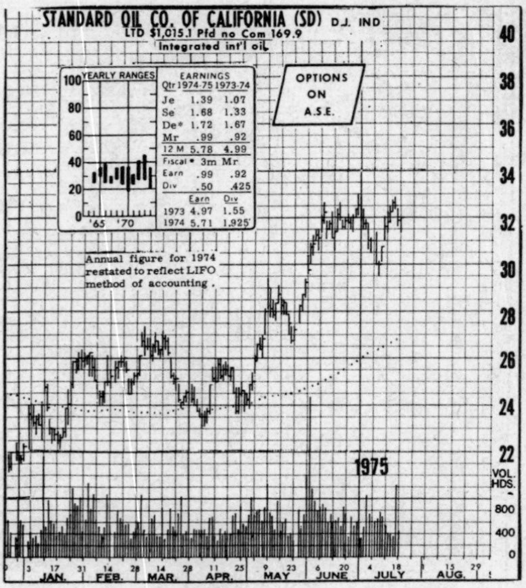
STANDARD OIL CO. OF CALIFORNIA (SD) D.J. IND
LTD $1,015.1 Pfd no Com 169.9
Integrated int'l oil
YEARLY RANGES
100
80
60
40
20
0
'65 '70
EARNINGS
Qtr 1974-75 1973-74
Je 1.39 1.07
Se 1.68 1.33
De* 1.72 1.67
Mr .99 .92
12 M 5.78 4.99
Fiscal • 3m Mr
Earn .99 .92
Div .50 .425
Earn Div
1973 4.97 1.55
1974 5.71 1.925
OPTIONS ON A.S.E.
Annual figure for 1974 restated to reflect LIFO method of accounting.
1975
40
38
36
34
32
30
28
26
24
22
VOL. HDS.
800
400
0
JAN.
FEB.
MAR.
APR.
MAY
JUNE
JULY
AUG.

CHART 15–25

Having cleaned out his book down to the 30 level in early July, it would seem that with the establishment of the second high in mid-July that this specialist has begun the process that will lower him safely and profitably to wholesale price levels.

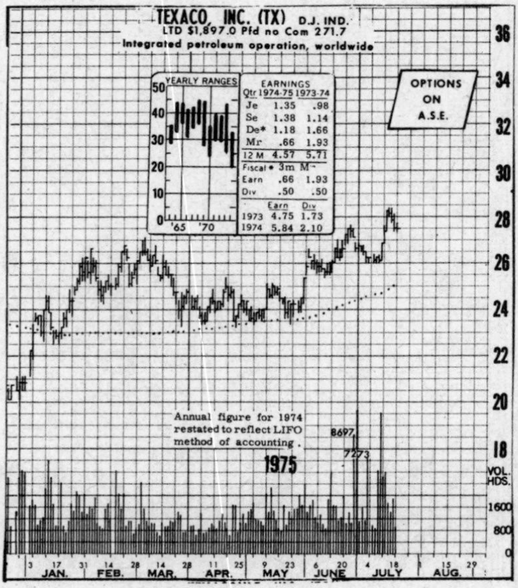
TEXACO, INC. (TX) D.J. IND.
LTD $1,897.0 Pfd no Com 271.7
Integrated petroleum operation, worldwide
YEARLY RANGES
50
40
30
20
10
0
'65 '70
EARNINGS
Qtr 1974-75 1973-74
Je 1.35 .98
Se 1.38 1.14
De* 1.18 1.66
Mr .66 1.93
12 M 4.57 5.71
Fiscal • 3m M
Earn .66 1.93
Div .50 .50
Earn Div
1973 4.75 1.73
1974 5.84 2.10
OPTIONS ON A.S.E.
Annual figure for 1974 restated to reflect LIFO method of accounting.
1975
8697
7273
36
34
32
30
28
26
24
22
20
18
VOL. HDS.
1600
800
0
JAN.
FEB.
MAR.
APR.
MAY
JUNE
JULY
AUG.

CHART 15–26

Sharply lower earnings were totally ignored when this specialist's turn came to maximize profits. This he did by distributing and selling short more than 2 million shares of stock in June and July.

SOURCE: Trendline's Daily Basis Stock Charts

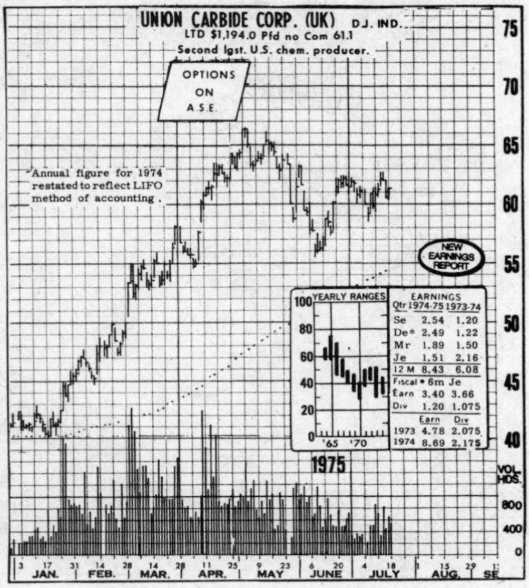
UNION CARBIDE CORP. (UK) D.J. IND.
LTD $1,194.0 Pfd no Com 61.1
Second lgst. U.S. chem. producer.
OPTIONS ON A.S.E.
Annual figure for 1974 restated to reflect LIFO method of accounting.
NEW EARNINGS REPORT
YEARLY RANGES
EARNINGS
Qtr 1974-75 1973-74
Se 2.54 1.20
De* 2.49 1.22
Mr 1.89 1.50
Je 1.51 2.16
12 M 8.43 6.08
Fiscal • 6m Je
Earn 3.40 3.66
Div 1.20 1.075
Earn Div
1973 4.78 2.075
1974 8.69 2.175
'65 '70
1975
VOL. HDS.
JAN. FEB. MAR. APR. MAY JUNE JULY AUG. SE

CHART 15–27

The existence of sharply higher March earnings helped this specialist lower stock prices in May and June on much lighter volume than would otherwise have been the case.

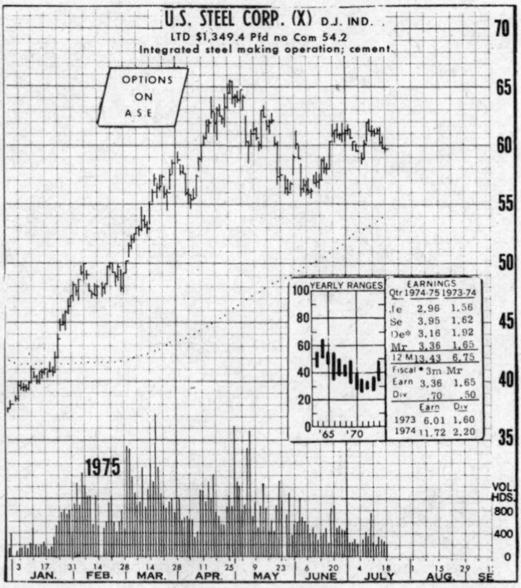
U.S. STEEL CORP. (X) D.J. IND.
LTD $1,349.4 Pfd no Com 54.2
Integrated steel making operation; cement.
OPTIONS ON A.S.E
YEARLY RANGES
EARNINGS
Qtr 1974-75 1973-74
Je 2.96 1.56
Se 3.95 1.62
De* 3.16 1.92
Mr 3.36 1.65
12 M 13.43 6.75
Fiscal • 3m Mr
Earn 3.36 1.65
Div .70 .50
Earn Div
1973 6.01 1.60
1974 11.72 2.20
'65 '70
1975
VOL. HDS.
JAN. FEB. MAR. APR. MAY JUNE JULY AUG. SE

CHART 15–28

The logic of dramatically higher earnings also provided investors with the incentive to buy U.S. Steel and hold on to it with passive complacency.

SOURCE: Trendline's Daily Basis Stock Charts

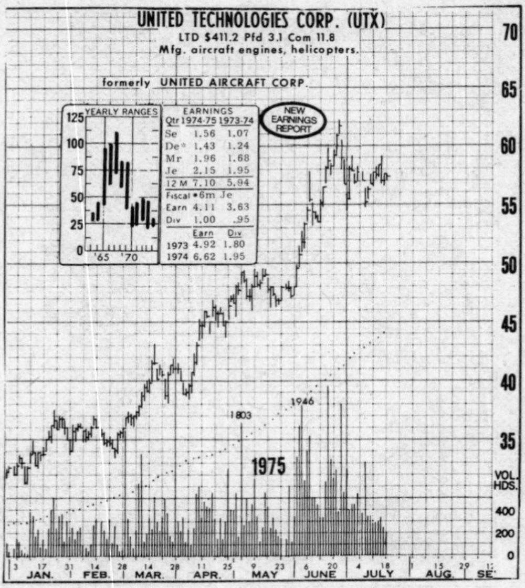
UNITED TECHNOLOGIES CORP. (UTX)
LTD $411.2 Pfd 3.1 Com 11.8
Mfg. aircraft engines, helicopters.
formerly UNITED AIRCRAFT CORP.
YEARLY RANGES
EARNINGS
NEW EARNINGS REPORT
1975
1803
1946
VOL. HDS.
JAN. FEB. MAR. APR. MAY JUNE JULY AUG. SE

This specialist is a genius at making investors think they've latched onto a certain profit which, almost overnight, then merges into a much more certain loss.

CHART 15–29

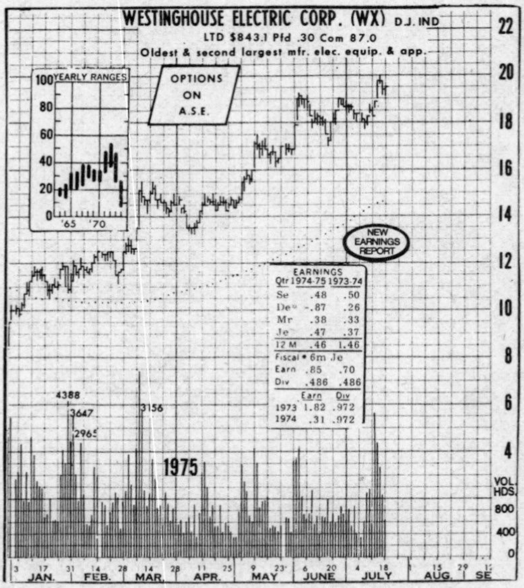
WESTINGHOUSE ELECTRIC CORP. (WX) D.J. IND
LTD $843.1 Pfd .30 Com 87.0
Oldest & second largest mfr. elec. equip. & app.
YEARLY RANGES
OPTIONS ON A.S.E.
NEW EARNINGS REPORT
EARNINGS
1975
4388
3647
2965
3156
VOL. HDS.
JAN. FEB. MAR. APR. MAY JUNE JULY AUG. SE

Once again, we see that the buy and sell orders on the specialist's book enables him to estimate the extent of public supply and demand as he raises price. The specialist in Westinghouse very wisely halted the advance in his stock just under the highly critical $20 price level. Had he closed at or above this price he would undoubtedly have precipitated heavy public selling at the very moment he was intent on establishing his own short positions.

CHART 15–30

SOURCE: Trendline's Daily Basis Stock Charts

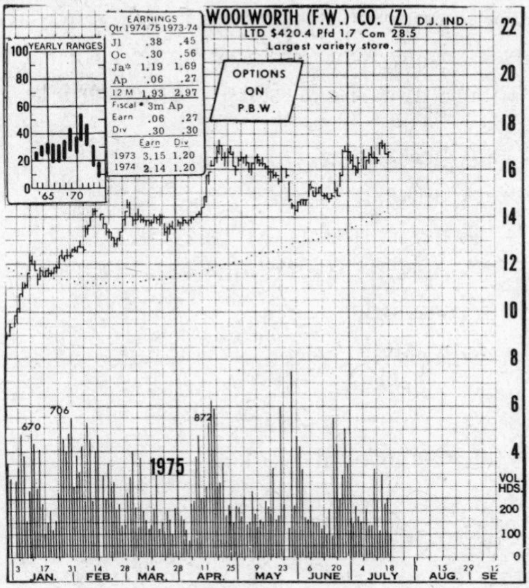
WOOLWORTH (F.W.) CO. (Z) D.J. IND.
LTD $420.4 Pfd 1.7 Com 28.5
Largest variety store.
OPTIONS ON P.B.W.
YEARLY RANGES
EARNINGS
1975
VOL. HDS.
JAN.
FEB.
MAR.
APR.
MAY
JUNE
JULY
AUG.

CHART 15–31

Once specialists have sold out their investment and trading accounts and established a major short position at a rally high, their sole objective is to lower stock prices to wholesale price levels as expeditiously as possible. Almost without exception, however, they are faced with inventory problems once they drop stock prices from the first high. That is why, like the specialist in Woolworth, they must invariably establish a second or a third high to unload the stock they acquired in the decline from the first high.

SOURCE: Trendline's Daily Basis Stock Charts

In reviewing the events leading up to the week ending July 18, it is interesting to observe that thirteen Dow stocks were either at, lower than, or within one to two points of their prices in the January–February period. This fact exposes the true condition of the market. The bullishness attributed to the Dow Average can be seen to be enormously exaggerated, since almost half the stocks in this average were already locked into a situation that was bearish in the most basic sense. These stocks are:

Allied Chemical
American Brands
American Can
American Telephone & Telegraph
Anaconda
Chrysler
General Foods
International Harvester
International Nickel
Johns Manville
Procter & Gamble
Sears
Texaco

Additional insight into the overall bearish tendency of Dow stocks is provided by examining what occurred in Dow stocks following the April high when their price movements began to rotate. The following eighteen stocks were the same price or lower on July 18 than at the Dow high of April 17:

Allied Chemical
Aluminum Co. of America
American Can
American Telephone & Telegraph
Anaconda
Bethlehem Steel
Chrysler
Du Pont
Eastman Kodak
General Electric
General Foods
Goodyear Tire & Rubber

International Harvester
International Nickel
Procter & Gamble
Sears
Union Carbide
U.S. Steel

On July 18 General Electric and Telephone were within 1½ points of their April 17 prices. Indeed, of the thirty Dow stocks, only ten were significantly higher on July 18 than April 17:

	April 17	*July 18*	*Increase in price*
American Brands	38⅜	42¼	3⅞
Esmark	27	34⅝	7⅝
Exxon	78¼	89	10¾
General Motors	41⅞	51⅜	9½
International Paper	47⅜	50⅞	3½
Johns Manville	20⅞	24⅝	3¾
Owens Illinois	38	44¾	6¾
Standard Oil of Calif.	25½	32	4½
United Technologies	46¼	57⅜	10⅛
Westinghouse	14½	19½	5
			65⅜

We see that the gains registered in these ten stocks, since the Dow's April high, average out to approximately 6½ points for each stock and that these gains advanced the Dow Average approximately 41 points. By examining the Dow's constituent elements, the reader can see, despite the rise in the Dow, not only how shaky the market's foundations had been, but how little it would now take to crumble them.

As we interpreted big block activity and specialist short selling, it reflected the fact that the retreat of the Dow from each mid-month high, which was then followed by another advance to a still higher monthly high, meant only that investors were favored by the immediate necessities of specialist inventory distributions and short selling. The elements of risk had not been erased. Each time the Dow had established a mid-monthly high, because of heavy specialist short selling, it could have begun a decline from which it might *not* have recovered. On each occasion Dow stocks rallied to their monthly highs, the event immediately became a metaphor for the crack of dice against the back of Las Vegas East crap table. One had only to substitute *The Wall Street Journal* for the drone of the stickman in the background encouraging tourists with his familiar refrain, "He's coming out again, the same lucky shooter." Over the very near term, however, the investor's luck would change; a decline would ultimately begin that would catch him by surprise. Instead of recovering as they had in the past when the Dow moved down from a new high, prices would continue to sink far below investor expectations.

Inevitably as prices move down from the final high, the investor's financial page will be advising him not to abandon faith in the underlying strength of the market. He will be told, "It is only logical to expect some sort of pullback, or at least a consolidation phase in the market." Compounding the investor's problem will be rallies in the Dow which will attempt to hide the fact that the over-all market is declining sharply. On some days the Dow may close sharply higher while the preponderance of declines over advances shows the market as a whole to be still disintegrating. Then, when the Dow continues its plunge past the levels at which the investor was advised to look for support, he will be told to look for support at levels that are still lower. When these are penetrated, he will be advised that the experts expect to find support at the old lows. When some or all of his stocks begin to penetrate their old lows, he will feel it is then too late to sell. Near the bottom he will hold on until the media grows pessimistic—then, thinking he should try to save something, the investor will sell everything.

We have seen that the investor's disappointments are proportionate to the degree in which his activities unknowingly assist in the development and refinement of the specialist's practices. When investors are buying, on balance, specialists are selling. When investors commit themselves to heavy selling, specialists are buying. Thus the public's bearishness is actually bullish, and its bullishness is, in fact, bearish.

It should now be clear that nothing is natural; nothing is as it seems to be. The movement of stock prices is not the reflection of economic law. The present and future trends of stock prices are, in the final analysis, prejudiced by the expectations and objectives of the Exchange establishment's elite clique. We have observed that the specialist's price movements are based on an awareness of what he already knows will take place. In this sense it can be said that the specialist's vision of things to come underlies and gives rise to the manner in which he utilizes price in order to generate the forces of public demand and supply. In fact, it is possible to say that the future of his stock's price is molded by the specialist into a highly flexible blueprint to be followed to its logical conclusions through time. The past history of these blueprints are outlined by stock charts which record a stock's high, low, and close.

I discovered a number of years ago that, curiously enough, there seemed to be a repetition of certain angles in the chart formations of stocks and an unusual symmetry to their chart patterns that could not possibly be explained in terms of public buying and selling. But, more than that, I felt that the unmistakable consistency in the angles and chart patterns of certain stocks could constitute the elements of a system. By utilizing triangles, parallel rulers, and a protractor,* I experimented with random samplings of charts until my intuitions hardened into an idea that could no longer be dismissed. The more I experimented, the more certain I became that my new approach to charting the market could prove to be of value to other investors.

*In order to obtain greater precision and speed I now use a Vemco V-Track Drafting Machine for plotting my charts.

I discussed the conventions and technologies that govern the use of my charting system in *The Wall Street Jungle* and *The Wall Street Gang*. Consequently, I will make no attempts to duplicate what I have already discussed at length. I have received many letters from readers who have found, as I did, that these techniques have assisted them enormously in determining the probable future course of individual stocks and the market in general. For the benefit of those, therefore, who are unfamiliar with my method of charting, I am including a group of charts with a brief description of how my charting techniques can be employed. In doing this, I once again must ask the investor to keep in mind the fact that while I consider the use of charts to be important, there is no question in my mind that they should be used merely as a rough tool in order to confirm the understanding of specialist intent that is to be gained from the analysis of the ticker tape's big block activity—particularly as it centers around critical price levels. The charts *are*, however, *most* important in that they do enable the investor to gain further insight into the fact that there is a predictable trajectory to the direction of stock prices.

The simplicity of this approach to charting can be visualized in the way in which three basic angles can be used in order to determine short- and long-term trends. As the reader will discover, although the angles differ considerably in terms of their long- or short-term functions, their versatility is such that they can be employed independently or interdependently. The reader's facility in using the angle theory of charting will develop with the education of his intuitions that comes with practice. Each angle is almost always useful in that it tells the chartist something about the future course of stock prices. However, the most profitable use of the technique will require the most effective application of the most effective angle. This knowledge will only come with time as the investor or trader begins to anticipate the kind of angle that can be best used and how best to use it in order to provide him with specific answers for the purchase and sale of stock. In this connection it should be kept in mind that the angles that can be most often counted on to provide answers to investment or trading problems in the present will be angles that, when applied to past price action, solved the same problems in the past.

In the chart of Colgate-Palmolive (Chart 15–32), the three basic angles are illustrated. They are the principal angle, the secondary angle, and the acute angle. What I call the "principal" angle is formed by drawing a line from the major long term low (in 1938—point A) to the preceding high (in 1937—point B). This gives me a 79½° angle. This angle is useful for short term trading purposes. It is applied to the chart by extending what I refer to as a "force line" from any of a stock's various high and low points in order to determine its angles of advance. The chartist can also employ the same angles on a downslanting basis to obtain angles of decline. It is possible to draw a principal angle from all major lows in a stock. To illustrate this point, I have elected to employ the principal angle from the low established in 1974 in Sears Roebuck (Chart 15–45) instead of the low established in 1938.* Each principal angle that the investor constructs, whether it be in a period like 1938 or 1974, has its particular advantages for providing insight into the probable direction of stock prices. For example, where the force lines of a principal angle derived from a low in the 1930s or 1940s might be useful in determining a long-term trend, the force lines of a principal (and the other) angle derived from a more recent low (say in 1970 or 1974) can often possess the advantage of functioning for the more immediate or short term.

My so-called "secondary" angle is formed (in Chart 15–32) by again drawing a force line from point A to the low preceding the major low at point C, which gives me a 63° angle. Secondary angles are oftentimes useful for intermediate-term trading pur-

*I illustrated the use of the 1938 low in Sears in *The Wall Street Gang*, page 216. In that example, I showed how the principal angle obtained from that low functioned until 1972. Interestingly enough, the principal angle established in 1938 is the same as the angle established in 1974—67½°.

poses when used on a semilogarithmic monthly chart. When used on a semilogarithmic yearly chart, the secondary angle is often excellent for plotting the course of a stock's price for investment purposes.

The "acute" angle is derived by measuring the difference between the secondary angle and the principal angle. To obtain this angle, merely subtract the secondary angle from the principal angle. In the Colgate-Palmolive chart (15–32), the acute angle is 16½°. The acute angle is best used for investment purposes on a yearly chart, and for both investment and trading purposes on a monthly chart.

Finally, there is an additional angle which can be obtained from the basic angles which I call a "complementary" angle. This is obtained by subtracting the principal (or the secondary) angle from 90°. Thus, in the chart of Colgate-Palmolive, the complementary angle of the principal angle is 10½° (90° − 79½° = 10½°; see Chart 15–44). The complement of the secondary angle is 27° (Charts 15–42 and 15–43).

As the reader will learn, when the larger (principal or secondary) angle is used, one obtains an image of the short-term trend of stock prices. The smaller (complementary) angle provides an image of the direction of stock prices over the longer term. For trading purposes, the larger angles will be most often employed. Investors, on the other hand, will be more inclined to seek the lower risk insights provided by the complementary angles.

In order to gradually introduce the reader to the angle theory, I have constructed my angles on Colgate-Palmolive only from the major low of 1938. By identifying all the angles and their manner of construction from this one low, the reader will be able to quickly recognize the same set of angles when they are presented in a different chart formation from the major low of another year. The additional charts of Colgate-Palmolive teach the reader to identify the three basic angles and the complements of the principal and secondary angles in simple learning tasks.

This will prepare him to then examine somewhat more complex applications of the angles.

The reader will be shown how to use the basic angles formed from one major low in one year in different combinations with each other and with the basic angles formed from the principal and secondary angles of other major lows in other years. Both investors and traders will also be shown the implications for buy and sell signals when these angles intersect or when price moves toward the apex formed by an intersection. As the reader gains experience with the use of the angles, the learning task will grow easier. As he develops a better understanding of their relationships, he will also discover how they can improve the timing of his investment and/or trading decisions.

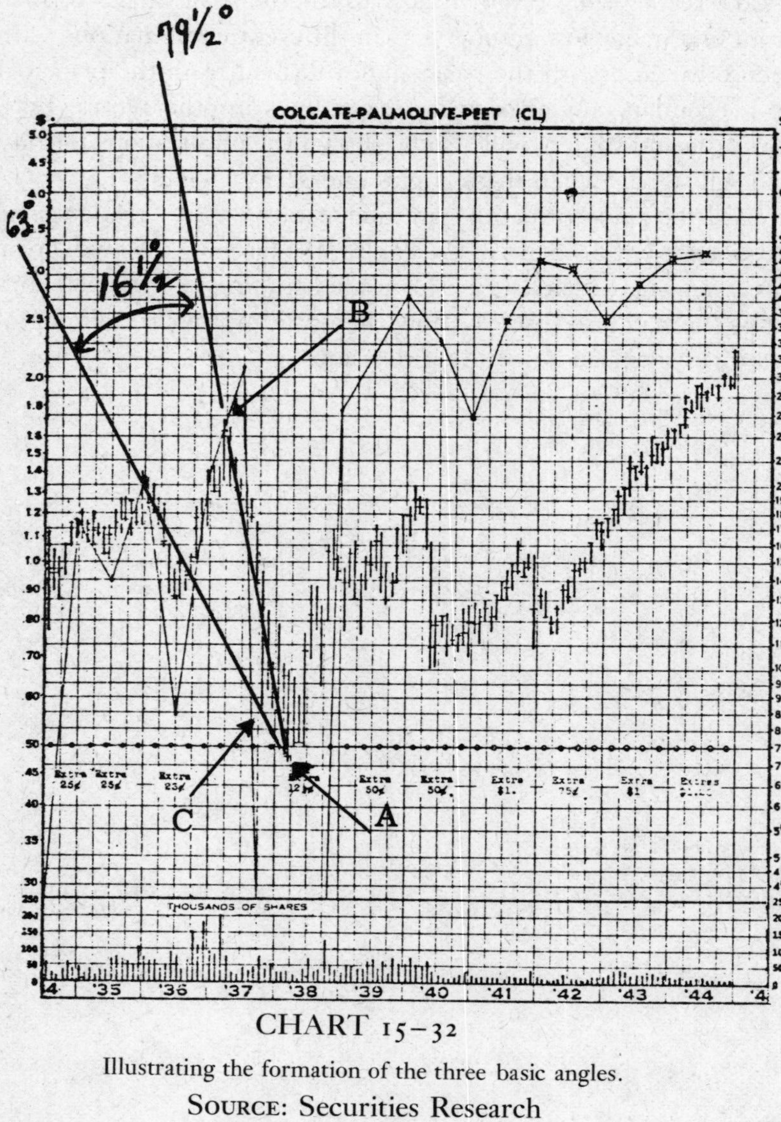
79½°
63°
16½°
COLGATE-PALMOLIVE-PEET (CL)
B
C
A
THOUSANDS OF SHARES
'35
'36
'37
'38
'39
'40
'41
'42
'43
'44

CHART 15–32

Illustrating the formation of the three basic angles.

SOURCE: Securities Research

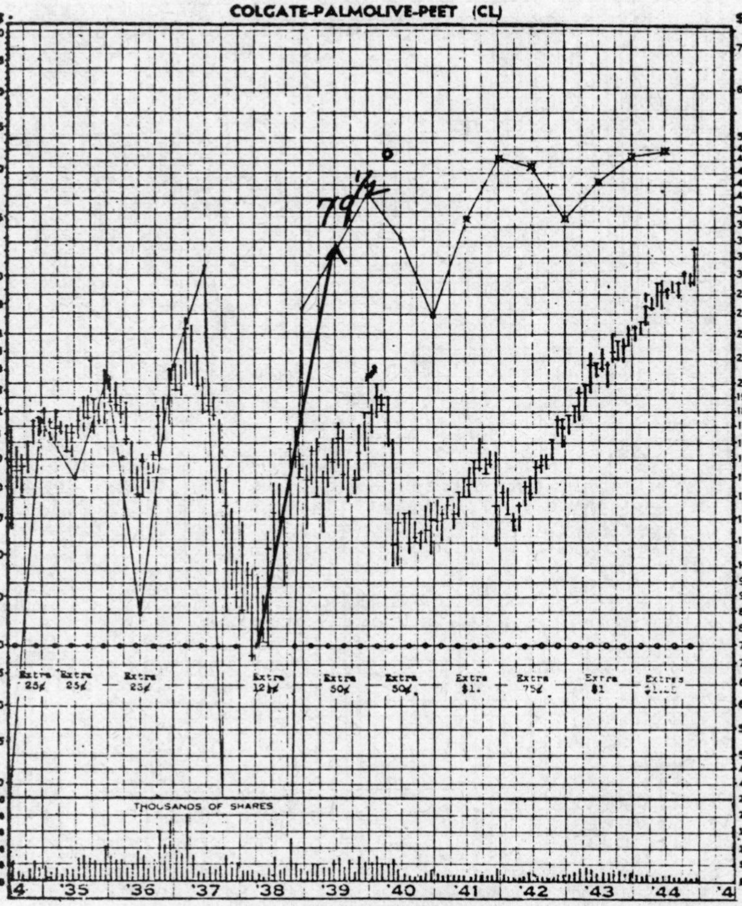
COLGATE-PALMOLIVE-PEET (CL)
THOUSANDS OF SHARES
Extra 25¢
Extra 25¢
Extra 25¢
Extra 12½¢
Extra 50¢
Extra 50¢
Extra $1.
Extra 75¢
Extra $1
'35
'36
'37
'38
'39
'40
'41
'42
'43
'44
79¼

CHART 15–33

This chart illustrates one possible application of the principal angle obtained from the 1938 low in forecasting the direction of stock prices over the intermediate term in 1938.

SOURCE: Securities Research

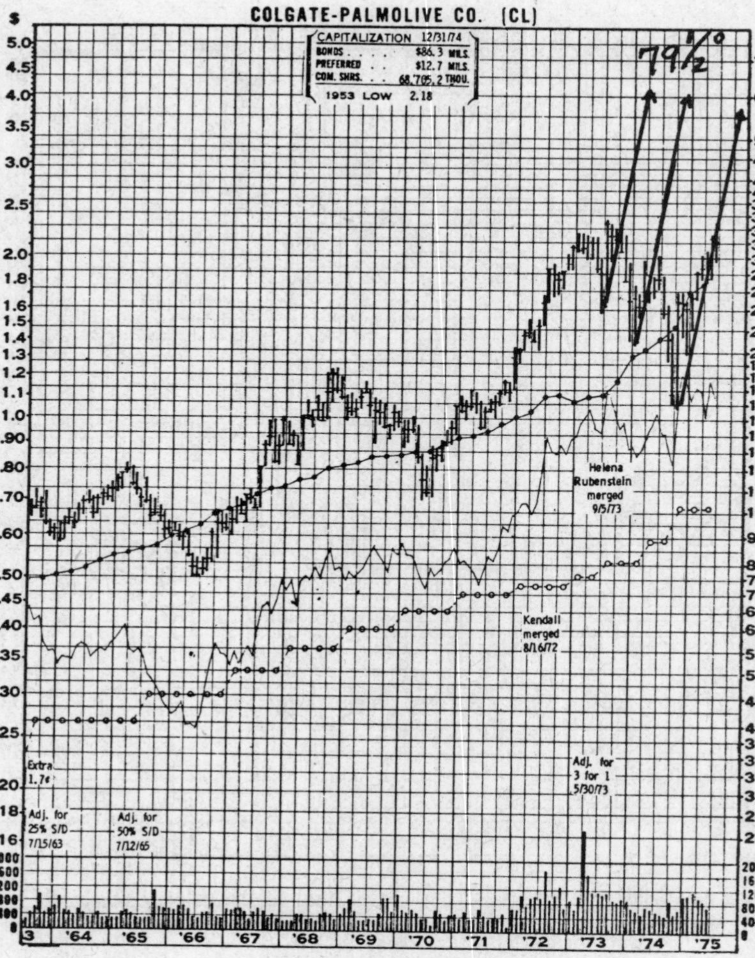
COLGATE-PALMOLIVE CO. (CL)
CAPITALIZATION 12/31/74
BONDS . . . . $86.3 MILS.
PREFERRED . . $12.7 MILS.
COM. SHRS. . . 68,705.2 THOU.
1953 LOW 2.18
79½
Helena Rubenstein merged 9/5/73
Kendall merged 8/16/72
Adj. for 3 for 1 5/30/73
Extra 1.7¢
Adj. for 25% S/D 7/15/63
Adj. for 50% S/D 7/12/65
'64 '65 '66 '67 '68 '69 '70 '71 '72 '73 '74 '75

CHART 15–34

This chart illustrates several possible applications of the principal angle obtained from the 1938 low in forecasting the direction of stock prices over the intermediate term in 1973, '74, and '75.

SOURCE: Securities Research

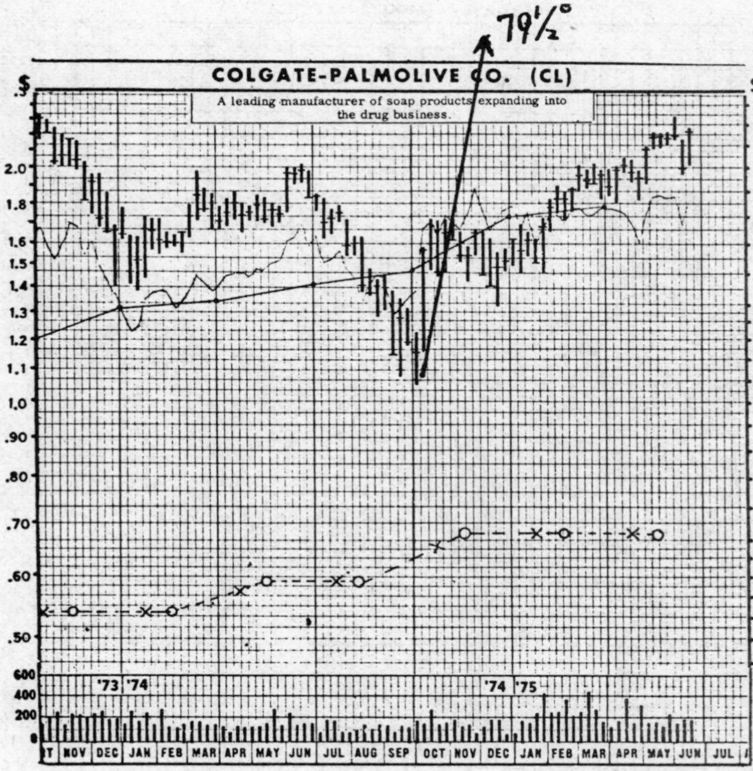

79½°
COLGATE-PALMOLIVE CO. (CL)
A leading manufacturer of soap products expanding into the drug business.
$
$
'73 '74
'74 '75
NOV DEC JAN FEB MAR APR MAY JUN JUL AUG SEP OCT NOV DEC JAN FEB MAR APR MAY JUN JUL

CHART 15–35

This chart illustrates one possible application of the principal angle obtained from the 1938 low in forecasting the direction of stock prices for short-term trading purposes in 1974.

Source: Securities Research

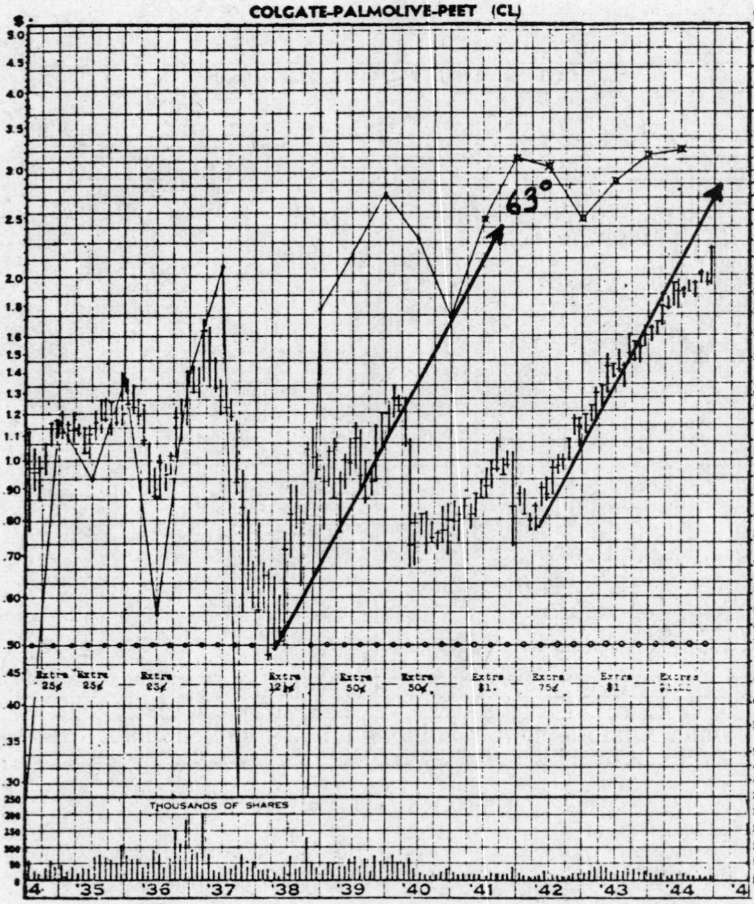
COLGATE-PALMOLIVE-PEET (CL)
63°
THOUSANDS OF SHARES
'35
'36
'37
'38
'39
'40
'41
'42
'43
'44

CHART 15–36

Illustrating how the secondary angle obtained from the 1938 low applied itself in 1938–39 and 1942–44 for long-term investment purposes.

SOURCE: Securities Research

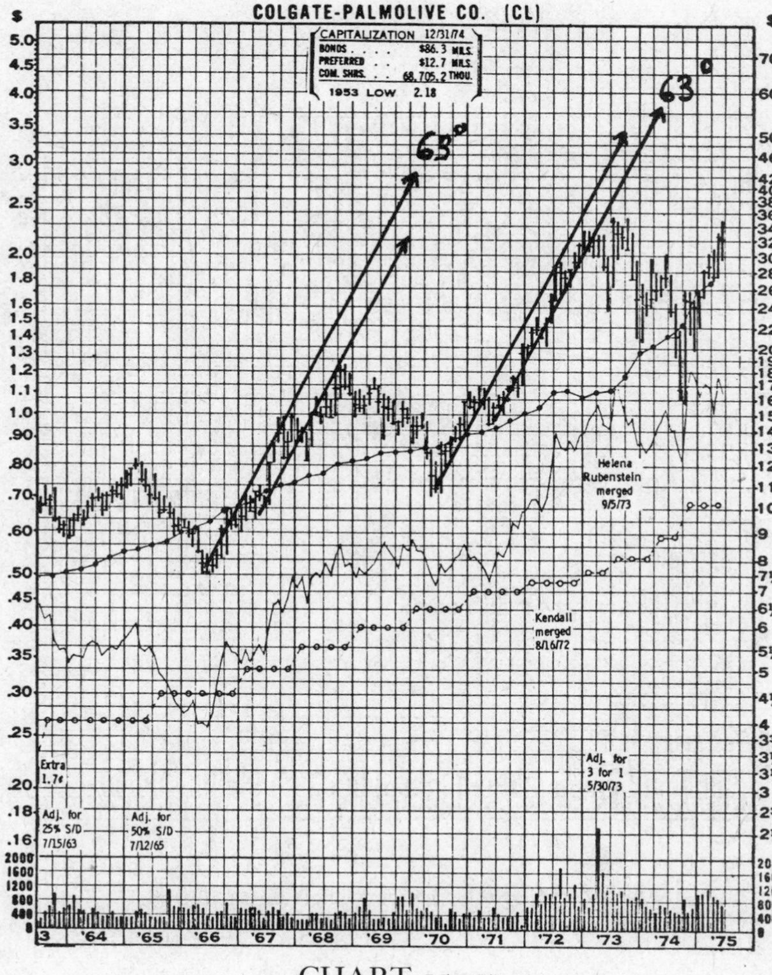
COLGATE-PALMOLIVE CO. (CL)
CAPITALIZATION 12/31/74
BONDS . . . . $86.3 MILS.
PREFERRED . . $12.7 MILS.
COM. SHRS. . . 68,705.2 THOU.
1953 LOW 2.18
63°
63°
Helena Rubenstein merged 9/5/73
Kendall merged 8/16/72
Adj. for 3 for 1 5/30/73
Extra 1.7¢
Adj. for 25% S/D 7/15/63
Adj. for 50% S/D 7/12/65
'64 '65 '66 '67 '68 '69 '70 '71 '72 '73 '74 '75

CHART 15–37

Illustrating how the secondary angle obtained from the 1938 low also functioned for long-term investment purposes in 1966–68 and 1970–73.

Source: Securities Research

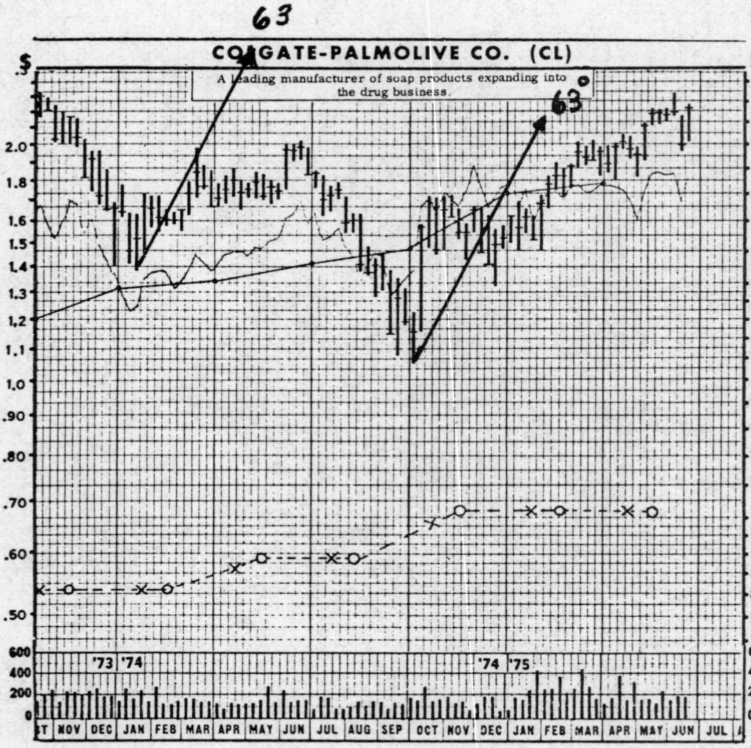
63
COLGATE-PALMOLIVE CO. (CL)
A leading manufacturer of soap products expanding into the drug business.
63°
$
$
2.0
1.8
1.6
1.5
1.4
1.3
1.2
1.1
1.0
.90
.80
.70
.60
.50
36
34
32
30
28
26
24
22
20
19
18
17
16
15
14
13
12
11
10
9½
9
8½
8
7½
7
600
400
200
0
'73 '74
'74 '75
NOV DEC JAN FEB MAR APR MAY JUN JUL AUG SEP OCT NOV DEC JAN FEB MAR APR MAY JUN JUL

CHART 15–38

Illustrating the application of the secondary angle obtained from the 1938 low for short-term trading purposes in 1974.

SOURCE: Securities Research

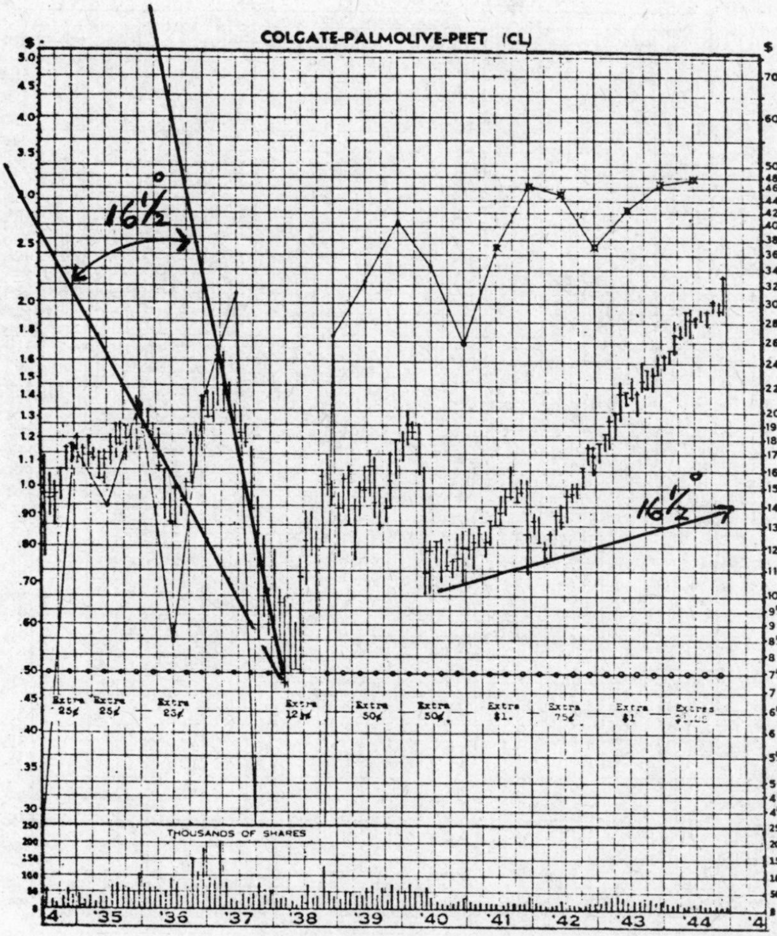
COLGATE-PALMOLIVE-PEET (CL)
16½°
THOUSANDS OF SHARES
'35
'36
'37
'38
'39
'40
'41
'42
'43
'44

CHART 15–39

Illustrating how the application of the acute angle obtained from the 1938 low provided the long-term investor with buy signals when the price touched the force line at 10½ in 1940, 11 in December, 1941, and 11½ in early 1942.

SOURCE: Securities Research

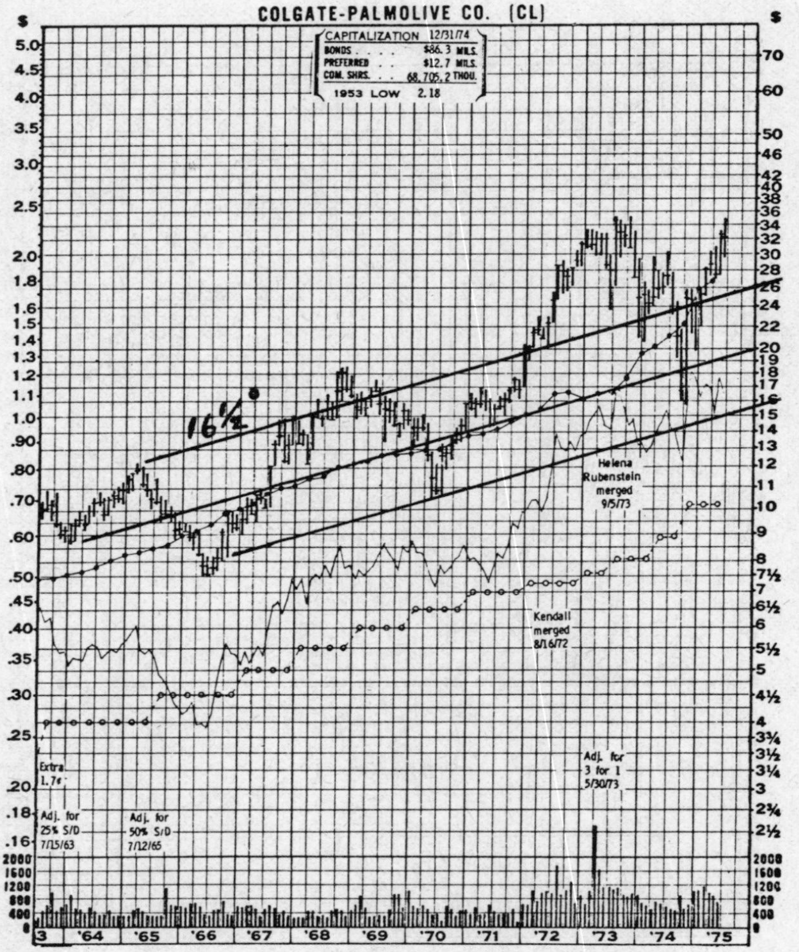
COLGATE-PALMOLIVE CO. (CL)
CAPITALIZATION 12/31/74
BONDS . . . . $86.3 MILS.
PREFERRED . . $12.7 MILS.
COM. SHRS. . . 68,705.2 THOU.
1953 LOW 2.18
16½°
Helena Rubenstein merged 9/5/73
Kendall merged 8/16/72
Extra 1.7¢
Adj. for 25% S/D 7/15/63
Adj. for 50% S/D 7/12/65
Adj. for 3 for 1 5/30/73
'64 '65 '66 '67 '68 '69 '70 '71 '72 '73 '74 '75

CHART 15–40

Illustrating the application of the acute angle obtained from the 1938 low to confirm the sale of an investment in this stock when price touched the uppermost acute force line at approximately 15 in 1967, and its repurchase in 1970 when price touched the lowest acute force line at 10½ in the second quarter of 1970.

SOURCE: Securities Research

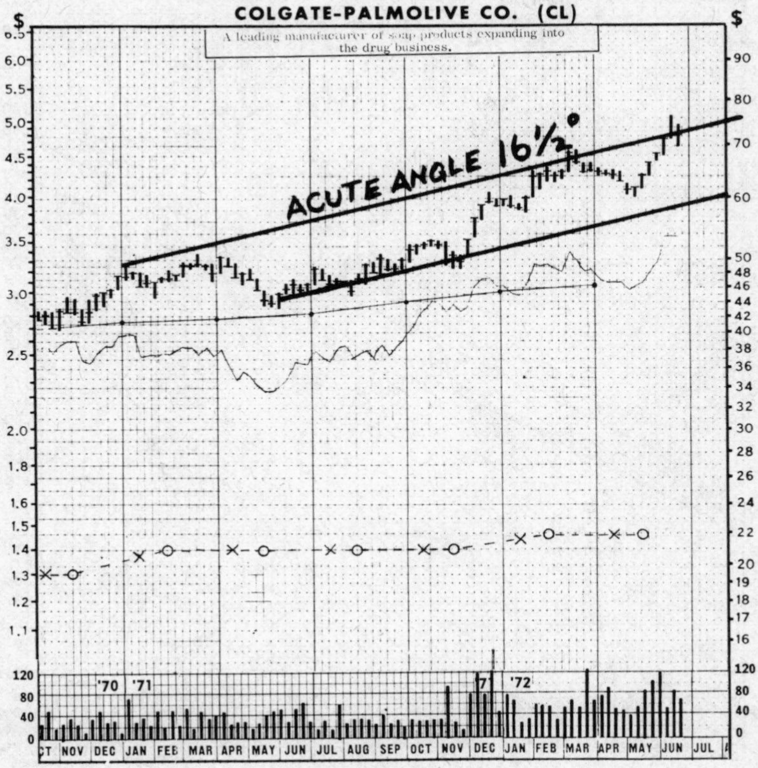
COLGATE-PALMOLIVE CO. (CL)
A leading manufacturer of soap products expanding into the drug business.
ACUTE ANGLE 16½°
$
6.0
5.5
5.0
4.5
4.0
3.5
3.0
2.5
2.0
1.8
1.6
1.5
1.4
1.3
1.2
1.1
90
80
70
60
50
48
46
44
42
40
38
36
34
32
30
28
26
24
22
20
19
18
17
16
120
80
40
0
'70
'71
'72
NOV
DEC
JAN
FEB
MAR
APR
MAY
JUN
JUL
AUG
SEP
OCT
NOV
DEC
JAN
FEB
MAR
APR
MAY
JUN
JUL

CHART 15–41

Illustrating how the application of the acute angle obtained from the 1938 low functioned to give the short-term trader buy signals when price touched the lower acute force line at approximately 45 in August, 1971, and at approximately 50 in November, 1971, and a sell signal when the price touched the upper acute force line at the 69 level in March, 1972.

SOURCE: Securities Research

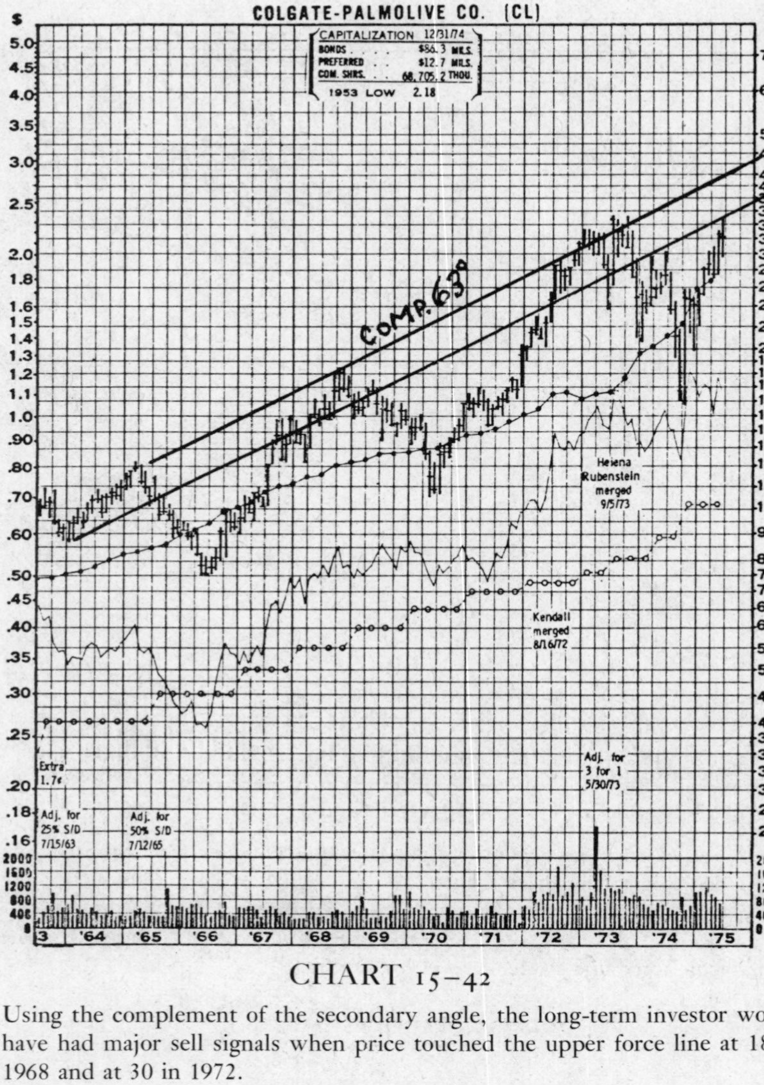
COLGATE-PALMOLIVE CO. (CL)
CAPITALIZATION 12/31/74
BONDS . . . . $86.3 MILS.
PREFERRED . . $12.7 MILS.
COM. SHRS. . . 68,705.2 THOU.
1953 LOW 2.18
COMP. 63°
Helena Rubenstein merged 9/5/73
Kendall merged 8/16/72
Adj. for 3 for 1 5/30/73
Extra 1.7¢
Adj. for 25% S/D 7/15/63
Adj. for 50% S/D 7/12/65
'64 '65 '66 '67 '68 '69 '70 '71 '72 '73 '74 '75

CHART 15–42

Using the complement of the secondary angle, the long-term investor would have had major sell signals when price touched the upper force line at 18 in 1968 and at 30 in 1972.

SOURCE: Securities Research

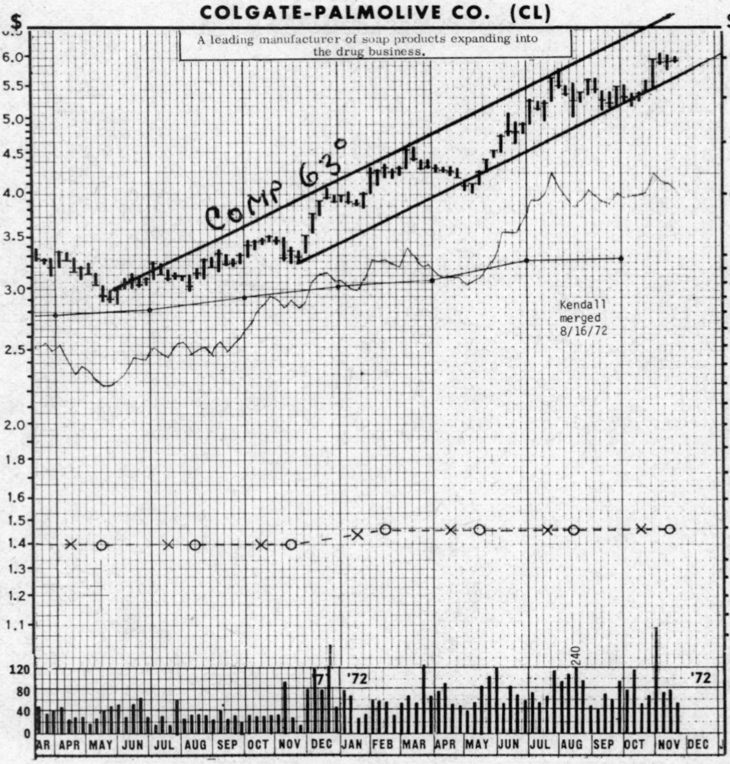
COLGATE-PALMOLIVE CO. (CL)
A leading manufacturer of soap products expanding into the drug business.
COMP 63°
Kendall merged 8/16/72
'71
'72
'72
240
AR APR MAY JUN JUL AUG SEP OCT NOV DEC JAN FEB MAR APR MAY JUN JUL AUG SEP OCT NOV DEC

CHART 15–43

Using the complement of the secondary angle, the short-term trader would have had a buy signal when price touched the lower force line at 64 in May, 1972, and a sell signal when price touched the upper force line at 86 in July, 1972.

SOURCE: Securities Research

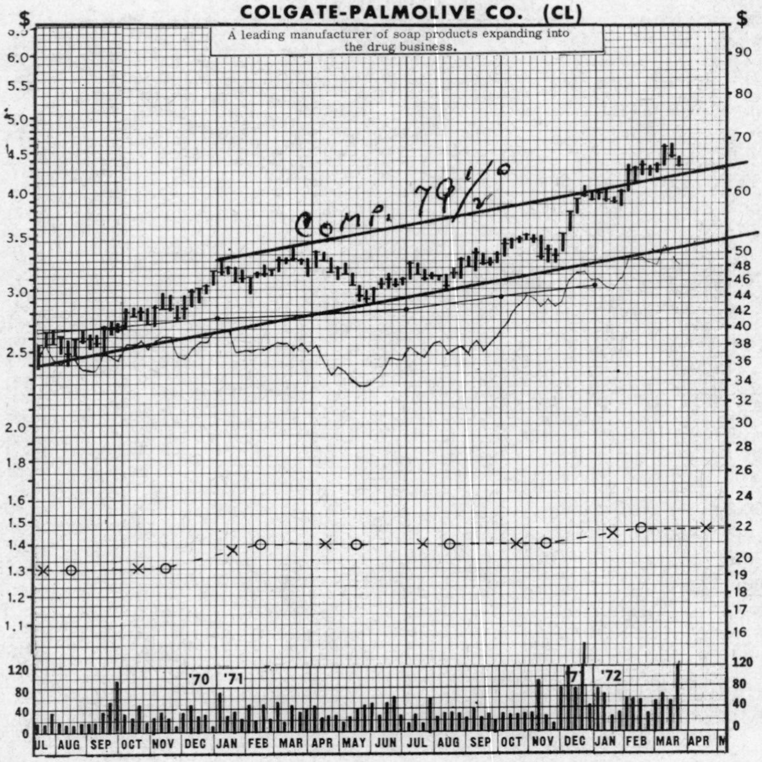
COLGATE-PALMOLIVE CO. (CL)
A leading manufacturer of soap products expanding into the drug business.
Comp. 79 1/2
'70 '71
'71 '72
JUL AUG SEP OCT NOV DEC JAN FEB MAR APR MAY JUN JUL AUG SEP OCT NOV DEC JAN FEB MAR APR

CHART 15–44

Using the complement of the principal angle, the short-term trader would have had buy signals when price touched the lower force line at 37 in August, 1970, 43 in May, 1971, and at 45 in August, 1971. A sell signal was provided when price touched the upper force line at 31 in March, 1971, and at 60 in December, 1971.

SOURCE: Securities Research

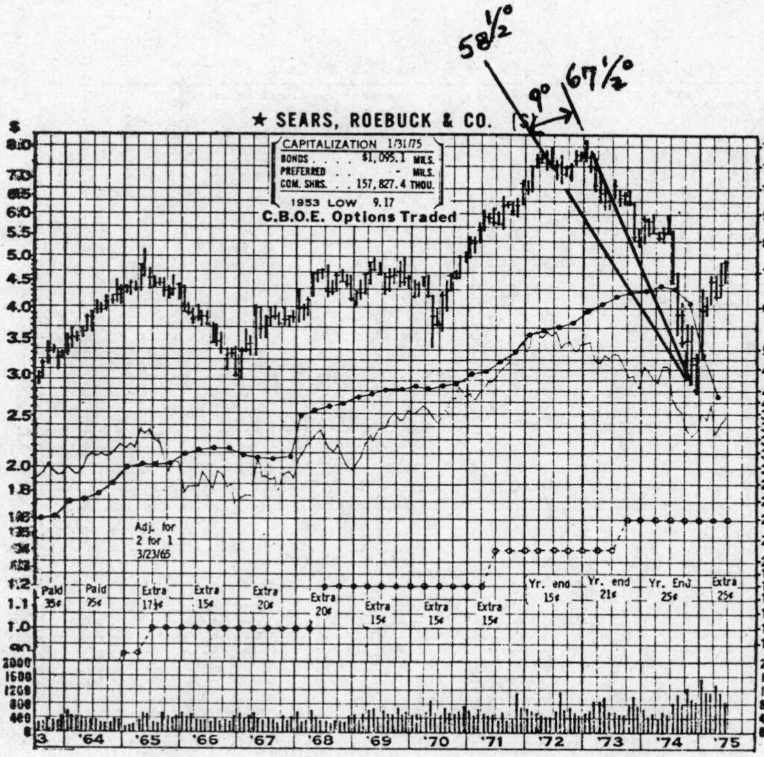
58½°
9°
67½°
★ SEARS, ROEBUCK & CO.
CAPITALIZATION 1/31/75
BONDS . . . . $1,095.1 MILS.
PREFERRED . . . - MILS.
COM. SHRS. . . 157,827.4 THOU.
1953 LOW 9.17
C.B.O.E. Options Traded
Adj. for 2 for 1 3/23/65
Paid 35¢
Paid 25¢
Extra 17½¢
Extra 15¢
Extra 20¢
Extra 20¢
Extra 15¢
Extra 15¢
Extra 15¢
Yr. end 15¢
Yr. end 21¢
Yr. End 25¢
Extra 25¢
'64 '65 '66 '67 '68 '69 '70 '71 '72 '73 '74 '75

CHART 15–45

Illustrating the three basic angles.

SOURCE: Securities Research

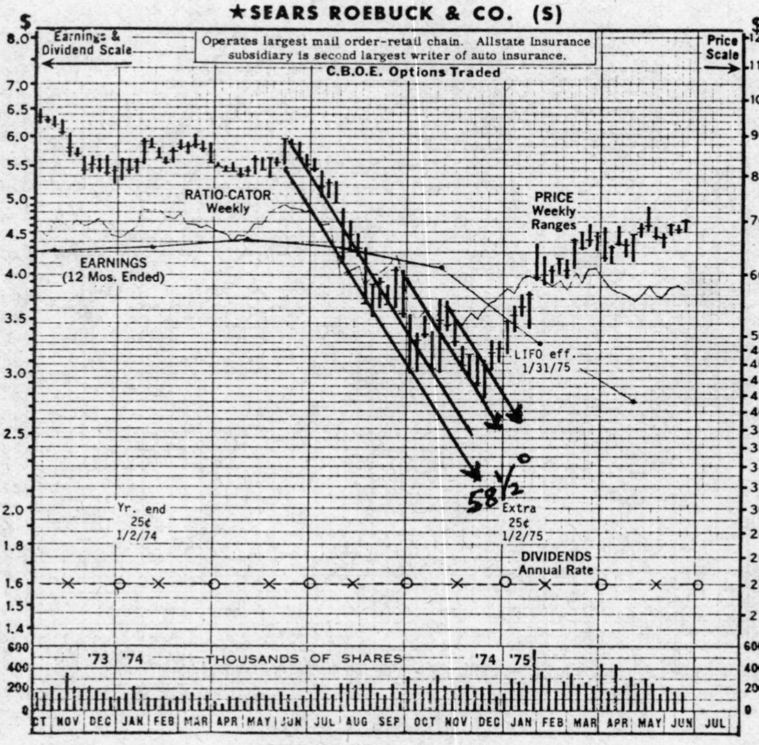
★SEARS ROEBUCK & CO. (S)
Earnings & Dividend Scale
Operates largest mail order-retail chain. Allstate Insurance subsidiary is second largest writer of auto insurance.
C.B.O.E. Options Traded
Price Scale
RATIO-CATOR Weekly
PRICE Weekly Ranges
EARNINGS (12 Mos. Ended)
LIFO eff. 1/31/75
58½
Yr. end 25¢ 1/2/74
Extra 25¢ 1/2/75
DIVIDENDS Annual Rate
THOUSANDS OF SHARES
'73 '74 '74 '75

CHART 15–46

Illustrating the secondary angle in a declining phase. Here we can see that the same angles employed to determine an advance can be used to determine a decline.

SOURCE: Securities Research

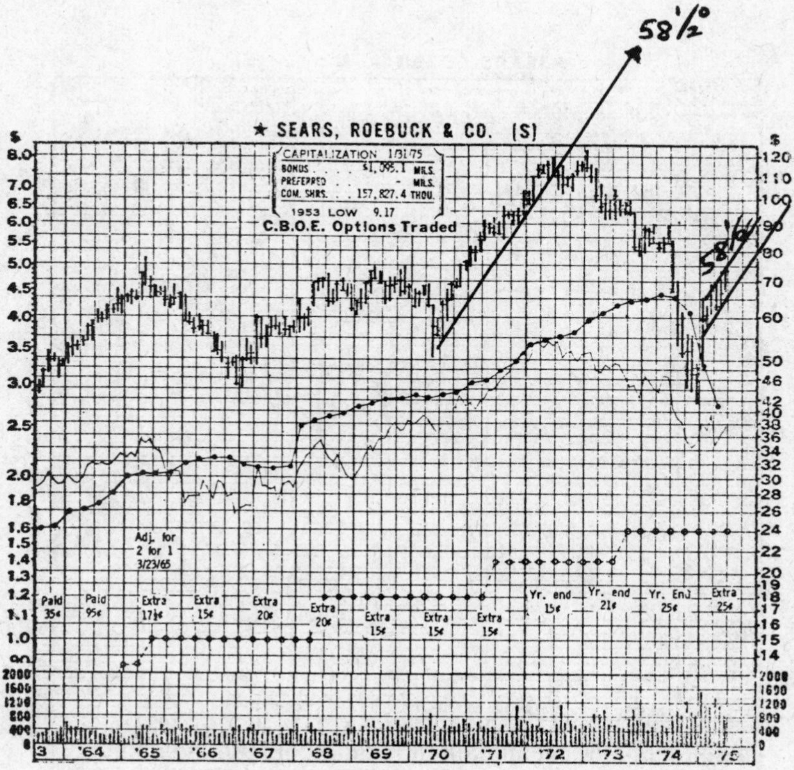
★ SEARS, ROEBUCK & CO. (S)
CAPITALIZATION 1/31/75
1953 LOW 9.17
C.B.O.E. Options Traded
58½°
Adj. for 2 for 1 3/23/65
'64
'65
'66
'67
'68
'69
'70
'71
'72
'73
'74
'75

CHART 15–47

The angle formations of the future have a relationship to the angle formations of the past, just as we have seen the angle formations of the past have a relationship to the angle formations of the future. Thus, we see here the secondary angle measured from the 1974 bottom functioning in 1970–71.

Source: Securities Research

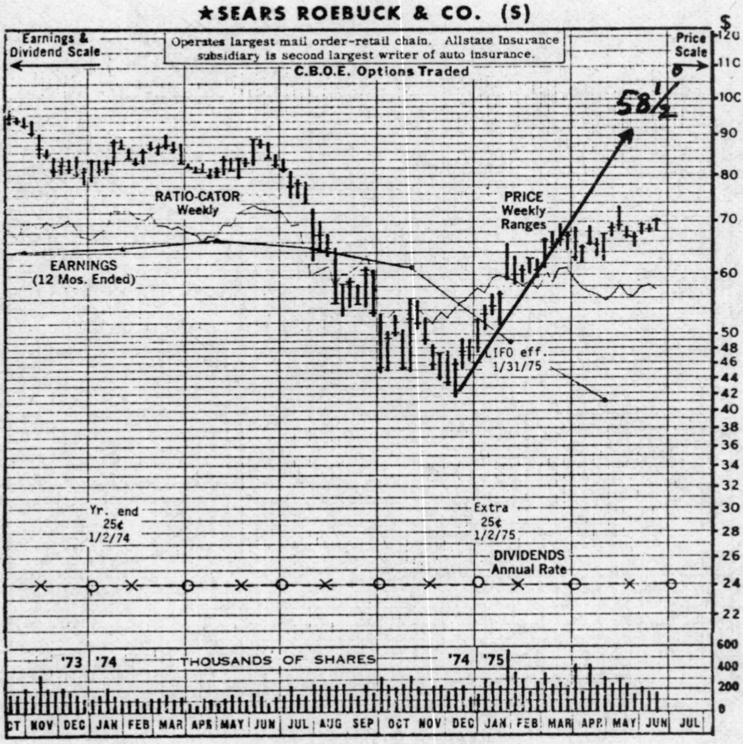
★SEARS ROEBUCK & CO. (S)
Earnings & Dividend Scale
Operates largest mail order-retail chain. Allstate Insurance subsidiary is second largest writer of auto insurance.
C.B.O.E. Options Traded
Price Scale
$
58½
RATIO-CATOR Weekly
PRICE Weekly Ranges
EARNINGS (12 Mos. Ended)
LIFO eff. 1/31/75
Yr. end 25¢ 1/2/74
Extra 25¢ 1/2/75
DIVIDENDS Annual Rate
'73 '74 THOUSANDS OF SHARES '74 '75
OCT NOV DEC JAN FEB MAR APR MAY JUN JUL AUG SEP OCT NOV DEC JAN FEB MAR APR MAY JUN JUL

CHART 15–48

Illustrating the use of the secondary angle on a monthly chart.

SOURCE: Securities Research

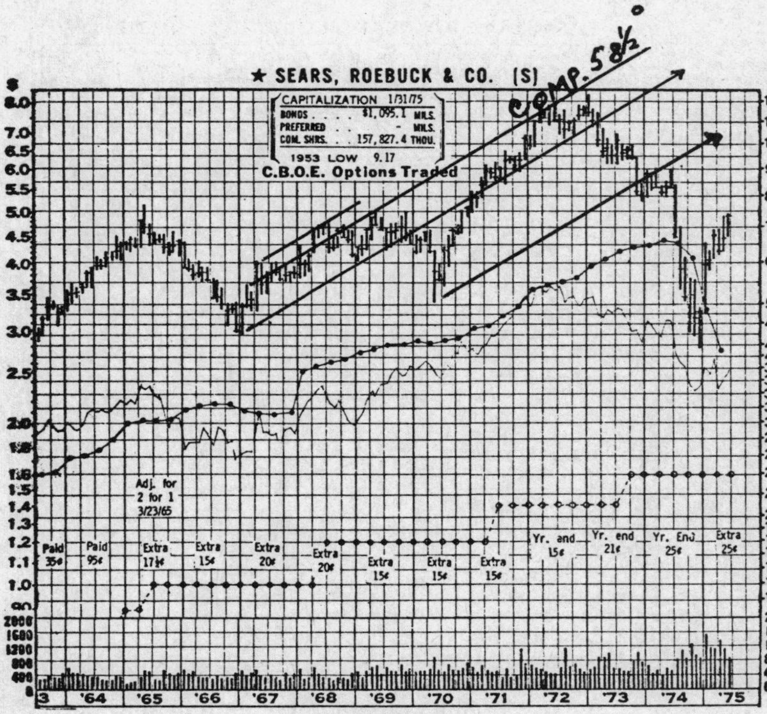
★ SEARS, ROEBUCK & CO. (S)
CAPITALIZATION 1/31/75
BONDS . . . . $1,095.1 MILS.
PREFERRED . . . - MILS.
COM. SHRS. . . 157,827.4 THOU.
1953 LOW 9.17
C.B.O.E. Options Traded
COMP. 58½
Adj. for 2 for 1 3/23/65
Paid 35¢
Paid 95¢
Extra 17½¢
Extra 15¢
Extra 20¢
Extra 20¢
Extra 15¢
Extra 15¢
Extra 15¢
Yr. and 15¢
Yr. end 21¢
Yr. End 25¢
Extra 25¢
'64
'65
'66
'67
'68
'69
'70
'71
'72
'73
'74
'75

CHART 15–49

This use of the complementary angle on a yearly chart illustrates the manner in which a highly active stock can be expected to proceed on the uptrend described by this channel for two to three years.

SOURCE: Securities Research

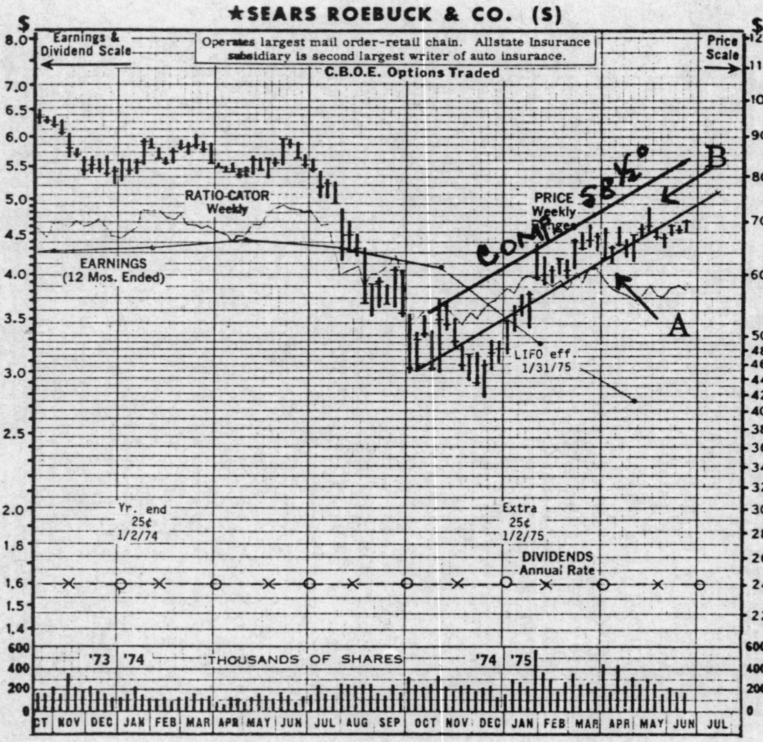
★SEARS ROEBUCK & CO. (S)
Earnings & Dividend Scale
Operates largest mail order-retail chain. Allstate Insurance subsidiary is second largest writer of auto insurance.
Price Scale
C.B.O.E. Options Traded
RATIO-CATOR Weekly
PRICE Weekly
COMP. 58½°
B
A
EARNINGS (12 Mos. Ended)
LIFO eff. 1/31/75
Yr. end 25¢ 1/2/74
Extra 25¢ 1/2/75
DIVIDENDS Annual Rate
'73 '74 THOUSANDS OF SHARES '74 '75
OCT NOV DEC JAN FEB MAR APR MAY JUN JUL AUG SEP OCT NOV DEC JAN FEB MAR APR MAY JUN JUL

CHART 15–50

Having approached a critical price level (70), Sears' price then moved sideways to penetrate the lower force line of the complement of the secondary angle (point A). This should suggest to the trader that the subsequent re-entry into the channel followed by an upside penetration of the critical price level (point B) is a sell signal (the breakout to a new high being a bear trap).

Source: Securities Research

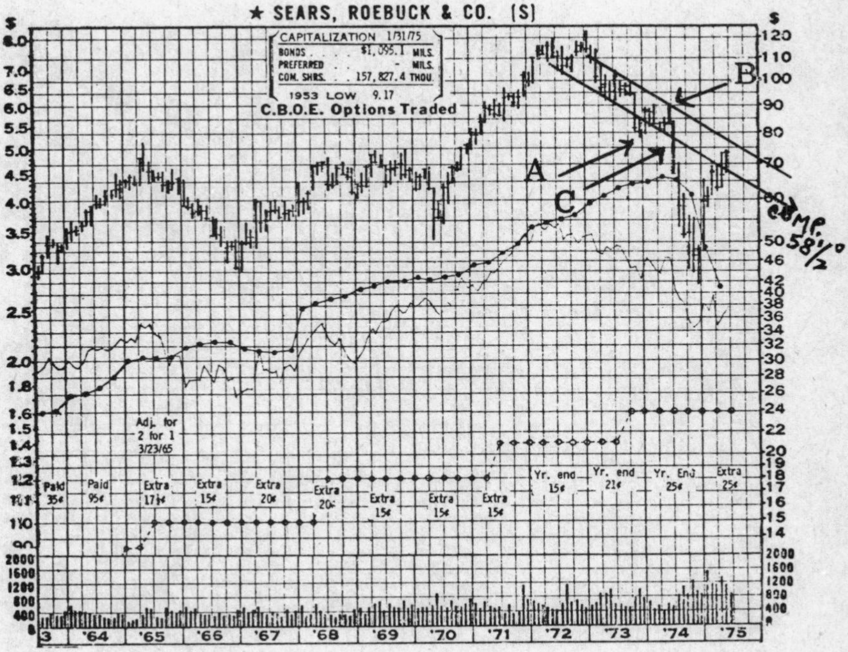
★ SEARS, ROEBUCK & CO. (S)
CAPITALIZATION 1/31/75
BONDS . . . $1,095.1 MILS.
PREFERRED . . - MILS.
COM. SHRS. . . 157,827.4 THOU.
1953 LOW 9.17
C.B.O.E. Options Traded
A
B
C
COMP. 58½
Adj. for 2 for 1 3/23/65
'64
'65
'66
'67
'68
'69
'70
'71
'72
'73
'74
'75

CHART 15–51

The value of the secondary angle when it is applied to the downtrend is that it can often provide the investor with the upside limits to which the stock will advance in the course of a rally high. The first penetration of the downside limits of the complementary angle channel (point A) is the signal that a second penetration (point C) is in the planning stages. On this first penetration, the specialist accumulates stock he will distribute at a critical price level (point B) subsequent to a re-entry into the channel. The sell signal is provided with the appearance of big blocks at or near the upper critical price level.

Source: Securities Research

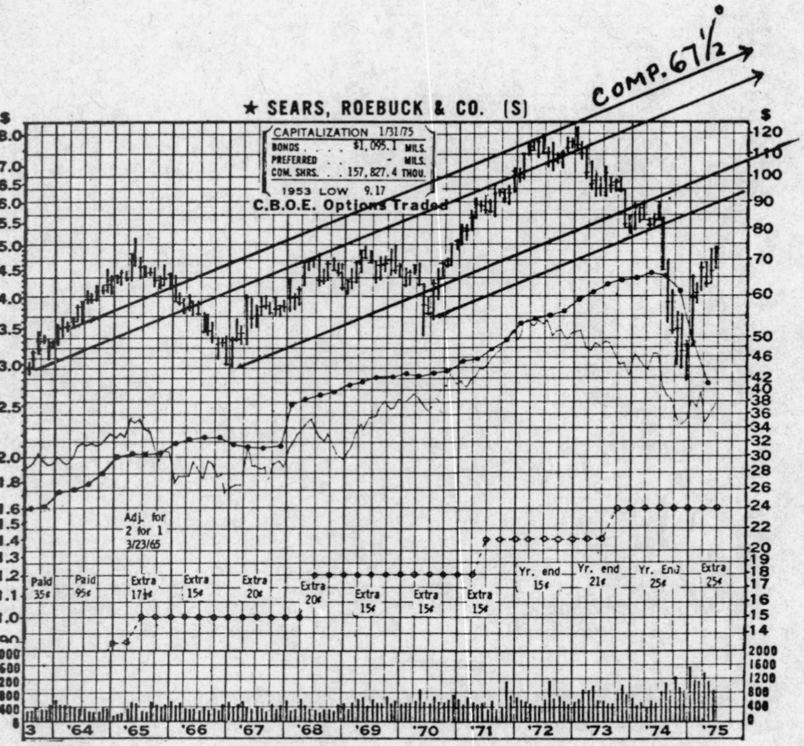
COMP. 67½
★ SEARS, ROEBUCK & CO. (S)
CAPITALIZATION 1/31/75
BONDS . . . . $1,095.1 MILS.
PREFERRED . . - MILS.
COM. SHRS. . . 157,827.4 THOU.
1953 LOW 9.17
C.B.O.E. Options Traded
Adj. for 2 for 1 3/23/65
Paid 35¢
Paid 95¢
Extra 17½¢
Extra 15¢
Extra 20¢
Extra 20¢
Extra 15¢
Extra 15¢
Extra 15¢
Yr. end 15¢
Yr. end 21¢
Yr. End 25¢
Extra 25¢
'64
'65
'66
'67
'68
'69
'70
'71
'72
'73
'74
'75

CHART 15–52

Employed on a long-term chart, the complement of the principal angle, when used in conjunction with price and volume figures, can provide the investor with an instrument for the timing of his buy and sell signals.

SOURCE: Securities Research

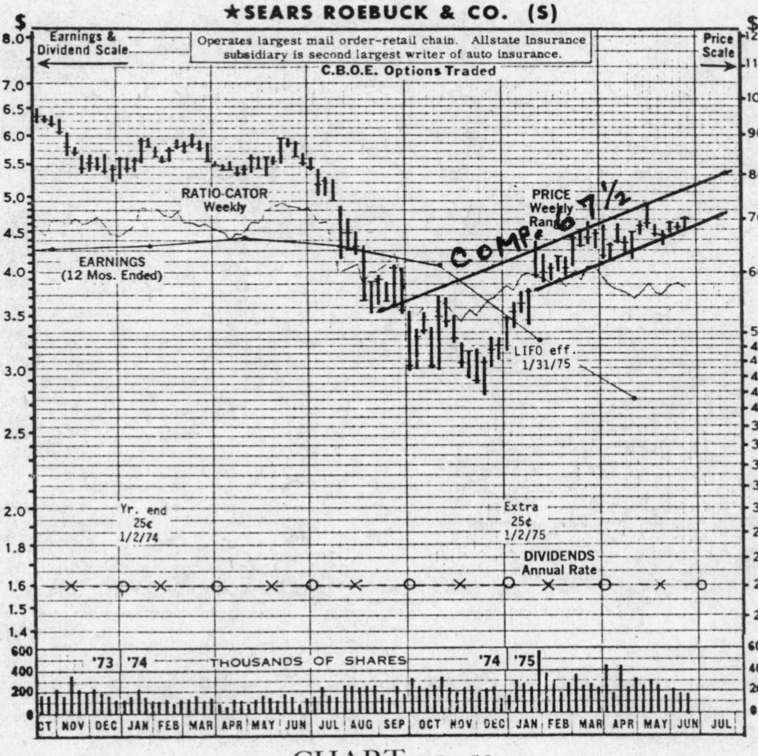
★SEARS ROEBUCK & CO. (S)
Earnings & Dividend Scale
Operates largest mail order-retail chain. Allstate Insurance subsidiary is second largest writer of auto insurance.
C.B.O.E. Options Traded
Price Scale
RATIO-CATOR Weekly
EARNINGS (12 Mos. Ended)
PRICE Weekly Range
COMP. 67½
LIFO eff. 1/31/75
Yr. end 25¢ 1/2/74
Extra 25¢ 1/2/75
DIVIDENDS Annual Rate
'73 '74 THOUSANDS OF SHARES '74 '75
CT NOV DEC JAN FEB MAR APR MAY JUN JUL AUG SEP OCT NOV DEC JAN FEB MAR APR MAY JUN JUL

CHART 15–53

Note how the two force lines of the complement of the principal angle establish an intermediate term trading channel.

SOURCE: Securities Research

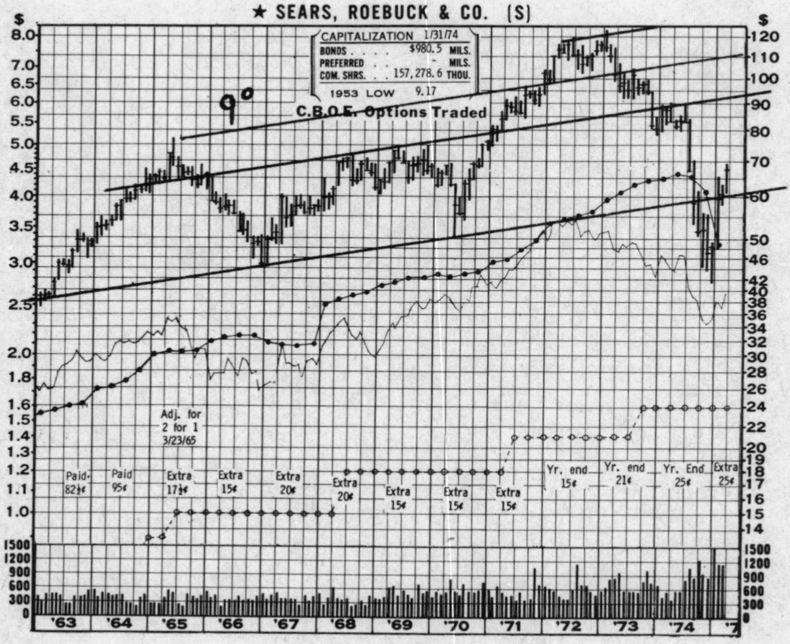
★ SEARS, ROEBUCK & CO. (S)
CAPITALIZATION 1/31/74
BONDS . . . . $980.5 MILS.
PREFERRED . . - MILS.
COM. SHRS. . . 157,278.6 THOU.
1953 LOW 9.17
C.B.O.E. Options Traded
9°
Adj. for 2 for 1 3/23/65
Paid 82½¢
Paid 95¢
Extra 17½¢
Extra 15¢
Extra 20¢
Extra 20¢
Extra 15¢
Extra 15¢
Extra 15¢
Yr. end 15¢
Yr. end 21¢
Yr. End 25¢
Extra 25¢
'63
'64
'65
'66
'67
'68
'69
'70
'71
'72
'73
'74

CHART 15–54

The chartist will find that the acute angle is an excellent tool as a forecaster of long-term price trends. It is, therefore, a most useful angle for the estimation of buy and sell signals for the long-term investor, especially when he uses it in conjunction with the price and volume figures on a yearly chart. This is illustrated by Charts 15-39, 15-40, and 15-54.

SOURCE: Securities Research

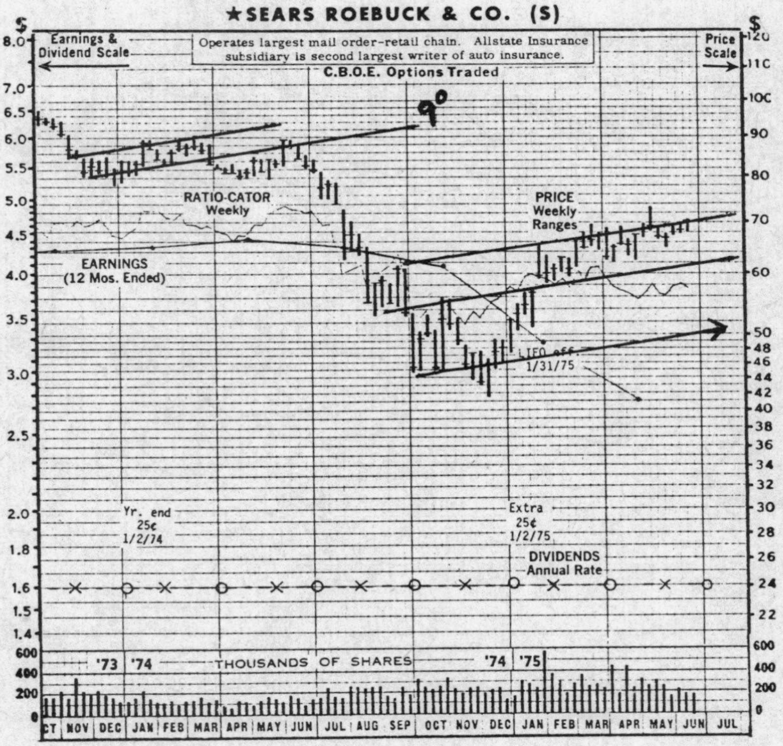
★SEARS ROEBUCK & CO. (S)
Earnings & Dividend Scale
Operates largest mail order-retail chain. Allstate Insurance subsidiary is second largest writer of auto insurance.
Price Scale
C.B.O.E. Options Traded
9°
RATIO-CATOR Weekly
PRICE Weekly Ranges
EARNINGS (12 Mos. Ended)
LIFO off 1/31/75
Yr. end 25¢ 1/2/74
Extra 25¢ 1/2/75
DIVIDENDS Annual Rate
'73 '74
THOUSANDS OF SHARES
'74 '75
CT NOV DEC JAN FEB MAR APR MAY JUN JUL AUG SEP OCT NOV DEC JAN FEB MAR APR MAY JUN JUL

CHART 15–55

While the acute angle is essentially oriented to calling buy and sell signals for investment purposes, oftentimes the use of the acute angle on the monthly chart is also for designating the timing of short-term purchases and sales.

SOURCE: Securities Research

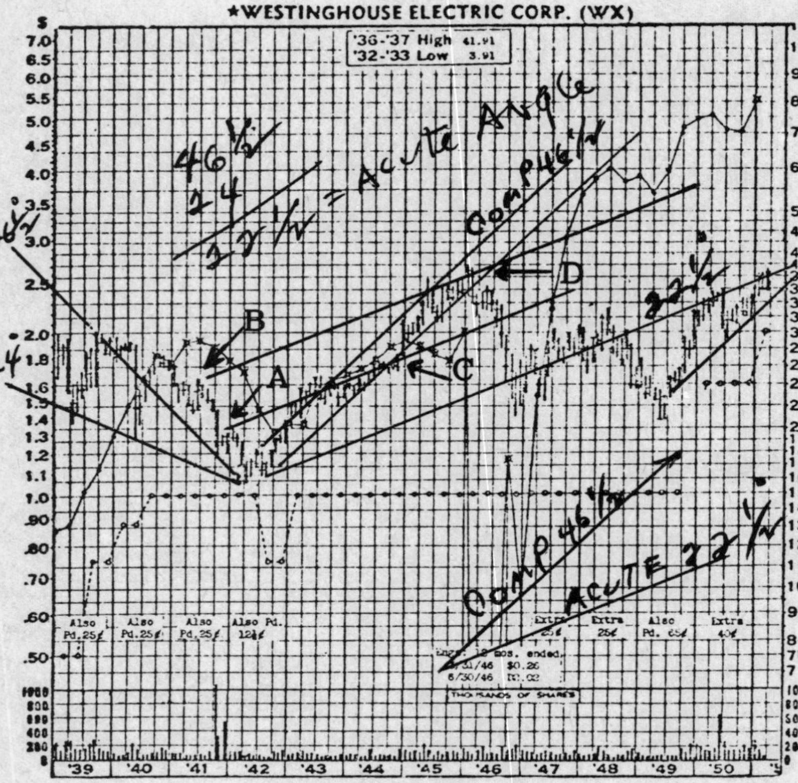
★WESTINGHOUSE ELECTRIC CORP. (WX)
'36-'37 High 41.91
'32-'33 Low 3.91
46½
24
22½ = Acute Angle
Comp 46½
B
A
C
D
22½
Comp 46½
Acute 22½
'39
'40
'41
'42
'43
'44
'45
'46
'47
'48
'49
'50

CHART 15–56

This chart illustrates the use of the three basic angles, principal, secondary, and acute. We see the manner in which the complement of the principal angle functions to establish an intermediate-term channel extending from 1942 through 1945. Careful note should be made of the manner in which the force line of the acute angle drawn from the high at point A acts to guide the direction of price until the breakout on the upside in December, 1944 (point C). The force line of the acute angle drawn from point B can be seen to then dominate the direction of trend from the point of intersection with the complement of the principal angle. It should also be noted that a change in the direction of price occurs as it moves to the apex of the angle formed by the intersection of the acute and complementary angles at point D.

Source: Securities Research

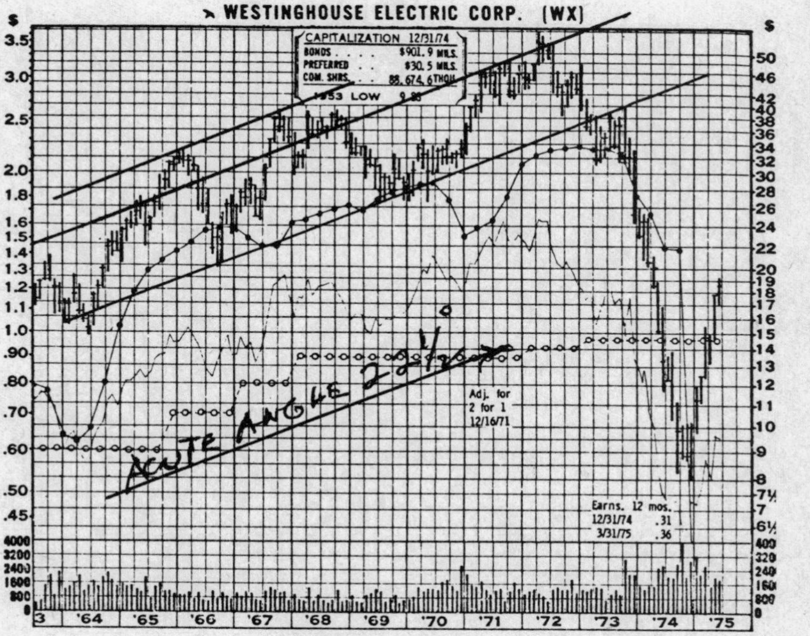
WESTINGHOUSE ELECTRIC CORP. (WX)
CAPITALIZATION 12/31/74
BONDS . . . . $901.9 MILS.
PREFERRED . . $30.5 MILS.
COM. SHRS. . . 88,674.6 THOU.
1953 LOW 9.85
ACUTE ANGLE 22½°
Adj. for 2 for 1 12/16/71
Earns. 12 mos.
12/31/74 .31
3/31/75 .36
'64
'65
'66
'67
'68
'69
'70
'71
'72
'73
'74
'75

CHART 15–57

This chart shows the manner in which the acute angle can, when used in conjunction with price and volume figures, assist the investor in the timing of his purchases and sales for long-term capital gains purposes. For example, the investor would have been given a buy signal as the price of Westinghouse advanced through the lower force line of the 22½° acute angle in July, 1964. He would then have had a sell signal when it touched the acute angle upper force line in the second quarter of 1965. Another buy signal was given when price touched the lower force line in the third quarter of 1966. The investor would then have anticipated the next sell signal when price touched the uppermost force line in the fourth quarter of 1967.

Source: Securities Research

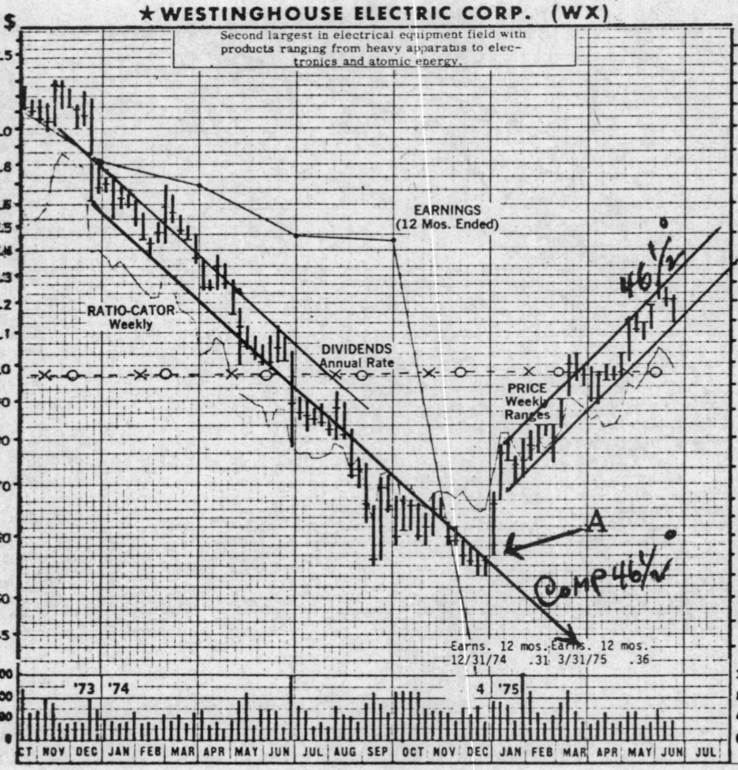
★ WESTINGHOUSE ELECTRIC CORP. (WX)
Second largest in electrical equipment field with products ranging from heavy apparatus to electronics and atomic energy.
EARNINGS (12 Mos. Ended)
RATIO-CATOR Weekly
DIVIDENDS Annual Rate
PRICE Weekly Ranges
46½
A
COMP 46½
Earns. 12 mos. 12/31/74 .31
Earns. 12 mos. 3/31/75 .36
'73
'74
4
'75
CT NOV DEC JAN FEB MAR APR MAY JUN JUL AUG SEP OCT NOV DEC JAN FEB MAR APR MAY JUN JUL

CHART 15–58

When deterioration has continued under a force line for a period of several months in the course of a downtrend, a sharp upside gap penetration of the force line (point A) should be considered a buy signal by the trader. It is often the case that when the complement of a principal angle functions in the course of a major downtrend the principal angle itself can be used to establish an intermediate-term uptrend channel.

SOURCE: Securities Research

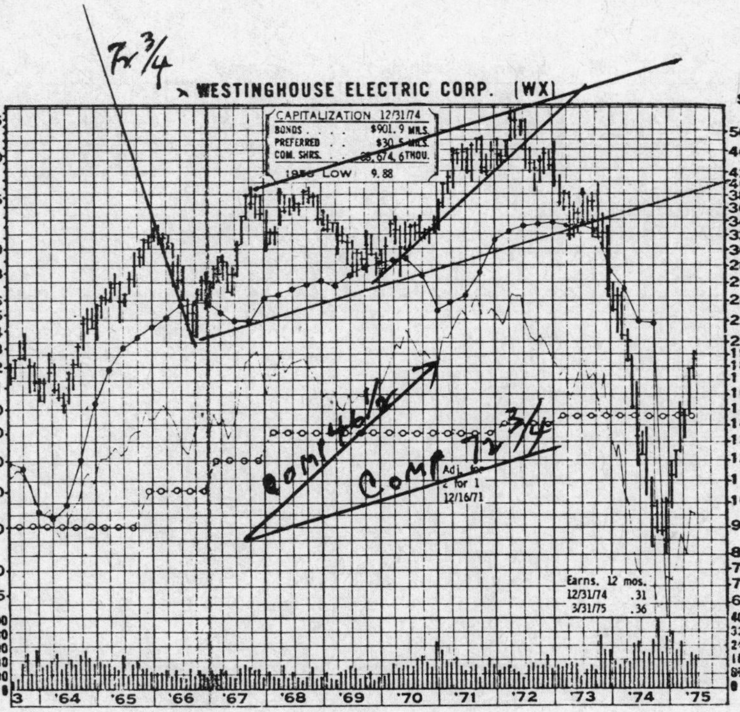
WESTINGHOUSE ELECTRIC CORP. (WX)
CAPITALIZATION 12/31/74
BONDS . . . . $901.9 MILS.
PREFERRED . . $30.5 MILS.
COM. SHRS. . . 88,674,6THOU.
Adj. for 2 for 1 12/16/71
Earns. 12 mos.
12/31/74 .31
3/31/75 .36
'64
'65
'66
'67
'68
'69
'70
'71
'72
'73
'74
'75

CHART 15–59

In order to refine and update the use of angles, it is always good policy to establish new principal (and secondary) angles from another low or a more recent low. In this chart we have projected our principal angle from the low of 1966. This has given us a complementary angle of 17¼°, which would have made it possible for us, among other things, to have timed the sale of Westinghouse with extraordinary precision in 1967 and 1972. The use of the complement of the principal angle drawn from the 1942 low with the complement of the principal angle drawn from the 1966 low enabled us to anticipate the sell signal (in 1972) as the price of the stock moved toward the apex of the vector formed by the intersection of the two lines.

Source: Securities Research

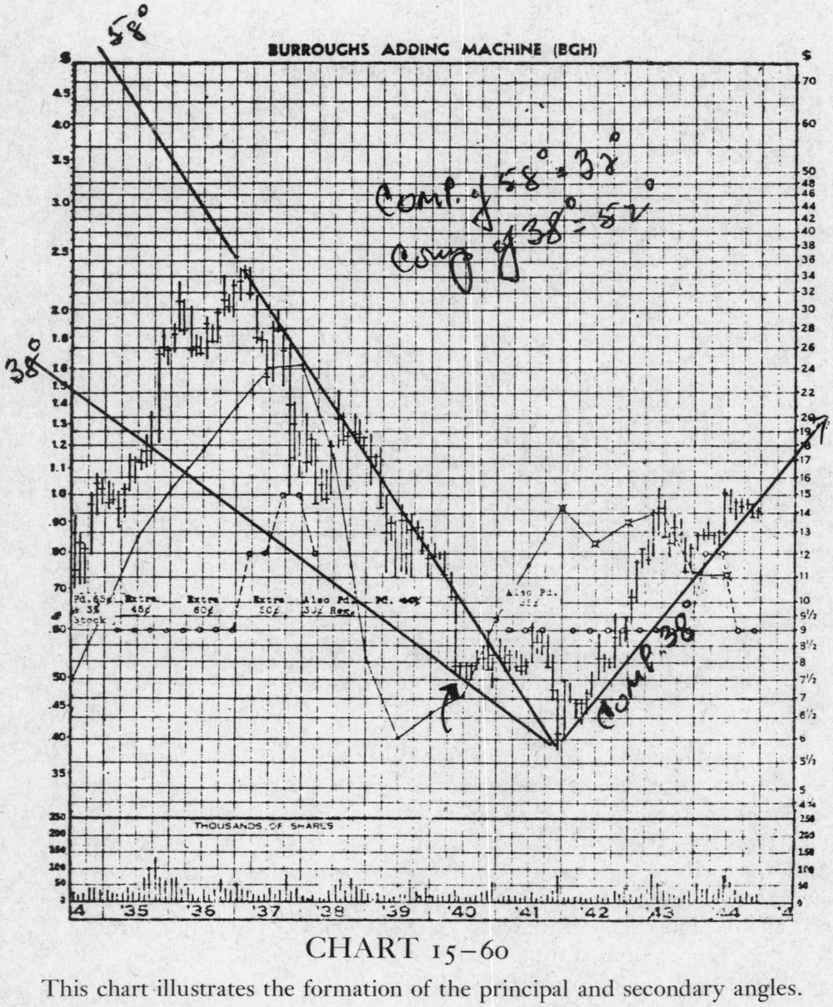
BURROUGHS ADDING MACHINE (BGH)
THOUSANDS OF SHARES
'35
'36
'37
'38
'39
'40
'41
'42
'43
'44

CHART 15–60

This chart illustrates the formation of the principal and secondary angles.

SOURCE: Securities Research

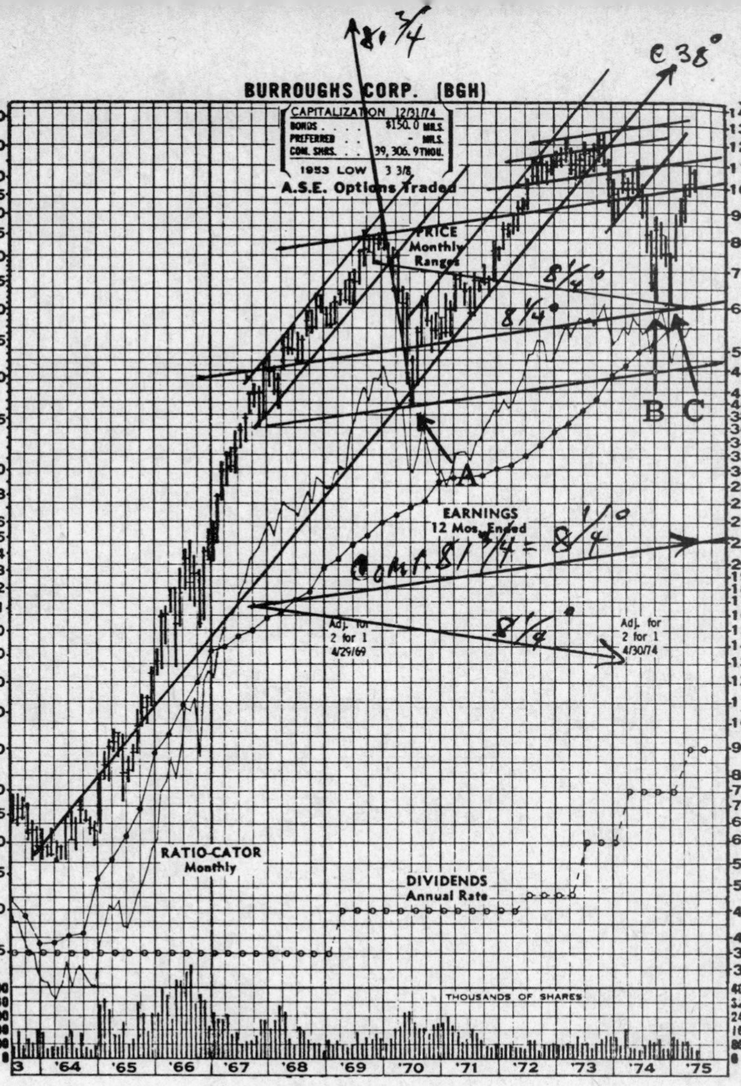
BURROUGHS CORP. (BGH)
CAPITALIZATION 12/31/74
BONDS . . . $150.0 MILS.
PREFERRED . . . - MILS.
COM. SHRS. . . 39,306.9 THOU.
1953 LOW 3 3/8
A.S.E. Options Traded
PRICE Monthly Ranges
EARNINGS 12 Mos. Ended
Adj. for 2 for 1 4/29/69
Adj. for 2 for 1 4/30/74
RATIO-CATOR Monthly
DIVIDENDS Annual Rate
THOUSANDS OF SHARES
A
B
C
'64
'65
'66
'67
'68
'69
'70
'71
'72
'73
'74
'75

CHART 15–61

This chart illustrates the use of the complement (8¼°) of the principal angle (81¾°) in one year (1970) with the complement (52°) of the secondary angle (38°) of another year (1941). Having established the long-term channel trends with the complement of the 38° angle, we can see the complement of the 81¾° angle enables us to anticipate and confirm the buy signals provided by price and volume figures in 1970 (point A). The value of the downtrending complement (8¼°) of the principal angle established in 1970 when utilized in conjunction with the uptrending complement (8¼°) of that same angle is that, although it is the downtrending angle that provides us with the first and second buy signals in 1974 in Burroughs (at points B and C), the proximity of the uptrending complementary angle serves to confirm the signal. It is also interesting to observe that the complement of the principal angle is sometimes more effective for indicating the long-term direction of stock prices than the acute angle.

Source: Securities Research

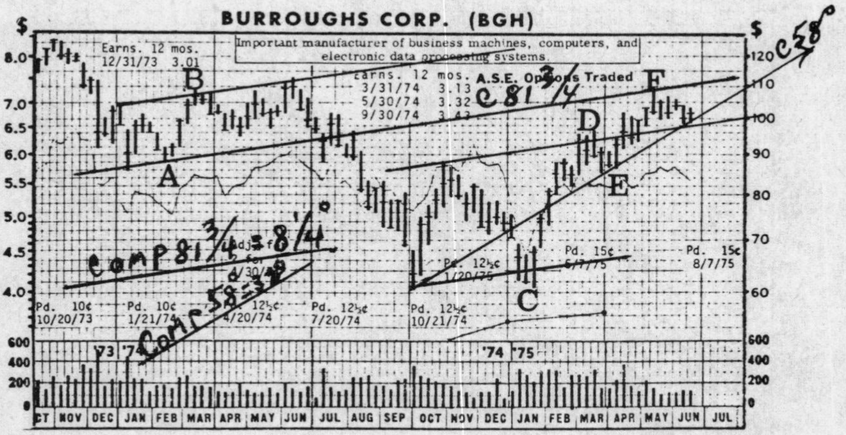
BURROUGHS CORP. (BGH)
Important manufacturer of business machines, computers, and electronic data processing systems.
Earns. 12 mos. 12/31/73 3.01
Earns. 12 mos. 3/31/74 3.13 5/30/74 3.32
A.S.E. Options Traded
C 81¾
C 58°
Comp 81¾ = 8¼°
Comp 58 = 32
A
B
C
D
E
F
Pd. 10¢ 10/20/73
Pd. 10¢ 1/21/74
Pd. 12½¢ 4/20/74
Pd. 12½¢ 7/20/74
Pd. 12½¢ 10/21/74
Pd. 15¢ 8/7/75
NOV DEC JAN FEB MAR APR MAY JUN JUL AUG SEP OCT NOV DEC JAN FEB MAR APR MAY JUN JUL

CHART 15–62

Once again we see the value of the complement (8¼°) of a principal angle (81¾°) when used as a trading tool in conjunction with the complement (32°) of another principal angle (58°). Buy signals were provided when the price touched the complement of the 81¾° force line at point A and a sell signal when it touched the same upper force line at point B. Another buy signal was given when price advanced through the complement of the 81¾° force line at point C and the sell signal given when it touched the force line at point D. A buy signal was again provided the trader when this stock touched the complement of the 58° principal angle at point E and a sell signal was given when it touched the complement of the 81¾° force line at point F.

Source: Securities Research

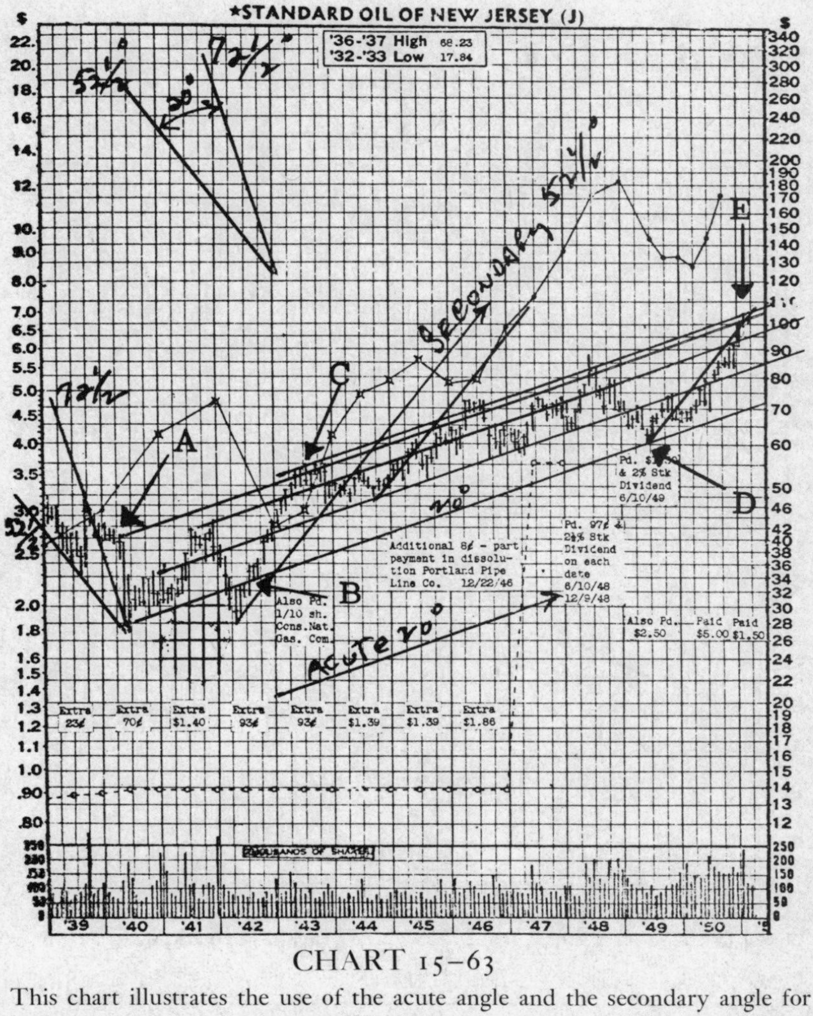

*STANDARD OIL OF NEW JERSEY (J)
'36-'37 High 68.23
'32-'33 Low 17.84
A
B
C
D
E
Secondary
Acute 20°
Additional 8¢ - part payment in dissolution Portland Pipe Line Co. 12/22/46
Also Pd. 1/10 sh. Cons.Nat. Gas. Com.
Pd. 97¢ & 2½% Stk Dividend on each date 6/10/48 12/9/48
& 2% Stk Dividend 6/10/49
Also Pd. $2.50
Paid $5.00
Paid $1.50
Extra 23¢
Extra 70¢
Extra $1.40
Extra 93¢
Extra 93¢
Extra $1.39
Extra $1.39
Extra $1.86
'39
'40
'41
'42
'43
'44
'45
'46
'47
'48
'49
'50

CHART 15-63

This chart illustrates the use of the acute angle and the secondary angle for long-term investment purposes. When price penetrated the acute force line at point B on the upside the investor would have had a buy signal. Then drawing an acute force line from point A, the investor would have had a sell signal when price touched this force line at point C. He would have had another buy signal at point D and a sell signal at point E.

SOURCE: Securities Research

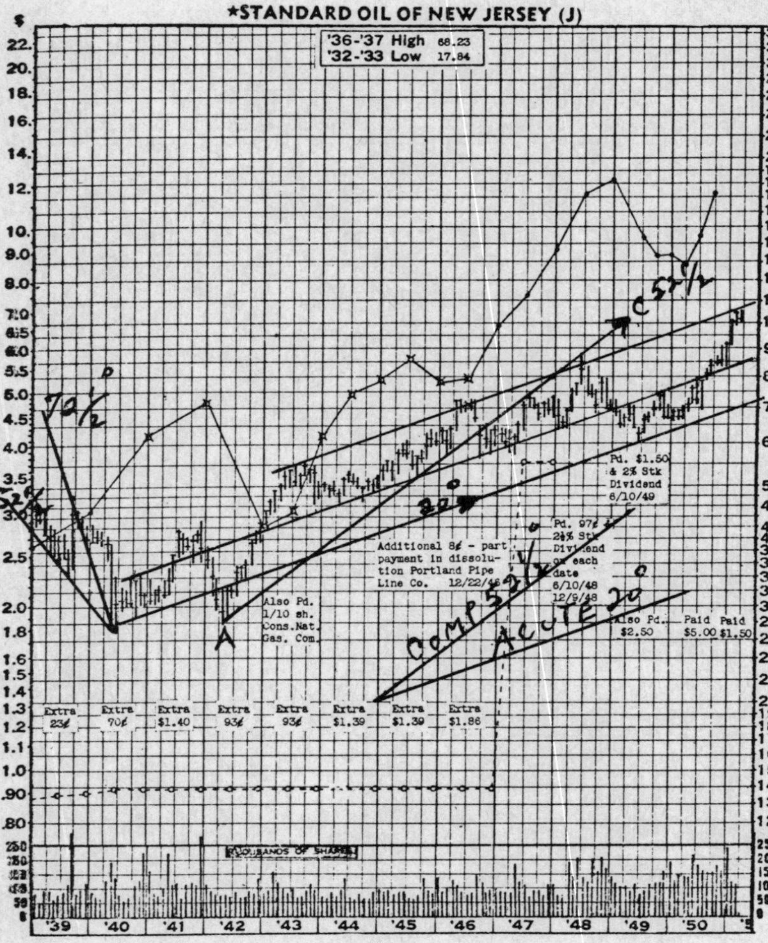
★STANDARD OIL OF NEW JERSEY (J)
'36-'37 High 68.23
'32-'33 Low 17.84
70½°
52½°
A
C 52½°
37½°
COMP 52½°
ACUTE 20°
Also Pd. 1/10 sh. Cons.Nat. Gas. Com.
Additional 8¢ - part payment in dissolution Portland Pipe Line Co. 12/22/48
Pd. $1.50 & 2% Stk Dividend 6/10/49
Pd. 97¢ + 2½% Stk Dividend on each date 6/10/48 12/9/48
Also Pd. $2.50
Paid $5.00
Paid $1.50
Extra 23¢
Extra 70¢
Extra $1.40
Extra 93¢
Extra 93¢
Extra $1.39
Extra $1.39
Extra $1.86
THOUSANDS OF SHARES
'39 '40 '41 '42 '43 '44 '45 '46 '47 '48 '49 '50

CHART 15–64

Employing the complement (37½°) of the secondary angle (52½°) instead of the secondary angle itself from point A, we find we have established a force line more suited to long-term investment purposes.

SOURCE: Securities Research

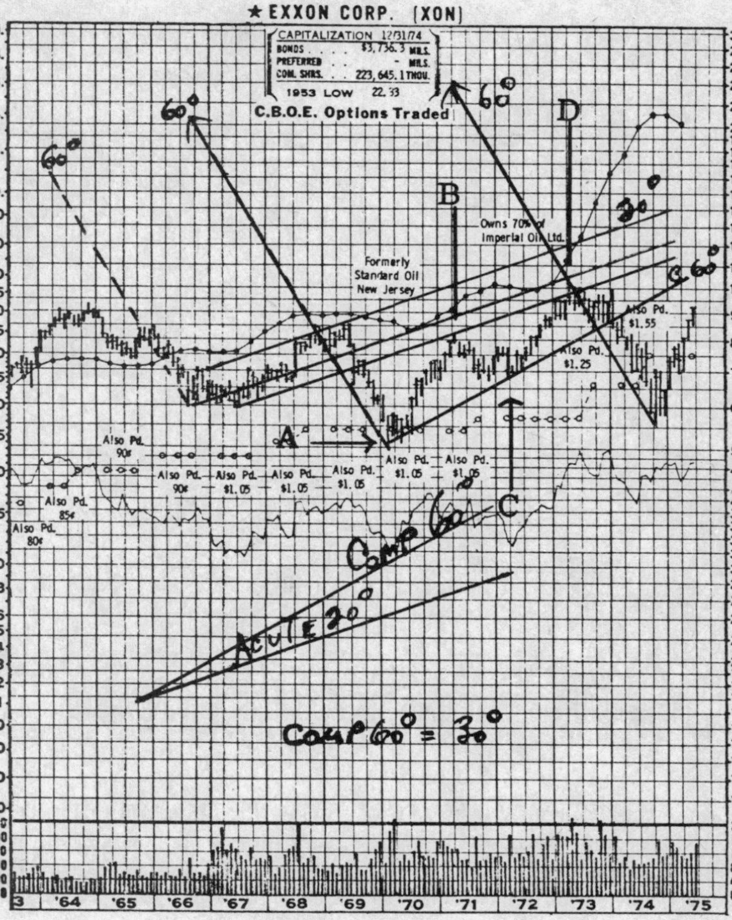
★ EXXON CORP. (XON)
CAPITALIZATION 12/31/74
BONDS . . . . $3,736.3 MILS.
PREFERRED . . . - MILS.
COM. SHRS. . . 223,645.1 THOU.
1953 LOW 22.33
C.B.O.E. Options Traded
60°
A
B
C
D
30°
Owns 70% of Imperial Oil Ltd.
Formerly Standard Oil New Jersey
Also Pd. $1.55
Also Pd. $1.25
Also Pd. 90¢
Also Pd. 85¢
Also Pd. 80¢
Also Pd. $1.05
COMP 60°
ACUTE 30°
COMP 60° = 30°
'64 '65 '66 '67 '68 '69 '70 '71 '72 '73 '74 '75

CHART 15–65

The long-term investment principle also obtains in this chart by employing the complement (30°) of the principal angle (60°) established in 1970. It is worth noting that the 60° principal angle tends to repeat itself from a number of this stock's important bottoms. When the investor extended the complement of the 60° principal angle from point A in 1970 he would have had a buy signal when the price of Exxon touched this line in March. He would then have had a sell signal when price touched the acute angle at point B. Another long-term buy signal was triggered when price touched the complement of the 60° force line in March, 1972, at point C and a sell signal when it touched the acute angle force line at point D.

SOURCE: Securities Research

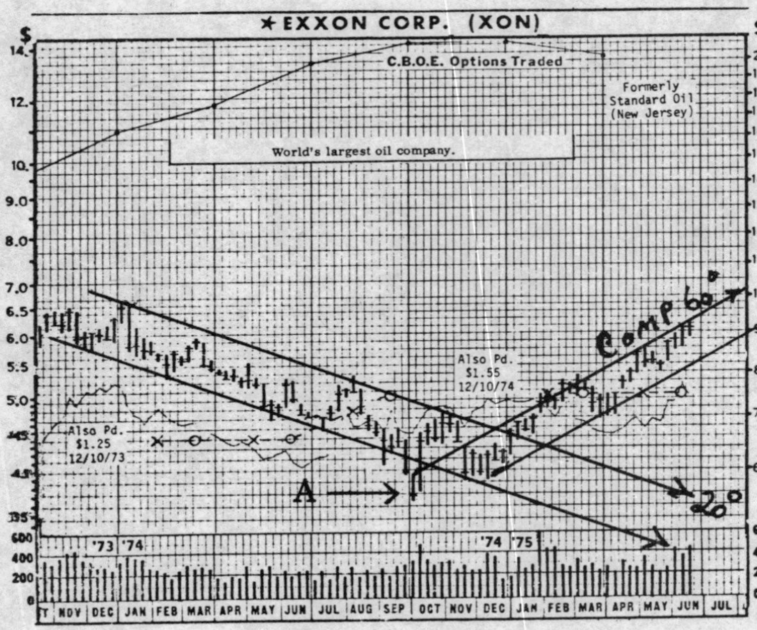
EXXON CORP. (XON)
C.B.O.E. Options Traded
Formerly Standard Oil (New Jersey)
World's largest oil company.
Also Pd. $1.55 12/10/74
Also Pd. $1.25 12/10/73
A
Comp 60°
20°
'73 '74
'74 '75
NOV DEC JAN FEB MAR APR MAY JUN JUL AUG SEP OCT NOV DEC JAN FEB MAR APR MAY JUN JUL

CHART 15–66

The use of the acute angle in this chart provides the trader with an excellent tool for short-selling purposes. Using the downward trend channel formed by the lower and upper acute force lines, the trader would have sold short at 100 in January, 1974, and covered when price touched the lower force line at 80 in February. He could then have sold short when price touched the upper force line at 77½ in August and covered when it touched the lower line at 64 in September. Had the trader bought on the signal provided by the volume figures at 55 at point A, he could then have sold when price once again touched the declining acute angle at 70 in November. It is interesting to observe that the complement of the 60° principal angle established in 1970 accommodated the 1975 uptrend in this stock. This becomes more understandable when one notes that the principal angle from the 1974 low was also 60°.

SOURCE: Securities Research

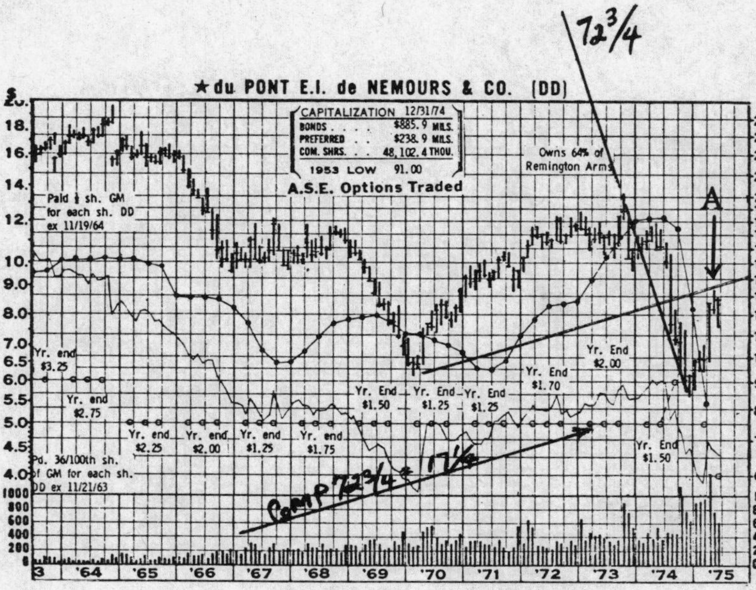
72 3/4
★du PONT E.I. de NEMOURS & CO. (DD)
CAPITALIZATION 12/31/74
BONDS . . . . $885.9 MILS.
PREFERRED . . $238.9 MILS.
COM. SHRS. . . 48,102.4 THOU.
1953 LOW 91.00
A.S.E. Options Traded
Owns 64% of Remington Arms
A
Paid ½ sh. GM for each sh. DD ex 11/19/64
Yr. end $3.25
Yr. end $2.75
Yr. end $2.25
Yr. end $2.00
Yr. end $1.25
Yr. end $1.75
Yr. End $1.50
Yr. End $1.25
Yr. End $1.25
Yr. End $1.70
Yr. End $2.00
Yr. End $1.50
Pd. 36/100th sh. of GM for each sh. DD ex 11/21/63
Comp 72 3/4 = 17 1/4
'64
'65
'66
'67
'68
'69
'70
'71
'72
'73
'74
'75

CHART 15–67

In the charts of Du Pont, United Technologies, and Eastman Kodak, we see that the complement of the principal angle drawn from the 1974 low of each stock provides us with a sell signal when price advances to touch the complementary force line at point A on each chart.

SOURCE: Securities Research

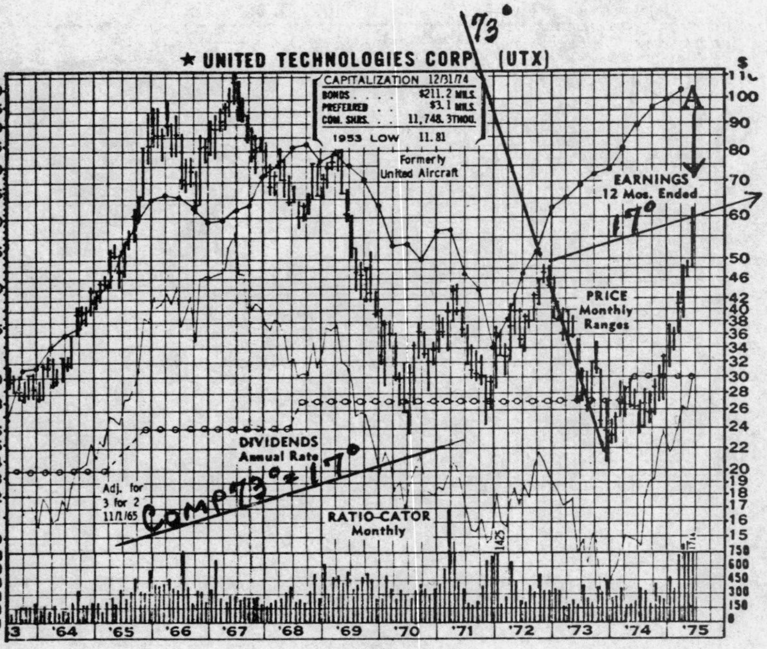
★ UNITED TECHNOLOGIES CORP (UTX)
CAPITALIZATION 12/31/74
BONDS . . . $211.2 MILS.
PREFERRED . . $3.1 MILS.
COM. SHRS. . . 11,748.3THOU.
1953 LOW 11.81
Formerly United Aircraft
EARNINGS 12 Mos. Ended
PRICE Monthly Ranges
DIVIDENDS Annual Rate
Adj. for 3 for 2 11/1/65
RATIO-CATOR Monthly
73°
17°
Comp 73° = 17°
A
'64 '65 '66 '67 '68 '69 '70 '71 '72 '73 '74 '75

CHART 15–68

SOURCE: Securities Research

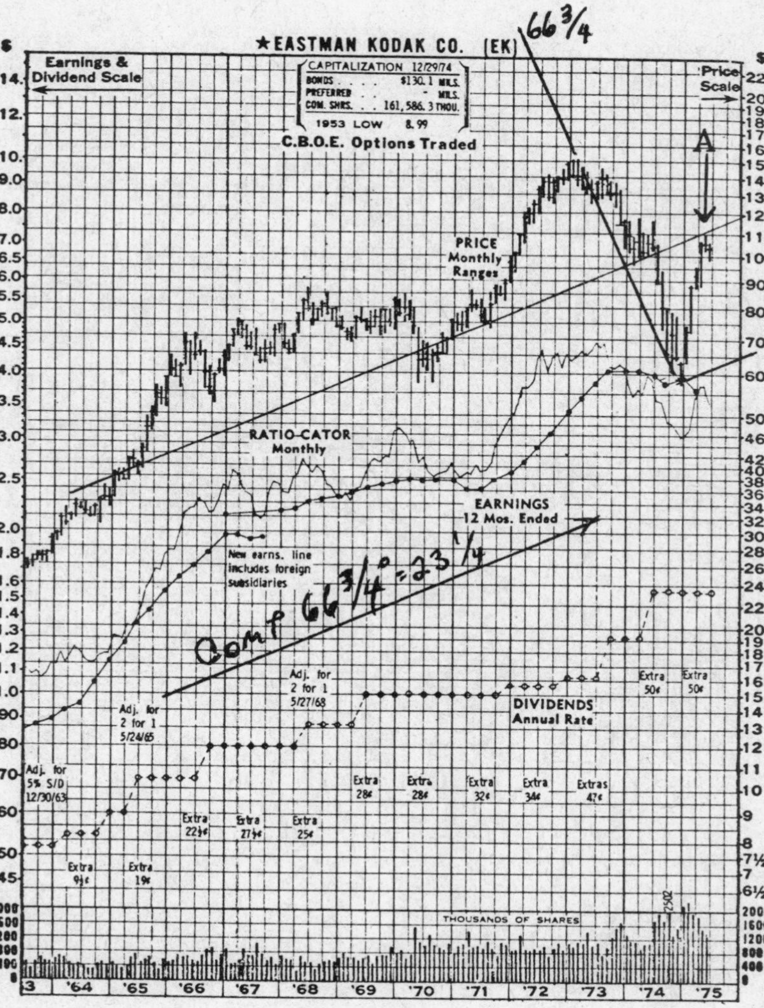
★EASTMAN KODAK CO. (EK)
66 3/4
Earnings & Dividend Scale
CAPITALIZATION 12/29/74
BONDS $130.1 MILS.
PREFERRED - MILS.
COM. SHRS. 161,586.3 THOU.
1953 LOW 8.99
C.B.O.E. Options Traded
Price Scale
A
PRICE Monthly Ranges
RATIO-CATOR Monthly
EARNINGS 12 Mos. Ended
New earns. line includes foreign subsidiaries
Comp 66 3/4° = 23 1/4
Adj. for 2 for 1 5/27/68
Adj. for 2 for 1 5/24/65
Adj. for 5% S/D 12/30/63
DIVIDENDS Annual Rate
Extra 50¢
Extra 50¢
Extra 28¢
Extra 28¢
Extra 32¢
Extra 34¢
Extras 47¢
Extra 22½¢
Extra 27½¢
Extra 25¢
Extra 9½¢
Extra 19¢
THOUSANDS OF SHARES
2502
'64 '65 '66 '67 '68 '69 '70 '71 '72 '73 '74 '75

CHART 15–69

SOURCE: Securities Research

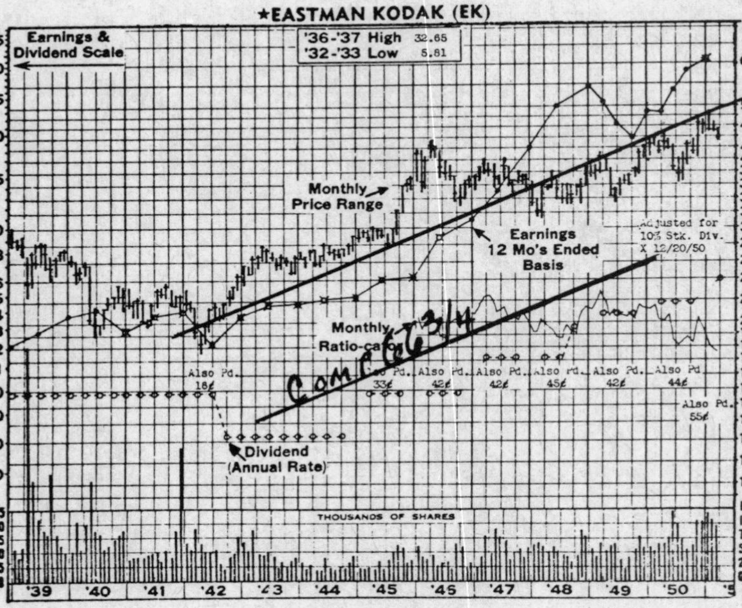
★EASTMAN KODAK (EK)
Earnings & Dividend Scale
'36-'37 High 32.65
'32-'33 Low 5.81
Monthly Price Range
Earnings 12 Mo's Ended Basis
Adjusted for 10% Stk. Div. X 12/20/50
Monthly Ratio-cat
Comp 6 3/4
Dividend (Annual Rate)
THOUSANDS OF SHARES
'39
'40
'41
'42
'43
'44
'45
'46
'47
'48
'49
'50

CHART 15–70

Note that the complement of the principal angle drawn from the 1974 low also functions from the 1942 low of Eastman Kodak. This illustrates the continuity of the formulas employed in the price blueprint. Also of interest is the manner in which the price of EK remained within the bounds of an internal trendline from 1947.

SOURCE: Securities Research

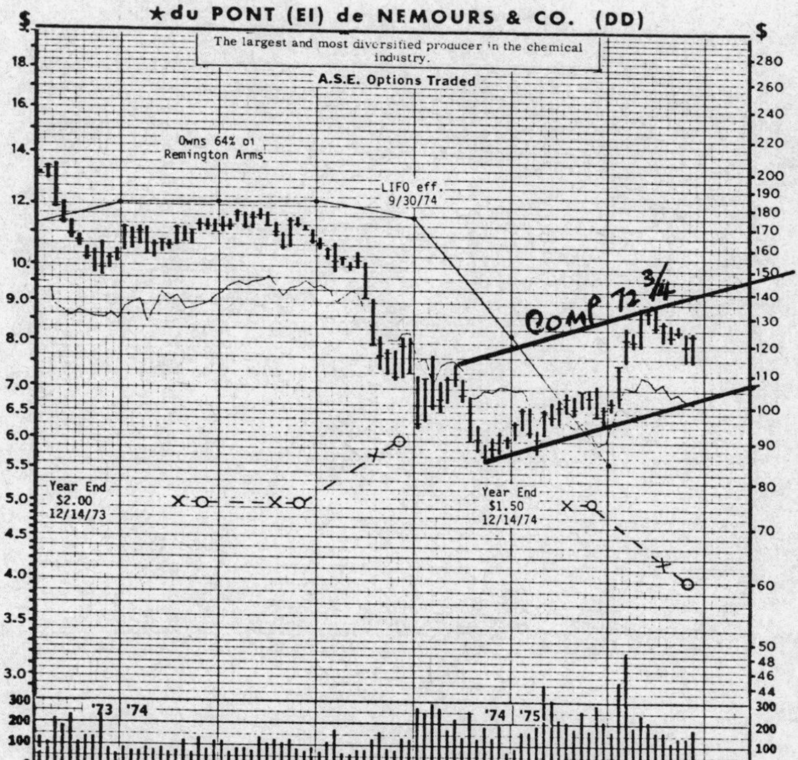
★du PONT (EI) de NEMOURS & CO. (DD)
The largest and most diversified producer in the chemical industry.
A.S.E. Options Traded
Owns 64% of Remington Arms
LIFO eff. 9/30/74
Comp 72 3/4
Year End $2.00 12/14/73
Year End $1.50 12/14/74
'73 '74
'74 '75
OCT NOV DEC JAN FEB MAR APR MAY JUN JUL AUG SEP OCT NOV DEC JAN FEB MAR APR MAY JUN JUL

CHART 15–71

Not surprisingly, we note that on Du Pont's monthly chart the complement of the principal angle provides the same sell signal as on the yearly chart.

SOURCE: Securities Research

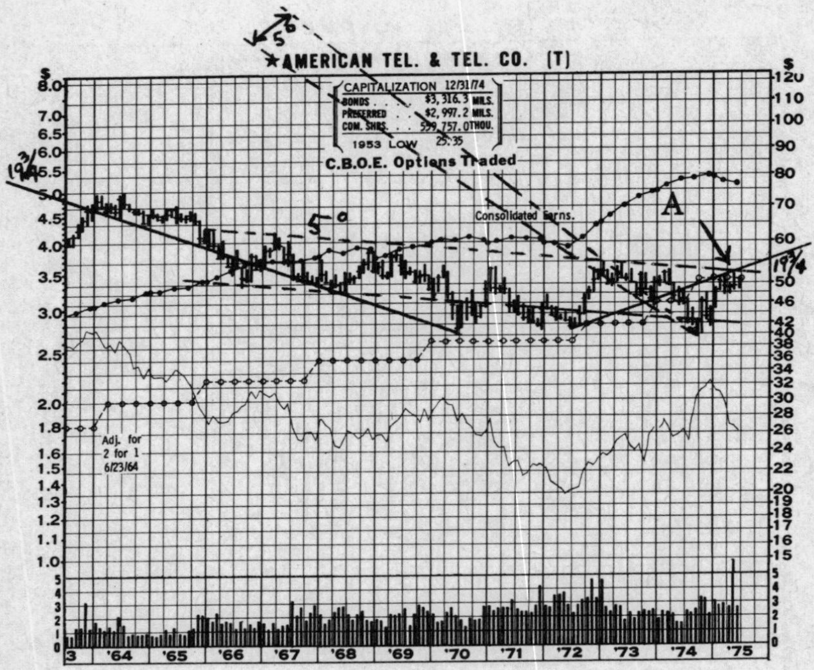
AMERICAN TEL. & TEL. CO. (T)
CAPITALIZATION 12/31/74
BONDS . . . $3,316.3 MILS.
PREFERRED . . $2,997.2 MILS.
COM. SHRS. . . 599,757.0 THOU.
1953 LOW 25.35
C.B.O.E. Options Traded
Consolidated Earns.
A
Adj. for 2 for 1 6/23/64
'64
'65
'66
'67
'68
'69
'70
'71
'72
'73
'74
'75

CHART 15–72

The charts of Telephone show us that the secondary angle of 19¾° from this stock's 1970 low when employed in conjunction with the 5° acute angle from the 1974 low establishes an unmistakable sell signal at the point of intersection (point A)—the $52 price level in May, 1975.

SOURCE: Securities Research

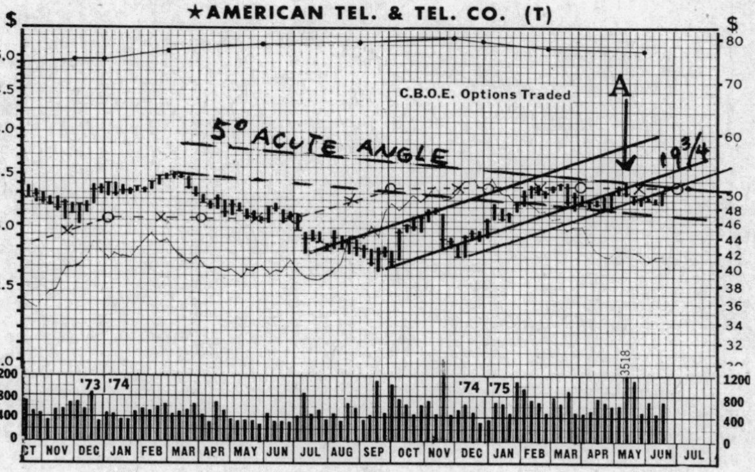
★AMERICAN TEL. & TEL. CO. (T)
C.B.O.E. Options Traded
5° ACUTE ANGLE
A
19 3/4
'73 '74
'74 '75
3518
CT NOV DEC JAN FEB MAR APR MAY JUN JUL AUG SEP OCT NOV DEC JAN FEB MAR APR MAY JUN JUL

CHART 15–73

SOURCE: Securities Research

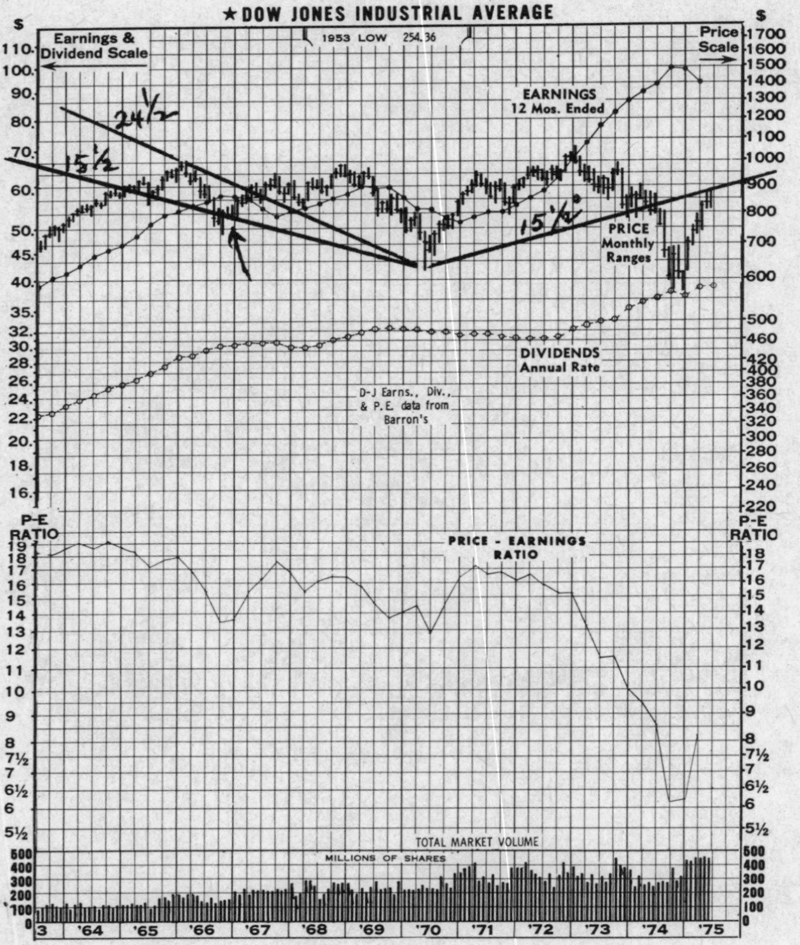
★DOW JONES INDUSTRIAL AVERAGE
Earnings & Dividend Scale
1953 LOW 254.36
Price Scale
EARNINGS 12 Mos. Ended
PRICE Monthly Ranges
DIVIDENDS Annual Rate
D-J Earns., Div., & P.E. data from Barron's
P-E RATIO
PRICE - EARNINGS RATIO
TOTAL MARKET VOLUME
MILLIONS OF SHARES
24½
15½
15½°
'64
'65
'66
'67
'68
'69
'70
'71
'72
'73
'74
'75

CHART 15–74

If the angle theory reveals the existence of predetermined plans of action for individual Dow stocks, it stands to reason that a chart of the Dow Average itself should provide us with an angle formula that prescribes the boundaries at which specialist short selling was destined to manifest itself at the May, 1975, high.

SOURCE: Securities Research

Obviously the implications of the angle theory raise a whole host of questions concerning the institutional arrangements that surround the Stock Exchange's practices. But they are questions that warrant a treatment that is separate and distinct from the purpose of this book. My objective is to provide the reader with insights that will enable him to successfully invest in the market's high-risk environment under low-risk conditions.

The chief value of the foregoing chart analysis to the reader is that it provides him with another tool for the successful timing of his investment decisions. When used in conjunction with the volume figures and my numbers theory, the reader can learn to recognize and anticipate the onset of specialist distribution and short selling at market highs and short covering and accumulation at market bottoms. Once the investor learns this, he will be able to buy when the specialist buys and sell when he sells. At such times the strategies the specialist employs to hide his practices will only serve to reveal them.

In the final chapter the reader will be given a series of test questions and review exercises. The purpose of this section is not so much to test how well he has retained each chapter's instructional objectives, but to strengthen his understanding of these objectives. It is my hope that, by constructively examining the reader's knowledge of basic theory through its application in practical test cases, I will enable him to be better able to apply my techniques when buying and selling stock. The primary objective of this last chapter, therefore, will be to provide the reader with opportunities for trying his hand at solving important investment problems on paper before trying to do it with cash.

16

Keys to Low Risk Investing or Questions and Answers to Test Your Skills

Ney's Seventeenth Axiom: When learning how to invest, do not use your savings.

Many readers will find this final chapter the most important in the book. It has been written to help the reader exercise those skills needed to employ my low risk system for investing.

The first set of exercises is designed to reinforce the reader's understanding of my theory. The questions will proceed from the very simple to the more complex. Thus we begin in Section 1 with easy-to-understand True-False questions.

We next proceed to multiple-choice questions which have been divided into Sections 2, 3, and 4. In some cases there is more than one correct answer. The reader should select the best answer. An answer sheet follows each section. This allows the reader to make sure he is on the right course before proceeding to more complex problems.

Section 5 contains hypothetical case histories with questions and answers in a multiple-choice format. These will test and reinforce the investor's ability to recognize buy and sell signals.

Finally, there is a section on charting which will test the reader's understanding of my charting methods. These, too, will proceed from simple to more complex applications of my theories.

I am confident that the reader who carefully works his way through this summary-and-exercise chapter will come away with a much greater facility for applying my techniques of successful stock market investing.

SECTION 1

Each of the following statements is either true or false. Mark T for true, F for false. Check your choices against the correct answers on page 340.

1. The market's major trends are known by specialists a long time in advance.

2. The single most important determinant of what constitutes a good investment is good earnings.

3. A careful analysis of a single stock can give the investor an indication of the trend of the market.

4. What has happened in the market in the past has very little to do with what happens in the market today.

5. The market declines from retail to wholesale price levels as a consequence of public selling.

6. As a trader or investor, the best way for you to succeed in the market is to follow the transactions of specialists.

7. The Dow Jones Average is a barometer investors should follow because it provides them with an excellent indication of the trend of the market.

8. The stocks in the Dow are no longer representative of industry as a whole. The movements of the Average are, therefore, of no consequence.

9. The Dow can establish new highs despite the fact that most stocks in the Dow have been moving lower for months.

10. It's more important to watch the price and volume movements of the five most active stocks in the Dow than it is the Dow Average itself.

11. One of the constructive features of owning Dow stocks is the probability that, in the course of a bull market, most Dow stocks will be among those that are the first to advance and the last to decline.

12. One of the good features of Dow stocks is that they provide more certain growth and better income than most other stocks.

13. Different investors should have different portfolios. Some should have portfolios oriented toward growth, others toward income.

14. So long as the income from your portfolio remains unchanged, it is of little consequence what happens to the stock prices of an income-oriented portfolio.

15. Institutional transactions play a major role in determining a stock's trend.

16. Heavy institutional buying is a major reason stock prices advanced in the first half of 1975.

17. Heavy institutional selling is a major cause of the volatility that has existed in the market since the beginning of the 1960s.

18. Institutions tend to perform much better in the market than the average individual because they can afford to pay big fees for investment advice.

19. Because they buy in big blocks, the costs of purchasing and selling stock are much lower for institutions.

20. The trust department of banks like Morgan Guaranty and Chase Bank lost billions of dollars in 1973–74 for investors who utilized their services.

21. The stock market's most important function is as a major source of equity capital.

22. The Exchange Act of 1934 was responsible for instituting major reforms of the Stock Exchange.

23. Specialists are allowed to keep the *specifics* of all their transactions secret.

24. The investor can only obtain two-month-old data on specialist short sales from the SEC.

25. The 1963 Special Study Report of the SEC maintained that the specialists' short sale transactions in specific stocks should be made public.

Answers to questions in Section 1

1.	T	13.	F
2.	F	14.	F
3.	T	15.	F
4.	F	16.	F
5.	F	17.	F
6.	T	18.	F
7.	F	19.	F
8.	F	20.	T
9.	T	21.	F
10.	T	22.	F
11.	T	23.	T
12.	T	24.	T
25.	T		

SECTION 2

The following multiple-choice questions are designed to reinforce the reader's understanding of concepts relating to portfolio selection. Always choose the *best* answer and then check your selections against the answers on page 343.

1. The individual with $5,000 to invest should select a portfolio of
   a. no more than three stocks and no less than two.
   b. three stocks.
   c. no more than four and no less than three stocks.

2. In pursuing a policy geared to the preservation of capital, an investor with $10,000 to $200,000 should select a portfolio of no less than four and no more than five or six stocks, of which the following set of four would qualify for inclusion:
   a. IBM, American Home Products, General Motors, Bristol Myers.
   b. IBM, General Motors, Eastman Kodak, Coca-Cola.
   c. Procter & Gamble, General Motors, Eastman Kodak, Sears.
   d. General Motors, Anaconda, Coca-Cola, American Home Products.

3. Investment advisory services supervising portfolios should be viewed skeptically when their advertisements include any but one of the following statements about their operating techniques. Choose the exception:
   a. We coordinate our investment strategies with client objectives.
   b. We constantly monitor the economy and capital market.
   c. We determine investment strategies based on analysis of Exchange insider activities.
   d. We utilize fundamental as well as technical analysis.

4. The special fees paid to the Exchange by institutions to execute their big blocks have run as high as
   a. 10 times the minimum commission.
   b. 29 times the minimum commission.

c. 19 times the minimum commission.
d. 50 times the minimum commission.

5. It is a good policy to select the stocks most favored by institutions for one's portfolio because
   a. continuing institutional demand for stock will keep their stock prices up.
   b. the companies they invest in are here to stay.
   c. Exchange insiders have a greater incentive to advance these stocks' prices.
   d. they provide better income.

6. Another good feature of buying Dow stocks is that if they decline in price, chances are
   a. their dividends will remain relatively unchanged.
   b. they will ultimately advance again in price once a new bull market gets underway.
   c. they will not stay down for long.

7. In order to buy and sell big blocks of the best high-quality stocks at optimum price levels, institutional portfolio managers
   a. try to establish good relationships with Stock Exchange insiders.
   b. do extensive research to determine which companies have the best management teams.
   c. pay insiders big fees.
   d. try to select the stocks with the best future earnings.

8. Many institutions customarily trade in big blocks that are transacted off the floor of the Stock Exchange. They, therefore, by-pass the specialist in that they conduct their business with large-block positioning firms such as Saloman Brothers and Goldman Sachs. Theses big-block houses
   a. set the prices of their stocks independently of the price established by the Exchange specialist in that stock.

b. save the institution commissions and special fees.
c. compete with the specialist in the ability to set the prices of stocks.
d. conform to the approximate price level established by the specialist when they cross their blocks.

9. Institutions prefer stocks like General Motors and American Telephone because
   a. they know it is easier to sell these stocks to the public.
   b. these stocks protect the reputation of the portfolio manager by providing a built-in cushion against possible losses.
   c. they like to invest in stocks other portfolio managers prefer.
   d. these stocks are leaders in their industries.

10. A major reason bank-managed portfolios have poor performance records is because the managers of these portfolios
    a. tend to look for growth situations.
    b. base their decisions on corporate fundamentals, such as earnings.
    c. can't sell their stocks without depressing the market.

Answers to questions in Section 2

1.	c	6.	b
2.	c	7.	c
3.	c	8.	d
4.	b	9.	b
5.	c	10.	b

SECTION 3

The following multiple-choice questions and answers are intended to strengthen the reader's understanding of the principles concerning the specialist's role and function in the market.

Always select the *best* answer and then check your choice against the answeres on page 349

1. According to the SEC's Special Study Report of 1963
   a. specialists should be commended for the manner in which they stabilized the market during the bear market of 1962.
   b. specialists are at the heart of the problem of organization, management, and disciplinary procedures of the Exchange.
   c. too much is expected of specialists.

2. To become a specialist, the best course of action is to
   a. be the son of a specialist.
   b. learn how to handle the job through long years of working with specialists.
   c. pass a special examination for specialists.
   d. have enough capital to be a specialist.

3. The average specialist controls as few as
   a. 3 stocks and as many as 10.
   b. 10 stocks and as many as 45.
   c. 5 stocks and as many as 30.

4. The number of specialists operating on the floor of the Stock Exchange is approximately
   a. 360
   b. 160
   c. 560

5. Investors can only succeed in making consistent gains in the market if
   a. they learn to look at the market as a merchandising operation controlled by insiders.
   b. they do their homework and learn which companies are favored by institutions.

   c. they learn what and when stocks are being sold by Exchange insiders.

6. Investors can do better in the market by sticking exclusively to stocks in which specialists
   a. maintain a small spread between the bid and ask price.
   b. have proven to be more predictable in their price movements because they control highly active stocks.
   c. have more capital to support their stocks in the face of public selling.
   d. are honest.

7. In the course of the bear market from 1971 through 1974, the income data provided on 28 specialist firms shows they
   a. were in desperate need of capital to support their stocks.
   b. took multimillion-dollar losses.
   c. had an income of $297 million in one year alone.

8. In the following list of specialist activities, which is the one thing that is not true?
   a. He invests for his family, friends and customers.
   b. He will meet with the heads of companies to discuss their stocks.
   c. He will discuss his stock with institutional traders in order to get them to do business with him.
   d. He adheres to Exchange rules which prohibit his showing his book to investment bankers and underwriters.

9. If a specialist runs short of capital he can
   a. sell stock to raise money.
   b. borrow money from another specialist.
   c. borrow money from the Federal Reserve.
   d. get a loan on his personal property.

10. The special access to information and privileges enjoyed by specialists
    a. enables them to better serve their customers and perform their duties.
    b. in no way interferes with their right to invest and trade for themselves.
    c. enables them to take greater risks to support the market.

11. In all likelihood, any Exchange reforms such as a central market or competing specialists would provide the investor
    a. with no additional benefits.
    b. with lower prices when buying and higher prices when selling.
    c. a more liquid market for stocks.

12. There are no basic differences between the practices of specialists in one stock and those of specialists in another stock, since
    a. the financial objectives are always the same.
    b. they all have to observe the same rules and regulations of the Stock Exchange.
    c. they are all closely regulated by the SEC.
    d. each specialist tries to maintain as fair and orderly a market as possible.
    e. once they have sold short at their stock's high, they are anxious to reaccumulate stock at the bottom.

13. In the course of a rally, if a specialist doesn't have enough stock in his trading account to supply investor demand
    a. he will supply it from his investment account.
    b. he will buy the stock from other investors by dropping prices to clean out his book.
    c. he will borrow the stock needed.

14. Specialists know, a long time in advance, the trend of stock prices because
    a. they can guess the future trend from the information on their books.
    b. they know what the demand for stock will be like.
    c. they are better able to gauge the future of interest rates than most investors.
    d. they are the ones who determine what the trend is going to be.
    e. they have charts that tell them what the trend will be.

15. The Board of Governors of the Stock Exchange has a broad-based selection of businessmen who are not stockbrokers. As heads of the media and major utilities, they
    a. seek to protect investor interests.
    b. serve their own interests by working closely in support of Stock Exchange practices and policies.
    c. feel investors would be better protected if the public had greater representation on the Board.

16. The rules preventing specialists from demoralizing the market by effecting short sales at or below the last sale price
    a. have been strengthened by the SEC.
    b. have exemptions allowing them to do this.
    c. were written by specialists.
    d. protect the investor against "bear raids."

17. The 1963 Special Study Report of the SEC pointed out that in the past specialists have sold short major blocks of stock from their trading accounts at a stock's high and then subsequently
    a. sold short additional stock in the course of the decline in order to pull down the market.

b. bought stock from institutional portfolio managers on payment of a special fee to cover their short sales.
c. delivered over their investment accounts to their trading accounts in order to establish a long-term capital gain.

18. A major reason for the regulatory problems in the investment industry is that
    a. the SEC is not given enough power to do its job properly.
    b. members of the SEC top brass cooperate with the Stock Exchange in order to move into top jobs in the securities industry.
    c. the SEC is inadequately staffed.

19. The SEC maintains a tight rein over investment advisers and stockbrokers across the country. In this same regard, the Commission's regulations concerning specialists
    a. are a major source of investor protection and investor confidence.
    b. contain many loopholes.
    c. are even more stringent than those governing anyone else in the investment business.

20. The stock market is
    a. controlled by the forces of supply and demand.
    b. an internal operation manipulated by Stock Exchange insiders for their own profit.
    c. controlled by the trend of interest rates.

21. The long-term trend of stock prices can be altered overnight
    a. because insiders have accumulated all the stock they want.

b. because of an important economic announcement.
c. because of "technical" corrections.

22. The market advances in response to
a. public demand.
b. insider buying.
c. lower interest rates.

23. One of the major factors the investor must contend with is that when the majority of Dow stocks decline in price,
a. the majority of all other listed stocks are also declining.
b. the market is reflecting the existence of negative economic news.
c. the Dow Average can still be making new rally highs.

Answers to questions in Section 3

1.	b	12.	e
2.	a	13.	c
3.	b	14.	d
4.	a	15.	b
5.	a	16.	b
6.	b	17.	c
7.	c	18.	b
8.	d	19.	b
9.	c	20.	b
10.	b	21.	a
11.	a	22.	b

23. c

SECTION 4

The following multiple-choice questions are designed to test the reader's ability to recognize the purpose and effect of specialists' merchandising strategies on stock prices. Always select the *best* answer and then check your choices against the answers on page 355.

1. From the following list, choose the factors that can tell the investor when specialists are covering their short sales and going long. (More than one answer.)
   a. The information will be published in *The Wall Street Journal*.
   b. The SEC provides investors with this information.
   c. There will have been a decline in stock prices.
   d. There will be an increase in Dow and NYSE volume.
   e. There will be heavy big block activity following a decline.

2. Once the specialist has sold his investment account at a rally high, he will then want to
   a. establish a major short position.
   b. clear out his book so he can acquire the stock needed to go higher.
   c. move as soon as possible to wholesale price levels to reaccumulate a new investment account for himself.

3. The main purpose of the short sale is that it
   a. provides investors with a chance to profit in a down market.
   b. enables specialists to control stock prices.
   c. enables specialists to profit in a down market.

4. The sharp increase in volume that took place in the Dow at the end of January, 1975, was in response to
   a. public demand.
   b. investor optimism over the court decision favoring IBM.

c. the fact that stock prices were raised dramatically.
d. economic factors signalling an economic upturn.
e. the announcement of lower interest rates.

5. When stock prices advance after heavy volume on the downside, it is because
   a. specialists want to unload inventory before taking stocks to lower price levels.
   b. there was a great deal of public short covering which caused prices to advance.
   c. institutional buyers took advantage of the decline in prices to accumulate stock at bargain prices.

6. Changes in the price of a stock are a reflection of
   a. a change in public supply-demand factors.
   b. a change in economic factors.
   c. a change in the specialist's inventory objectives.
   d. a change in trend.

7. Heavy volume on the downside indicates that
   a. market conditions are deteriorating fast.
   b. market conditions are being influenced by negative economic factors.
   c. a reversal in stock prices is in the offing.

8. When specialists want to merchandise their stock, one of the things they have to do is
   a. create demand for stock.
   b. conduct a sale by lowering stock prices.
   c. conduct a sale by raising stock prices.

9. When there is a sharp decline in stock prices, specialists do all of the following except
   a. clear out their books of stock.

b. cover their short sales.
c. accumulate stock.
d. take big losses.

10. The significance of a decline in Dow volume as stock prices decline is
 a. an indication of underlying strength.
 b. that stock prices are going lower.
 c. that the specialist has covered his short sales.

11. To indicate a temporary reversal, Dow volume should exceed
 a. 1.4 million shares a day.
 b. 2.5 million shares a day.
 c. 3.0 million shares a day.

12. Specialist short covering and accumulation for a major reversal could be indicated by three to four or more consecutive days of Dow volume in excess of
 a. 1.4 million shares a day.
 b. 1.8 million shares a day.
 c. 2.8 million shares a day.

13. An increase in volume after a run-up in price
 a. indicates underlying strength caused by investor demand.
 b. indicates specialist short selling.
 c. is a consequence of good corporate or economic news.

14. The announcement of the IBM court decision was considered to be of such great economic importance that
 a. it forced the specialist to open IBM 25 points higher to meet public demand.
 b. it caused a complete reversal in the public's attitude toward stocks.

c. it provided a rationale for raising prices and pulling the public into the market.
d. it created great optimism among investors because it showed that government was becoming pro-business.

15. Despite the importance to Wall Streeters of the court decision concerning IBM, the stock did not perform as well as stocks like Eastman Kodak and Du Pont. This was because
    a. the public did not attribute too much importance to the announcement.
    b. there was a great deal of public selling in the stock.
    c. the specialist sold the stock short.
    d. the earnings of IBM were not what analysts expected.

16. The specialist is aware of how the public conforms to certain price behavior patterns. Hence, if he is raising prices from 70 to 100, he will
    a. distribute big blocks just above 100.
    b. distribute big blocks just under 100.
    c. examine his book to see whether there are more buy orders or sell orders above 100.

17. If very big blocks appear at the 59 price level and still more at the 60 level after a sharp advance from the 25 price level, it is an indication
    a. the stock is going higher.
    b. the stock is being set up for a decline.
    c. institutional interest is coming into the stock.

18. The appearance of big blocks at the 20 price level after a sharp decline from the 30 price level is
    a. a bullish signal suggesting the stock could make a good trading vehicle.

b. bearish.
c. a signal the stock should be sold short.

19. When a stock declines from the 90 level, touches the 60 level on high volume, and then, after proceeding to 59, advances to 70 and declines once more to the 60 level on light volume, chances are
  a. it will bounce up off the 60 level.
  b. it will go through the 60 level.
  c. it will test the 59 level again.

20. Chances are that, if there are a lot more sell orders at 60 than buy orders, a specialist who has advanced his stock from the 30 price level to 59 will
  a. advance it just above 60 to collect the sell orders and then proceed higher to unload them.
  b. open his stock above the 60 level to avoid the sell orders.
  c. advance his stock no higher than 59⅞.

21. Recalling the circumstances involved in the Telephone offering, investors should have been warned not to buy the stock on the thirteenth, fourteenth, or fifteenth because
  a. Telephone's price has been declining for years.
  b. of the high volume on the twelfth and thirteenth.
  c. of the decline in the Dow of more than 2 points on May 12 on 1,550,350 shares.

22. The price action in Telephone on the fourteenth and fifteenth left no doubt the stock would decline on the sixteenth because
  a. it had advanced too fast.
  b. the specialist indicated he was selling short on those days.

c. the specialist didn't let the public sell short on those days.

23. There was still another major indicator on May 14 that was signaling a forthcoming decline in Telephone:
    a. The advance on high volume in the Dow.
    b. The advance on high volume in GM.
    c. Texaco declined 1/4 point to 24 3/4 on 148,800 shares.

Answers to questions in Section 4

1.	c, d, e	12.	b
2.	a	13.	b
3.	b	14.	c
4.	c	15.	c
5.	a	16.	c
6.	c	17.	b
7.	c	18.	a
8.	c	19.	b
9.	d	20.	c
10.	b	21.	b
11.	a	22.	b

23. b

SECTION 5

Section 5 concentrates exclusively on the practical application of theory to market events. In working through this section, the reader will be able to test as well as strengthen his ability to evaluate the future trend of stock prices.

Five hypothetical market scenarios are presented, followed by multiple-choice questions and answers. The scenarios should be carefully read. There are clues in each description of market events that can be used to determine what the investor or trader should do and what the likely course of events is to be. When working through the multiple-choice questions, always select the *best* answer. These are provided at the end of each case study.

Case History A

It is a Friday in early November. The Dow has just touched 500. The market has been in a protracted decline for a year and a half and has not rallied for several months. Stock prices have declined about 50 percent from their highs. Unemployment, interest rates, and inflation have been rising. The Bureau of Labor Statistics has just published the information that there has been a slight improvement in employment. This information has been headlined by the media. The Dow advances 28 points on a volume of 1.4 million shares with NYSE volume at 20 million shares.

1. Stock prices advanced on Friday
   a. because of public demand.
   b. because specialists had acquired large inventories they wished to unload.
   c. because of the good economic news.

2. The advance on Friday
   a. was planned by specialists to cheer up investors over the weekend.
   b. was caused by specialist short covering.
   c. was caused by public short covering.

3. This was not a time for investors to buy because
   a. it would have been impossible for the market to advance long-term in the face of such negative economic news.
   b. there had been no indication of major specialist short covering and accumulation.
   c. November is never a good month to buy stocks.

4. One reason stock prices will decline subsequent to the termination of the rally is that
   a. economic factors are continuing to deteriorate.
   b. specialists will want to accumulate stock at bottom dollar from investors who sell in December for tax purposes.
   c. of heavy profit taking by traders.

5. If one is a trader, he should
   a. enter an order to buy on Monday morning's opening.
   b. wait until he sees if prices move down Monday.
   c. realize that the rally will be so short it's not worth participating in it.

Answers to questions on Case History A

1. b
2. a
3. b
4. b
5. a

Case History B

It is a Thursday in October. After two months of consistent decline, the Dow has suddenly dropped 20 points, putting it under the 500 level, on 2.1 million shares. General Motors has dropped 1 point to 24, Telephone 1 point to 29, Procter & Gamble has declined 2 points to 39, Eastman Kodak 2 points to 48, and Du Pont 3 points to 52. NYSE volume is 27 million shares.

1. The investor who is now in 50 percent cash and holds all these stocks should
   a. sell them and go into 100 percent cash.
   b. do nothing.
   c. commit 50 percent of his reserves into the purchase of more of these stocks.

   d. commit all his reserves into the purchase of these stocks.

2. Under the same circumstances, the trader should
   a. consider a purchase of General Motors and/or Procter & Gamble.
   b. wait to see if the Dow drops to 400.
   c. wait another day to see what happens.

3. Assuming the Dow closes on another drop of 20 points on Friday on Dow volume on 2.2 million shares
   a. traders should enter their orders to buy at the Monday opening.
   b. investors and traders should enter their orders to buy at the Monday opening.
   c. investors still holding stock should sell.

4. If the Dow closes down 2 points on 17 million shares, with Dow volume at 1.7 million shares, and most Dow stocks remain unchanged, this indicates
   a. there will not be a long-term advance.
   b. traders should enter their orders to purchase Procter & Gamble at the Monday opening.
   c. investors should enter their buy orders for the Monday opening.

5. If there is a sharp advance on Friday, it will indicate
   a. the market has embarked on a major rally.
   b. the market has embarked on a short-term rally.
   c. nothing, unless the Dow can negate the sell signal caused by the penetration of the 500 level by going back up to close above the 500 level.

6. If there is a sharp advance on Friday, it indicates

a. public demand, including short covering, has advanced stock prices.
b. that we can look to General Motors for an indication of which way the market is headed.
c. traders should immediately enter their orders to buy at the market.

7. If there is a sharp advance on Friday, the following week should begin
   a. with a big advance in the Dow on heavy volume.
   b. a probable advance in the Dow in the first hour followed by a possible decline thereafter.
   c. another sharp drop in stock prices as General Motors moves down to the 20 level.

8. If there is a sharp advance on Friday and Monday, it indicates
   a. the probability that another major upturn has begun.
   b. that the Dow will once again move back down to the old lows.
   c. that traders should stay on the sidelines.

Answers to questions on Case History B

1.	b	5.	b
2.	c	6.	c
3.	b	7.	a
4.	b	8.	b

Case History C

The Dow has been declining for approximately two months. During the most recent two-week period the Dow has dropped 80 points on 12-, 13-, and an occasional 15-million-share day. For the whole of this period, Eastman Kodak, Procter & Gamble, and Sears have been declining. Then, on a Thursday, General Motors closes at 52⅞, Eastman Kodak at 69, Procter & Gamble at 75. For the whole of this period the media has been bullish, then two weeks ago, it turned bearish as short-term interest rates advanced.

Then on Friday, the Dow declines 32 points, putting it under the 700 level on a volume of 26 million shares. Eastman Kodak drops 6 points to 63 on 94,000 shares, opening on a downside gap of 2 points; Procter & Gamble declines to 71 on 45,000 shares; General Motors opens at 48⅝ and closes at 49 on a volume of 150,000 shares, having established an intraday high of 49½. 900 stocks are down, 300 are up, and 300 unchanged.

1. On Monday Eastman Kodak opens at 62 on heavy volume and declines to 61 where two big blocks of 15,000 and 25,000 shares appear on the tape. There is a probability that
   a. Eastman Kodak will now advance from 61.
   b. after the specialist has cleared out his book down to the 57–58 level, we will see a sharp rally in this stock.
   c. the stock will now decline at least down to 50.

2. On Monday, the probability is that Procter & Gamble will decline under 70
   a. on volume of 125,000 shares.
   b. on volume of 80,000 shares.
   c. on volume of 225,000 shares.

3. On Monday, General Motors will probably
   a. move down to 40–41.
   b. drop to somewhere in the 47–48 price level, where it will reverse its decline.
   c. open on an upside gap.

4. On Monday, stock prices could

a. be off 30 points and then rally at the end of the first hour.
b. rally as soon as the market opens.
c. open unchanged and close up or down 2 points or so.

5. On Monday, the probability is that volume will
   a. be in excess of 30 million for the day.
   b. once again decline to 15 million shares as stock prices rally after an early morning decline.
   c. be light during the first hour and heavy for the rest of the day.

6. In the Friday decline of General Motors from its intraday high
   a. the volume indicator was more important than price.
   b. the price decline was more important than volume.
   c. the action of each was equally important.

7. On Monday, the probability is the media will be
   a. very bullish.
   b. very bearish.
   c. inconclusive.

8. On Monday, traders
   a. should enter their orders to buy General Motors at the opening.
   b. should sell General Motors at the opening.
   c. should wait to see how General Motors closes on Monday before doing anything.

Answers to questions on Case History C

1.	b	5.	a
2.	b	6.	c
3.	b	7.	b
4.	a	8.	a

Case History D

In two weeks' time, Eastman Kodak declines from the 69 price level to the 60 level on fairly light volume. Then, on the tenth trading day, a Friday, it drops to about 59 and closes at about 59¾ on approximately 120,000 shares. The Dow Industrial Average, meanwhile, has dropped under the 700 level earlier in the week and drops almost 10 points on the day Eastman Kodak declines to 59. On that day, Dow volume registers 1.6 million shares while NYSE volume is relatively light. For the four preceding days, Dow volume has averaged about 1.2 million shares. For the whole of this period, daily volume in General Motors has been in excess of 100,000 shares a day at the 30 price level. During this same period Telephone drops from the 46 to the 42 price level on very heavy volume; Texaco is trading at the 20 level on volume in excess of 100,000 shares a day, with volume moving to 130,000 and 150,000 on some days. The media has been bullish for the whole of the previous month; now it is suddenly quoting institutional portfolio managers who are turning bearish on the economy. It has been rumored that interest rates will rise and on that Friday CitiBank does, in fact, raise its prime rate ⅛ percent.

1. Investors should
   a. buy Eastman Kodak.
   b. wait to see if Eastman Kodak goes lower on higher volume.
   c. wait to see an indication of a sequence of four to five days of high volume in the Dow on the downside, or approximately 2 million-or-more-share days for two or three days running, before buying any stocks.

2. General Motors and Telephone indicate
   a. they are in a buying range for investors.
   b. they are in a buying range for traders.

c. that General Motors should be bought by traders, but not Telephone.

3. The media's sudden bearishness is a sign that
   a. one should sell immediately.
   b. one should buy immediately.
   c. many stocks will be moving into buying ranges.

4. The specialist in Eastman Kodak will probably
   a. advance back up over 60 before declining further.
   b. drop his price to 58 on a sharp increase in volume before rallying.
   c. launch Eastman Kodak on a bull move.

5. Short sellers should
   a. not cover.
   b. cover at the market at the Monday opening.
   c. wait until Monday to see whether the Dow drops further before deciding to cover.

6. Short sellers in Telephone and General Motors should
   a. cover at the market on Monday.
   b. not cover yet.
   c. wait to see what happens in Eastman Kodak on Monday before covering.

7. Short sellers in other Exchange stocks
   a. should cover on Monday at the opening.
   b. should add to their short position in anticipation of a sharply lower Dow on Monday.
   c. should wait to see what happens to General Motors on Monday before covering.

8. If institutional portfolio managers turn bearish
   a. it's an indication their selling could send the market lower.

b. their recommendations should not be followed, as most institutional portfolio managers tend to follow the herd.
c. it is worth considering their opinions because they pay big fees for competent investment advice.

9. The rise in interest rates is
   a. used as a rationale for the decline in stock prices.
   b. meant to cause fear among investors of much lower stock prices.
   c. a signal stock prices will now advance.

Answers to questions on Case History D

1. c	5. b
2. b	6. a
3. c	7. a
4. b	8. b
9. a	

Case History E

On a Tuesday, the day after the Dow advances to a new high after a succession of highs in the course of a three-month rally, it declines 23 points on a Dow volume of 1.9 million shares while NYSE volume is 25.5 million shares. Prior to this decline, General Motors has been advancing at the rate of approximately ¼ of a point or ⅛ of a point each day for the previous six days of trading. On the day of the decline it drops 2½ points from 52 to 49½ on 125,000 shares. In the course of the same decline Telephone declines ½ point to 40⅛ on 160,000 shares. The day before, *The Wall Street Journal's* comments about the future of the economy are highly optimistic. On the following day, the boom talk of *The Wall Street Journal* has undergone a metamorphosis. Now it describes a whole host of factors that its experts cite as being responsible for the decline, including predictions that unemployment, having improved somewhat during the past three months, will once again move back to 13 percent of the work force. The head of CitiBank predicts a rise in interest rates to 14 percent, and new-car sales figures reveal that sales have slumped to 50 percent of the amount for the comparable period a year earlier. These factors are also cited as reasons for the sharp drop in the price of General Motors' shares.

1. The likelihood is that
   a. after a sharp rally on Wednesday to unload stock, General Motors will resume its decline.
   b. after a sharp additional decline Wednesday, morning, General Motors will continue its advance on Wednesday and Thursday.
   c. General Motors will continue its decline at least down to the 40–41 level.

2. The trader who owns 200 shares of General Motors
   a. should sell them at the Wednesday opening.
   b. should buy more at the Wednesday opening.
   c. should wait to see what happens Wednesday.

3. There seems no doubt that Tuesday's decline
   a. represents profit taking by traders.
   b. indicates specialists have cleaned out their books of stock prior to advancing stock prices.
   c. is the beginning of a major drop in stock prices.

4. Were this the beginning of a three-day shakeout the media would
   a. become even more bearish.
   b. become bullish.
   c. quote institutional portfolio managers who are both bullish and bearish.

5. The price action in General Motors prior to Tuesday's decline

a. suggests the rally has not yet come to an end.
b. is highly unusual in a stock like General Motors.
c. is an indication of strength in an overall weak market.

6. The significant feature of the high volume decline in Telephone
   a. is its ominous implications of institutional selling.
   b. is its bullishness.
   c. is its bearishness.

7. The decline in General Motors has
   a. overall bullish implications for the market as a whole.
   b. overall bearish implications for the market as a whole.
   c. no bearing on what the rest of the market will do.

Answers to questions on Case History E

1.	b	4.	a
2.	b	5.	a
3.	b	6.	b
7.	a		

SECTION 6

This charting section is designed to enable the reader to practice my charting techniques in order to use them to determine buy and sell signals. Each set of questions will be presented with a chart which the reader can use to construct his angles or determine the buy and sell signals. Each set of answers will accompany a duplicate chart which will have the appropriate notations.

Q. Construct the principal, secondary, and acute angles on Chart 16–1. Complete the following list from the measurements you obtain:

principal °
secondary °
acute °
complement of principal °
complement of secondary °

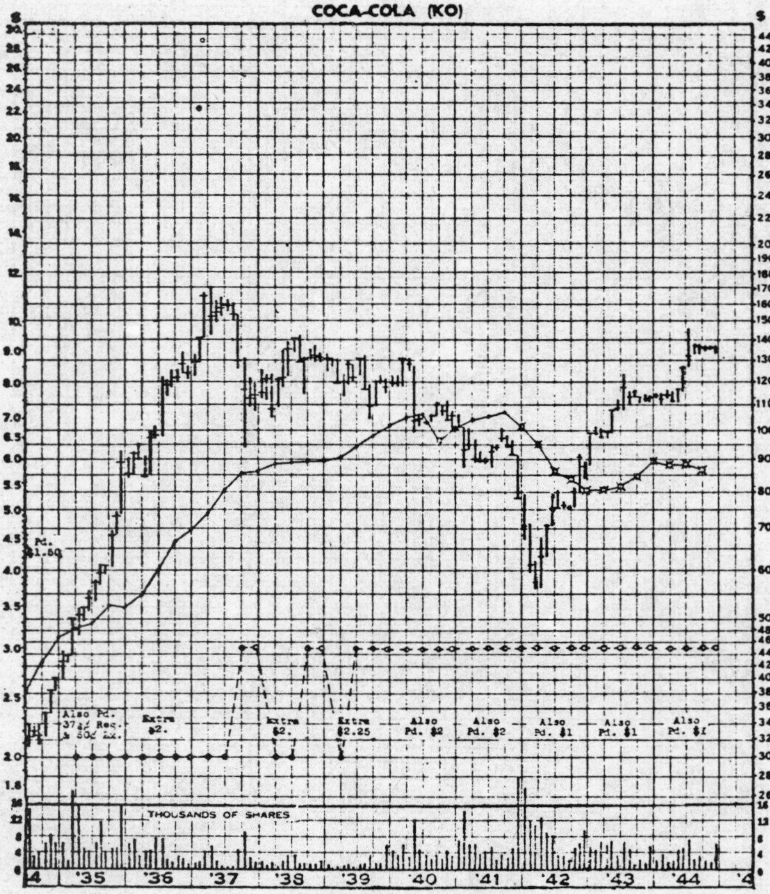
COCA-COLA (KO)
THOUSANDS OF SHARES
Extra $2.
Extra $2.25
Also Pd. $2
Also Pd. $2
Also Pd. $1
Also Pd. $1
Also Pd. $1
'35
'36
'37
'38
'39
'40
'41
'42
'43
'44

CHART 16–1
SOURCE: Securities Research

A. principal 44°
secondary 26½°
acute 17½°
complement of principal 46°
complement of secondary 63½°

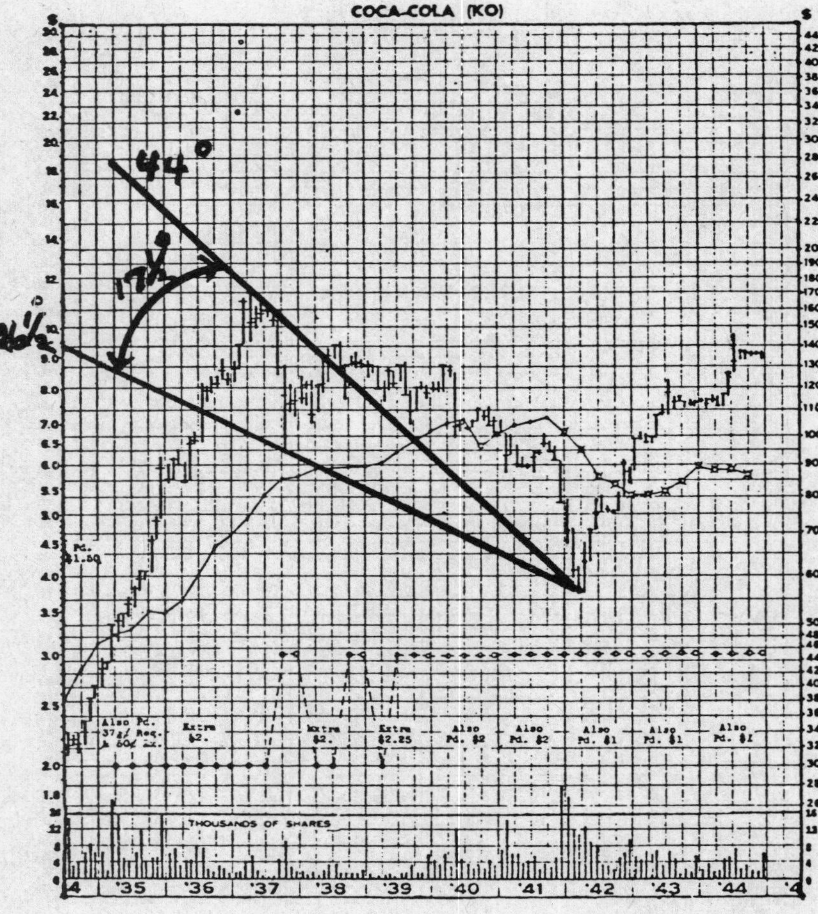
COCA-COLA (KO)
44°
17½°
26½°
THOUSANDS OF SHARES
'35
'36
'37
'38
'39
'40
'41
'42
'43
'44

CHART 16–2
SOURCE: Securities Research

Q. When we apply the force lines of the secondary angle obtained from the 1942 low in Coca-Cola to the 1963–1975 yearly chart we obtain a major sell signal in one year and a major buy signal in the following year. Determine when and at what price the investor would have timed his transactions.

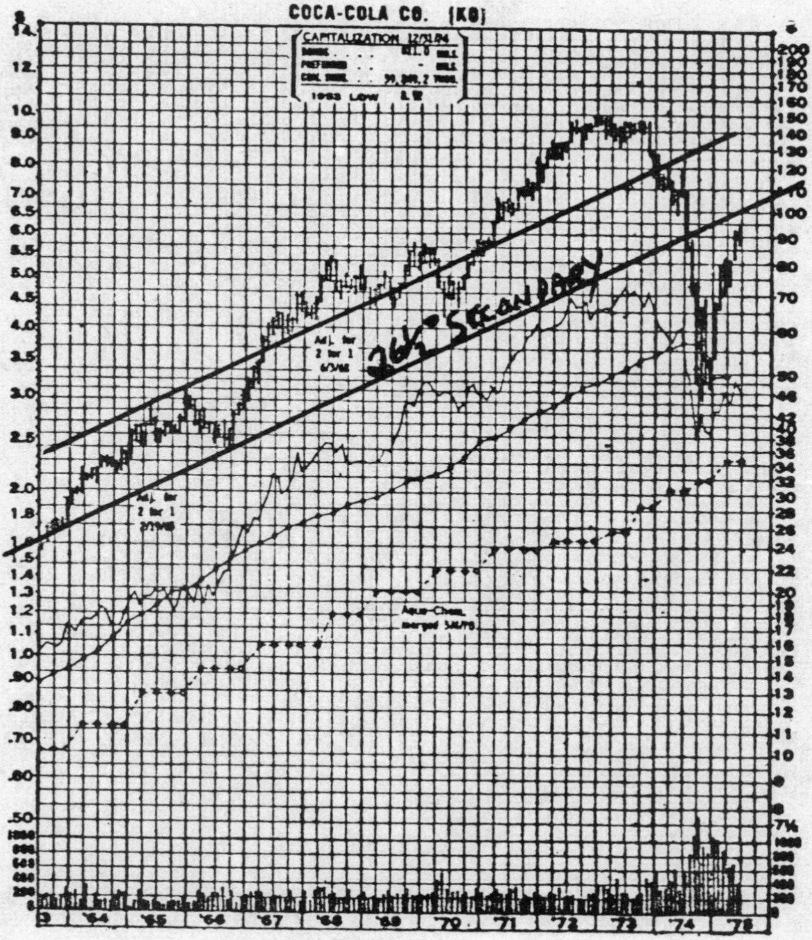
COCA-COLA CO. (KO)
CAPITALIZATION
1963 LOW
26½° SECONDARY
'64
'65
'66
'67
'68
'69
'70
'71
'72
'73
'74
'75

CHART 16–3
SOURCE: Securities Research

A. When price touched the upper force line at the 45 level in December, 1965 (point A), the investor was provided with a sell signal. When price touched the lower force line at 36 in November, 1966 (point B), the investor was provided with a buy signal.

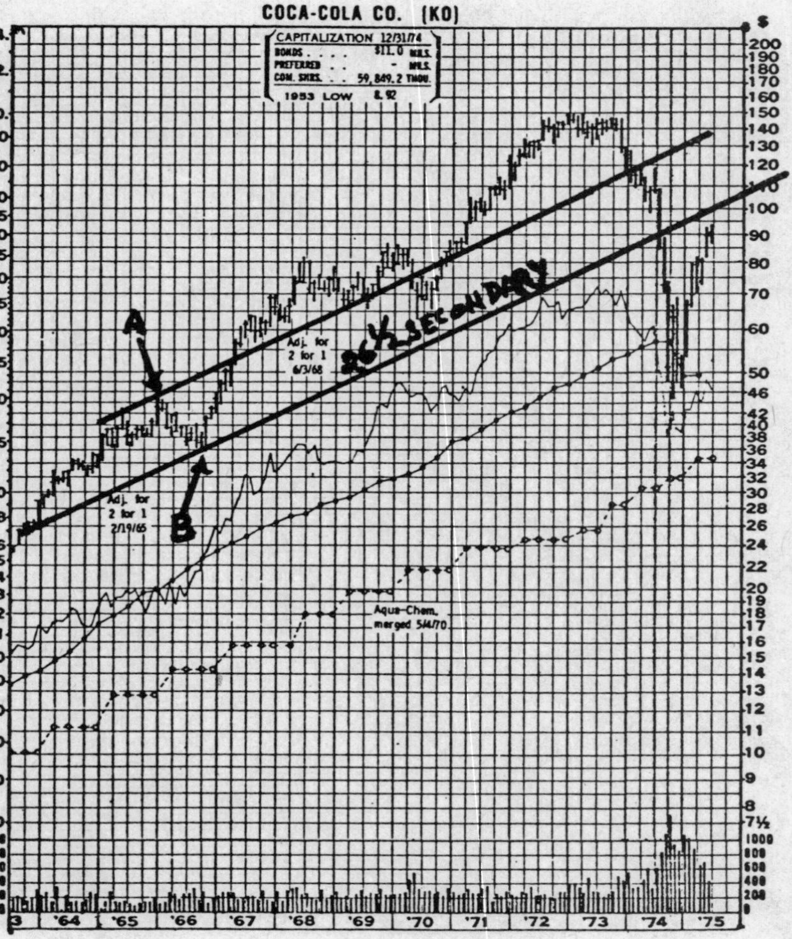
COCA-COLA CO. (KO)
CAPITALIZATION 12/31/74
BONDS . . . . $11.0 MILS.
PREFERRED . . - MILS.
COM. SHRS. . . 59,849.2 THOU.
1953 LOW 8.92
A
B
Adj. for 2 for 1 2/19/65
Adj. for 2 for 1 6/3/68
26½ SECONDARY
Aqua-Chem. merged 5/4/70
'64
'65
'66
'67
'68
'69
'70
'71
'72
'73
'74
'75

CHART 16–4
SOURCE: Securities Research

Q. By applying the force lines of the principal and acute angles obtained from the 1942 low in Coca-Cola to the 1963–1975 yearly chart we obtain a major sell signal. Determine when and at what price the investor would have sold.

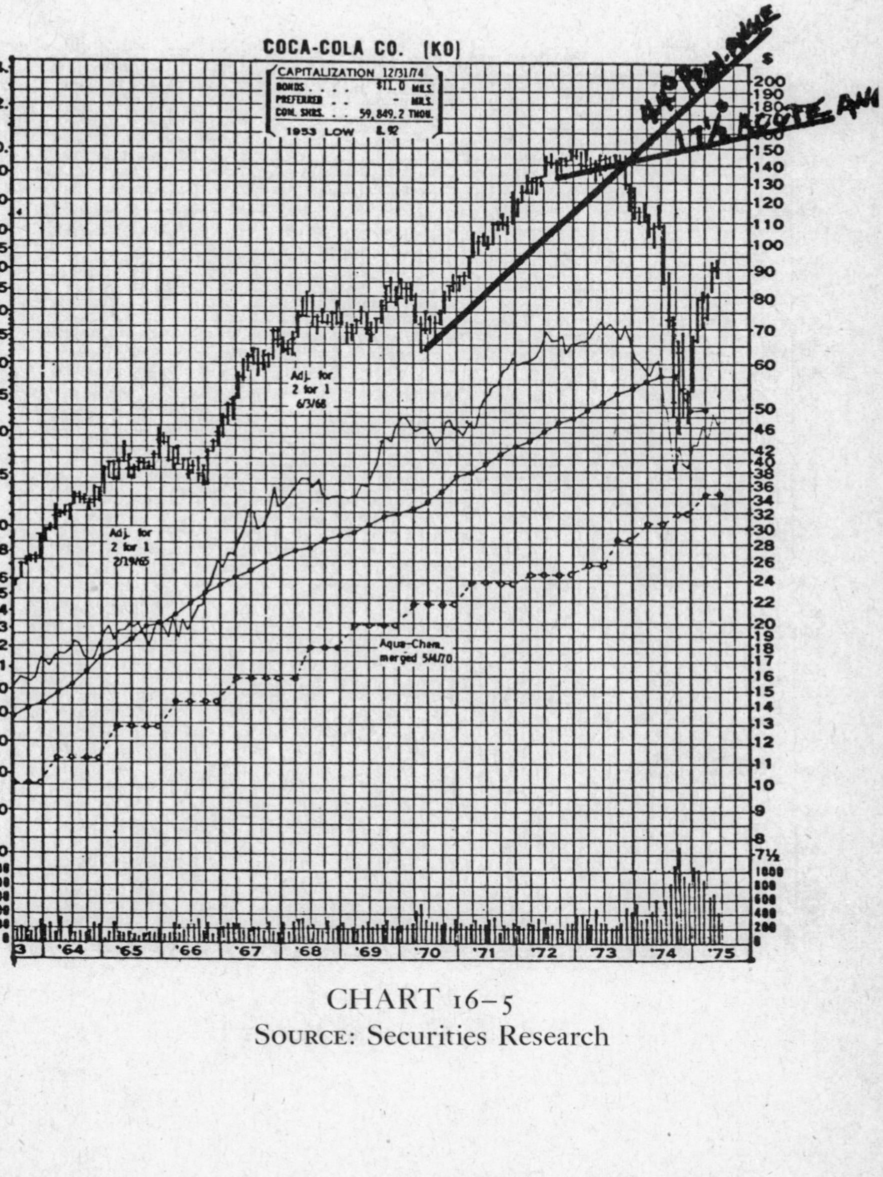
COCA-COLA CO. (KO)
CAPITALIZATION 12/31/74
BONDS . . . . $11.0 MILS.
PREFERRED . . . - MILS.
COM. SHRS. . . 59,849.2 THOU.
1953 LOW 8.92
Adj. for 2 for 1 6/3/68
Adj. for 2 for 1 2/19/65
Aqua-Chem. merged 5/4/70
'64
'65
'66
'67
'68
'69
'70
'71
'72
'73
'74
'75

CHART 16–5
SOURCE: Securities Research

A. When the price reached the apex formed by the intersection of the 44° and 17½° angles in October, 1973, the investor would have identified a major sell signal at the 140 price level.

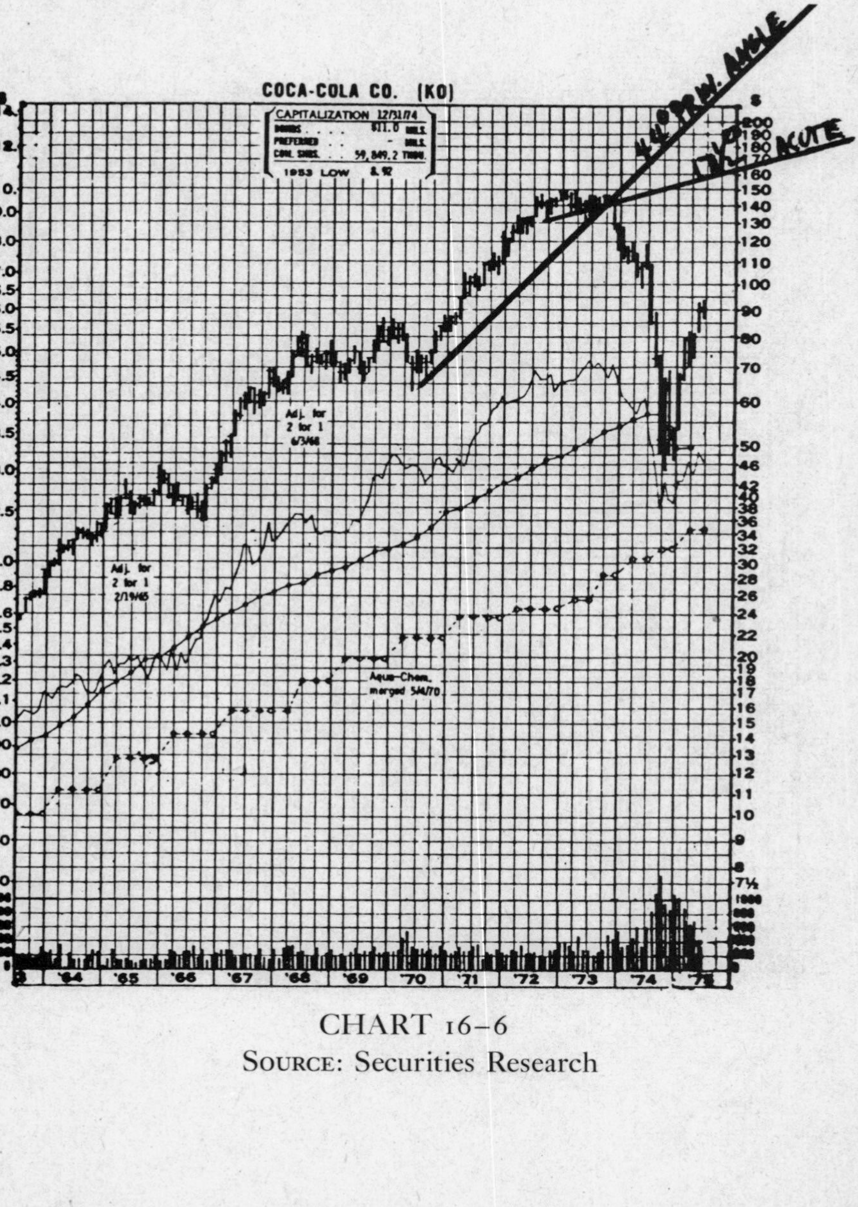
COCA-COLA CO. (KO)
CAPITALIZATION 12/31/74
1953 LOW 8.92
ACUTE
Adj. for 2 for 1 2/19/65
Adj. for 2 for 1 6/3/68
Aqua-Chem. merged 5/4/70
'64
'65
'66
'67
'68
'69
'70
'71
'72
'73
'74

CHART 16–6
SOURCE: Securities Research

Q. What angle constructed from the 1942 low would have enabled the investor to call a sell signal at the 1965 high and a buy signal at the 1970 low?

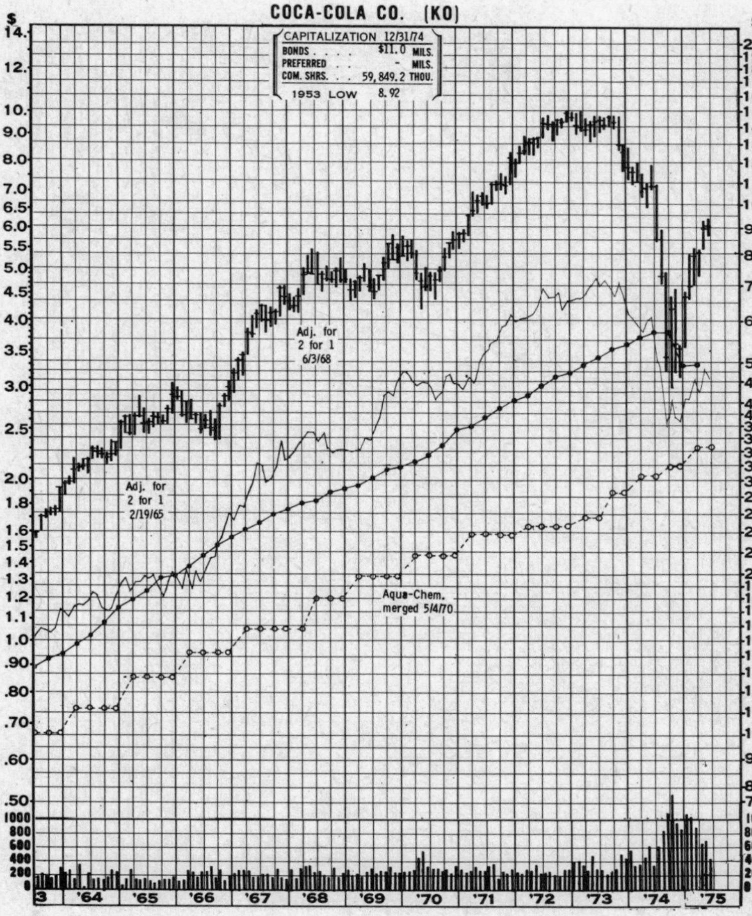
COCA-COLA CO. (KO)
CAPITALIZATION 12/31/74
BONDS . . . . $11.0 MILS.
PREFERRED . . - MILS.
COM. SHRS. . . 59,849.2 THOU.
1953 LOW 8.92
Adj. for 2 for 1 6/3/68
Adj. for 2 for 1 2/19/65
Aqua-Chem. merged 5/4/70
'64 '65 '66 '67 '68 '69 '70 '71 '72 '73 '74 '75

CHART 16–7
SOURCE: Securities Research

A. By extending the force line of the 17½° acute angle from the May high of 1965 it is possible to obtain a major sell signal at the December, 1965, high at the 45 level and a major buy signal at 63 at the May, 1970, low.

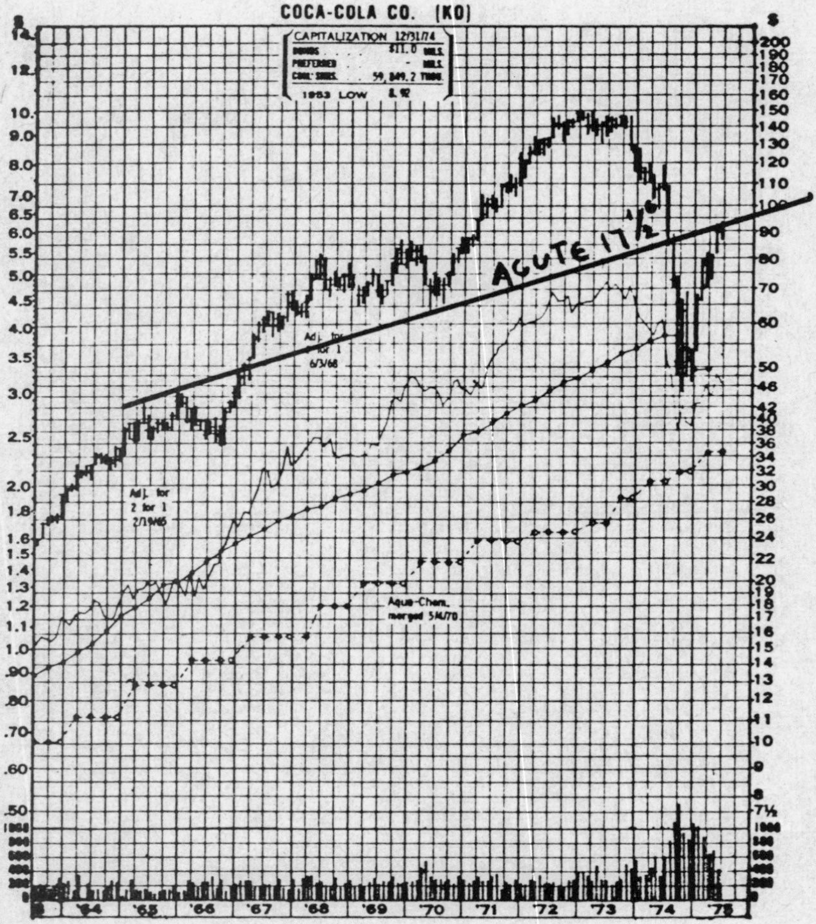
COCA-COLA CO. (KO)
CAPITALIZATION 12/31/74
1953 LOW 8.92
ACUTE 17½°
Adj. for 2 for 1 6/3/68
Adj. for 2 for 1 2/19/65
Aqua-Chem. merged 5/4/70
'64 '65 '66 '67 '68 '69 '70 '71 '72 '73 '74 '75

CHART 16–8
SOURCE: Securities Research

No school of thought has yet been developed that discusses these charting techniques. Simply put, the charts point to the fact that a creed is in operation on the floor of the Stock Exchange that is indifferent to the needs and welfare of those the Exchange was meant to serve. They reveal that stock prices move through time according to prearranged formulas that have nothing to do with the laws of supply and demand.

As matters now stand, the Stock Exchange is as fascinating a study in folklore and primitive self-interest as anything that an early nineteenth-century frontier-town gambling casino had to offer. For more than a decade, observation of the facts about the Stock Exchange caused me to regard its practices as immoral and uncontrollable. I was, however, able to employ my study of the general principles surrounding the activities of Stock Exchange insiders to develop a methodology for minimizing risks and maximizing profits in the market.

It is my belief that this book will serve the needs of the small investor by creating some order out of the tangled folklore that surrounds the market. I have attempted to introduce him to a practical way of understanding and utilizing the market in order to add to income. By providing him with a better understanding of what constitutes a logical frame of reference for investing in the market on a low-risk basis, I hope to enable him to develop the skills that will better prepare him for the hazardous moment when he commits his money into the market.

Appendix A

DOW STOCKS

Symbol	Stock	Specialist
(A)	Anaconda	Blair S. Williams & Co.
(AA)	Alcoa	Asiel & Co.
(AC)	American Can	Lief, Werle & Co.
(ACD)	Allied Chemical	Picoli & Co.
(AMB)	American Brands	Adler, Coleman & Co.
(BS)	Bethlehem Steel	Walter N. Frank & Co.
		Travers & Hume
(C)	Chrysler	Zuckerman, Smith & Co.
(DD)	Du Pont	Robb, Peck, McCooey & Co., Inc.
(EK)	Eastman Kodak	Robb, Peck, McCooey & Co., Inc.

(ESM)	Esmark	Phelan, Silver & Co.
(GE)	General Electric	Stokes, Hayt & Co.
(GF)	General Foods	Williams, Eisele & Co.
(GM)	General Motors	Blair S. Williams & Co.
(GT)	Goodyear	Robb, Peck, McCooey & Co., Inc.
(HR)	Int'l Harvester	Phelan, Silver & Co.
(IP)	Int'l Paper	Weil & Duffy
(JM)	Johns-Manville	Walter N. Frank & Co.
		Travers & Hume
(N)	Int'l Nickel	Weil & Duffy
(OI)	Owens-Illinois	Adler, Coleman & Co.
(PG)	Procter & Gamble	Zuckerman, Smith & Co.
(S)	Sears	Sprague & Nammack
(SD)	Standard Oil of California	Ziebarth, Geary & Co.
(T)	American Telephone & Telegraph	Le Branche & Co.
(TX)	Texaco	Asiel & Co.
(UA)	United Aircraft	Benjamin Jacobson & Sons
(UK)	Union Carbide	Wagner, Stott & Co.
(WX)	Westinghouse	Benton, Corcoran, Leib & Co.
(X)	U.S. Steel	Benton, Tompane & Co.
(XON)	Exxon	Ernest & Co.
		Ware & Keelips
		Homans & Co.
(Z)	Woolworth	de Cordova, Haupt, Andrews & Co.

Appendix B

	10/01/74		*10/02/74*		*10/03/74*		*10/04/74*	
	close	volume						
Dow (Dow Jones Ind. Av.)	604.82	1,804,600	601.53	1,115,900	587.61	1,718,900	584.56	1,630,400
NY (N.Y. Stk. Ex. Comp.)	vol-16,890,000			12,230,000		13,150,000		15,910,000
A (Anaconda)	H–14⅞		15⅛		14⅞		15	
	L–13¾		14¾		14½		14½	
	C–14⅞	V–13,200	14¾	18,600	14⅞	13,600	15	24,200
AA (Alcoa)	38½		39¼		37⅞		37	
	37¼		37⅞		36⅞		36½	
	38	37,200	38	22,900	36⅞	42,000	36¾	18,100
AC (American Can)	23⅜		24¼		24⅛		24⅝	
	22¾		23⅛		23¾		24	
	23⅛	5,000	24	4,900	24	3,700	24⅝	9,400
ACD (Allied Chemical)	27		27		26½		24¾	
	25½		26⅜		24¾		23	
	26⅜	25,300	26⅞	9,200	25⅛	17,000	24⅜	28,700
AMB (American Brands)	29¼		29½		29½		29¼	
	28¾		28¾		29⅛		29	
	28⅞	9,000	29¼	4,300	29⅛	4,500	29⅛	5,900
BS (Bethlehem Steel)	25⅝		25⅞		25¾		24⅞	
	24⅝		25½		24⅝		24¼	
	25½	31,700	25½	20,400	24¾	44,500	24⅝	35,200

	10/01/74		10/02/74		10/03/74		10/04/74	
C (Chrysler Corp.)	12⅛		12¼		12¼		12	
	12		12⅛		11⅞		11¼	
	12	44,200	12⅛	19,200	12	51,400	11⅝	85,700
DD (Du Pont)	107		105½		100⅝		98½	
	102		100¾		96		93½	
	105	64,900	100⅞	29,800	97⅞	64,600	94¾	75,400
EK (Eastman Kodak)	66⅜		66⅜		63¾		62½	
	63¼		64⅞		61¼		60½	
	65½	135,400	64⅞	57,500	62⅝	72,600	60¾	114,500
ESM (Esmark)	24¾		24½		23⅜		23	
	23½		23¾		23		22⅛	
	24¾	5,200	23¾	4,800	23	10,400	22¾	4,000
GE (General Electric)	33		34⅝		33⅝		33¼	
	30½		33⅜		32⅝		32	
	33	124,600	34¼	57,100	33⅜	70,500	32⅞	88,400
GF (General Foods)	17⅛		17¾		17⅜		17⅝	
	16½		17¼		16⅞		16½	
	17⅛	28,300	17¼	10,800	17⅛	12,100	16¾	78,800
GM (General Motors)	36⅜		36⅜		35⅝		35½	
	35¼		35½		35⅛		35	
	35¾	94,400	35¾	83,600	35⅜	61,300	35⅛	92,800

GT (Goodyear Tire)	13¾		14		13⅞		14	
	13⅜		13¼		13⅝		13½	
	13¾	23,500	13¾	26,000	13¾	70,000	13⅝	59,100
HR (Int'l Harvester)	19¾		20		20		19⅞	
	18⅝		19½		19½		19⅜	
	19¾	38,100	19⅞	13,400	19¾	16,300	19⅝	23,300
IP (Int'l Paper)	35⅞		37		36⅛		35⅝	
	34⅝		35⅞		35⅜		35	
	35⅞	22,300	36¾	12,800	35½	50,600	35⅝	26,300
JM (Johns Manville)	15¼		15½		15⅜		15¼	
	14¾		15		15		14⅞	
	15	17,800	15	6,100	15	5,800	15	7,500
N (Int'l Nickel)	22½		22¾		22⅝		22½	
	21⅞		22¼		22¼		21½	
	22¼	10,700	22⅝	7,300	22¼	8,200	21⅝	68,700
OI (Owens Illinois)	29¾		29⅞		29½		29¾	
	29¼		29⅝		29¼		29¼	
	29⅝	9,700	29⅝	4,300	29¼	4,900	29¼	8,600
PG (Procter & Gamble)	71¼		70¾		70		69¼	
	68¾		69¼		68⅛		67	
	70	64,300	69¾	34,100	68¼	30,000	68¾	31,300
S (Sears)	51½		50¾		49⅞		46¾	

	10/01/74		10/02/74		10/03/74		10/04/74	
	49½		49¾		47¾		44⅝	
	50½	96,000	49⅞	32,600	48½	45,200	45⅛	81,700
SD (Std. Oil Of Cal.)	22		21¾		20⅞		21¾	
	21½		21		20⅛		20⅛	
	21½	71,100	21	95,400	20⅜	72,700	21⅝	80,300
T (Amer. Tel. & Tel.)	41⅛		40½		40½		40⅞	
	40		40⅛		40		40⅛	
	40	419,500	40⅜	167,400	40¼	196,300	40¾	135,700
TX (Texaco)	21¼		21¼		20½		21⅝	
	20⅜		20⅜		20		20⅛	
	20⅞	104,100	20⅝	123,300	20⅛	164,000	21½	96,000
UTX (Utd Technologies)	26⅜		26⅞		26¾		25⅞	
	25¾		26¼		25½		25¼	
	26¼	8,000	26½	17,700	25½	21,500	25⅝	4,000
UK(Union Carbide)	35⅞		35⅜		35⅜		34	
	34½		35		33⅝		33¼	
	35¼	44,200	35¼	28,300	33⅝	56,500	34	28,100
WX (Westinghouse)	10⅛		10⅛		9⅞		9¼	
	9¾		9⅞		9		8¾	
	10	95,000	9⅞	88,800	9⅛	409,900	9	188,200

X (U.S. Steel)	38⅝		36¾		36⅛		37¼	
	35⅞		36⅛		35⅜		35⅝	
	36⅞	92,300	36¼	48,400	36	34,000	37¼	40,000
XON (Exxon)	58¾		58½		56½		56⅜	
	57½		55⅞		54⅞		54⅞	
	58⅜	51,900	56¼	52,100	54⅞	57,600	55¾	79,400
Z (Woolworth)	10⅞		10⅞		10⅞		10⅞	
	10½		10⅝		10⅝		10⅝	
	10¾	17,700	10⅝	14,800	10¾	7,200	10⅞	11,100

	10/07/74		*10/08/74*		*10/09/74*		*10/10/74*		*10/11/74*	
Dow	607.56	1,408,600	602.63	1,404,300	631.02	1,486,400	648.08	2,218,400	658.17	1,804,500
NY		15,000,000		15,460,000		18,820,000		26,360,000		20,090,000
A	16		16¼		16½		17¼		17	
	15⅜		15⅞		15⅜		16		16½	
	15⅞	12,300	15⅞	18,800	16⅛	13,100	16¾	28,100	17	14,900
AA	37⅞		37⅝		36		36¾		36⅜	
	36¾		33⅜		33½		35		34¾	
	37¾	31,500	33⅜	114,900	36	51,300	35½	73,900	35¾	62,300
AC	24¼		24⅞		25⅛		26		26¼	
	23¾		24⅛		24⅛		24⅞		25½	
	24	4,700	24⅞	7,200	25	10,300	25¾	15,500	26⅛	5,600

	10/07/74		10/08/74		10/09/74		10/10/74		10/11/74	
ACD	25¾		25⅝		27¾		32½		32⅞	
	24½		25		24½		29¾		31⅛	
	24¾	36,900	25⅛	14,100	27¾	18,400	31¼	63,000	32⅜	34,000
AMB	30¾		31¼		31⅜		33½		33½	
	29⅛		30½		29⅞		31¼		32½	
	30½	5,700	30½	7,100	31¼	6,200	32⅞	10,000	32⅞	7,700
BS	25¾		26		27⅛		28		27⅞	
	25⅛		25		24¾		27⅛		27	
	25¾	31,000	25¼	52,100	27⅛	49,500	27⅛	43,900	27⅞	36,000
C	12⅛		12⅜		12⅜		12⅜		11⅞	
	11¾		11⅞		11⅝		11⅝		11½	
	12⅛	38,800	11⅞	31,800	12¼	43,400	11⅝	94,200	11⅝	59,100
DD	98⅞		98⅜		101½		106½		108	
	95¾		97⅛		95⅞		103		104⅛	
	98	49,800	97⅜	26,100	101½	48,800	104¾	69,800	108	55,800
EK	64⅛		64¼		69¾		73½		74⅞	
	62		63⅛		62⅞		69¾		70⅞	
	63¾	81,000	63½	90,600	69¾	97,500	72⅜	179,800	74	114,100
ESM	24		24⅜		24¼		25⅛		26¼	
	22½		23¾		23¾		24		25	
	24	2,600	23¾	6,300	24¼	3,900	25	10,300	26⅛	9,100

GE	34⅝		34⅝		36⅜		38⅞		38	
	32⅝		33¼		33⅛		36¾		36½	
	34⅝	65,200	33¾	79,700	36⅜	82,200	37⅝	152,900	37⅜	115,400
GF	17⅛		18⅛		19½		21⅜		21	
	16⅝		17⅜		17¾		20		19½	
	17⅛	33,800	17⅞	15,100	19½	15,400	20⅝	33,600	19⅝	21,000
GM	35¾		35½		36⅝		37½		36¾	
	35⅛		35		35		35⅝		35⅞	
	35⅜	181,900	35⅛	104,100	36⅝	109,500	35⅞	116,300	36	104,100
GT	14½		14½		14¾		14⅞		14¼	
	13⅝		13⅝		13½		14⅛		13¼	
	14½	31,700	14	18,000	14¾	26,500	14¼	15,600	14⅛	24,700
HR	20½		20½		21⅜		22⅜		21⅞	
	19½		20⅛		19¾		21½		20⅞	
	20⅜	22,600	20¼	16,100	21⅜	25,300	21¾	40,000	21	33,600
IP	37⅝		38		39¾		43¼		43¼	
	36¼		36½		37⅛		40½		41⅛	
	37⅝	29,900	37⅝	29,000	39¾	24,200	42	89,000	42¾	27,400
JM	15½		15¾		16		17		16½	
	15		15⅜		15⅜		16⅛		16	
	15½	11,600	15⅝	19,400	16	10,200	16⅜	23,600	16½	7,800
N	22⅝		22⅞		23⅞		24⅝		24⅝	

	10/07/74		10/08/74		10/09/74		10/10/74		10/11/74	
	21¾		22½		22⅜		24		24	
	22½	17,300	22⅝	15,500	23¾	36,000	24⅜	19,100	24⅜	9,900
OI	29⅞		30½		31¼		32⅞		33⅞	
	29⅛		29⅝		30¼		31½		32¾	
	29⅞	13,200	30½	24,200	31¼	6,300	32⅛	10,300	33⅝	4,500
PG	70¾		71½		70¾		74¾		77⅜	
	69		69½		67		71¼		72¾	
	70¾	47,100	69⅝	26,300	69⅝	79,800	72½	55,200	77¼	32,100
S	46¾		46⅞		47¾		50		50⅝	
	45		45		44½		48⅛		47½	
	46⅜	48,100	45⅜	39,300	47¾	51,600	48¾	52,200	49¼	48,100
SD	23		23⅜		24½		24⅝		24	
	21⅞		22½		22⅝		23¾		23⅛	
	23	80,600	23	48,000	24	67,000	24¼	73,900	23⅝	97,900
T	41¾		42⅝		44⅛		44⅝		44¾	
	41		41⅞		42⅛		44		44	
	41⅝	133,600	42½	135,300	43½	156,700	44¼	155,900	44½	145,000
TX	22¾		22¾		23		23½		23	
	21⅞		21⅞		21⅜		22½		22⅜	
	22¾	113,700	22¼	105,500	23	115,700	22¾	127,200	22⅞	100,500

UTX	26⅜		26⅝		26⅞		28⅞		28⅞	
	26		26		25¼		27½		28	
	26⅜	3,400	26⅛	3,400	26⅞	16,000	28⅞	34,500	28⅝	116,900
UK	37		37⅞		38⅛		40½		41⅝	
	34½		35¾		35¼		38¼		39¾	
	37	26,100	35¾	32,000	38	37,300	40	74,800	41⅝	76,700
WX	10		10		10		10⅛		10	
	9¼		9½		9¾		9⅞		9⅛	
	10	110,500	9¾	206,300	10	122,900	10	169,300	9⅛	243,900
X	38⅞		39⅜		40⅝		41⅞		41½	
	37⅝		38⅜		38⅛		40½		40½	
	38¾	27,900	38½	28,900	40½	32,700	41⅛	57,700	41¼	56,300
XON	59½		60⅞		64¼		66⅞		66¼	
	56¼		58½		58⅞		64⅛		63	
	59⅜	81,300	60½	63,600	64	101,300	64⅛	136,200	65⅜	89,700
Z	11⅛		11		10⅞		11⅛		11⅛	
	10⅝		10¾		10½		10¾		10⅞	
	10⅞	34,600	10¾	25,500	10¾	27,400	11	192,600	11⅛	45,400
	10/14/74		*10/15/74*		*10/16/74*		*10/17/74*		*10/18/74*	
Dow	673.50	2,005,500	658.40	1,621,400	642.29	1,623,000	651.44	1,247,400	654.88	1,571,900
NY		19,770,000		17,390,000		14,790,000		14,470,000		14,500,000

	10/14/74		10/15/74		10/16/74		10/17/74		10/18/74	
A	18½		18		16⅞		16½		16⅝	
	16¾		16½		16¼		15⅞		15⅞	
	17⅞	23,500	16½	23,000	16¼	8,200	16	14,800	16⅜	12,900
AA	39½		37⅞		36½		35⅝		35⅜	
	36¼		35½		34⅞		35		34⅝	
	38	43,000	36	45,500	35	56,400	35⅜	33,300	34¾	29,000
AC	26⅝		26½		26		26		26⅛	
	25⅞		25¾		25⅛		25½		25⅝	
	26¼	8,400	25⅞	15,000	25½	6,200	26	4,400	26	4,200
ACD	34¾		34		33		31½		33¼	
	32½		32⅞		31⅜		30		31⅝	
	33¼	34,800	33½	37,300	31½	41,700	31	25,100	33¼	36,100
AMB	33½		33		32⅞		32¾		32¾	
	33		32		32⅛		32⅛		32⅛	
	33¼	6,900	32⅜	6,500	32½	5,400	32¼	6,900	32⅜	8,700
BS	28		27⅜		27		27⅝		28	
	27¼		26⅛		26		26½		26⅞	
	27¼	48,700	26¼	121,300	26½	45,800	27⅜	29,400	27⅛	59,600
C	12⅜		12⅜		11⅞		11½		11⅝	
	11¾		11⅞		11⅜		11⅛		11	
	12⅜	78,000	12	67,000	11½	68,800	11⅜	69,500	11	45,900

DD	116¼		113		109½		107⅞		109¼	
	109⅛		108		106		105½		99	
	113	50,400	108½	38,500	107	39,300	106¼	43,900	100	122,600
EK	78½		76¾		72½		69¾		71¾	
	74¾		73		64½		66		69⅛	
	76	148,000	73⅜	144,700	64½	224,700	69⅛	175,500	69⅞	136,300
ESM	26⅞		26¾		26		25¾		26¾	
	26½		25⅞		25⅝		25⅛		25½	
	26½	8,600	25⅞	42,700	25¾	6,700	25⅛	2,000	26½	7,300
GE	38½		37½		36⅞		36⅜		37⅛	
	37⅜		36		35⅝		35¼		36½	
	37⅞	82,700	36½	64,800	35¾	54,100	35⅞	58,900	36½	101,200
GF	20¾		20⅞		20		19¾		19⅝	
	19⅝		20¼		19¼		19		19¼	
	20⅝	15,500	20¼	19,100	19¼	29,900	19⅝	6,600	19½	27,600
GM	38		37¾		37		36⅝		36⅝	
	36⅛		36⅝		36⅛		35⅞		35½	
	37⅛	92,600	37⅜	93,300	36⅛	74,200	36¼	63,900	35⅝	111,700
GT	14⅜		14⅝		14⅛		14¼		14¾	
	14⅛		13⅞		13½		13⅝		14⅛	
	14⅜	57,400	14	83,800	13⅝	265,100	14¼	38,000	14⅝	28,600
HR	21⅜		20⅜		19⅞		20		20½	

	10/14/74		10/15/74		10/16/74		10/17/74		10/18/74	
	20⅜		19¼		19½		19½		19¾	
	20⅜	27,800	19½	33,300	19¾	11,500	20	13,400	19⅞	20,600
IP	44⅛		42⅞		41⅜		41¼		41¾	
	42⅝		40¾		40⅛		40½		40⅝	
	42⅞	76,900	41	33,200	40⅞	23,100	41	52,200	41	22,100
JM	16⅞		17		16½		16⅜		16⅝	
	16⅜		16⅝		15		15¼		16¼	
	16⅝	9,500	16¾	7,800	15½	77,200	16⅛	20,300	16½	6,100
N	24¾		24⅜		24		24⅝		24¾	
	24⅜		24		23½		23⅛		24	
	24¾	9,900	24	23,700	23½	18,400	24⅝	22,100	24⅛	27,500
OI	34¾		34		33⅝		33		33¾	
	33⅝		33⅛		32¾		32⅝		32¾	
	34	11,800	33¼	7,100	33¼	4,100	32⅝	5,000	32¾	6,700
PG	81⅜		81¾		80¼		81⅜		83⅞	
	77½		78½		79¼		78		82	
	79⅝	35,200	80⅜	24,500	79¼	19,800	80¾	33,100	82⅝	24,500
S	53¼		53		52		51⅞		51⅜	
	50½		51⅛		49⅞		50¼		50	
	51¾	36,100	51⅜	39,300	50¾	54,200	50⅝	40,700	50¼	45,100
SD	24½		24¼		24		24⅛		25	

	23¾		23¾		23¼		23⅛		24⅛	
	24⅜	87,500	24	44,200	23⅝	35,400	24	42,100	25	78,700
T	45⅜		45⅛		45⅛		45¼		45⅝	
	44¾		44⅝		44½		44⅝		45⅜	
	45	229,200	44⅞	89,300	44⅞	77,300	45¼	81,100	45½	145,000
TX	23⅜		23¼		22⅞		22⅞		23⅜	
	22⅞		22½		22½		22⅛		22¾	
	23	139,100	22¾	88,800	22⅝	60,300	22¾	70,800	23¼	89,400
UTX	29¾		29⅝		28½		28⅜		28⅞	
	28⅛		27⅞		27½		27⅛		27¾	
	29¼	26,400	27⅞	37,600	27⅞	6,800	28⅜	9,300	28½	9,500
UK	43		42¾		40		41¼		43½	
	41⅜		40¾		38		38¾		41⅞	
	42¼	88,300	41	105,600	38⅝	69,100	41¼	43,400	43½	98,500
WX	10		10		9¾		9½		9⅞	
	9¼		9⅝		9⅜		9⅛		9⅜	
	9¾	353,500	9¾	177,400	9⅜	141,000	9⅜	151,200	9⅞	106,400
X	42¾		41⅜		40½		41½		42¾	
	41¼		39¾		39½		40		41¾	
	41⅝	49,300	40⅛	87,200	40	30,400	41½	22,900	42	92,800
XON	68½		68		66		66⅛		67⅝	

	10/14/74		10/15/74		10/16/74		10/17/74		10/18/74	
	65½		65		64¾		64¼		66⅝	
	66	86,200	66	86,500	64⅞	39,500	65⅞	43,100	67¼	48,400
Z	11¼		11¼		11		11		11	
	11		11		10¾		10⅝		10⅝	
	11¼	40,300	11⅛	35,000	10⅞	28,400	11	24,500	11	18,900
	10/21/74		10/22/74		10/23/74		10/24/74		10/25/74	
Dow	669.82	1,488,400	662.86	1,653,300	645.03	1,539,500	636.26	1,431,100	636.19	1,239,200
NY		14,500,000		18,930,000		14,200,000		14,910,000		12,650,000
A	17		17¾		17		16¼		16¾	
	16⅛		17⅛		15		15		16⅛	
	17	11,100	17¼	17,600	15¼	63,800	16	21,400	16⅜	15,000
AA	36¼		38		35¾		34⅞		35¼	
	34		35		35		34		34	
	36	44,800	35⅞	42,600	35⅛	13,100	34¼	10,700	34⅜	34,100
AC	26½		26¾		26⅛		26		25¾	
	25¾		26		25⅞		25½		25⅛	
	26½	12,900	26⅜	6,100	25⅞	4,000	25¾	4,800	25⅛	11,800
ACD	33⅝		34⅜		33		29⅞		30¼	
	32½		33¼		30⅞		29⅛		29⅝	
	33⅝	38,200	33¼	23,900	31	21,600	29⅜	28,200	30¼	25,300

AMB	33¼		33¼		32⅜		30½		30	
	32¼		32⅜		30⅝		29¼		29⅜	
	33	5,700	32⅜	6,100	30⅞	8,300	29½	9,000	29⅜	6,100
BS	27¾		27⅞		27		26¾		27⅜	
	26⅞		26¾		26⅜		26		26½	
	27⅝	30,600	26⅞	28,800	26¾	14,800	26⅛	23,000	26¾	25,800
C	11⅛		10⅞		10⅝		10½		10¼	
	10½		10⅝		9⅝		9½		10⅛	
	10¾	117,300	10¾	79,100	9¾	184,300	10⅛	127,000	10¼	62,000
DD	107½		106½		105		102½		103	
	98⅛		101⅝		99½		98½		100¾	
	105½	74,300	103½	45,700	104	65,600	102½	56,000	101¾	29,200
EK	75		75½		72		70¼		70¾	
	68¼		72½		69¼		67⅜		68½	
	74⅜	65,900	72¾	101,600	69⅞	99,400	70	86,400	69	50,300
ESM	27⅜		27¾		26⅞		26⅛		26⅞	
	26		27		26¼		25⅝		25⅜	
	27¼	7,000	27	14,500	26¼	4,700	26	4,100	26¼	5,600
GE	38		38⅜		36¾		36⅛		36⅛	
	36⅝		37		35¾		34⅞		34⅝	
	38	81,700	37⅛	150,700	36½	75,100	35½	103,300	34⅞	68,900

	10/21/74		10/22/74		10/23/74		10/24/74		10/25/74	
GF	20		20¼		19¾		19⅛		19⅜	
	19½		19⅝		19⅜		18⅜		18¾	
	19¾	12,600	19¾	18,900	19⅝	5,100	18¾	11,900	19	9,400
GM	35⅝		35⅜		34¼		33⅛		33⅝	
	34⅝		34⅜		33		32⅝		32⅜	
	35	153,600	34½	127,100	33¼	162,500	33	153,900	33⅛	167,900
GT	15		15⅛		14⅞		14½		14⅞	
	14½		14¾		14⅜		14¼		14¼	
	14⅞	91,300	14⅞	19,900	14½	18,800	14¼	15,600	14⅜	32,000
HR	20⅜		20⅝		19⅞		19¾		19¾	
	19¾		19¾		19⅜		19		19⅛	
	20¼	23,700	20	24,500	19½	21,100	19⅜	19,300	19⅛	13,300
IP	41¾		42		40¾		39⅝		39½	
	40¾		41		39⅜		38¾		38⅝	
	41¾	25,600	41¼	78,900	39⅞	37,500	39⅛	69,900	39	83,800
JM	16¾		16¼		15⅞		15¾		16	
	16⅛		15⅞		15⅝		15¼		15½	
	16¼	6,000	15⅞	7,300	15⅝	4,500	15¾	6,400	15¾	6,000
N	24½		24¾		24¼		23⅝		23¾	
	24⅛		24⅜		23⅝		23¼		23¼	
	24¼	8,400	24½	18,100	24	32,100	23¼	11,700	23½	22,800

OI	33⅜		33⅞		33½		33⅜		33½	
	32⅜		33¼		33		32⅞		33	
	33⅜	3,900	33⅜	10,800	33	4,500	33	8,600	33½	2,100
PG	86¼		88¼		86⅝		85		85⅜	
	82⅜		86½		84¼		82¾		83¼	
	85¾	25,700	87	48,400	85	43,500	83½	33,200	83¾	40,900
S	50¾		50⅞		49¼		47⅛		47⅝	
	48		49⅜		46¾		45		45¼	
	50¾	55,800	49⅜	59,100	47⅛	52,800	46⅜	53,200	45⅜	32,100
SD	25¼		25⅜		24¾		23⅞		24¼	
	24⅝		24⅝		23⅝		23¼		23¼	
	25¼	42,800	24⅞	44,900	24	68,300	23⅝	52,700	23¾	42,000
T	46		46⅝		45¾		45½		45¾	
	45¼		45¾		45¼		44¾		45⅛	
	46	77,000	45⅞	170,600	45½	89,100	45½	97,700	45¼	62,300
TX	24		24¼		23¾		22⅞		23¼	
	23		23½		22⅜		22		22½	
	24	83,800	23⅞	83,700	22½	94,000	22½	90,300	22⅞	87,100
UTX	29		29⅜		29		28⅜		28⅛	
	28¾		28¾		28⅝		27¾		27¾	
	29	11,200	28⅞	45,100	28¾	6,400	27⅞	7,100	27¾	6,600

	10/21/74		10/22/74		10/23/74		10/24/74		10/25/74	
UK	43¼		43⅝		42¼		41¾		42½	
	42⅝		42¾		41⅝		40¾		41½	
	43¼	36,600	42¾	51,400	41¾	65,700	41½	46,700	41⅞	37,700
WX	9⅞		9⅞		9⅜		9⅜		9½	
	9½		9¼		9		9		8⅞	
	9¾	247,300	9¼	170,400	9	140,300	9¼	168,500	9	149,000
X	42½		42⅝		40		38¾		39⅛	
	41⅜		40½		38¾		37½		38½	
	42¼	34,100	40½	47,400	39	59,100	38¾	37,600	38⅞	33,400
XON	68½		69⅞		68⅜		66⅞		66⅜	
	66⅞		68⅝		66⅝		65¼		65¼	
	68⅜	37,300	68⅞	75,300	66¾	71,100	65¾	49,100	65⅞	46,100
Z	11⅛		10¾		10¾		10¾		10¾	
	10⅝		10½		10½		10½		10⅜	
	10⅞	22,200	10¾	34,500	10¾	8,400	10½	23,500	10½	31,400
	10/28/74		*10/29/74*		*10/30/74*		*10/31/74*		*11/01/74*	
Dow	633.84	962,500	659.34	1,394,900	673.03	1,809,700	665.52	1,544,700	665.28	1,268,900
NY		10,540,000		15,610,000		20,130,000		18,840,000		13,470,000
A	16⅜		16⅝		16⅝		16¼		16⅜	
	15⅞		16⅛		16		16		15⅞	

	16¼	8,200	16⅝	10,500	16¼	11,200	16	78,000	16⅛	10,600
AA	35¼		35⅝		37		36		33⅛	
	33¾		35¼		35¼		33		31½	
	34½	11,400	35⅜	18,000	36⅜	39,500	33	48,200	32	53,800
AC	25⅜		25⅜		25½		25⅝		25¾	
	24½		24¾		25		25¼		25⅛	
	24¾	4,200	25	3,900	25⅛	5,100	25¼	6,200	25½	5,400
ACD	31		32½		31¼		32⅜		31⅝	
	29⅞		31½		29⅞		30⅞		30⅜	
	31	11,700	31½	30,000	30¾	65,600	31½	22,900	31⅝	18,500
AMB	29⅝		30		32¼		33⅛		32½	
	29¼		29⅜		30⅜		31		31⅝	
	29⅜	6,800	30	8,800	31⅜	8,800	32⅝	10,700	32½	5,900
BS	27⅝		28⅛		29⅛		29		28¼	
	26⅝		27½		27⅞		28		27⅝	
	27½	14,900	28	68,400	28⅝	56,700	28¼	33,200	28⅛	29,800
C	10		10		10⅛		10¼		10	
	9⅝		9⅞		10		10		9⅞	
	9¾	91,600	10	81,700	10	63,900	10⅛	47,300	9⅞	37,600
DD	101⅝		104		107½		109¼		108⅞	
	100⅛		101½		104		106¼		106½	
	100⅝	20,500	104	31,000	106½	54,700	107	33,100	108⅛	32,500

	10/28/74		10/29/74		10/30/74		10/31/74		11/01/74	
EK	69		73⅞		75¾		76		72⅝	
	67½		70		73¼		71½		71⅛	
	68½	33,500	73⅞	73,100	74¾	128,000	71⅝	103,000	72	57,100
ESM	26¼		27		27⅞		28½		30½	
	26		26⅛		27		27⅞		28¾	
	26⅛	3,100	27	7,700	27¾	4,500	28½	6,000	29¾	23,800
GE	35⅞		37⅜		38¼		38⅝		39	
	34⅜		36		36⅝		37¼		37¾	
	35⅝	44,600	37¼	87,400	37¾	109,000	38¼	93,600	39	67,000
GF	19		19		19		19½		19¾	
	18⅜		18⅝		18½		18⅝		19⅛	
	18¾	12,300	19	6,900	19	17,500	19⅜	14,500	19⅝	9,400
GM	32½		34¾		34⅝		34¼		33¾	
	31⅝		32⅛		33¾		33½		33¼	
	31⅞	185,900	34¾	167,100	34⅛	133,100	33⅝	110,300	33⅜	148,500
GT	14¼		14¼		14⅜		14½		14¼	
	13⅞		14		14		13¾		13⅞	
	14⅛	56,600	14	30,400	14¼	41,000	14	82,700	14¼	65,400
HR	19		19⅜		20¼		20⅝		20¼	
	18⅝		19		19¼		20⅛		19⅞	
	18⅞	16,500	19¼	22,300	20	30,200	20⅜	27,300	20⅛	17,300

IP	39		40⅜		42¼		42		40½	
	38½		39⅜		40½		41		39¾	
	38¾	5,000	40⅜	39,500	41½	43,600	41¼	38,000	39¾	42,900
JM	15½		15⅝		16¾		17		16⅜	
	15⅛		15⅛		15¾		16⅛		16⅛	
	15¼	6,500	15½	4,700	16¾	23,400	16¼	20,600	16¼	2,100
N	23⅝		23⅛		23¾		24¼		23¾	
	23⅛		22¾		23⅜		23½		23⅜	
	23⅜	2,000	23⅛	31,400	23⅝	7,900	23⅝	17,700	23⅝	9,300
OI	33		34		35¼		35⅞		35½	
	32⅛		32¾		33⅞		34⅜		35⅛	
	32¾	4,800	33¾	5,100	34½	9,100	35⅝	5,400	35⅛	8,600
PG	84½		89		93		92		89	
	82⅛		85¾		88¼		86¾		86¼	
	83½	12,500	89	49,200	91⅞	47,300	86¾	50,500	86½	15,800
S	46¼		49⅝		54		56		53½	
	44⅝		46½		49⅝		51⅝		51¼	
	45⅝	34,300	49½	74,100	53⅜	90,700	52	73,000	52½	53,700
SD	23⅞		24⅛		25⅜		25⅝		25⅛	
	23½		23¼		23¾		25		24½	
	23½	15,400	24	39,700	25⅛	104,800	25	78,600	25	46,400

	10/28/74		10/29/74		10/30/74		10/31/74		11/01/74	
T	45⅛		46⅛		46½		46¾		46½	
	44⅝		45¼		45⅞		46		45⅞	
	44⅞	85,100	45⅞	87,600	46¼	154,700	46¼	121,100	46½	159,200
TX	23⅜		24¼		24		24		23⅜	
	22⅝		23¼		23⅝		22¾		22⅜	
	23⅜	59,600	24¼	97,000	23¾	102,800	22¾	108,500	22⅞	106,100
UTX	28¼		28⅞		28⅝		28⅞		28⅝	
	27⅜		28¼		28¼		28⅜		28¼	
	28¼	3,000	28¾	6,000	28⅝	4,900	28⅝	6,100	28⅜	3,800
UK	42		44¼		46		45⅜		44⅞	
	41⅛		42¼		44⅛		44⅞		44⅛	
	42	24,700	44¼	78,300	45½	178,100	44⅞	98,300	44⅜	40,600
WX	9⅛		9		9¼		9⅝		9⅜	
	8¾		8¾		8⅞		9⅛		9⅛	
	8⅞	117,800	8⅞	129,800	9⅛	119,100	9½	148,200	9¼	85,100
X	39⅜		41⅝		42¾		43		42⅜	
	38¾		39½		41⅛		42		41⅛	
	39	17,700	41⅝	35,400	42¼	64,900	42¼	34,700	41¼	43,600
XON	65⅞		68¾		71		70⅜		69⅛	
	64⅝		66		68⅞		68¼		67¾	
	65⅞	37,200	68⅝	57,700	69⅞	73,500	68½	77,500	68⅞	58,500

Z	10½		10½		10⅞		11		10⅞	
	10¼		10¼		10⅜		10⅝		10⅝	
	10¼	15,100	10½	12,200	10¾	15,400	10¾	19,700	10⅞	10,600
	11/04/74		*11/05/74*		*11/06/74*		*11/07/74*		*11/08/74*	
Dow	657.23	966,300	674.75	1,225,100	669.12	1,871,400	671.93	1,320,600	667.16	1,187,900
NY		12,740,000		15,960,000		23,930,000		17,150,000		15,890,000
A	16¾		17⅞		18¼		18¼		17⅞	
	16		16⅞		17¼		17½		17¼	
	16¾	5,500	17¾	9,900	17¼	10,500	17⅞	11,500	17¾	10,400
AA	32¼		33¼		33⅞		32⅝		32⅛	
	31		31¾		32⅛		30¾		30¾	
	31¾	16,700	33¼	49,000	32¼	26,000	30¾	25,100	31	39,100
AC	25⅝		26⅛		26½		26		26⅛	
	25⅛		25⅝		25⅞		25¾		25½	
	25⅝	4,400	26⅛	12,800	26	21,400	25¾	4,400	25⅞	12,900
ACD	31¼		32½		34¼		34		34⅜	
	30⅜		30⅜		32		31¾		33½	
	30¾	10,000	32½	12,400	32¼	32,800	33⅞	21,700	34¼	14,200
AMB	32½		32½		33½		33¼		32½	
	32		31¾		32½		32½		31⅝	
	32	4,200	32⅜	5,500	33	11,000	32½	11,900	31⅞	6,700

	11/04/74		11/05/74		11/06/74		11/07/74		11/08/74	
BS	27⅜		26¾		27		26⅞		26⅜	
	26⅝		26¼		26¼		26⅛		25½	
	26⅞	18,300	26½	21,300	26¾	26,100	26¼	23,300	26¼	26,400
C	10		10¼		10¼		10		10⅛	
	9¾		9¾		9⅝		9¾		9¾	
	9⅞	37,300	10¼	70,400	9⅞	73,100	9⅞	36,100	10⅛	53,700
DD	108		110⅜		112¾		111		109⅜	
	106⅛		106¾		107¼		107½		107½	
	107¼	29,200	110⅜	37,200	107¼	83,600	109½	34,600	108⅛	36,100
EK	72⅞		75		77½		75¾		75	
	70½		71⅝		73¼		73¼		74⅛	
	71¾	57,500	74⅞	70,900	73¼	93,500	74	63,800	74⅜	48,700
ESM	29½		30		30¼		30¾		29⅞	
	29¼		29¼		29¾		29⅜		29¾	
	29⅜	10,200	29⅞	9,100	29¾	11,600	30⅛	9,300	29⅞	2,500
GE	38⅝		39⅞		40½		39¾		39⅜	
	38		37¾		38½		38⅜		38⅜	
	38½	54,400	39⅞	60,200	38½	96,700	39⅜	80,500	38¾	57,200
GF	19⅞		19¾		20⅜		19⅞		19¼	
	19⅜		19⅛		19¾		19⅜		18⅝	
	19½	8,100	19¾	8,300	19⅞	29,400	19⅜	25,100	18¾	15,200

GM	34⅛		35½		36¼		35		34¾	
	32⅝		33⅝		35⅝		34½		33⅞	
	34	92,600	35⅜	97,500	35¾	137,500	34⅞	145,300	34¼	120,500
GT	14⅛		14¾		15		14⅞		14¾	
	13¾		14		14½		14¼		14⅛	
	14	38,100	14½	20,200	14½	36,500	14¾	15,600	14¼	15,100
HR	20⅛		20⅜		20⅝		19⅞		19⅞	
	19⅝		19¾		19¾		19¾		19⅝	
	20	16,300	20⅜	19,600	19¾	31,000	19⅞	18,900	19¾	26,100
IP	39½		39⅞		41⅝		40⅝		40⅜	
	39⅛		38⅝		40		40		39⅞	
	39¼	11,600	39⅞	16,000	40½	53,900	40	59,900	40	20,300
JM	16⅛		16⅞		17⅛		16⅝		16⅜	
	15¾		15¾		16⅜		16¼		16¼	
	16	14,100	16⅞	17,000	16⅜	12,600	16¼	10,100	16¼	5,400
N	23¼		23⅛		23¼		22⅝		22⅜	
	22¾		22½		22½		22¼		22⅛	
	22⅞	38,600	23	11,100	22⅝	62,800	22⅜	14,500	22¼	25,400
OI	35		35		36⅛		36		36	
	34¼		34¼		35½		35⅝		35¼	
	34½	7,400	35	2,500	35¾	9,100	36	9,900	35¼	2,000

	11/04/74		11/05/74		11/06/74		11/07/74		11/08/74	
PG	87¼		90½		92½		91		93	
	84½		87⅜		88		87⅜		90⅞	
	87¼	24,400	90¼	17,700	88⅜	40,000	91	21,400	91⅜	27,200
S	52		53¾		55⅞		55		53¾	
	50⅝		50⅝		53⅞		52⅝		51½	
	51⅛	33,000	53⅝	27,300	54	69,100	53⅝	45,200	51¾	43,800
SD	24⅞		25⅛		25½		24¾		24¾	
	24		24¼		24½		24		23⅝	
	24¾	29,400	24⅞	55,800	24½	58,200	24¼	48,200	23⅝	45,400
T	46⅜		47		47¾		47⅝		47⅝	
	46		46¼		47		47⅛		47	
	46⅜	66,500	47	129,400	47¼	223,900	47⅛	162,700	47⅜	103,300
TX	22⅝		23		23¾		22½		22⅜	
	22¼		22¼		22¼		22		21⅝	
	22¼	79,500	23	60,000	22⅜	115,500	22¼	110,200	22	105,600
UTX	28½		28½		29⅛		29¾		29⅞	
	28		27		27⅞		27½		29¼	
	28	6,700	28⅛	16,500	28	18,900	29⅝	15,700	29⅝	7,200
UK	43¾		43½		45		44½		44⅜	
	42		41⅜		43⅞		43½		43⅝	
	42	52,200	43⅜	91,100	44⅛	125,500	44⅛	82,700	44	61,700

WX	9⅜		10		10¼		9⅞		9¾	
	9		9⅛		9½		9½		9½	
	9⅛	75,500	9⅞	161,300	9½	175,000	9⅞	69,700	9¾	76,700
X	40⅜		40⅛		41		40		38¾	
	38¾		39¾		39⅝		38½		37⅞	
	39⅞	76,000	40	32,000	40	57,300	38¾	71,200	38	119,800
XON	68⅜		68¾		70¼		69¾		69	
	66¾		67¼		68⅝		68½		68⅛	
	67⅞	38,100	68⅝	43,600	69	112,200	68⅞	61,600	68¾	50,100
Z	11		11¼		11⅛		11		11	
	10⅝		11		10⅞		10⅝		10¾	
	11	10,400	11	39,600	10⅞	16,700	10⅞	10,500	10⅞	8,500
	11/11/74		*11/12/74*		*11/13/74*		*11/14/74*		*11/15/74*	
Dow	672.64	895,900	659.18	1,035,000	659.18	1,316,800	658.40	1,021,600	647.61	966,900
NY		13,220,000		15,040,000		16,040,000		13,540,000		12,480,000
A	18		17¾		17½		17¾		17⅜	
	17⅝		17⅛		17¼		17⅛		17	
	17⅝	8,800	17¼	10,700	17½	14,200	17¼	10,300	17	11,300
AA	31½		31½		31¾		33¼		32¾	
	31⅛		31		31		32		30⅞	
	31½	18,900	31	62,400	31⅝	30,500	32¼	33,200	31	27,000

	11/11/74		11/12/74		11/13/74		11/14/74		11/15/74	
AC	26		26¼		26½		26¾		26⅞	
	25⅜		25⅞		25⅞		26⅜		26⅝	
	26	4,000	25⅞	3,400	26½	4,100	26¾	6,700	26⅝	7,200
ACD	34⅜		34⅜		33		33		33¼	
	33¼		33⅛		32		32¼		32⅛	
	34¼	9,300	33⅛	16,400	32⅝	27,700	32⅜	6,900	33¼	4,400
AMB	32½		32⅞		32⅜		32⅛		31⅜	
	31¾		32½		31¾		31½		30¾	
	32½	3,500	32¾	7,200	32¼	4,900	31⅝	4,300	31⅛	6,600
BS	26⅞		26⅝		26		26⅞		26⅜	
	25⅞		25¼		25⅛		26¼		25⅝	
	26½	15,800	25½	35,900	25¾	28,900	26⅜	24,500	26	33,400
C	10⅛		10⅛		10		9⅞		9⅝	
	9⅞		9⅞		9¾		9⅝		9⅛	
	10	42,900	9⅞	29,900	9¾	29,300	9⅝	28,700	9⅛	80,500
DD	108¼		107½		105¾		108		104½	
	107¼		103		101⅝		104⅝		102	
	107¾	20,300	103¼	45,100	104¾	39,300	104⅞	26,000	103	16,700
EK	75⅞		75⅝		74⅛		74¾		71⅞	
	74		73		72¾		71¼		69½	
	75¾	30,800	73⅝	65,400	73½	78,200	71¼	75,500	69¾	63,600

ESM	30¼		29⅞		29¾		29¾		29½	
	29¾		29¼		28⅝		29½		29	
	30	3,100	29¼	7,600	29½	7,200	29½	2,200	29¼	12,400
GE	39⅞		39⅝		38		38⅛		37¼	
	38⅛		38		36⅝		37¼		35¾	
	39⅝	27,300	38⅛	42,200	37	98,300	37½	55,400	36	42,000
GF	18⅞		18¾		18⅝		19¼		18¾	
	18¼		18½		18¼		18⅛		18⅛	
	18⅞	13,400	18⅝	10,600	18⅜	10,000	18½	17,600	18⅜	9,900
GM	34¼		34⅛		34¾		35⅛		33⅞	
	33⅝		33½		33		33⅝		33	
	34⅛	78,800	33⅝	69,200	34¾	136,800	33¾	108,500	33¼	78,400
GT	15		14⅞		14⅞		15		15	
	14⅛		14⅜		14½		14¾		14½	
	15	25,000	14⅝	27,300	14¾	22,400	15	47,000	14¾	34,300
HR	20⅛		20⅝		20⅛		20¼		20⅝	
	19½		19¾		19⅝		19¾		19⅞	
	20⅛	21,700	20⅛	19,100	19⅞	10,400	19⅞	11,300	20⅝	14,300
IP	40¾		40½		41¼		41⅜		40¼	
	40		40		39⅞		40		38¾	
	40½	7,300	40⅛	25,200	41¼	21,800	40¼	20,100	39	18,500

	11/11/74		*11/12/74*		*11/13/74*		*11/14/74*		*11/15/74*	
JM	17¼		17⅛		17		17⅝		17⅝	
	16½		16¾		16⅜		17		17	
	17⅛	19,900	16¾	3,800	17	7,700	17½	13,800	17¼	12,800
N	22⅜		22½		22⅛		22⅜		22⅜	
	22		21⅞		21½		21⅞		21⅞	
	22¼	8,300	21⅞	25,400	21¾	16,800	22	20,800	22⅜	9,600
OI	35½		35⅜		35		35¾		35⅝	
	35		35⅜		34⅛		35		35¼	
	35½	3,100	35⅜	900	35	11,000	35¾	5,200	35⅝	4,100
PG	92⅛		91⅞		90⅝		89¾		87⅜	
	91⅜		89⅞		88¾		87⅜		84⅞	
	91¾	12,300	89⅞	20,900	88⅞	28,900	87½	24,700	84⅞	31,000
S	52⅝		52¾		51¾		52		50½	
	50⅞		51		50⅝		50¾		48⅞	
	51⅞	21,100	51⅛	30,200	51½	45,500	50¾	49,300	49⅛	42,400
SD	23¾		23¾		23⅜		23¼		22⅞	
	23⅛		23¼		23		22⅝		22¼	
	23⅝	40,500	23½	29,200	23⅛	41,700	22¾	43,400	22¾	29,900
T	47¾		48		47¾		47⅞		47¾	
	47		47½		47⅜		47⅝		47⅜	
	47¾	106,600	47¾	69,600	47⅝	109,500	47⅝	80,800	47½	92,300

TX	22¼		22¼		21⅜		22		21⅞	
	21⅝		21⅝		21		21⅜		21½	
	22¼	97,200	21¾	105,700	21¼	154,600	22	81,000	21½	94,700
UTX	31⅛		31½		30¾		30½		30½	
	29		30		29⅝		29¾		29⅝	
	30¾	13,300	30⅛	23,300	30⅜	7,600	30¼	13,800	29⅞	2,700
UK	44⅛		44		42⅞		43¼		43¼	
	43⅞		42½		41⅝		42⅝		42½	
	44	37,300	42¾	35,600	42¼	54,700	43⅛	28,700	42½	27,900
WX	10⅛		10⅛		9⅞		9⅞		9¾	
	9⅝		9½		9½		9⅝		9½	
	10	135,900	9½	122,400	9⅞	141,900	9¾	52,600	9½	81,400
X	38⅛		38⅛		38⅞		39¼		38½	
	36⅞		36½		36½		38¼		37¾	
	38⅛	42,700	37	47,600	38¼	56,700	38½	56,200	38	23,600
XON	69		69¼		67⅞		66⅞		66⅝	
	68¼		68¼		65⅞		65⅝		65	
	68¾	18,600	68⅜	34,300	65⅞	67,300	66¾	62,300	65	45,400
Z	11		11⅛		11		11⅛		11⅛	
	10⅞		10⅞		10⅞		10⅞		10⅞	
	11	8,200	10⅞	8,500	10⅞	8,900	11⅛	10,800	10⅞	8,600

	11/18/74		11/19/74		11/20/74		11/21/74		11/22/74	
Dow	624.92	1,386,700	614.05	1,483,100	609.59	1,089,900	608.57	1,869,900	615.30	1,224,500
NY		15,230,000		15,720,000		12,430,000		13,820,000		13,020,000
A	16¾		15⅞		16		16		16⅛	
	15⅛		15⅝		15½		15½		15⅞	
	15⅞	13,800	15⅞	4,900	15⅞	4,900	15⅞	4,900	16⅛	3,700
AA	30¾		29¾		29¼		30		30½	
	29¼		28⅝		28¾		28¾		30	
	29¼	57,000	28¾	37,100	28¾	14,700	29½	17,700	30½	42,800
AC	26½		26⅛		26⅛		26		26	
	25⅞		25⅞		26		25¾		25¾	
	26⅛	6,600	26	6,000	26	5,100	25¾	3,700	26	3,900
ACD	32½		32⅜		32⅜		32		31⅝	
	32		31½		31		31		31¼	
	32¼	6,600	31½	28,900	31	10,300	31⅛	10,300	31¼	16,500
AMB	31⅝		29⅞		29⅜		29⅞		30½	
	29¾		29		28⅞		29		29⅞	
	29¾	11,200	29	8,100	29¼	5,400	29⅝	4,300	30¼	3,100
BS	26		25⅞		26⅜		26⅜		27⅜	
	25⅜		25¼		25⅝		25⅝		26½	
	25⅜	20,400	25¾	21,800	25¾	19,100	26⅜	19,400	26¾	24,400

C	9⅛		8⅞		8⅞		8⅞		8⅞	
	8½		8½		8⅝		8⅝		8½	
	8½	128,600	8⅝	70,200	8¾	50,400	8¾	39,900	8½	54,300
DD	102½		99		98		94		94½	
	99¼		96¼		93⅞		92¼		90	
	99⅝	51,200	97	34,300	94	32,500	92¼	86,200	90	47,600
EK	68½		68		68		68¼		68¼	
	67		66		66		65⅜		67⅛	
	67¼	80,800	66⅝	68,500	66¼	60,800	66⅜	66,600	67⅞	67,700
ESM	28¾		28⅞		28½		27⅞		28⅛	
	28¼		28⅜		27¾		27		27½	
	28¾	6,000	28½	5,500	27¾	3,100	27⅝	5,800	27⅝	3,200
GE	35⅛		34⅝		34¾		34⅝		35⅞	
	33¾		33⅝		33½		33¼		34⅝	
	34	69,500	34⅛	59,600	33¾	43,500	34¼	65,800	35¼	48,600
GF	18½		18⅝		18⅜		18¾		18¾	
	17¾		17⅞		18		18⅛		18⅛	
	18	22,500	17⅞	26,500	18⅜	23,200	18¼	10,600	18⅛	22,700
GM	32½		31⅝		31⅜		31⅛		31¼	
	31½		31		31		30⅝		30⅞	
	31¾	162,000	31¼	157,800	31¼	104,700	30⅞	90,900	30⅞	93,700

	11/18/74		11/19/74		11/20/74		11/21/74		11/22/74	
GT	14⅝		14¼		14		13⅝		14⅛	
	14¼		13¾		13½		13½		13¾	
	14¼	28,100	13¾	70,900	13¾	23,900	13½	20,600	14	14,500
HR	20½		20½		20¼		20⅝		20½	
	20		19½		19½		19⅝		20⅛	
	20	14,700	19½	23,500	19¾	13,400	20¼	16,600	20⅛	15,200
IP	38¼		38⅛		37¾		36⅞		37⅜	
	37¾		37¼		36⅞		36⅛		36¾	
	38	21,300	37½	21,100	37	27,400	36¾	33,100	37¼	20,700
JM	16⅞		16⅝		16¾		16¾		17¼	
	16⅜		15¾		16⅜		16¼		16⅝	
	16⅜	7,500	16⅝	25,800	16⅝	20,700	16⅝	66,300	16⅞	9,800
N	22		21⅞		21⅞		21⅜		21½	
	21¾		21⅝		21½		21		21	
	21⅞	18,200	21¾	10,100	21½	20,300	21	8,900	21¼	14,500
OI	35¼		35¼		34⅞		33⅝		34¼	
	35⅛		34¾		33½		33¼		33¼	
	35⅛	6,400	34¾	5,700	33½	14,100	33¼	3,200	33¾	5,800
PG	84½		81½		79⅜		81⅝		83½	
	82		78½		78		78⅜		81½	
	82⅛	27,900	78½	35,600	78¾	34,400	80¾	19,700	82½	32,000

S	48⅜		46⅞		47		46⅛		47½	
	46½		45⅝		45⅛		45		45¾	
	46½	43,200	46	43,100	45⅛	59,100	45⅝	42,000	45⅞	41,900
SD	22⅝		21⅞		21⅝		21½		21⅝	
	22		21		21		21		21	
	22⅛	41,600	21½	48,900	21¼	67,800	21½	49,600	21¼	43,900
T	47⅛		46½		46¼		43¼		43¾	
	46		45½		45⅝		42½		43	
	46	105,900	45⅝	113,900	45⅝	60,100	42⅝	870,300	43⅝	263,400
TX	21½		20⅞		20⅝		20½		20⅞	
	20⅝		20¼		20⅛		20⅛		20⅜	
	20¾	191,400	20½	156,200	20⅜	118,900	20⅜	105,200	20¾	100,000
UTX	29¼		29		29		29		30	
	28¼		28⅜		28⅜		28¼		28⅝	
	29	14,900	28½	23,200	28¾	8,800	28¼	2,600	30	25,800
UK	42		40¾		40¼		39⅝		40¾	
	40¾		39¼		39¼		38¾		40	
	40⅞	50,600	39½	75,900	39½	30,700	39⅜	21,800	40¼	48,400
WX	9⅜		9¼		9⅛		9⅜		9⅜	
	9		8¾		8⅞		8⅞		9	
	9	88,100	8¾	168,700	8⅞	100,100	9¼	61,900	9	82,400

	11/18/74		11/19/74		11/20/74		11/21/74		11/22/74	
X	37⅝		37		37⅝		38		38½	
	36⅝		36		36⅜		36⅝		38	
	36⅞	35,700	36¼	66,400	37⅛	34,800	37¾	27,000	38	15,600
XON	64⅝		62⅛		60⅞		59⅛		60¼	
	62½		60½		59⅛		58¼		59¼	
	62½	42,600	60⅞	45,900	59½	60,100	58⅞	83,400	59½	44,600
Z	10⅞		10¾		10⅝		10½		10⅜	
	10⅝		10½		10⅜		10⅛		10⅛	
	10¾	12,400	10½	19,000	10⅜	17,600	10⅛	11,600	10⅛	13,800
	11/25/74		11/26/74		11/27/74		11/28/74		11/29/74	
Dow	611.94	1,064,900	617.26	1,507,600	619.29	1,517,400	HOLIDAY		618.66	815,800
NY		11,300,000		13,600,000		14,810,000				7,400,000
A	16⅛		15⅝		15⅞				15⅝	
	15¼		15¼		15⅜				15⅛	
	15¼	6,100	15⅜	3,100	15½	4,700			15⅜	3,200
AA	30¾		30½		31¼				31⅛	
	29⅜		29¼		30				30½	
	29⅝	36,000	29¾	10,600	30⅜	30,200			31⅛	4,400
AC	26		26⅛		26¼				26¼	

	25¾		25⅞		26		25⅞	
	25⅞	3,800	25⅞	6,200	26	6,200	25⅞	8,400
ACD	31½		32¼		32¼		32¾	
	31		31⅛		31¾		31¾	
	31½	15,300	31⅞	7,600	32	5,300	32¾	10,000
AMB	30⅜		30⅜		31		31	
	29⅞		29⅞		30⅛		30½	
	30¼	5,900	30⅜	6,400	30⅞	7,900	30½	4,700
BS	27⅜		27⅜		27⅞		26¾	
	26⅞		27		27		26⅜	
	27¼	23,800	27	20,900	27	16,700	26½	7,400
C	8⅝		8¾		8½		7⅞	
	8½		8½		7¾		7⅝	
	8⅝	58,300	8½	46,800	7¾	216,800	7⅞	71,100
DD	90¾		93¾		94⅝		92¾	
	87½		89½		92		89¾	
	89⅜	39,700	92½	41,300	92	29,700	90½	21,500
EK	69½		69⅛		69⅛		66	
	66¾		67⅝		64½		64	
	68⅞	62,300	68	61,700	65¾	74,200	64⅝	55,100
ESM	27⅞		28¾		28¼		27⅞	
	27⅝		28		27¼		27½	
	27¾	1,400	28	25,500	27¾	7,700	27½	1,400

	11/25/74		11/26/74		11/27/74		11/28/74		11/29/74	
GE	36⅜		35¼		36⅝				37⅛	
	34⅞		34		35¼				36¼	
	35⅜	45,500	35⅛	349,000	36⅜	80,900			37⅛	34,800
GF	18⅜		18		19				19	
	17⅝		17½		17¾				18⅜	
	17¾	18,500	17⅝	23,100	18⅝	19,200			18¾	11,800
GM	31		31		31¼				30¾	
	30⅛		30		30⅝				30½	
	30¼	100,200	30½	117,100	30⅝	107,000			30½	59,900
GT	14		14⅛		14				13⅝	
	13¾		13¾		13¾				13⅛	
	13¾	16,000	14	18,700	13¾	30,800			13¼	19,200
HR	20⅜		20⅝		21				20¾	
	19⅞		20		20¼				20⅜	
	20⅛	15,100	20½	16,800	20⅝	22,900			20⅝	7,200
IP	37⅞		38¼		38				37⅛	
	37⅛		37⅛		37				36¼	
	37⅛	23,600	37½	34,700	37	35,800			37⅛	13,700
JM	17		17		17¼				17	
	16⅝		16⅝		16⅞				16⅞	
	16⅝	7,800	16⅞	7,100	17¼	7,500			17	2,800

N	21⅛		21¼		21⅜		21⅜	
	20¾		20⅞		21		21	
	20⅞	28,700	21	9,900	21¼	9,900	21⅜	7,200
OI	33¾		32⅞		33		32¾	
	32½		32½		32⅜		32¼	
	33	8,900	32⅞	11,600	32⅜	8,000	32½	1,600
PG	83		85¾		85⅜		83⅛	
	81⅛		82⅝		83¾		81¾	
	83	27,500	84	28,500	84	22,400	82¾	8,300
S	45⅝		46½		47¼		47¼	
	43¾		43⅞		45¾		46⅝	
	44	53,800	45⅞	83,600	46¼	54,600	47¼	37,000
SD	21½		21⅝		22		21½	
	21		21⅛		20¾		21	
	21⅜	34,700	21½	64,000	21½	112,300	21⅛	75,700
T	43		43		43⅝		43¼	
	42⅜		42⅝		43⅛		42⅞	
	42⅝	138,600	42⅞	130,800	43½	119,700	43¼	50,400
TX	20¾		20¾		21¼		21½	
	20⅜		20⅜		20⅝		20¾	
	20⅝	105,600	20⅝	125,400	20⅞	147,900	21½	102,700

	11/25/74		11/26/74		11/27/74		11/28/74		11/29/74	
UA	30⅞		30¼		30⅜				30	
	29¾		29¼		29½				29⅜	
	30	22,100	30	14,100	29¾	10,800			30	8,600
UK	40⅛		40⅜		43				41¾	
	39¾		39¾		40½				41	
	40⅛	23,200	40¼	68,600	41¼	44,100			41⅝	30,400
WX	9¼		9⅛		9⅛				9	
	9		9		8⅞				8¾	
	9⅛	73,600	9	63,300	9	150,500			8⅞	104,100
X	38¼		38¾		40				39	
	37¾		37⅞		39				38⅝	
	37¾	15,300	38¾	17,100	39⅛	26,400			38¾	10,400
XON	60⅜		61½		63⅝				63	
	59⅛		58⅞		60⅝				61⅝	
	59⅞	43,500	60⅛	73,200	61½	69,200			62¾	26,100
Z	10⅜		10¼		10⅛				10⅛	
	10⅛		10		9⅞				9⅞	
	10⅛	13,500	10⅛	20,900	10	37,600			9⅞	16,700
	12/02/74		12/03/74		12/04/74		12/05/74		12/06/74	
Dow	603.02	1,097,000	596.61	1,275,400	598.64	1,391,200	587.06	1,275,900	577.60	1,592,200

NY		11,140,000		13,620,000		12,580,000		12,890,000		15,500,000
A	15½		15⅛		15⅛		14⅜		13⅞	
	14⅞		14¾		14⅜		13⅝		13¼	
	15	7,700	14¾	9,300	14½	12,000	13¾	29,500	13¼	10,900
AA	31½		30¾		30		27⅜		26⅝	
	30⅝		29¾		26¾		26		26	
	31	26,100	29⅞	37,900	27⅛	99,800	26	74,300	26⅜	43,600
AC	26		25⅞		25⅞		25⅞		25⅛	
	25⅝		25½		25⅜		25⅛		24⅝	
	25⅝	3,800	25⅝	7,500	25⅝	5,900	25⅜	11,900	24⅞	5,900
ACD	32⅜		32		31½		31⅝		30⅜	
	31⅞		31		31		30⅞		29⅜	
	32	3,400	31	17,500	31½	13,100	31	9,000	29⅞	21,200
AMB	30⅞		30⅞		32		32		30⅞	
	30⅛		30½		31		31¼		30⅜	
	30⅞	4,800	30¾	6,500	31⅝	5,900	31¼	7,100	30⅜	7,600
BS	26½		25¾		25¾		25⅞		25¼	
	25⅜		25⅛		25¼		25⅛		24⅜	
	25½	14,300	25⅝	21,400	25½	16,400	25¼	22,700	24½	28,600
C	7⅞		7¾		7⅝		7⅝		7⅜	
	7⅝		7½		7½		7¼		7	
	7¾	38,000	7½	63,700	7⅝	60,800	7¼	71,100	7⅛	67,900

	12/02/74		12/03/74		12/04/74		12/05/74		12/06/74	
DD	89½		88¼		89¼		89¼		87⅝	
	88⅛		87		87½		86¼		84½	
	88⅝	23,400	87¼	49,700	88¼	21,300	86⅝	27,300	86¼	61,700
EK	62⅞		62½		63½		62½		60⅞	
	61⅝		61¼		61½		60⅜		59⅛	
	62	70,400	61¾	50,900	62⅛	86,800	60⅜	53,700	59⅝	120,500
ESM	27½		26¾		26⅝		26¾		26½	
	26¾		26⅛		26⅜		26		25¾	
	26¾	5,800	26¼	2,400	26½	1,400	26	5,000	26	6,100
GE	36¾		35¾		35¾		35⅞		34⅜	
	36½		34⅞		35⅛		34½		33⅜	
	36½	30,400	35⅛	51,700	35⅜	38,300	34⅝	63,300	33⅝	68,700
GF	18⅝		18¾		18½		18⅛		17⅞	
	18⅛		18⅛		17⅝		17⅝		17⅜	
	18⅜	8,700	18½	10,400	17¾	19,000	17⅝	10,600	17¾	14,700
GM	30⅜		30		30		29½		29⅞	
	30		29⅝		29⅜		29		28⅞	
	30	104,000	29⅝	108,900	29½	114,500	29⅛	127,000	29⅜	156,300
GT	13⅛		12¾		12¾		12⅝		12⅜	
	12¾		12⅜		12⅜		12¼		12	
	12¾	18,500	12½	27,400	12⅝	32,600	12⅜	33,200	12⅛	24,300

HR	20⅞		20⅛		20⅛		20½		20¾	
	20¼		19½		19⅝		19⅞		19¾	
	20⅜	16,800	20	20,100	19⅞	21,800	20⅛	17,000	20⅜	19,100
IP	36⅞		35¼		35½		35¼		33	
	34⅝		35		34⅝		32½		31⅝	
	35½	22,700	35	19,900	35¼	27,700	32¾	54,100	31¾	83,400
JM	17⅛		17		17		17⅛		16⅞	
	16⅞		16¼		16⅞		16¾		16½	
	16⅞	5,200	17	31,300	17	8,800	16¾	6,600	16⅝	10,400
N	21¼		20⅝		20¾		20½		19⅞	
	20¾		20½		20½		20⅛		19¾	
	20¾	19,700	20½	25,000	20½	16,300	20⅛	23,400	19⅞	17,400
OI	32¼		30¼		31		31⅜		30⅜	
	30		30		30¼		30⅝		30⅛	
	30	7,900	30¼	4,600	31	16,300	30¾	5,500	30⅛	3,800
PG	82½		80¾		82½		82½		79⅞	
	80½		79¾		81¼		80¼		78¼	
	81¼	13,800	80¾	14,300	81¾	13,500	80⅜	16,500	78⅜	38,400
S	47¼		47		47⅜		46⅞		44⅛	
	45⅝		45¼		46½		44½		43	
	45⅞	31,900	46½	39,500	46¾	33,700	44⅝	39,100	43⅜	50,400

	12/02/74		12/03/74		12/04/74		12/05/74		12/06/74	
SD	21⅜		20¾		20¾		20⅞		21	
	20⅝		20¼		20⅜		20½		20½	
	20¾	38,300	20½	58,800	20¾	70,600	20⅞	69,600	20½	66,600
T	43		42⅛		42¼		42¼		41⅝	
	42¼		41¾		41⅝		41⅝		41¼	
	42¼	54,600	41⅞	160,300	41⅞	127,600	41¾	104,700	41¼	90,200
TX	21½		21		21¼		21		20½	
	20⅞		20¾		20½		20⅜		20⅛	
	21	100,200	20⅞	96,600	20⅝	133,800	20½	116,900	20½	120,300
UTX	29¾		29		28¾		29½		29	
	28½		27		28¼		28¼		28	
	28¾	14,100	28⅛	17,600	28⅝	23,500	28¼	12,400	28½	14,500
UK	41¼		39⅝		40⅛		39⅝		38½	
	39½		38⅞		39¼		38⅞		37¼	
	39⅝	32,000	38⅞	33,500	39⅝	48,100	39	21,500	37⅜	53,400
WX	8⅞		8¾		8¾		8¾		8⅝	
	8⅝		8½		8½		8⅝		8¼	
	8⅝	300,700	8¾	176,500	8¾	225,200	8⅝	141,900	8½	213,100
X	38¾		37½		37⅝		37⅝		36¾	
	37⅞		36¾		36½		36⅜		36	
	38	31,300	37¼	43,600	37⅝	47,900	36½	25,900	36¼	40,100

XON	62½		61⅞		62		62½		60¼	
	61⅝		61⅛		61⅛		60⅞		59	
	61⅝	32,000	61½	33,800	61½	32,600	60⅞	61,500	59⅝	61,900
Z	10		9⅝		9⅝		9¾		9½	
	9⅝		9⅜		9¼		9⅝		8⅞	
	9⅝	16,500	9½	34,800	9½	16,400	9⅝	13,600	8⅞	71,200
	12/09/74		*12/10/74*		*12/11/74*		*12/12/74*		*12/13/74*	
Dow	579.94	1,327,500	593.87	1,469,800	595.35	1,388,400	596.37	1,380,200	592.77	1,093,900
NY		14,660,000		15,690,000		15,700,000		15,390,000		14,000,000
A	13⅝		13¾		13⅝		14		14⅛	
	13⅛		13⅜		13¼		13⅛		13¾	
	13⅜	22,200	13⅜	10,900	13¼	22,100	14	15,400	13¾	8,800
AA	26½		27¾		27¾		27¾		27½	
	25⅞		26¾		27		27⅛		27¼	
	26¼	17,000	27½	25,700	27⅛	16,700	27⅜	22,600	27½	21,800
AC	25		26⅛		26¼		27		27	
	24⅜		25⅛		25⅝		26		26⅝	
	24⅞	8,800	26⅛	8,600	26⅛	7,200	26¾	8,400	26⅞	7,900
ACD	29⅜		30		30¾		29⅞		29¼	
	28¾		28⅞		30⅛		29¼		28¾	
	28¾	11,500	29¾	11,300	30¼	13,100	29¼	22,600	28¾	9,800

	12/09/74		12/10/74		12/11/74		12/12/74		12/13/74	
AMB	30⅞		31¼		31⅛		31¼		31⅝	
	30⅛		30⅝		30⅝		30¾		31	
	30⅝	7,300	30⅝	6,500	30¾	9,200	31¼	7,900	31¼	4,700
BS	24¾		24⅞		25		25½		25⅛	
	24⅛		24⅜		24½		24¾		24¾	
	24¼	19,000	24¾	14,400	24¾	14,800	24⅞	39,600	24⅞	14,500
C	7⅛		7¾		8⅜		8¾		8⅝	
	7		7⅛		7⅝		7⅞		8⅜	
	7	85,300	7⅝	86,100	8⅛	84,200	8½	103,000	8⅜	50,000
DD	87⅞		91		90		88¾		89¾	
	86		87½		87¾		86		87½	
	86⅞	30,200	88⅞	31,800	87¾	15,800	88¾	27,200	88⅛	32,900
EK	62⅞		63⅜		63		62⅜		61⅛	
	59⅛		61½		61¼		60⅛		59	
	61⅞	69,800	61½	100,500	61⅜	54,400	60½	62,700	59	75,800
ESM	26⅝		27¾		28¼		28		28⅛	
	26⅛		26¾		27¼		27½		27¾	
	26⅝	2,600	27⅝	6,000	28⅛	6,600	27⅞	2,100	28	2,100
GE	33⅞		34⅞		35¼		33¾		33⅜	
	32⅞		33⅝		33¾		32¼		32⅛	
	33¼	65,600	34⅜	61,800	33¾	71,900	32⅝	85,100	32⅞	49,500

GF	17⅞		17⅞		17¾		17⅞		17⅞	
	17		17⅛		17¼		17⅛		17¼	
	17¼	24,000	17⅜	21,800	17¼	12,400	17½	23,200	17¼	14,800
GM	29⅞		30¾		31¾		32⅛		32⅜	
	29		29¾		30⅜		30⅞		31⅝	
	29⅜	158,400	30½	185,100	31¼	163,000	32	188,000	31⅞	96,700
GT	12⅜		12⅝		12⅜		12⅝		12½	
	11¾		12⅛		12		12		12	
	12⅛	26,800	12¼	29,000	12	54,000	12⅛	15,400	12	36,300
HR	20½		20½		20¾		20¼		19¾	
	20		19¾		19⅞		19¾		18⅝	
	20¼	19,400	20	18,000	20	21,600	19⅞	24,400	18⅝	38,700
IP	32⅜		33⅝		34⅜		34⅜		34⅜	
	31¾		32¾		33¼		33½		33⅝	
	32⅛	19,000	33⅛	18,700	34	38,400	34¼	32,400	33⅝	38,200
JM	16⅞		17¼		17⅝		17¼		17¼	
	16⅝		16¾		17⅛		16⅞		16¾	
	16⅝	10,100	17⅛	6,500	17⅜	5,600	16⅞	12,400	17	17,500
N	20⅛		20⅜		20⅜		20¼		20½	
	19¾		19¾		20⅛		19⅞		20	
	20⅛	40,200	20⅜	47,200	20¼	20,300	20⅛	25,400	20⅜	25,600

	12/09/74		12/10/74		12/11/74		12/12/74		12/13/74	
OI	30¼		30¾		31		30½		29⅞	
	30		29¾		30¼		30		28¾	
	30	2,700	30¾	9,100	30½	8,200	30	3,900	29	4,100
PG	80¾		83½		83		82¾		80¾	
	78¼		80		80¾		80½		78⅛	
	80	26,400	81⅞	28,300	81¾	29,300	80¾	20,300	80	44,900
S	43¾		44¾		45¼		46¼		46¼	
	41½		43¼		44⅛		44⅜		45⅜	
	42½	55,200	44⅛	48,200	44¾	43,100	46¼	42,300	45⅞	33,400
SD	21		21⅞		23		23¼		23	
	20½		21⅛		21¾		22		22¼	
	21	85,000	21¾	84,400	22⅜	73,800	23	56,500	22⅜	43,800
T	42⅛		43⅞		43¾		44		44⅛	
	41⅜		42⅝		43¼		43⅜		43½	
	42⅛	114,000	43½	155,600	43⅝	123,000	43⅞	149,600	43⅞	70,200
TX	20⅝		21⅛		21½		21¾		22	
	20⅛		20⅝		20¾		21⅛		21⅜	
	20⅝	120,000	21	117,300	21¼	150,200	21⅝	138,400	21⅞	118,300
UTX	29½		30⅜		30		29⅜		29	
	28½		29½		29¼		28⅞		28½	
	29⅜	14,300	29⅞	11,900	29⅝	4,600	29⅛	3,100	28½	15,600

UK	38¼		39		39½		39⅜		39¾	
	37		37¾		38⅝		38⅜		38¼	
	37⅝	35,600	38⅞	63,200	38¾	31,400	38¾	20,600	39¾	18,800
WX	8½		8⅝		8¾		8⅝		8⅝	
	8¼		8⅜		8½		8½		8⅜	
	8⅜	87,400	8⅝	120,700	8⅝	123,900	8½	76,300	8⅜	80,200
X	36¼		36⅞		36⅞		37⅜		37⅛	
	35½		36¼		36½		36⅝		36¾	
	35¾	27,500	36½	30,800	36⅝	26,000	37⅛	26,500	36¾	31,000
XON	59¾		61⅛		63⅛		62¼		62⅞	
	58⅛		59¼		60⅞		61		61⅜	
	59⅜	71,500	60⅞	59,300	61⅝	100,800	61¼	97,800	62½	61,500
Z	9		8½		8½		8⅜		8⅜	
	8⅜		8¼		8⅛		8		8⅛	
	8⅜	50,700	8⅜	51,100	8⅜	42,800	8¼	27,000	8¼	26,500
	12/16/74		*12/17/74*		*12/18/74*		*12/19/74*		*12/20/74*	
Dow	586.83	1,340,600	597.54	1,291,100	603.49	1,444,000	604.43	1,617,000	598.48	1,325,900
NY		15,370,000		16,880,000		18,050,000		15,900,000		15,840,000
A	14		13⅝		13¾		13½		13½	
	13½		13¼		13⅜		13¼		13¼	
	13¾	19,300	13¼	7,600	13½	22,600	13¼	14,100	13⅜	8,000

	12/16/74		12/17/74		12/18/74		12/19/74		12/20/74	
AA	27¼		27¼		28¼		28⅛		28¾	
	26¾		26⅞		27		27⅝		28	
	27	37,200	27	23,300	27⅞	23,600	27¾	30,600	28¾	12,000
AC	27¾		27¾		28⅛		28⅛		28	
	27⅛		27¼		27¾		27⅝		27⅞	
	27⅜	6,600	27¾	11,200	27¾	13,000	28⅛	10,500	27⅞	5,900
ACD	29⅜		29⅝		30⅝		30½		30⅛	
	28⅞		28		30		29⅞		29½	
	28⅞	10,300	29¼	18,100	30⅛	12,000	30½	5,000	29½	17,800
AMB	31⅝		31¼		31½		31½		31½	
	31		30⅞		31⅛		31		30¼	
	31⅛	6,800	31⅛	10,000	31½	12,300	31¼	6,300	30¼	7,100
BS	25		24½		24⅞		24⅞		24⅞	
	24⅝		24¼		24½		24⅜		24½	
	24⅝	21,900	24½	13,800	24¾	10,500	24⅝	15,300	24⅝	17,800
C	8⅜		8⅛		8		7⅝		7⅝	
	8		7⅞		7⅝		7½		7¼	
	8	64,200	8	59,400	7⅝	70,300	7½	72,800	7¼	65,400
DD	88⅜		88¼		90½		92⅝		91⅜	
	87		87		89¼		89¾		89¾	
	87	35,700	88¼	32,100	90¼	56,300	91¼	45,000	90	22,900

EK	60¼		59⅝		61¼		61¾		61	
	58¼		57⅝		59¾		59½		59¾	
	58¼	82,300	59⅝	114,400	59¾	126,500	60¾	83,000	60½	46,500
ESM	28⅜		28		28		28¼		28	
	27⅝		27½		27½		27½		27⅝	
	27⅝	4,000	27¾	3,200	27¾	1,100	28¼	2,000	27⅞	700
GE	33⅜		32⅝		33¾		33¾		33⅝	
	31		30¾		32½		33¼		32¼	
	31	137,900	32⅝	62,900	33¼	69,900	33⅜	69,200	32¼	109,900
GF	17¼		16¾		16⅞		16⅞		17	
	16½		16¼		16⅜		16⅜		16½	
	16¾	30,800	16¾	26,200	16⅜	24,200	16⅞	174,200	17	30,500
GM	32¼		33⅜		33⅝		33⅛		32⅛	
	31½		31⅝		32⅞		32¼		31	
	31¾	160,000	33⅜	137,800	33⅜	127,500	32¼	201,600	31¼	139,900
GT	12⅜		12½		12⅞		12¾		12¾	
	12		12⅛		12½		12½		12½	
	12⅛	35,200	12½	34,600	12¾	57,100	12⅝	46,400	12¾	67,500
HR	19		19		19½		19¾		19⅝	
	18½		18⅛		19		19		19⅛	
	18½	21,100	18¾	29,900	19⅜	19,200	19¼	23,900	19½	19,500

	12/16/74		12/17/74		12/18/74		12/19/74		12/20/74	
IP	34		34½		34⅞		35		34¾	
	33½		33½		34⅜		34½		33¾	
	33¾	29,300	34½	39,900	34⅞	12,800	34½	29,900	33⅞	22,800
JM	17¼		17¼		17½		17		17	
	16⅞		17		17⅛		16⅝		16¾	
	17	13,200	17⅛	4,100	17⅛	25,200	17	12,800	16¾	5,600
N	20⅜		19⅞		20⅛		20		19⅜	
	19¾		19½		19⅞		19⅝		18⅞	
	19¾	22,300	19¾	12,800	20	19,000	19¾	30,700	19¼	40,300
OI	29¼		29¼		30¾		30½		30¾	
	29		28¾		29¼		30		30¼	
	29	1,800	29¼	6,200	30½	12,100	30¼	9,500	30½	1,900
PG	79⅝		80½		80¾		80¾		80½	
	77¾		77½		79¾		79		79½	
	77¾	26,900	80⅛	24,000	79⅞	42,000	80½	61,100	79¾	19,000
S	46⅛		47⅛		48½		49¼		48¾	
	45⅛		45⅜		47½		47¾		47½	
	45¼	34,500	47⅛	41,000	48½	61,600	48⅝	56,300	47½	41,200
SD	22⅝		22⅞		23⅛		22½		22⅛	
	22		21⅞		22⅝		21⅝		21⅜	
	22⅜	58,100	22⅞	71,700	22¾	65,300	21¾	60,200	21¾	67,300

T	44⅛		44¼		44⅜		44⅞		44½	
	43⅝		43½		43¾		43⅞		44	
	43⅝	66,200	43⅞	102,200	43¾	109,500	44⅜	101,300	44⅜	93,100
TX	22¼		22		22⅛		21⅝		20¾	
	21⅝		21½		21⅝		20¾		20½	
	21⅞	122,600	22	140,100	21⅝	176,300	20⅞	153,900	20¾	146,000
UTX	28¾		29½		31⅛		31¾		32¼	
	28		28¼		29⅞		30½		31⅝	
	28¼	4,300	29⅜	10,900	30¾	20,800	31¾	15,100	31¾	13,500
UK	40⅛		40¾		41⅞		42⅛		42	
	39¼		39¾		41⅛		41⅛		41⅜	
	39⅞	42,900	40¾	34,900	41¼	46,700	41⅞	31,100	41½	49,700
WX	8⅝		8½		8½		8½		8¼	
	8¼		8¼		8¼		8¼		8	
	8½	120,700	8½	91,700	8½	94,700	8¼	135,400	8¼	165,500
X	37		37¼		38¼		37⅞		38	
	36⅝		36⅜		37½		37½		37½	
	36⅝	23,400	37¼	24,300	37⅝	19,400	37¾	13,700	37½	22,100
XON	62⅝		63½		64¼		63		62¾	
	61⅞		62		63		62		61¾	
	62	78,500	63½	81,100	63	61,300	62¾	83,300	61¾	49,000

	12/16/74		*12/17/74*		*12/18/74*		*12/19/74*		*12/20/74*	
Z	8⅜		8½		8½		8½		8⅜	
	8⅛		8¼		8¼		8¼		8⅛	
	8⅜	22,600	8⅜	20,600	8¼	30,700	8¼	22,700	8⅜	17,500
	12/23/74		*12/24/74*		*12/25/74*		*12/26/74*		*12/27/74*	
Dow	589.64	1,521,000	598.40	968,700	HOLIDAY		604.74	899,500	602.16	1,072,800
NY		18,040,000		9,540,000				11,810,000		13,060,000
A	13⅜		13¾				13⅞		13½	
	13⅛		13⅛				13⅜		13⅛	
	13¼	15,700	13¾	5,400			13½	12,000	13⅜	12,900
AA	29⅜		29½				30		29¾	
	28½		29				29½		29⅜	
	29⅛	22,400	29⅛	8,000			29¾	13,500	29⅜	17,100
AC	28½		28¾				29		29	
	27⅝		28⅛				28½		28⅝	
	28	9,900	28⅝	3,300			28⅞	8,200	29	8,800
ACD	29½		27⅞				27¾		28	
	27¾		27½				27½		27	
	27¾	32,900	27¾	8,700			27½	10,300	27¼	10,100
AMB	29⅞		30				30⅜		30⅜	
	29⅛		29½				29⅝		30	

	29½	10,800	29⅞	3,900	30	5,000	30⅜	5,600
BS	24⅝		24⅞		25¼		25⅛	
	23½		24¼		24⅝		24⅞	
	24	33,700	24⅞	8,800	25	34,800	24⅞	29,900
C	7¼		7⅝		7¾		7⅝	
	7⅛		7⅛		7½		7¼	
	7⅛	96,500	7⅝	43,800	7½	62,300	7⅜	97,200
DD	89½		91¼		91½		91	
	88⅛		88¾		90⅞		90⅛	
	89	31,300	90½	10,700	91⅜	12,100	90½	8,800
EK	60¾		62¼		61⅞		61½	
	59		60⅛		60¾		60⅝	
	59⅝	97,200	61¼	42,900	61⅜	48,400	61	27,600
ESM	27⅞		28		28½		28¼	
	27½		27⅝		27⅞		27⅜	
	27⅞	1,900	28	1,800	28	1,600	27⅝	1,800
GE	32¼		32⅜		33¼		32⅞	
	31⅛		31¾		31⅞		32⅛	
	31¾	79,300	32	52,200	32⅝	66,400	32⅜	47,600
GF	17⅛		16⅞		17¾		17¾	
	16⅜		16⅜		16⅞		17⅛	
	16½	24,800	16⅞	10,800	17½	16,300	17⅜	14,000

	12/23/74		12/24/74		12/25/74	12/26/74		12/27/74	
GM	30⅞		30¾			31⅝		31½	
	30		29⅞			30⅝		30½	
	30	152,900	30½	61,300		31½	106,400	30¾	99,500
GT	12¾		12⅝			12¾		12¾	
	12½		12⅝			12½		12½	
	12½	34,600	12⅝	9,200		12¾	7,200	12½	28,400
HR	19½		19¼			19¼		19	
	18⅞		18⅞			18⅞		18⅝	
	19¼	25,200	19¼	12,900		19⅛	27,500	18⅝	14,200
IP	33⅞		32⅞			33		33⅜	
	32		32⅜			32½		32¾	
	32¼	35,200	32½	9,600		32⅞	13,200	33⅜	7,800
JM	16⅞		16¾			17⅜		18	
	16⅝		16⅝			16⅝		17⅛	
	16⅝	30,200	16¾	500		17¼	3,900	17⅞	5,300
N	19⅝		19⅝			20¼		20⅛	
	19⅛		19⅛			19⅞		19⅞	
	19⅛	9,200	19⅝	6,400		20⅛	13,500	20	5,100
OI	30½		30½			32¼		32	
	30¼		30⅜			31		31½	
	30⅜	9,400	30½	1,200		32	8,500	31¾	4,800

PG	79¾		81		81½		80½	
	78⅝		80		80		79⅝	
	79½	12,300	80	15,600	80⅝	17,900	79¾	26,000
S	47⅜		48¾		48⅞		49⅛	
	46⅜		47½		48		48⅛	
	47¼	51,000	48	26,200	48⅝	19,300	48⅛	29,000
SD	21⅞		22		22⅜		22	
	21⅛		21¼		21⅝		21⅝	
	21⅜	63,600	22	42,300	22	37,700	21⅞	36,200
T	44⅜		44⅛		44¾		44½	
	43⅜		43⅜		44¼		44⅛	
	43⅜	121,200	44⅛	78,100	44½	58,400	44⅛	60,700
TX	20⅝		20¾		21⅛		20⅞	
	20⅛		20⅛		20½		20⅛	
	20⅛	260,700	20¾	95,700	20½	145,300	20⅞	260,500
UTX	31⅝		31¾		32½		32⅝	
	30¾		30⅞		31½		32	
	31	9,500	31½	4,000	32¼	7,000	32¼	5,300
UK	41½		41⅞		41¾		41½	
	40½		41⅜		41		41⅛	
	41	26,800	41¾	15,000	41⅛	11,700	41¼	18,900

	12/23/74		12/24/74		12/25/74		12/26/74		12/27/74	
WX	8¼		8⅜				8½		8⅜	
	8		8⅛				8¼		8¼	
	8¼	112,800	8⅜	66,600			8⅜	64,100	8⅜	111,400
X	37⅜		37¼				38		38	
	36½		36⅞				37⅛		37⅝	
	37⅛	17,700	37	13,500			37⅝	5,100	37¾	14,100
XON	62		62⅜				63⅝		63⅞	
	61		61¼				62⅜		62⅞	
	61¼	49,300	62⅜	23,100			63⅜	35,700	63⅜	30,900
Z	8⅜		8½				9		9⅛	
	8⅛		8¼				8⅝		8¾	
	8⅜	42,600	8⅜	287,100			8¾	26,200	9⅛	32,900
	12/30/74		12/31/74		01/01/75		01/02/75		01/03/75	
Dow	603.25	1,529,400	616.24	1,579,500	HOLIDAY		632.04	1,196,600	634.54	1,388,700
NY		18,520,000		20,970,000				14,800,000		15,270,000
A	13⅝		13¾				14¾		14½	
	13⅛		13⅛				13½		14	
	13¼	14,700	13½	17,700			14½	5,000	14¼	11,900
AA	29½		30				30¼		30⅜	
	29		29⅜				29⅝		29⅝	

	29⅛	9,500	29⅞	22,000	29⅞	16,000	29⅞	17,300
AC	29		29¼		30		30¼	
	28⅝		28⅝		29⅛		29⅝	
	28⅞	17,700	29	8,700	29¾	7,100	30	9,200
ACD	26½		28½		29½		29¼	
	25¾		25¾		28⅝		28½	
	26	17,300	28⅜	14,200	29¼	16,300	28½	52,900
AMB	30⅜		30⅜		31½		32	
	29¾		29⅞		30½		31¼	
	30⅜	7,100	30¼	7,300	31½	8,600	32	4,400
BS	25⅛		25⅛		25⅜		25⅜	
	24⅞		24⅝		24¾		24¾	
	24⅞	24,400	24⅞	18,100	24⅞	18,600	25¼	32,000
C	7¼		7⅜		8		8	
	7⅛		7⅛		7⅜		7¾	
	7⅛	137,000	7¼	153,000	8	71,000	8	47,300
DD	91⅞		92¾		95⅛		95½	
	90¼		92		92½		93⅝	
	91¾	14,100	92¼	31,700	95⅛	18,800	95	24,300
EK	61		62⅞		65¼		65⅜	
	60		61¼		63⅜		63	
	61	48,200	62⅞	55,300	63¾	70,200	64¼	96,700

	12/30/74		12/31/74		01/01/75		01/02/75		01/03/75	
ESM	28¼		28⅛				29		29¼	
	27½		27¾				28⅛		28¾	
	27⅝	3,300	27⅞	3,900			29	3,400	28¾	21,300
GE	32⅜		33⅜				34¼		33⅞	
	31½		32⅝				33⅜		32⅜	
	32	95,700	33⅜	68,500			33¾	68,000	32⅝	135,900
GF	17½		17⅞				18⅞		19½	
	16⅞		17⅛				18⅜		18⅜	
	17¼	29,700	17⅞	29,200			18⅞	23,500	19⅛	15,700
GM	30½		30⅞				32⅛		33⅞	
	30		30⅜				31¼		32⅛	
	30¼	144,400	30¾	173,600			31⅞	95,800	33⅝	92,500
GT	12¾		13				13⅜		13⅞	
	12⅜		12½				12¾		13⅛	
	12¾	58,600	12⅞	31,500			13⅜	19,600	13⅞	27,300
HR	18⅞		19⅞				20½		20¾	
	18⅝		18⅞				19¾		20	
	18¾	22,200	19¾	30,000			20¼	15,200	20⅝	17,100
IP	34		35¾				37		36¾	
	33⅛		34¼				36½		35¾	
	33⅞	15,000	35¾	21,300			36⅝	18,400	36	18,400

JM	19¼		19½		20⅛		20⅛	
	18		19		19¾		19⅝	
	19¼	12,700	19½	11,400	19¾	15,800	20	12,100
N	20⅝		21½		22¼		22⅛	
	20		20¾		22		21⅝	
	20½	25,700	21½	11,700	22¼	25,200	22	13,100
OI	32¼		33¾		34		34	
	31⅝		32⅛		33⅜		33¾	
	32¼	19,200	33¾	7,700	34	1,500	33¾	4,600
PG	80¼		81½		83		82¾	
	79⅝		79¼		82¼		81	
	79⅝	8,300	81½	13,400	82¼	83,200	81⅛	57,400
S	48⅝		49⅛		51		52½	
	47⅜		48⅛		48⅜		50⅝	
	48¼	29,800	48¼	23,200	50⅜	48,000	52⅜	67,200
SD	21⅞		22⅜		24		24⅛	
	21½		21⅝		22⅛		23⅜	
	21¾	63,500	22¼	56,400	23⅝	28,700	23½	42,300
T	44¼		45		46		46⅜	
	43⅞		44⅛		44¾		45⅝	
	44	74,500	44⅝	114,200	46	108,900	46⅛	96,600

	12/30/74		12/31/74		01/01/75		01/02/75		01/03/75	
TX	21⅛		21⅛				22¼		23⅜	
	20½		20½				21⅛		21⅞	
	20⅞	287,500	20⅞	279,100			22¼	161,500	23	183,400
UTX	32½		32¾				32¾		32⅞	
	31¾		32¼				32		32⅛	
	32¼	11,200	32⅝	5,400			32	7,100	32¾	15,100
UK	41⅜		42¼				42⅜		42¼	
	41		41				41⅝		40¾	
	41⅛	12,300	41⅜	27,600			42⅜	20,200	40¾	17,200
WX	9½		10¼				10¼		10⅛	
	8½		9⅝				9⅞		9¾	
	9½	222,900	10	239,300			10⅛	138,500	9⅞	144,900
X	37⅝		38⅜				38⅞		39⅞	
	37⅜		37¾				38¼		38¼	
	37⅝	14,200	38	40,200			38½	10,300	39⅝	18,000
XON	63⅜		64⅝				66½		67¾	
	62⅜		63				65		66⅛	
	63⅛	49,400	64⅝	30,500			66¼	39,900	67¼	54,600
Z	9¼		9½				9⅞		10⅛	
	8⅞		9				9⅜		9½	
	9	39,300	9⅜	33,400			9⅞	32,300	10⅛	38,000

	01/06/75		*01/07/75*		*01/08/75*		*01/09/75*		*01/10/75*	
Dow	637.20	1,399,300	641.19	1,189,200	635.40	1,529,100	645.26	1,584,000	658.79	2,237,900
NY		17,550,000		14,330,000		15,600,000		16,340,000		25,890,000
A	14⅝		14½		15		14⅞		15½	
	14⅜		14⅜		14½		14½		15	
	14⅝	10,600	14½	6,300	14¾	10,600	14⅞	7,200	15⅜	14,800
AA	30⅛		30		29½		28⅞		29½	
	29⅝		29⅜		29		27⅝		28¾	
	30	43,200	29½	36,900	29	10,200	28¼	32,600	28¾	34,500
AC	30		30		30		30⅛		31	
	29⅜		29½		29½		29⅜		30¼	
	29¾	13,700	29⅞	7,300	29⅝	10,400	29⅞	40,900	31	20,600
ACD	28¾		28⅞		29		28¼		30	
	28⅛		28		27½		27⅝		29	
	28½	12,200	28¾	15,300	27¾	19,800	28⅛	7,900	30	20,800
AMB	33⅜		33⅛		33⅜		33¼		34¼	
	32½		32⅞		32⅞		32¾		33½	
	33	13,500	33	5,900	33	13,600	33¼	2,900	34¼	12,500
BS	25⅞		26⅝		26½		26¾		27¼	
	25¼		25⅝		26¼		26		26⅞	
	25¾	22,200	26½	26,300	26⅜	15,100	26½	25,800	27⅛	26,400

	01/06/75		01/07/75		01/08/75		01/09/75		01/10/75	
C	8½		9¼		9½		9⅜		9½	
	8⅛		8⅜		9¼		9⅛		9¼	
	8½	75,800	9¼	96,300	9⅜	119,600	9¼	75,500	9¼	98,800
DD	96¼		97⅛		97		97¾		99½	
	94		93⅜		94¾		94		98	
	94	37,000	97	17,200	94¾	22,100	97¾	39,200	98⅝	38,000
EK	65⅜		64⅞		65⅜		65¾		69¾	
	64⅛		63½		63⅜		63⅛		66⅜	
	64⅛	77,000	64¾	44,800	63⅜	54,600	65¾	54,200	67¼	117,600
ESM	29		28⅛		28		28		28⅛	
	28¾		27⅞		27¼		27¾		27⅜	
	28⅞	1,100	28⅛	1,300	28	2,100	28	1,500	27⅜	3,100
GE	33		34		34½		34½		36	
	32⅜		32⅜		33⅝		33½		34⅜	
	32⅝	80,200	33⅝	56,800	33¾	76,800	34⅛	86,500	35⅞	148,500
GF	19⅝		19⅞		20¼		20⅝		21⅛	
	19⅛		19⅛		19½		19⅞		20⅜	
	19⅜	27,000	19⅞	40,400	20	410,400	20⅛	257,200	20⅞	98,400
GM	35⅝		35¾		35¾		37⅛		37¾	
	33¾		34½		35¼		35⅛		36½	
	35⅛	131,200	35⅜	122,400	35½	154,800	37⅛	114,300	36⅝	127,500

GT	14¼		14¼		14		14		14¾	
	14		14		13¾		13⅝		14¼	
	14	31,000	14	101,100	13⅞	14,400	14	36,600	14⅝	110,300
HR	20⅞		20⅝		20½		20½		21	
	20½		20⅛		20⅛		20⅛		20½	
	20½	35,600	20½	15,400	20⅜	13,600	20½	18,000	20¾	35,900
IP	36⅞		37⅜		36⅞		36⅞		37¼	
	35¾		36½		36½		35¾		37⅛	
	36⅞	12,100	36⅝	25,200	36½	14,400	36⅞	19,600	37⅛	19,700
JM	20⅜		20		20¾		20⅛		20⅝	
	20		19¾		19⅞		19¾		20⅛	
	20	10,000	20	15,500	20⅛	22,600	20⅛	21,900	20¼	18,600
N	22⅛		21¾		21⅞		22		22½	
	21½		21½		21½		21⅜		22⅛	
	21¾	16,500	21½	6,900	21¾	12,200	22	18,500	22½	23,500
OI	34¼		33⅞		34¼		33½		34¼	
	33½		33⅜		33⅝		32¾		33¾	
	33½	5,100	33⅝	4,500	33⅝	1,500	33½	18,500	33⅞	7,000
PG	82½		81¾		81½		80¼		82½	
	81		80½		79½		78½		81	
	81⅛	34,900	80¾	30,800	79½	37,000	80	36,100	81⅞	32,800

	01/06/75		01/07/75		01/08/75		01/09/75		01/10/75	
S	52⅞		51¾		51⅝		52⅜		54⅞	
	51⅝		50⅞		50¾		50¾		53¼	
	51⅝	58,000	51½	41,000	51⅛	35,300	52⅜	89,600	53⅜	72,400
SD	24		23½		23⅝		24		25⅛	
	23⅛		22¾		23⅛		22½		24½	
	23¼	33,800	23⅜	35,100	23⅛	23,500	24	46,400	24¾	172,000
T	46½		46⅝		46⅝		47⅛		48¼	
	46¼		46⅛		46½		46½		47⅝	
	46½	75,400	46⅝	98,100	46⅝	54,500	47⅛	179,800	48	248,500
TX	23⅞		23¾		23¾		24		24⅝	
	23½		23⅜		22⅞		22⅝		24	
	23⅝	165,900	23¾	100,000	23	114,900	24	123,000	24⅜	223,700
UTX	33⅝		33½		32¾		32¾		33⅞	
	33		32⅝		31¼		31¼		33	
	33½	11,300	33	5,600	31⅜	7,800	32⅝	5,100	33¾	38,800
UK	41⅝		41¼		41⅜		41		42¼	
	40⅞		40⅞		40¾		40⅝		41	
	41	24,300	41⅛	24,100	41¼	32,300	41	34,200	41½	45,900
WX	10⅜		10¾		11¼		11¼		11¾	
	10		10⅛		10¾		10⅝		11¼	
	10¼	194,500	10¾	98,600	10⅞	143,800	11¼	95,500	11½	203,000

X	40		39¾		39¾		39⅞		41⅛	
	39⅜		39⅛		39⅛		39¼		40⅛	
	39½	16,200	39½	19,400	39⅜	13,800	39⅞	24,700	41	48,900
XON	68		67½		67¼		67¼		69	
	66¼		66		66½		65½		67⅞	
	66¼	77,400	66⅞	46,400	66½	51,300	67¼	42,100	69	107,500
Z	10¾		11¼		11¼		11⅝		12⅜	
	10		10⅝		11		11		11¾	
	10¾	52,400	11	44,300	11⅛	16,100	11⅝	28,700	12⅛	67,000
	01/13/75		*01/14/75*		*01/15/75*		*01/16/75*		*01/17/75*	
Dow	654.18	1,816,100	648.70	1,443,100	653.39	1,550,800	655.74	1,422,200	644.63	1,076,900
NY		19,780,000		16,610,000		16,580,000		17,110,000		14,260,000
A	16		16		15⅞		16¾		16⅞	
	15⅜		15½		15½		16		16	
	15⅝	13,700	15¾	14,900	15¾	7,500	16⅝	12,400	16⅛	17,400
AA	29¼		29¼		28⅞		28⅝		28¾	
	28½		28⅝		28½		28¼		28¼	
	28¾	52,000	29	26,700	28⅝	10,500	28⅝	161,400	28⅜	10,800
AC	31⅜		30¾		30¾		30⅝		30½	
	30¾		30¼		30¼		30⅜		29⅝	
	30¾	14,200	30½	6,300	30⅜	5,000	30⅜	6,600	29¾	6,800

	01/13/75		01/14/75		01/15/75		01/16/75		01/17/75	
ACD	30½		28⅜		27¾		28¼		28⅛	
	28¼		27½		27		27¾		27¼	
	28¼	32,800	27½	17,700	27¾	84,000	28	35,900	27¼	15,600
AMB	35¼		34⅛		33⅞		34		34	
	33⅝		33⅝		33½		33⅝		33½	
	33⅞	11,900	33⅞	6,200	33½	6,900	33⅞	6,100	33½	6,800
BS	27½		27⅝		27¾		27⅞		27⅞	
	27⅛		27¼		27⅛		27½		27⅜	
	27¼	27,900	27½	24,500	27¾	18,900	27⅞	16,400	27¾	15,600
C	9⅝		9½		9¼		9		8⅞	
	9⅜		9¼		8¾		8⅝		8⅝	
	9⅜	109,900	9¼	58,100	8⅞	76,900	8⅞	39,800	8¾	44,000
DD	99¾		95⅞		95¾		95½		95⅝	
	95¾		94¼		94		94⅛		91¾	
	96	39,400	94⅝	25,400	94¾	33,900	95⅜	15,700	92¼	47,100
EK	67¾		66¾		67⅜		68⅜		66¾	
	65¾		65¼		65⅜		66¾		63¾	
	65⅞	89,100	65½	50,000	67⅜	80,800	67⅜	96,900	64¼	81,900
ESM	28		27⅞		27¾		27½		27½	
	27¾		27⅝		27¼		27½		27⅛	
	28	3,700	27¾	700	27⅜	800	27½	600	27¼	1,000

GE	36⅞		36¾		36		36⅜		36⅜	
	36		35¼		34⅝		35⅝		34⅝	
	36⅜	94,900	35½	77,500	36	92,200	36⅜	96,900	34¾	54,400
GF	21¾		21¼		20⅝		20½		20⅞	
	21		20¾		19⅝		19⅞		20¼	
	21⅜	81,800	20⅞	30,000	19⅞	32,500	20½	17,800	20⅜	20,500
GM	37¼		36⅞		37⅜		37⅞		37½	
	36¾		36¼		36¼		37		37⅛	
	37	157,900	36⅝	152,300	37⅜	137,800	37⅝	122,400	37¼	83,000
GT	15¼		14¾		15		15⅛		15	
	14¾		14¼		14⅜		14¾		14¾	
	14⅞	38,800	14½	22,500	15	72,800	14⅞	28,600	14¾	84,400
HR	20⅞		20⅝		20½		20⅝		20½	
	20¼		20⅛		20		20¼		20⅜	
	20½	22,500	20⅜	16,100	20⅜	21,600	20½	14,300	20⅜	10,100
IP	37¾		37		36½		36⅜		36½	
	36⅜		36		36		36⅛		35⅛	
	36⅝	14,400	36	20,300	36⅜	23,600	36⅜	35,700	35⅛	13,400
JM	20⅜		19¾		21⅝		22		21⅜	
	19½		19¼		19¼		21		20⅝	
	19½	64,500	19¾	18,500	21⅝	83,200	21¼	30,300	20¾	23,800

	01/13/75		01/14/75		01/15/75		01/16/75		01/17/75	
N	22⅞		22⅝		22¾		23		23⅛	
	22⅝		22¼		22⅜		22¾		22⅝	
	22⅝	10,800	22⅜	94,000	22⅝	13,700	23	3,800	22⅞	23,300
OI	33⅞		33		32⅞		33½		33⅝	
	33¼		32⅝		32½		32¾		33	
	33¼	3,400	33	1,900	32½	2,700	33½	4,400	33	7,000
PG	82⅞		83¼		83⅛		84⅞		85	
	81½		81½		81½		83¼		84¼	
	81¾	24,600	81¾	81,300	83⅛	30,400	84⅝	23,800	84¼	22,600
S	54⅝		54¾		55⅝		56⅝		56⅛	
	53½		53⅜		53⅞		55⅝		54½	
	53¾	55,800	54⅛	44,100	55⅝	60,800	56¼	54,900	54⅝	56,700
SD	24⅞		23⅜		23		23		22⅞	
	23¾		22¾		22⅜		22½		22⅜	
	23⅞	51,100	23	96,300	23	61,400	22¾	57,900	22½	37,100
T	48		47⅞		48		46¾		46⅝	
	47⅝		47⅜		46¾		46⅛		46¼	
	47⅝	94,900	47⅝	101,200	47¼	137,400	46⅜	202,000	46⅜	80,500
TX	24⅝		23¾		23⅛		23⅛		23	
	23⅞		23⅛		22½		22¾		22½	
	23⅞	321,800	23¼	263,100	23	171,100	22⅞	91,100	23	92,300

UTX	34⅞		33⅞		33⅞		33¾		34⅜	
	33¾		32¾		32⅝		33¼		33¾	
	33⅞	36,700	32¾	17,700	33⅞	28,800	33¾	7,300	33¾	14,900
UK	42⅞		42⅛		41⅝		41		40⅝	
	41¾		41⅜		40⅝		40⅜		40⅛	
	42⅛	49,400	41¾	29,900	41¼	32,800	40⅜	23,700	40¼	78,800
WX	11⅞		11¾		11¾		11⅞		11½	
	11½		11¼		11⅜		11¼		11¼	
	11⅝	173,300	11⅝	131,400	11¾	121,700	11½	120,500	11¼	69,000
X	40⅞		40½		40⅞		41		41	
	40¼		39⅞		39⅞		40¼		40½	
	40⅜	21,600	40	18,900	40⅞	18,900	40¾	26,300	41	14,000
XON	69¾		69¼		69¼		69⅛		68⅜	
	68⅝		68⅛		68¼		68¼		67	
	68⅝	54,200	68¾	50,300	69⅛	41,100	68⅜	48,400	67⅛	33,600
Z	12⅜		12⅛		11⅝		11⅞		11¾	
	12		11¾		11⅛		11⅜		11½	
	12	48,800	11¾	29,900	11⅜	46,100	11¾	20,500	11½	10,500
	01/20/75		*01/21/75*		*01/22/75*		*01/23/75*		*01/24/75*	
Dow	647.45	1,074,200	641.90	1,210,200	652.61	940,300	656.76	1,354,500	666.61	1,819,400
NY		13,450,000		14,780,000		15,330,000		17,960,000		20,670,000

	01/20/75		01/21/75		01/22/75		01/23/75		01/24/75	
A	16⅛		16		16		16		17	
	15¾		15¾		15¾		15⅝		16⅝	
	15⅞	5,100	15¾	4,100	15¾	5,700	16	5,500	17	16,100
AA	28¾		29		29		29¾		30⅝	
	27⅛		28		28¼		28¾		29⅜	
	28¾	15,200	28½	41,900	29	5,700	29½	13,000	30	57,800
AC	30¼		30⅜		30⅛		30½		30¾	
	29½		29¾		29⅝		30		30⅜	
	30⅛	7,100	30¼	5,500	29⅞	3,100	30¼	9,500	30½	11,800
ACD	28¼		29⅜		28⅝		29⅝		30½	
	27⅛		28⅜		27⅞		28⅝		29⅝	
	28¼	31,400	28½	19,500	28½	9,100	29¼	9,600	30½	18,400
AMB	34		34¼		34		34⅞		35⅛	
	33⅜		33⅝		33½		34		34⅜	
	34	18,500	33¾	9,100	34	8,600	34⅜	9,500	35⅛	16,000
BS	27⅞		27⅞		28⅛		28¾		29⅞	
	27		27¼		27¼		28		28⅞	
	27⅝	60,900	27¼	13,600	28	31,500	28⅝	34,200	29⅜	40,500
C	8⅞		9⅛		9¼		9½		10⅛	
	8⅝		8⅞		9		9¼		9⅝	
	8¾	38,600	9⅛	43,100	9⅛	59,500	9½	56,600	10	251,900

DD	92¾		92⅝		90½		91		90⅝	
	91¾		87⅛		87¼		89¼		88¼	
	92⅜	28,200	87⅜	55,700	90½	41,700	89⅜	37,600	90½	34,900
EK	65⅜		66¼		68		68¾		66	
	63¼		63¾		63		66⅜		63¼	
	65⅜	57,000	63⅞	72,300	68	61,900	67	140,000	65⅛	125,500
ESM	27		27		27⅝		28		27⅝	
	26⅛		26⅜		26¾		27		26½	
	26¼	4,900	26⅝	2,700	27⅝	2,500	27¼	6,800	26⅝	56,100
GE	35		35⅝		35⅞		36		35⅜	
	34		34½		34⅜		34		34⅝	
	35	40,200	34⅝	69,300	35⅞	48,200	34½	85,900	35⅜	128,000
GF	20¼		20⅜		19⅝		20⅝		21½	
	19¾		19⅛		18⅝		19⅞		21	
	20	18,900	19⅛	26,900	19⅝	18,800	20½	18,800	21⅜	20,500
GM	37⅛		37¼		37½		37⅝		38½	
	36½		36⅜		36		37		36¾	
	37⅛	80,600	36½	76,000	37⅜	95,100	37	75,300	38½	100,000
GT	14⅞		15⅛		15		15½		15½	
	14⅝		14¾		14¾		15		15¼	
	14¾	19,800	14¾	29,800	15	13,800	15¼	33,100	15½	80,300

	01/20/75		01/21/75		01/22/75		01/23/75		01/24/75	
HR	20½		20½		20⅝		20½		20¼	
	20¼		20¼		20¼		20		19⅞	
	20⅜	9,500	20½	22,100	20½	13,300	20	27,400	20⅛	24,300
IP	35¼		35¾		35½		36¼		36⅞	
	34⅝		35¼		35¼		35⅜		36½	
	35⅛	22,600	35¾	16,100	35½	13,400	36	38,700	36⅞	15,100
JM	21⅛		21⅞		21⅝		21⅝		21⅝	
	20½		21¼		21¼		21		21⅛	
	21⅛	6,900	21⅞	22,900	21⅜	23,800	21⅛	28,800	21⅜	20,700
N	23⅛		23⅝		23¾		24⅛		24⅛	
	22⅝		23¼		23¼		23⅝		23¾	
	23⅛	10,200	23⅝	35,600	23¾	17,100	23⅞	7,500	23⅞	18,000
OI	33¼		33¼		32⅞		33½		35⅞	
	32		32⅞		32¾		33		33¾	
	32⅝	10,800	33	1,300	32⅞	2,100	33½	10,100	35⅝	14,600
PG	83⅝		84		83¾		85¾		84⅜	
	82⅜		82		81¼		83		83¾	
	83	28,200	82	27,200	83¾	26,500	84½	35,000	84	40,700
S	54⅞		54⅞		53		55¾		57¼	
	53¾		52⅝		51⅜		53¼		54½	
	54¾	33,500	52⅝	57,200	53	45,900	54⅞	39,000	56⅞	53,900

SD	22¾		23		23⅞		24⅝		25	
	22⅛		22⅝		22⅝		23¼		24	
	22⅝	42,700	22⅞	52,200	23⅞	36,500	24	66,500	24⅞	73,200
T	46¼		47⅛		47		47⅜		47¼	
	46		46⅜		46⅜		47		37	
	46¼	61,500	46¾	136,200	47	58,300	47⅛	104,400	47⅛	103,500
TX	23¼		23⅞		24		24⅞		24½	
	22¾		23¼		23¼		23⅞		23¾	
	23¼	242,500	23⅝	95,100	24	71,500	24⅜	112,000	24⅜	170,700
UTX	35		35¾		36¼		37½		36½	
	34		35		34¾		36		35⅞	
	35	8,000	35¼	25,000	36¼	41,200	36⅝	51,400	35⅞	25,100
UK	41¾		42⅜		41⅜		41¾		42½	
	40¼		41		40¼		41		41⅜	
	41¾	32,600	41⅛	51,500	41⅛	40,000	41½	80,700	42½	66,500
WX	11¼		11⅛		11⅛		11⅜		11¼	
	10⅝		10½		10¾		11		10⅞	
	10⅞	74,400	10⅞	102,900	11⅛	64,900	11	65,800	11⅛	62,000
X	40⅞		41⅝		41¼		42½		44	
	40⅜		40¾		40½		40¾		42	
	40⅞	16,100	40⅞	18,300	40¾	35,000	42	55,700	43⅝	58,500

	01/20/75		01/21/75		01/22/75		01/23/75		01/24/75	
XON	67⅞		68⅜		68⅛		69⅜		70¼	
	66⅝		67¼		66⅜		68⅛		68¾	
	67⅞	33,400	67⅜	57,500	68⅛	34,000	68¾	79,600	69⅝	87,800
Z	11¾		11⅞		11¾		11⅞		12	
	11½		11½		11½		11⅝		11⅝	
	11¾	14,500	11⅝	19,600	11⅝	11,600	11⅞	16,500	11⅞	27,000
	01/27/75		01/28/75		01/29/75		01/30/75		01/31/75	
Dow	692.66	2,866,100	694.77	2,929,600	705.96	2,180,900	696.42	2,733,800	703.69	1,987,500
NY		32,130,000		31,760,000		27,410,000		29,740,000		24,640,000
A	18		18⅛		17⅝		17½		15⅝	
	17⅝		17¼		16⅞		15½		15⅛	
	17¾	19,000	17¼	26,300	17⅜	15,100	15⅝	47,300	15½	20,500
AA	32⅝		34		33⅝		34⅜		34	
	31½		32⅞		32⅞		33		32¾	
	32⅜	62,600	33¼	38,900	33⅝	36,300	33	45,800	33¾	22,700
AC	31⅛		31¼		31⅜		31¼		31¼	
	30⅝		31		30¾		30¾		30⅞	
	31	14,800	31¼	19,800	30⅞	18,700	30⅞	23,500	31¼	9,500
ACD	32½		33½		32¼		33		32½	
	31½		32½		31½		32⅛		31¾	

	32	39,100	32⅝	42,500	32	19,500	32⅛	19,400	32¼	12,600
AMB	36½		37		36¾		36⅝		36¾	
	35⅜		36¼		36⅛		35½		35½	
	36½	21,700	36⅜	15,900	36⅜	17,100	35⅞	11,200	36⅝	13,400
BS	30½		30⅜		30⅝		31¼		31¾	
	29¾		29¾		30⅛		30⅝		30⅞	
	30⅛	81,900	30	142,100	30⅝	56,300	30⅞	108,800	31⅝	48,800
C	11½		11⅞		11⅝		11⅝		11½	
	10½		11¼		11¼		11¼		11⅛	
	11½	226,700	11½	217,700	11⅝	114,500	11¼	128,900	11½	85,200
DD	95½		95½		97¾		96⅜		99	
	92½		93¼		91⅞		93¾		93⅞	
	95½	63,100	93¾	63,800	96	90,300	94⅜	73,900	98⅜	47,300
EK	69½		70		72¾		74		74¼	
	68⅛		68¾		69⅛		71⅞		71⅝	
	69¼	161,100	69⅛	154,000	72⅝	170,600	72	123,500	72½	145,100
ESM	27		27¼		27		26¾		26⅜	
	26⅝		26¾		26⅛		26¼		26¼	
	27	11,600	26⅞	14,800	26¼	19,900	26¼	11,900	26⅜	12,800
GE	36¾		37⅞		39½		39¾		38⅞	
	35⅝		36⅞		37⅝		38		38	
	36⅜	142,200	37¾	209,700	39⅛	136,300	38⅜	180,200	38⅝	80,700

	01/27/75		01/28/75		01/29/75		01/30/75		01/31/75	
GF	24⅜		23⅜		22⅞		23⅜		23⅞	
	22⅝		22⅝		22⅜		23		23⅛	
	23¼	174,100	22⅝	44,200	22⅝	57,900	23¼	71,300	23½	44,300
GM	40		40⅛		40⅛		40		38⅞	
	39⅛		39⅜		39⅜		38½		38	
	39⅜	192,800	39½	205,600	39⅞	136,700	38½	109,700	38½	115,900
GT	16		16⅜		16⅜		16⅜		16⅛	
	15⅝		16		16		15¾		15½	
	16	74,800	16⅛	95,800	16⅛	31,600	15¾	36,200	16	22,800
HR	20⅜		20¾		20⅞		21⅝		21¼	
	19⅞		20⅜		20⅜		20¾		20¾	
	20⅜	52,000	20⅝	36,200	20⅞	61,500	21	42,000	21	95,900
IP	38½		38¾		38½		39		38⅝	
	37¼		37½		37¾		37¾		37⅞	
	37¼	70,400	38	74,900	38	45,800	37¾	55,700	38	48,300
JM	22¾		22⅝		22⅝		22¾		22	
	21⅞		21¾		21¾		21⅛		21⅛	
	22⅝	42,100	22¼	42,300	22¼	45,900	21⅛	97,500	21⅞	18,900
N	24¾		25		25⅜		25½		25¼	
	24¼		24⅝		24⅝		25		24½	
	24⅜	28,100	24¾	24,400	25⅛	38,000	25⅛	28,000	25	43,800

OI	36⅝		36½		37¾		37⅜		37¼	
	35⅝		36		36		37		36¾	
	36¼	15,200	36	8,600	37	12,200	37⅛	9,000	37⅛	9,100
PG	87⅞		89⅞		91¾		92¼		91½	
	84½		88¼		88⅛		90		89⅞	
	87¾	42,900	88¼	44,900	90¾	52,900	90½	50,500	91⅜	24,300
S	60½		60⅞		64		65½		60⅝	
	59		59¾		60		60		59	
	59⅛	144,200	60⅝	103,800	63⅞	90,600	60	157,500	59½	84,100
SD	25⅞		26		26¼		26⅜		26¼	
	24¾		25⅜		25½		25½		25⅝	
	25⅞	118,600	25⅞	92,600	26	89,400	25⅞	100,200	26	42,500
T	48⅛		48⅞		48¾		49		48⅝	
	47⅜		48¼		48⅛		48⅜		48⅛	
	48	242,700	48⅜	296,200	48⅜	151,000	48½	240,500	48½	153,100
TX	25		25⅜		26		26¼		26¼	
	25⅝		24⅞		25⅛		25¼		25¼	
	24⅞	148,500	25¼	212,600	25⅞	197,300	25⅝	148,800	26¼	204,700
UTX	37		36⅞		36⅝		36		35	
	36		36		35½		35		33¾	
	36¾	36,300	36¾	37,700	36	11,900	35	30,900	34	17,800

	01/27/75		01/28/75		01/29/75		01/30/75		01/31/75	
UK	45		44⅞		44¾		45⅞		45¾	
	43½		43¾		43¼		44¾		44¾	
	44⅝	200,700	43¾	191,200	44¾	95,500	45	88,500	45½	91,500
WX	11¾		12		11⅞		11⅞		11⅝	
	11⅜		11¾		11		10¾		10¾	
	11¾	140,000	11⅞	180,500	11⅞	159,700	10⅞	438,800	11¼	296,500
X	45¼		45⅝		46		47		47¼	
	44¼		44¾		44⅜		45¾		46⅜	
	44¾	77,000	45	82,800	45⅞	77,200	46⅜	78,800	47¼	38,900
XON	72⅞		73½		74⅜		75		73⅜	
	70⅞		72⅜		72⅛		72½		71¾	
	72⅛	151,300	72⅝	158,500	74	95,700	72½	123,400	73⅛	76,000
Z	12⅜		12⅝		12⅜		12⅝		12½	
	11⅞		12¼		12⅛		12¼		12¼	
	12⅜	70,600	12¼	50,800	12⅜	45,500	12⅜	52,100	12⅜	60,500
	02/03/75		*02/04/75*		02/05/75		*02/06/75*		*02/07/75*	
Dow	711.44	1,961,000	708.09	2,589,900	717.85	2,230,400	714.17	2,499,100	711.91	1,615,700
NY		25,400,000		25,040,000		25,830,000		32,020,000		20,060,000
A	16		16½		17		17		16	
	15⅜		15⅞		16⅜		16⅛		15½	

	15⅞	21,600	16½	15,900	16⅝	17,800	16¼	19,800	15¾	30,500
AA	33⅞		33¾		34⅜		34½		33¼	
	33⅜		32¾		33¾		33¾		32⅜	
	33⅝	25,700	33⅝	16,200	33¾	58,500	34	47,100	33⅛	42,100
AC	31¼		31⅛		31¼		32⅝		32½	
	30⅝		30¾		30½		31⅝		31⅞	
	31⅛	39,100	31	19,700	31¼	20,200	32¼	41,400	32⅛	14,700
ACD	32⅞		32⅜		33⅜		34¼		34½	
	32		31¼		31⅛		33⅛		33	
	32⅜	13,800	31⅝	12,400	33⅜	17,700	33⅛	16,200	34½	17,400
AMB	37		36⅞		36⅝		37½		37½	
	35⅝		35⅞		35¾		36½		36⅛	
	36¾	13,100	36½	10,100	36¼	12,300	37⅛	18,400	37⅜	11,900
BS	32¾		31½		31⅝		31⅝		30⅞	
	31½		30⅛		30⅝		30½		29¾	
	32½	90,600	31	65,800	31⅜	64,100	30¾	45,400	30¾	61,900
C	11½		10¾		10⅜		10¼		10	
	11⅛		10		9⅞		9⅞		9⅝	
	11¼	79,600	10	231,400	10¼	158,400	10	85,700	9¾	61,500
DD	101¾		99¼		99⅛		99⅞		96⅞	
	96¾		97		97⅛		97¼		94⅞	
	99⅝	73,900	97¾	80,000	98⅞	32,900	97⅜	68,200	96⅝	53,000

	02/03/75		02/04/75		02/05/75		02/06/75		02/07/75	
EK	74½		74¾		76⅞		78½		78½	
	72		72⅜		73¾		75⅞		75¾	
	74½	104,600	74½	130,400	76¾	134,000	76⅛	155,800	78½	92,000
ESM	27⅜		27¾		27⅝		28⅝		28	
	26⅛		27¼		27		27½		27¼	
	27¼	16,900	27⅜	8,500	27½	10,700	28	13,600	28	11,900
GE	39½		39⅛		39¾		40⅞		39¾	
	38⅝		38½		38⅛		39¾		38¼	
	39⅜	107,200	38⅝	123,800	39¾	121,400	40⅛	123,200	39¾	73,100
GF	23¾		23⅛		23¾		23⅞		22¾	
	23⅛		22⅝		22⅞		22¾		22	
	23½	40,300	22⅞	18,400	23⅜	38,400	22¾	53,000	22½	11,500
GM	38¾		36⅜		37¼		37⅜		35¾	
	38⅛		35½		35⅜		35⅛		34⅞	
	38⅜	99,900	35⅝	607,800	37¼	225,100	35⅜	195,800	35¾	162,600
GT	16⅜		16		16⅜		16⅜		15⅞	
	15⅞		15¾		15¾		15⅞		15¼	
	16¼	14,600	16	33,800	16	24,600	16	29,200	15¾	26,500
HR	21⅞		21¾		21¾		23⅛		22⅞	
	20⅞		21		21¼		22⅜		22½	
	21½	31,000	21½	36,700	21¾	26,700	22½	67,300	22⅞	24,500

IP	38¼		38⅜		39¾		40⅜		39¾	
	37⅝		37⅞		38⅛		39¾		38¾	
	38¼	16,300	38¼	87,500	39¾	62,700	40	50,500	38¾	59,300
JM	23¾		23½		23¾		24¼		23¾	
	21⅞		22⅞		22⅞		23⅜		23¼	
	23⅝	95,800	23¼	63,400	23¾	40,200	24	78,200	23½	49,300
N	25		25⅛		25½		25¾		25⅛	
	24¾		24⅝		24⅞		25⅜		24⅜	
	25	6,100	25	14,900	25½	11,500	25⅜	19,600	24½	60,900
OI	37¼		37¼		37		37		36	
	36¾		36¾		36½		36½		35½	
	37	9,900	37	16,400	36½	3,900	36½	3,300	35⅝	1,800
PG	91⅞		91¼		95⅛		95¾		93⅜	
	90¾		90¼		91⅝		93½		91½	
	91	25,000	91¼	29,700	95	51,700	93½	42,200	92⅞	34,400
S	60⅜		60¼		61⅛		63¼		60¼	
	58⅛		58⅜		59		60¾		59¼	
	58⅞	52,000	60	57,900	60⅞	106,400	60⅞	94,400	60	69,100
SD	26⅛		26¼		26⅛		26		24⅞	
	25¾		25¼		25¼		25		24⅛	
	26⅛	62,500	26¼	126,300	25⅝	82,100	25	107,800	24½	66,100

	02/03/75		02/04/75		02/05/75		02/06/75		02/07/75	
T	48⅞		49⅛		50		50½		50	
	48¼		48½		49¼		48¾		48⅜	
	48⅞	124,000	49⅛	112,600	50	339,300	48¾	266,700	49⅞	111,300
TX	26⅛		26⅝		26¼		26⅛		25¼	
	25⅜		25⅛		25⅝		25¼		24⅝	
	25⅝	136,300	26⅝	160,000	25⅞	158,900	25⅜	191,700	24⅞	101,900
UTX	36¼		36		36⅜		36⅜		35¾	
	34		34⅞		35¾		36		34⅞	
	35¾	24,400	35⅞	15,600	36⅛	21,300	36	24,900	35¾	10,300
UK	46		46⅞		47⅛		47¾		46⅞	
	45		45½		46¼		47		46⅜	
	46	85,200	46¾	85,600	47⅛	74,000	47	140,400	46⅝	54,600
WX	12⅛		11⅞		11¾		12¼		11⅞	
	11¼		11½		11⅜		11¾		11⅜	
	11⅞	364,700	11⅝	142,100	11¾	97,800	11⅞	193,000	11¾	106,700
X	48⅜		48		48⅝		49⅞		50	
	46¾		47¼		46⅞		49		48½	
	48⅛	91,900	47⅝	126,600	48⅝	91,300	49¼	142,300	50	121,800
XON	74⅝		75⅞		74½		74⅜		73½	
	73⅛		73⅛		73⅛		73⅛		72¼	
	74¼	64,500	75¾	97,000	73¾	91,900	73¼	116,200	73¼	49,100

Z	12⅝		12¾		12¾		13		12¾	
	12½		12½		12½		12¾		12½	
	12⅝	30,400	12⅝	43,400	12¾	36,400	12¾	47,500	12⅝	24,000
	02/10/75		*02/11/75*		*02/12/75*		*02/13/75*		*02/14/75*	
Dow	708.39	1,452,500	707.60	1,420,700	715.03	1,407,000	726.92	2,857,400	734.20	1,765,200
NY		16,120,000		16,470,000		19,790,000		35,160,000		23,290,000
A	15⅞		15¾		15¾		16		15¾	
	15⅝		15½		15½		15⅝		15⅛	
	15⅝	28,600	15½	13,200	15⅝	22,600	15¾	62,500	15¾	38,200
AA	33¼		32¾		33¼		34½		35¼	
	32		32⅜		32⅛		33¾		33¾	
	32¾	17,300	32½	5,600	33¼	16,400	34¼	45,000	34⅝	21,100
AC	32¼		32		32		32¾		33½	
	31¾		31½		31⅝		32		32⅛	
	32	11,500	31¾	16,400	31⅝	4,300	32½	26,200	33½	37,800
ACD	35⅜		35		35¾		37		36½	
	34¼		34⅛		34⅞		35¾		35¾	
	34⅞	19,800	34¾	10,100	35½	10,100	36¼	24,800	36¼	13,500
AMB	38⅜		38⅛		38¾		39⅝		39⅞	
	37¼		37⅜		37⅞		38⅞		39	
	38¼	23,500	37⅞	15,300	38¾	21,200	39¼	21,100	39¾	29,100

	02/10/75		02/11/75		02/12/75		02/13/75		02/14/75	
BS	31		30		30		30½		30¼	
	30⅛		29⅜		29½		29⅞		29⅝	
	30¼	57,000	30	62,800	30	36,100	30¼	68,500	30	44,700
C	9¾		10¼		11		11⅛		10⅝	
	9½		9½		10⅛		10½		10	
	9½	64,200	10¼	86,400	10¾	112,200	10⅝	157,600	10¼	87,600
DD	97¾		96⅜		98½		102		100	
	96		94¾		95¾		99		98⅝	
	96	38,800	96⅛	39,700	98½	15,000	99½	88,500	99¾	37,000
EK	79¼		78¾		80⅞		85¾		86⅞	
	77⅜		77⅛		77⅞		82		83¼	
	77⅞	81,400	78¾	72,100	80⅞	73,400	83⅝	208,700	86⅛	167,600
ESM	28		27⅞		27⅞		28⅛		28½	
	27½		27¼		27½		27⅝		27⅞	
	27⅞	8,100	27⅞	4,000	27¾	6,100	27⅞	38,300	28¼	19,200
GE	40¾		40		41⅜		43⅛		43¼	
	39⅝		39⅝		40		41⅝		42¼	
	40	56,300	40	74,000	41⅜	52,000	42⅛	194,500	42⅞	120,600
GF	23⅛		22⅝		22½		22½		22½	
	22⅛		21¾		22⅛		22		21½	
	22⅝	42,500	22½	23,500	22¼	26,900	22	48,300	22½	29,300

GM	35¾		35⅞		36⅞		37⅞		38⅜	
	35⅛		35⅛		35⅞		37⅜		37⅜	
	35½	125,300	35⅞	153,600	36⅞	96,200	37⅝	193,000	38	113,800
GT	15⅞		15½		15⅝		16⅛		16⅛	
	15½		15¼		15¼		15⅞		15⅝	
	15½	31,200	15⅜	26,800	15½	17,900	16	114,400	15¾	25,800
HR	23½		23½		23⅞		24½		24½	
	23		23		23¼		23⅞		23¾	
	23	44,100	23¼	24,400	23¾	30,300	24	43,400	24¼	26,000
IP	39⅛		38¾		38⅝		39½		41¼	
	38½		38		38		38⅞		39½	
	38¾	42,200	38⅜	97,100	38⅝	19,000	39⅜	44,700	40¾	67,900
JM	23⅝		22⅞		22		23		22⅞	
	23		21⅞		21⅛		22⅛		21¾	
	23¼	68,100	22¼	92,600	22	18,600	22½	42,500	22⅞	59,500
N	24¼		23¾		23¼		24½		24¼	
	23⅝		23		22⅞		23⅜		23¾	
	23¾	19,700	23⅜	10,800	23¼	14,900	24	59,300	24¼	10,800
OI	35¾		35		35		37½		37¾	
	35⅛		34½		34½		36		37	
	35⅛	3,400	34⅝	8,600	35	5,300	37½	15,800	37¾	5,600

	02/10/75		02/11/75		02/12/75		02/13/75		02/14/75	
PG	94		94		94		95		96¼	
	92¾		93		93		93¾		93¾	
	93⅜	16,400	93⅞	36,200	94	14,600	93⅞	76,300	96¼	51,000
S	59⅞		60⅜		59⅝		61⅞		61⅜	
	58¾		58½		58½		60⅜		59⅝	
	59	49,300	60	36,100	59½	62,300	60⅜	90,900	60⅜	58,500
SD	24⅝		24⅝		25		26⅛		25½	
	24		24		24⅛		24⅞		24¾	
	24⅜	53,100	24⅜	39,500	25	51,500	25	108,900	25¼	58,600
T	49⅞		49⅞		50¾		51¼		51	
	49½		49⅝		49⅝		50½		50⅝	
	49½	101,600	49¾	63,800	50⅝	157,300	50¾	291,000	50¾	84,000
TX	25¼		25		25¼		25½		25⅛	
	24⅜		24¼		24¾		24⅞		24⅝	
	24⅝	99,400	25	88,600	25¼	153,800	25	170,400	25	117,900
UTX	35⅞		35¾		36⅛		37		36¾	
	34⅞		35		35¼		36¼		36	
	35¼	7,500	35½	5,700	36	9,600	36¾	27,200	36	31,500
UK	46½		45⅞		45⅜		48⅛		48¾	
	45⅞		45¼		44¾		45⅝		46¾	
	46⅛	75,700	45½	48,000	45¼	65,200	47⅜	150,600	48	109,000

WX	11⅞		11¾		12		12⅜		12½	
	11⅝		11½		11⅝		12		12⅛	
	11⅝	58,300	11¾	56,400	12	74,600	12¼	156,300	12½	137,000
X	49⅜		48¼		47⅝		48¼		48⅛	
	48⅝		47⅝		47		47¼		47⅛	
	49	104,300	47⅝	106,800	47⅜	56,700	47¼	103,300	48	48,900
XON	73⅝		73⅜		72⅞		73⅞		74	
	72½		72⅛		71⅝		72½		73⅛	
	73⅛	45,800	72¾	52,900	72⅜	138,400	73¾	139,000	73⅝	61,100
Z	13⅝		13⅝		14		14⅜		14⅜	
	13⅛		13¼		13⅞		14		14⅛	
	13½	58,100	13⅝	49,700	14	24,400	14¼	46,400	14¼	52,600
	02/17/75		*02/18/75*		*02/19/75*		*02/20/75*		*02/21/75*	
Dow	HOLIDAY		731.30	1,985,900	736.39	1,749,100	745.38	1,744,300	749.77	2,224,500
NY				23,990,000		22,190,000		22,260,000		24,440,000
A			15¾		15¾		16		16⅛	
			15¼		15		15½		15⅞	
			15½	35,500	15¾	24,800	16	11,400	16	31,700
AA			36½		36¼		38½		40	
			34¾		35⅜		36		38¾	
			35⅞	16,700	36	16,200	38½	31,900	39½	45,400

	02/17/75		02/18/75		02/19/75		02/20/75		02/21/75
AC	34		34½		34⅛		33⅝		
	33⅛		33¾		33⅜		33¼		
	34	27,300	33⅞	24,600	33⅝	11,500	33⅝	15,300	
ACD	36		35¾		35¾		35¾		
	35⅛		34⅝		34¾		34¼		
	35⅜	29,300	35¾	14,600	35⅝	15,800	34¼	12,400	
AMB	39¾		39¾		39¾		39⅞		
	39⅜		39¼		39⅜		39½		
	39½	19,200	39⅝	9,200	39¾	12,000	39½	9,100	
BS	30⅛		30⅜		31½		31⅝		
	29¾		29⅝		30⅜		31¼		
	30	24,900	30⅛	44,200	31⅜	57,800	31⅜	38,700	
C	9⅞		9¾		9⅜		9⅞		
	9½		9⅜		9⅛		9¼		
	9¾	233,300	9⅜	183,500	9⅜	149,500	9¾	132,000	
DD	101¼		101¼		103½		103¼		
	98		98¾		100¼		101½		
	100¾	60,700	100⅞	38,500	102¼	59,000	102⅜	42,900	
EK	87		84¾		85⅜		88⅞		
	83¾		82⅜		83¼		87½		
	83⅞	119,800	84⅝	109,200	85⅜	122,000	88⅛	153,700	

ESM	28⅞		29⅛		29⅞		30⅜	
	28⅛		28⅞		29		29⅝	
	28½	15,500	29	20,600	29⅞	14,500	29⅝	25,400
GE	43¼		42⅞		43¾		45⅝	
	42⅜		40⅝		42⅝		44¼	
	42⅜	109,000	42⅞	117,200	43⅝	129,600	44¾	146,100
GF	23		23		23⅞		25	
	22¼		22½		22¾		24	
	22½	40,900	23	21,800	23⅞	25,300	24¾	102,800
GM	38¼		37¾		37⅞		39	
	37½		37¼		37⅛		37¼	
	37¾	102,800	37⅜	68,200	37⅜	70,400	39	211,200
GT	15¾		15¾		15⅞		16⅛	
	15⅜		15⅜		15½		15½	
	15½	62,000	15¾	26,500	15½	28,300	16	80,200
HR	25⅜		26½		27		27	
	24		25½		26⅜		26⅜	
	25	65,800	26½	67,700	26¾	49,400	26¾	53,300
IP	42		41⅜		41¼		41⅞	
	40¼		40⅝		40		41½	
	40¾	54,600	41	83,600	40⅞	93,800	41⅝	53,300

	2/17/75	02/18/75		02/19/75		02/20/75		02/21/75	
JM		23		22⅜		22½		22¼	
		22⅛		22		22		21⅝	
		22⅛	35,600	22	14,200	22	14,800	21⅝	9,900
N		24½		24¼		24⅝		24⅜	
		23¾		23⅞		24⅛		24⅛	
		23⅞	10,600	24¼	9,500	24⅛	19,800	24¼	20,500
OI		39		38¾		38⅝		39¾	
		37¾		38		38		38¾	
		39	6,800	38½	6,600	38⅜	2,700	39⅛	7,600
PG		95		94		93⅞		94	
		92¾		92		93		92	
		92¾	47,000	93	28,300	93¼	36,500	92	56,000
S		61⅛		62⅞		62⅞		62⅞	
		60⅛		60½		61¾		61⅞	
		60¾	52,400	62⅝	53,600	62½	42,400	62⅞	40,800
SD		25⅞		25⅞		26⅛		26	
		25		25⅛		25⅝		25⅝	
		25⅝	44,600	25⅞	79,700	25⅞	68,200	26	59,800
T		51⅛		51⅛		51⅜		50⅞	
		50½		50		50⅞		50⅝	
		50½	124,700	50¾	162,700	51¼	156,400	50¾	224,100

TX	25⅜		26		26½		26¾	
	24⅞		25		25⅝		26⅜	
	25⅛	286,400	25⅞	206,700	26½	154,300	26¾	204,500
UTX	35⅞		35⅝		35		35¼	
	35¼		34⅝		34½		34½	
	35½	29,100	34¾	21,200	34⅞	16,100	34¾	33,100
UK	48½		48⅛		49		49⅞	
	47⅛		47		48⅛		49¼	
	47⅞	88,000	48	73,900	49	85,300	49⅞	129,500
WX	12½		12⅜		12½		12½	
	12¼		12⅛		12⅛		12¼	
	12⅜	94,200	12⅜	90,300	12½	55,200	12½	76,700
X	48⅜		48¼		49⅞		50	
	47⅛		47⅜		48¼		49½	
	47⅞	47,300	48¼	59,000	49¾	95,500	50	105,300
XON	74¾		75⅜		77¾		78¼	
	73⅜		73⅝		76⅛		77¼	
	74⅛	66,100	75¼	48,800	77¾	75,600	77¼	74,800
Z	14⅛		14		13¾		13½	
	13⅞		13½		13¼		13⅛	
	14⅛	35,800	13¾	24,200	13⅜	39,300	13⅜	30,400

	02/24/75		02/25/75		02/26/75		02/27/75		02/28/75	
Dow	736.94	1,493,400	719.18	1,474,400	728.10	1,399,300	731.15	1,187,600	739.05	1,129,100
NY		19,150,000		20,910,000		18,790,000		16,430,000		17,560,000
A	15⅞		15½		15		15⅜		15⅜	
	15⅜		15		14⅝		14¾		14⅞	
	15½	15,400	15⅛	16,800	15	25,800	15⅛	28,300	15⅜	11,100
AA	39¼		38		36⅝		36⅜		35⅞	
	38⅜		36¼		35¾		35¾		34¾	
	38½	35,600	36¼	23,700	36	27,500	35¾	33,500	34¾	14,100
AC	33⅝		32¾		33½		33¾		34	
	32¾		32		32¼		32⅝		33⅜	
	33	19,900	32⅜	25,600	32⅝	17,300	33½	15,100	34	12,300
ACD	34½		33½		34⅛		34⅜		35¼	
	33½		32		33		33⅞		33¾	
	33¾	22,900	33	19,400	34⅛	8,300	34	7,300	35¼	13,900
AMB	39⅝		38⅜		37½		37⅞		38¼	
	38		36¼		36⅛		37½		37½	
	38¾	15,100	36⅜	15,300	37	13,000	37⅞	7,500	38	15,000
BS	31⅜		30½		30⅜		30¼		29¾	
	30⅞		29¾		29⅝		29⅜		29⅛	
	31⅛	28,600	29⅞	28,900	30⅜	35,000	29⅝	3,600	29⅝	28,600

C	10		9¾		9⅞		10⅜		10⅜	
	9⅝		9½		9½		9¾		10⅛	
	9¾	126,500	9⅝	52,800	9⅞	36,900	10⅛	91,600	10¼	38,800
DD	103		100½		99		99¾		99	
	101		98½		97½		98¾		98	
	101	33,900	98⅞	41,600	99	31,500	98⅞	45,100	99	23,400
EK	87¾		85		85¾		86⅜		88	
	86⅛		82⅞		83¾		84⅝		84½	
	86⅛	79,100	84	126,400	85½	93,900	85⅜	99,300	87¾	81,700
ESM	29¾		28⅜		27½		28		27⅞	
	28¼		27¼		27		27½		27½	
	28¼	11,800	27½	7,500	27½	10,400	27¾	5,800	27¾	5,600
GE	44⅝		43⅝		42¾		43⅝		44⅞	
	43¾		42¼		41⅞		42⅜		42⅞	
	43⅞	115,100	42¼	139,900	42½	131,400	43	79,400	44⅛	77,000
GF	24¾		23¾		24		24¼		24	
	23⅝		23⅛		23⅛		23¾		23½	
	23¾	35,300	23¼	33,100	23⅞	21,200	23¾	20,700	23¾	13,000
GM	38⅞		38⅛		38¼		38⅝		39	
	38⅜		37⅛		37¼		37⅞		37⅞	
	38⅝	110,300	37¼	87,500	37¾	91,800	38¼	72,100	39	65,300

	02/24/75		02/25/75		02/26/75		02/27/75		02/28/75	
GT	16		15⅝		15½		15¾		15⅝	
	15¾		15⅜		15⅛		15⅜		15¼	
	15¾	35,500	15½	29,500	15½	28,900	15½	37,200	15⅝	33,600
HR	26½		25⅜		25¾		26½		26½	
	25½		24⅝		25		26		25⅝	
	25⅝	40,700	25	50,000	25¾	33,500	26	27,100	26⅜	26,000
IP	41¾		41		40¼		40⅜		40⅛	
	40¼		40⅜		39⅞		39⅞		39½	
	40¾	53,300	40⅜	55,500	40	77,600	40	26,200	40	31,100
JM	21⅝		20½		20¼		20⅝		21⅝	
	20⅜		20		19¾		20¼		20½	
	20¾	36,300	20¼	11,700	20¼	16,400	20⅜	12,200	21⅝	7,400
N	24⅜		24¼		23⅝		23⅝		23⅝	
	24		23¾		23⅜		23½		23⅜	
	24⅛	9,400	23¾	13,500	23½	13,300	23⅝	11,700	23⅝	12,900
OI	38⅞		38⅜		38⅞		39⅝		40	
	38½		37½		37¼		39		39⅛	
	38⅝	8,700	37½	6,300	38⅞	6,100	39⅝	17,100	39¼	14,000
PG	93⅜		92¼		93⅜		94¼		94⅜	
	91½		91		90⅝		93⅜		93¼	
	92¼	36,300	91	25,400	92¾	19,200	94	26,100	94⅜	26,800

S	62¾		61¾		61		61¼		60⅞	
	61¾		59⅝		59¾		59⅞		59¾	
	62½	52,300	60	74,700	60½	72,600	60½	35,000	60¾	40,100
SD	25⅞		25⅛		25⅛		25⅜		25⅜	
	25⅜		24½		24½		24⅞		25⅛	
	25½	57,900	24½	57,700	25	33,600	25¼	42,100	25⅜	45,100
T	50½		50⅛		50		50¼		50½	
	50		49⅝		49¾		49⅞		50	
	50	99,400	49⅞	100,200	49⅞	64,600	50	76,200	50⅜	112,100
TX	26⅝		26		25⅝		26		26⅛	
	26⅛		25		25		25½		25⅛	
	26¼	97,300	25⅛	113,300	25⅜	113,200	25¾	70,400	26⅛	88,900
UTX	35		34¼		35⅝		35¾		36	
	34¼		33½		33⅞		35¼		35¼	
	34¼	12,300	34⅛	27,800	35½	10,900	35⅝	6,900	36	6,600
UK	49⅝		47⅞		48⅜		49⅜		50	
	48½		47¼		47¼		48⅞		48¾	
	48½	63,600	47½	49,300	48¼	121,600	49⅛	67,700	50	92,300
WX	12½		12⅛		11⅝		11¾		12½	
	12⅛		11½		11⅛		11⅝		11¾	
	12⅛	95,200	11½	110,500	11⅝	101,500	11¾	50,400	12½	96,100

	02/24/75		02/25/75		02/26/75		02/27/75		02/28/75	
X	50		49⅛		49⅞		49½		49⅛	
	49¼		48¼		48½		47⅝		47½	
	49¼	59,400	48⅞	43,500	49¾	59,800	47⅞	78,100	49⅛	48,300
XON	77		76⅜		77⅛		77¾		77¾	
	76¼		75⅜		75⅝		76⅞		76¾	
	76¼	54,000	75¾	66,300	76¾	60,000	77	47,700	77⅜	34,200
Z	13⅜		13⅛		13⅛		13⅜		13⅞	
	13		12¾		12¾		13		13⅜	
	13⅛	32,300	12⅞	20,700	13⅛	22,500	13⅜	13,200	13⅞	13,800
	03/03/75		*03/04/75*		*03/05/75*		*03/06/75*		*03/07/75*	
Dow	753.13	1,931,100	757.74	2,712,400	752.82	1,981,400	764.71	1,658,000	770.10	1,799,000
NY		24,100,000		34,140,000		24,120,000		21,780,000		25,930,000
A	15¾		16¾		16½		16¾		17	
	15¼		16		15⅞		16		16⅝	
	15¾	29,500	16⅛	35,500	16¼	11,600	16⅜	29,900	17	26,600
AA	35½		36¼		36⅞		37⅞		40	
	34½		35¾		35⅞		36½		37¾	
	35⅜	43,500	36	89,700	36⅞	17,500	37⅞	23,400	38¼	36,000
AC	34¼		34¼		34⅛		34⅜		34⅜	
	33⅝		33⅝		33¾		33⅝		34⅛	

	33¾	19,200	34	53,100	33⅞	9,800	34⅜	30,400	34⅛	9,400
ACD	36½		38¼		37⅝		36¼		36⅞	
	34¾		37⅛		36⅜		35⅜		35⅞	
	36½	15,900	37¼	62,200	36⅞	38,400	36	19,400	36⅝	10,200
AMB	38¾		39½		39⅝		39¾		40	
	37¾		38⅝		39		39⅛		39⅜	
	38⅝	9,800	39	22,700	39½	12,300	39⅜	10,700	39⅞	11,700
BS	31		31⅜		31⅜		32⅞		33¼	
	29¾		30⅝		30¾		31⅛		32¾	
	31	56,800	30⅝	65,700	31⅛	29,300	32⅝	121,600	33	66,000
C	10¾		11		10¾		10⅞		11¼	
	10⅜		10⅝		10½		10½		11	
	10⅝	69,500	10⅝	80,300	10⅝	47,900	10⅞	41,900	11⅛	110,400
DD	101⅝		104¾		102⅞		103		104¾	
	99¼		101⅜		100		100		103⅛	
	101⅝	31,100	101½	63,200	102	42,500	103	74,500	104¾	48,300
EK	91		94		92⅝		91⅞		94	
	87¾		91		90¼		89⅞		91⅞	
	91	104,800	91⅛	218,500	90⅝	122,200	91⅞	136,700	92⅞	116,700
ESM	28		28¼		28⅜		27⅞		28½	
	27¾		27¾		27¾		27½		28⅛	
	28	5,000	28⅛	31,500	27¾	15,700	27⅞	4,200	28½	7,000

	03/03/75		03/04/75		03/05/75		03/06/75		03/07/75	
GE	44⅞		46¼		45¼		45⅝		46⅝	
	44⅛		44¾		43⅝		43⅞		45⅛	
	44⅞	109,400	45	109,800	44	95,300	45½	64,700	46⅜	81,300
GF	24⅛		24¾		24⅝		24⅞		25	
	23⅝		23⅞		23¾		24		24¾	
	23⅞	28,600	24	55,200	24½	27,800	24¾	52,000	24⅞	39,100
GM	40⅛		41		40¾		40¾		41½	
	39⅜		39⅝		39⅝		39⅝		40⅝	
	39⅞	198,100	39⅝	153,500	40	126,700	40⅝	90,300	41¼	126,100
GT	15⅝		16		15¾		16¼		16½	
	15¼		15⅝		15⅛		15½		16⅛	
	15½	28,900	15⅝	40,400	15⅝	58,600	16¼	63,100	16½	62,700
HR	26⅞		26⅝		26⅛		26⅛		26¾	
	26⅜		25⅝		25⅝		25⅜		26⅛	
	26½	19,800	25⅞	33,500	25⅝	21,200	26	21,500	26⅜	20,500
IP	40¼		40		38½		39¼		39⅞	
	39⅞		38¾		37½		37⅝		38⅞	
	39⅞	29,900	38¾	72,700	37⅝	113,000	39¼	32,900	39¾	128,300
JM	22⅜		22¼		22¼		22		22¼	
	21⅜		21⅝		21⅝		21⅝		21⅞	
	21⅜	13,100	21⅝	16,100	21¾	13,200	21¾	12,900	21⅞	17,200

N	23⅞		24⅝		24⅝		24¼		24	
	23½		24		24		24		23⅜	
	23⅞	10,400	24⅜	22,900	24⅛	12,600	24	7,300	24	39,700
OI	39⅜		38½		38⅛		38		38⅜	
	38½		38⅛		37⅞		37⅝		38	
	38½	4,500	38⅛	16,000	37⅞	11,400	38	9,500	38	2,700
PG	95½		98½		97¼		97¾		98⅞	
	94⅜		96½		95¼		94¾		97⅛	
	95⅜	31,900	96¾	33,800	95¼	43,400	97¾	51,200	98¼	43,400
S	63⅞		65¾		65		65½		66⅜	
	61⅛		64⅜		63		63½		64⅞	
	62⅞	56,400	65	82,000	64¼	80,000	64⅞	75,400	66¼	64,400
SD	26⅛		27⅛		27⅜		26⅞		26⅞	
	25¼		26½		26⅛		26⅜		26	
	26⅛	60,500	26¾	108,600	26½	46,600	26½	36,300	26⅛	39,200
T	50⅝		51¼		51¼		51		51	
	50¼		50⅞		50½		50½		50¾	
	50⅝	108,400	51	231,500	50⅝	220,000	50¾	108,600	50⅞	124,400
TX	26½		27		27⅛		26⅝		26⅜	
	26		26⅜		26⅜		26⅛		25⅝	
	26½	101,000	26½	248,700	26½	157,600	26⅛	114,300	25⅞	97,800

	03/03/75		03/04/75		03/05/75		03/06/75		03/07/75	
UTX	36⅞		37⅜		37⅛		37		37⅜	
	36⅛		36½		36¼		36⅛		36¾	
	36⅞	112,000	37	32,700	36⅞	17,400	37	8,000	37⅜	21,600
UK	53⅜		55		55		53¼		54⅝	
	50½		53⅜		52⅛		52		52⅞	
	53⅜	224,700	53½	268,100	52½	214,600	53⅛	146,800	54⅛	106,900
WX	12⅞		13⅛		13		12⅝		13½	
	12⅜		12½		12⅜		12⅜		13	
	12¾	116,700	12¾	173,500	12⅝	125,500	12⅝	92,400	13½	183,000
X	50¼		51¾		52⅜		52½		53	
	49⅛		50½		51¼		51¾		52½	
	50¼	190,900	51½	183,900	52	137,900	52½	107,700	53	92,000
XON	78		79⅝		78¾		76¼		76½	
	77¼		78¼		75¼		74⅝		75⅛	
	78	73,100	78¼	72,500	75¼	65,000	75⅞	48,700	76¼	53,600
Z	14¼		14¾		14⅝		14		14⅛	
	13⅝		14⅜		14		13⅝		13¾	
	14¼	27,700	14½	34,600	14	46,300	13⅞	21,700	13⅞	12,800
	03/10/75		03/11/75		03/12/75		03/13/75		03/14/75	
Dow	776.13	1,973,300	770.89	2,235,600	763.69	1,623,600	762.98	1,374,800	773.47	1,651,000

NY		25,890,000		31,280,000		21,560,000		18,620,000		24,840,000
A	17½		17⅞		17⅛		17		17⅛	
	16⅞		17⅛		16⅝		16⅝		16¾	
	17½	43,100	17⅛	27,700	17	24,600	16⅞	17,300	16¾	11,000
AA	37⅞		37½		37½		37½		39¼	
	36⅞		36⅞		36⅞		36⅞		37½	
	37⅝	16,900	36⅞	47,200	37½	41,300	37½	18,600	38⅞	29,400
AC	34½		34½		34		33⅞		34¼	
	34⅛		34		33½		33⅜		33¾	
	34⅜	19,200	34¼	12,400	33¾	14,000	33¾	10,000	34⅛	21,900
ACD	36⅞		36⅞		36⅜		36¼		36½	
	36⅛		36⅜		35½		35⅜		35¾	
	36⅝	31,800	36⅜	56,000	36¼	15,700	36	38,900	36¼	21,500
AMB	39⅞		39⅞		39⅜		38¾		39⅞	
	39⅛		39⅛		38¼		38		38¾	
	39¾	12,400	39¼	9,500	38⅝	9,700	38¾	8,400	39⅝	12,400
BS	33½		33⅞		33⅜		33		33⅞	
	32⅝		32⅞		32⅝		32⅛		32¾	
	33⅛	56,300	33⅛	82,500	32⅝	51,100	32⅞	37,500	33⅞	91,400
C	11⅜		11⅝		11⅝		11½		11½	
	11		11⅛		11		11¼		11⅜	
	11⅜	93,100	11⅛	106,200	11½	101,000	11⅜	45,000	11⅜	51,800

	03/10/75		03/11/75		03/12/75		03/13/75		03/14/75	
DD	104¾		105		102¾		102		103	
	102¾		101		101		99¼		100¾	
	104½	31,600	101¾	39,300	102	27,500	101	35,800	102⅝	38,000
EK	93¼		91⅞		90½		91⅜		92¾	
	91		89		88¾		88⅝		90⅞	
	92	88,200	89⅝	94,300	89¼	102,400	91	59,100	92⅛	67,900
ESM	28½		28⅛		28		27		28	
	27¾		27⅝		27⅛		26¾		26⅞	
	27⅞	7,300	28⅛	5,400	27¼	8,500	27	7,300	27¾	5,700
GE	48⅞		49½		48		46¼		46⅝	
	45¼		48		46		45¼		46	
	48⅞	121,100	48¼	125,100	46¼	130,600	45½	87,400	46⅜	56,800
GF	25⅜		25⅝		25⅝		25⅜		25⅝	
	24¾		25⅛		24⅝		25		25¼	
	25¼	65,500	25⅛	34,700	25½	33,700	25¼	18,200	25½	37,800
GM	41⅞		43		43⅜		42½		44⅛	
	40½		41⅝		41⅞		41¾		42⅞	
	41⅞	122,800	42¼	184,700	42⅜	155,500	42⅜	96,400	44⅛	160,500
GT	16⅞		16⅞		16⅞		17⅛		17⅜	
	16½		16½		16¼		16⅝		17	
	16⅞	56,200	16½	43,400	16½	25,900	17	83,900	17⅛	45,400

HR	26⅝		26⅞		25¾		25¼		26⅛	
	25¾		26		25¼		25		25	
	26⅝	24,600	26	31,200	25¼	36,400	25¼	34,300	25¾	26,800
IP	40¼		41½		41⅝		42⅛		43	
	39⅞		40⅛		40⅜		41⅛		42¼	
	40¼	51,400	41	73,600	41⅜	37,500	42⅛	64,300	42⅞	80,500
JM	22¼		22⅜		22¼		22¼		22½	
	21⅞		22		21⅝		22		22	
	22¼	12,800	22⅛	20,100	22⅛	20,500	22¼	20,300	22¼	15,200
N	24⅛		24⅛		23⅞		23½		23⅜	
	23¾		23⅞		23⅝		23¼		23	
	24	8,100	24	23,000	23¾	54,100	23⅜	20,900	23	62,200
OI	38		38⅛		37¼		37		37¾	
	37½		37⅝		37		36¾		37	
	37⅞	3,800	37⅝	6,700	37¼	10,500	36⅞	15,000	37⅝	3,400
PG	98¾		98¾		97⅜		95		96⅞	
	98		97¼		94		93¾		95¼	
	98⅜	31,600	97⅜	22,300	94	37,100	95	23,000	95½	30,500
S	67⅞		67⅝		66¼		65⅞		65⅝	
	65⅞		66¼		65⅛		64½		64¾	
	67⅝	50,600	66½	68,500	65½	54,800	65⅜	32,600	64⅞	39,200

	03/10/75		03/11/75		03/12/75		03/13/75		03/14/75	
SD	26⅝		27⅛		26¾		26⅜		27⅛	
	25⅞		26¼		26⅛		26		26⅛	
	26½	65,800	26¾	74,500	26⅜	37,400	26⅜	35,700	26⅞	84,500
T	51⅛		51⅝		51⅜		51⅛		51½	
	50¾		51¼		51⅛		50¾		51	
	51⅛	138,700	51¼	158,400	51⅛	113,900	51⅛	148,700	51½	89,500
TX	26⅜		26¾		25⅞		25½		26⅜	
	25⅞		26		25½		25¼		25⅜	
	26⅜	105,800	26⅛	106,500	25½	78,300	25⅜	66,100	25⅞	109,000
UTX	37⅞		39		39¾		40		40⅛	
	37		37¾		38⅜		39		39	
	37⅞	63,300	38¾	88,400	39½	13,200	39⅛	20,000	39⅞	33,400
UK	54⅞		55⅜		54½		53½		54	
	53⅝		54½		53		52¾		53⅛	
	54¾	150,100	54⅝	154,200	53⅝	131,100	53¼	71,100	53⅝	80,900
WX	15⅛		15½		14⅞		14¾		15⅛	
	13⅝		14⅝		14½		14⅛		14⅝	
	15⅛	317,100	14⅞	313,600	14¾	118,300	14¾	92,100	15	107,700
X	53⅛		54¾		54⅛		53½		55⅛	
	52⅜		52¾		53⅛		52½		53⅜	
	52⅞	96,900	53⅝	156,000	53¼	81,400	52⅞	118,800	55	160,400

XON	77⅛		78¼		77½		76½		77⅜	
	76⅛		77⅛		76¾		75⅝		75⅝	
	77	44,900	77⅝	50,200	76¾	41,400	76	36,300	76⅛	62,800
Z	14⅜		14⅛		14		13⅞		13⅞	
	13⅞		13¾		13¾		13⅝		13⅝	
	14	42,300	13⅞	20,000	13⅞	16,200	13⅞	12,300	13¾	13,500
		03/17/75		*03/18/75*		*03/19/75*		*03/20/75*		*03/21/75*
Dow	786.53	1,715,100	779.41	2,249,200	769.48	1,781,500	764.00	1,866,100	763.06	1,321,600
NY		26,780,000		29,180,000		19,030,000		20,690,000		15,940,000
A	17⅝		17⅜		17¼		18		17⅝	
	17		16⅞		16⅞		17		17¼	
	17⅜	24,300	17	26,200	17¼	9,300	17¼	31,300	17⅝	5,700
AA	39½		41		38¾		39¼		38⅞	
	38½		39⅛		37¼		38¼		38⅛	
	39½	46,200	39⅛	60,300	38¾	45,200	38⅝	34,700	38⅝	16,400
AC	34⅜		34⅜		34⅛		33¼		33	
	34		34⅛		33⅛		32½		32½	
	34⅜	9,900	34⅛	10,200	33⅛	16,100	32⅞	13,600	32⅞	8,600
ACD	37		37½		36¾		36½		35⅝	
	36⅜		36⅝		36⅛		35¾		35¼	
	37	13,800	37	28,500	36½	38,200	36¼	14,400	35⅝	7,600

	03/17/75		03/18/75		03/19/75		03/20/75		03/21/75	
AMB	40		40		39⅜		39½		39½	
	39½		39½		38¾		39⅛		38¼	
	40	11,900	39½	10,700	39⅜	8,300	39½	6,500	38⅝	9,700
BS	34½		35		34¼		34½		34¼	
	33⅝		34⅛		33½		33⅜		33½	
	34½	91,600	34¼	118,800	34	66,800	33⅞	37,500	34	36,000
C	11½		11⅛		10¾		11⅞		11⅜	
	11		10¾		10½		10⅝		10¾	
	11	81,600	10⅞	63,600	10¾	37,900	10¾	137,700	11⅛	36,800
DD	104⅞		106		102		99⅞		98⅞	
	102⅝		102		99¾		98		96¾	
	104¾	36,900	102½	52,100	99⅞	75,300	98⅜	68,300	96⅞	58,000
EK	94⅞		95⅝		93¾		95		93	
	92½		93⅛		92⅜		92½		91¼	
	94⅞	79,700	93¼	134,000	93½	65,600	92⅝	79,200	92¼	51,000
ESM	28⅞		29½		28¼		28⅜		27¾	
	28		28½		27⅞		27⅝		27⅛	
	28⅞	13,400	28¾	14,300	28	10,400	27⅝	3,400	27½	2,000
GE	48¾		49¼		47¼		47⅜		46¾	
	46⅜		48		46⅜		46		45¾	
	48¾	109,400	48	105,500	47	158,600	46⅜	93,800	46½	63,100

GF	25½		26		25¾		25⅝		24⅞	
	25¼		25⅝		24¾		24½		23¾	
	25½	30,900	25¾	77,800	24¾	18,600	25	29,000	24⅝	19,100
GM	45⅞		45¾		43		44		43⅛	
	44⅜		43⅞		42¼		42⅝		42½	
	45⅞	163,900	44	179,700	42⅝	148,200	42⅞	143,400	43	126,700
GT	17⅛		17⅛		17		17		17	
	17		16⅝		16⅝		16¾		16¾	
	17⅛	66,600	16¾	51,100	16⅞	51,000	16⅞	36,500	16⅞	31,900
HR	26⅛		25⅝		25⅜		25½		25⅛	
	25½		25¼		24⅞		24¾		24¾	
	25⅝	17,700	25¼	19,300	25¼	20,400	24⅞	19,500	24⅞	11,500
IP	43¼		44⅛		43⅞		43⅝		41⅝	
	42⅝		43⅛		42⅞		42½		40¾	
	43⅛	57,700	43⅜	76,200	43¾	44,600	42½	44,300	40⅞	56,000
JM	22⅝		22⅞		22⅝		22⅞		22⅝	
	22⅛		22½		22⅛		22⅜		22	
	22⅝	19,500	22⅝	22,800	22⅜	12,800	22¾	63,800	22½	19,100
N	23¼		23⅛		23		23⅜		23⅜	
	22⅞		22⅞		22¾		22⅞		23	
	23	25,400	22⅞	33,000	23	10,900	23	15,600	23⅜	10,900

	03/17/75		03/18/75		03/19/75		03/20/75		03/21/75	
OI	39⅜		39⅞		39¾		40⅞		40	
	38		39½		39¼		39½		39½	
	39⅜	23,100	39¾	20,700	39¾	11,900	40⅛	23,300	39¾	10,200
PG	95⅞		96¾		95		94¼		92¼	
	94¼		95¼		94¼		90¾		89¾	
	95⅞	36,500	95⅜	72,200	94¼	26,700	90¾	37,000	92¼	43,500
S	66⅞		69¼		67⅛		67½		66⅞	
	65		66⅝		65⅝		66		66⅛	
	66⅞	47,100	66¾	100,100	66⅞	45,400	66⅜	34,700	66⅜	37,600
SD	27		26⅞		26		25⅜		25¼	
	26⅜		26⅛		25⅛		24⅞		24⅝	
	26¾	34,300	26¼	49,800	25¼	81,500	25⅛	52,200	25⅛	43,400
T	51⅝		51¾		51½		50⅜		49⅜	
	51¼		51⅜		50¾		49		48⅝	
	51½	86,300	51½	113,600	50⅞	146,700	49⅛	351,400	48⅞	191,100
TX	26⅛		25⅞		25½		25⅜		24¾	
	25½		25⅜		25		24⅝		24¼	
	25½	98,100	25½	97,500	25½	115,500	24¾	110,500	24¾	115,800
UTX	41¾		43⅛		41		41⅜		40⅞	
	40		41⅜		40⅛		40¼		40⅜	
	41½	23,500	41½	52,900	40⅛	29,000	41	21,000	40½	33,500

UK	55⅜		55⅞		54		54⅜		55¼	
	53⅞		55		53		53¼		53¼	
	55¼	103,900	55	162,900	53¼	134,700	53⅝	98,100	55	95,500
WX	15½		15⅜		14¾		15		14¾	
	15		14¾		14⅜		14⅝		14¼	
	15¼	168,000	14¾	136,300	14¾	83,900	14⅝	92,200	14⅝	53,500
X	56¼		57⅝		56¾		57½		57½	
	55⅛		56½		55½		56⅛		56⅝	
	56	131,000	57⅛	244,000	56⅜	154,700	56½	108,100	57⅜	89,400
XON	76¼		75⅝		72⅞		74¼		73⅜	
	75⅜		72¾		70⅞		72		72⅜	
	75⅜	43,100	73	75,700	72	101,700	72⅞	49,600	73	27,800
Z	13⅞		14⅛		14		14⅛		14⅛	
	13⅝		13¾		13¾		13⅝		13¾	
	13¾	19,800	14	35,100	13⅞	11,600	14	15,500	14	10,200
	03/24/75		*03/25/75*		*03/26/75*		*03/27/75*		*03/28/75*	
Dow	742.43	1,549,000	747.89	1,679,000	766.19	1,358,700	770.26	1,413,100	HOLIDAY	
NY		17,810,000		18,500,000		18,530,000		18,300,000		
A	17½		17		17⅜		17½			
	16¾		16¾		16¾		17¼			
	17	16,000	16¾	9,500	17⅜	11,600	17⅜	26,400		

	03/24/75		03/25/75		03/26/75		03/27/75		03/28/75
AA	38		37½		37⅝		37⅝		
	37¼		36½		37¼		37⅛		
	37¼	43,700	37½	30,300	37¼	25,800	37⅜	20,000	
AC	32⅜		32¼		33		33		
	32		31⅝		32		32½		
	32¼	12,600	32⅛	5,300	32¾	9,300	32¾	6,900	
ACD	35		35⅝		37⅛		37¾		
	34½		34		35⅝		36⅝		
	35	11,500	35⅝	14,100	37⅛	15,300	36⅝	27,400	
AMB	38⅜		38⅛		39⅜		38½		
	37¼		37¼		38¼		38⅛		
	37½	8,400	37¾	8,200	38⅞	12,100	38½	6,000	
BS	33⅜		33⅜		34¼		34¾		
	32⅝		32½		33⅜		34⅛		
	33¼	41,300	33	37,400	34	37,900	34⅜	68,000	
C	11		10⅝		11		11		
	10⅝		10¼		10¾		10⅜		
	10¾	36,500	10⅝	48,000	10⅞	43,900	10⅝	62,100	
DD	95⅞		96		98¾		100¼		
	94¼		94		96		98¾		
	94¾	57,800	95⅜	68,400	98¾	25,500	99	63,000	

EK	90¾		90½		92⅜		93½	
	89½		88⅛		91		92⅝	
	89⅝	78,700	89½	121,100	92¼	106,200	92⅞	49,500
ESM	27		27		27⅛		27	
	26¾		26¼		26⅝		26½	
	26¾	4,300	26½	6,000	27	7,400	26½	45,700
GE	45⅛		45½		46⅞		47¼	
	43¼		44⅛		45¾		46½	
	44⅝	108,000	45½	139,100	46⅞	86,900	46¾	87,200
GF	24		23⅝		24¼		25	
	23¼		22¾		23¼		24¼	
	23¾	20,900	23	25,700	24	44,100	24½	18,200
GM	42¼		42⅛		42⅝		43	
	41⅝		41¼		41¾		41⅞	
	41⅞	117,700	41⅞	108,200	42⅝	70,700	42⅛	73,600
GT	16⅞		16¾		17¼		17½	
	16½		16⅝		16¾		17¼	
	16¾	23,000	16¾	54,800	17¼	52,200	17¼	25,800
HR	24¾		25		25¾		26⅛	
	24½		24⅛		24⅞		25¾	
	24⅝	14,100	24⅞	14,900	25⅝	15,800	26⅛	27,800

	03/24/75		03/25/75		03/26/75		03/27/		03/28/75
IP	40		40¼		41⅝		42⅛		
	39⅜		39		41		41½		
	39⅝	68,200	40	68,300	41½	51,600	41¾	41,800	
JM	22¼		21½		21½		22⅜		
	21½		20¾		20¾		22		
	21½	28,800	20¾	14,400	21½	12,100	22⅜	9,500	
N	23⅛		23⅛		23¾		24		
	22⅞		22⅞		23⅛		23⅝		
	22⅞	11,900	23⅛	14,600	23¾	18,200	23⅞	18,100	
OI	39⅜		38⅞		39½		39¼		
	38¾		38⅛		38⅝		38⅝		
	38¾	5,600	38¾	7,700	38⅝	9,900	38⅝	8,500	
PG	91¼		93		94¾		96½		
	89⅝		90¼		93¼		94¾		
	90¾	20,000	92½	40,500	94⅝	28,000	96	36,000	
S	65⅜		65½		66½		68		
	64¼		64⅛		65		65⅝		
	64⅞	37,600	65⅛	52,600	65⅞	71,400	67¼	73,400	
SD	24⅞		24⅛		24⅜		24⅝		
	24⅛		23⅞		24		24⅛		
	24¼	75,100	24⅛	100,200	24⅜	38,300	24½	44,300	

T	48½		49⅛		50⅛		50¼	
	48		47⅝		49⅛		49½	
	48¼	125,300	49⅛	143,700	49½	104,200	49¾	101,300
TX	24⅜		24¾		24⅝		24⅞	
	23⅝		23¼		24		24¼	
	24	145,100	24⅛	135,800	24½	74,200	24¾	77,900
UA	40⅛		40¾		41⅜		41⅞	
	38½		38⅛		40½		40⅝	
	38¾	49,100	40½	38,500	41⅜	17,100	41	12,600
UK	54⅜		55¼		56¾		58¼	
	53¾		53½		55⅛		56⅝	
	54	96,900	55	99,900	56⅜	153,500	58⅛	167,600
WX	14⅝		14⅜		14¾		15	
	14⅛		14		14¼		14½	
	14⅜	112,500	14¼	91,100	14⅝	66,100	14½	82,800
X	56½		56¼		58		58¾	
	55½		54½		56¼		57⅝	
	55⅞	81,900	56	95,200	57½	98,900	58½	75,700
XON	71¾		72¼		74		74¾	
	70⅝		69¾		71¾		73½	
	71	77,500	71½	68,700	74	40,000	73⅝	34,900

	03/24/75		03/25/75		03/26/75		03/27/75		03/28/75
Z	13¾		13⅝		13¾		13⅞		
	13¼		13		13¼		13½		
	13⅜	19,000	13½	16,600	13⅝	10,500	13½	21,100	

03/31/75			03/31/75			03/31/75		
Dow	768.15	1,187,100	ESM	26¾		S	68¾	
				26½			67½	
NY		16,270,000		26¾	4,300		67½	33,300
A	17¾		GE	46¾		SD	24⅞	
	17½			45⅞			24⅛	
	17⅝	14,800		46	61,300		24¼	33,200
AA	37⅞		GF	24⅞		T	50	
	37¼			24			49⅜	
	37¼	30,300		24⅜	20,600		49⅜	72,900
AC	33⅜		GM	42¼		TX	24⅝	
	32⅞			41			24	
	33¼	8,900		41⅛	73,700		24⅛	98,200
ACD	37½		GT	17⅜		UA	41½	
	36⅝			17⅛			40⅝	
	36⅝	18,400		17⅜	35,900		41	29,000
AMB	38⅞		HR	26½		UK	58⅛	
	38⅛			25¾			56¾	

	38¼	7,900		25⅝	16,800		56¾	97,200
BS	34¾		IP	42⅜		WX	14⅞	
	34⅛			41⅝			14½	
	34⅛	40,400		41¾	24,500		14¾	54,300
C	10⅞		JM	22⅜		X	59½	
	10½			21⅝			58½	
	10½	30,900		21⅞	5,900		58¾	102,200
DD	99¾		N	25¼		XON	74⅝	
	98¾			23¾			73⅞	
	99⅛	31,700		25	98,200		74	36,200
EK	94		OI	39		Z	13⅞	
	91⅞			38½			13⅝	
	92¼	53,900		38½	4,500		13¾	17,200
			PG	97				
				95¼				
				95¾	30,500			

	04/01/75		04/02/75		04/03/75		04/04/75	
Dow	761.58	1,229,900	760.56	1,215,500	752.19	1,180,300	747.26	1,228,600
NY		14,480,000		15,600,000		13,920,000		14,170,000
A	17⅞		17⅜		17⅜		16⅞	
	17⅛		16¾		16¾		16½	
	17⅛	28,100	16¾	17,000	16¾	7,700	16¾	41,600
AA	37¾		37⅝		37		36¼	
	36¾		37⅛		36		35⅞	
	37⅛	29,800	37¼	27,700	36¼	23,300	36	17,100
AC	33⅜		33⅝		33½		33⅜	
	33		33⅛		33⅛		32¾	
	33¼	5,800	33½	12,000	33⅜	5,400	32¾	6,600
ACD	36⅞		36½		36½		36½	
	35⅝		35¾		36		35½	
	36⅛	9,000	36⅛	8,800	36¼	11,000	35½	29,400
AMB	38⅞		39¼		39½		39⅜	
	38⅛		38⅛		38¼		37⅝	
	38⅝	5,700	39	5,200	38⅝	11,000	39	13,300
BS	34½		34¾		34⅜		33⅞	
	33¾		33⅞		33⅝		33¼	
	34	40,200	34½	50,900	33¾	22,600	33⅞	34,200

C	10⅝		10⅞		10½		10⅜	
	10⅜		10⅜		10¼		10¼	
	10½	24,600	10½	35,000	10⅜	22,300	10¼	28,100
DD	100¼		101¼		102⅜		101½	
	98½		99		100¾		99¾	
	99½	38,200	101	36,600	100⅞	24,300	101	33,700
EK	92⅜		92⅞		91		90⅜	
	90⅞		90¼		89½		88⅝	
	91⅜	70,500	91¼	84,400	89¾	82,100	89⅛	77,000
ESM	26⅞		26½		26¼		26⅛	
	26⅛		26		26		25¾	
	26⅜	5,600	26⅜	8,500	26	8,000	25¾	1,900
GE	46¼		46½		45⅞		45⅜	
	45⅝		45¼		45¼		45	
	45⅞	54,700	45⅝	74,800	45⅜	57,400	45⅛	58,100
GF	24½		24⅛		23⅜		22⅞	
	23⅛		23		22⅝		22⅝	
	23⅝	54,000	23	60,000	23	25,800	22¾	19,400
GM	41		41⅛		40⅞		40⅞	
	40¼		40⅜		40½		40⅛	
	40⅜	101,100	40⅝	67,900	40¾	73,500	40¼	72,300

	04/01/75		*04/02/75*		*04/03/75*		*04/04/75*	
GT	17⅜		17½		17½		17¼	
	17¼		17¼		17⅛		17	
	17⅜	16,200	17⅜	39,400	17⅛	40,400	17⅛	15,800
HR	25¾		25⅜		25⅜		25	
	25		25		24⅞		24⅝	
	25½	37,800	25	36,900	25⅛	18,000	24⅝	14,200
IP	42		42¼		41⅞		42⅛	
	41⅝		41¼		41⅜		41⅝	
	41⅝	23,700	41½	38,600	41⅞	16,500	42⅛	14,500
JM	21¾		20¾		20¾		20⅜	
	20¼		20		20¼		20⅛	
	20½	16,800	20¾	22,400	20½	8,200	20¼	10,400
N	24⅞		25		24⅞		24¾	
	24⅝		24¾		24⅝		24⅝	
	24¾	15,900	24¾	29,500	24⅝	18,700	24¾	13,600
OI	39¼		39⅜		39		38¾	
	38⅝		38¾		38½		38⅜	
	39	5,000	39	4,900	38¾	12,500	38⅝	3,600
PG	95¼		94⅞		92⅞		92	
	93¾		92½		91		90	
	93¾	13,200	93	21,300	91¼	18,700	91	41,500

S	67⅞		68½		67½		65½	
	67⅛		67½		66		62½	
	67⅜	42,600	67¾	46,000	66	202,300	63	123,700
SD	24¾		24¼		23⅞		23⅝	
	24		23¾		23½		23⅛	
	24	49,500	23¾	45,900	23½	48,300	23½	45,000
T	49⅛		49⅛		48⅞		48⅝	
	48⅝		48⅞		48⅜		48¼	
	49	97,600	49	96,200	48¾	81,800	48¼	90,300
TX	24½		24⅝		24⅛		23⅞	
	24		24		23⅝		23⅜	
	24⅜	99,500	24	68,900	23¾	83,800	23½	139,600
UTX	40⅞		39⅞		39⅜		39¾	
	40		38⅞		38¾		38½	
	40	22,600	38⅞	36,200	39	11,600	39⅝	23,700
UK	56½		56⅞		56¼		56¼	
	55⅞		56		55¾		55½	
	56	80,500	56	84,700	55¾	65,100	55¾	67,800
WX	14⅜		14½		14⅛		13⅝	
	14⅛		14⅛		13½		13⅜	
	14⅜	63,000	14¼	42,100	13½	62,900	13½	67,500

	04/01/75		04/02/75		04/03/75		04/04/75	
X	58⅜		58⅜		57⅝		56¼	
	57½		57⅝		55¾		55	
	57¾	62,100	57⅝	70,300	55⅞	72,500	55¾	62,600
XON	74¾		74⅜		73¼		71⅝	
	73¾		73¼		71⅝		70⅜	
	74	100,000	73⅜	31,900	71¼	37,000	70¾	40,000
Z	13¾		14		13⅞		13⅞	
	13½		13⅝		13¾		13⅝	
	13¾	16,600	13⅞	11,500	13¾	7,600	13⅞	22,100

	04/07/75		04/08/75		04/09/75		04/10/75		04/11/75	
Dow	742.88	1,043,200	749.22	1,112,500	767.99	1,324,500	781.29	2,123,400	789.50	1,671,300
NY		13,860,000		14,320,000		18,120,000		24,990,000		20,160,000
A	16¾		17		17½		18		17¾	
	16½		16⅝		16⅞		17½		17¼	
	16½	27,200	17	34,500	17⅜	21,700	17¾	25,500	17¼	34,400
AA	36⅜		35⅝		37		38⅛		38¾	
	35½		35		35¼		36⅞		37⅝	
	35⅞	11,600	35⅜	39,100	36⅞	37,800	37⅞	48,300	38¾	34,300
AC	32		31⅝		31⅞		31⅞		31¼	
	31⅛		31¼		31⅜		31		30¼	

	31¼	12,900	31½	8,700	31⅞	9,300	31¼	38,200	30⅝	12,300
ACD	35¼		34¾		35		35¾		35¾	
	34⅜		34		34		35		35⅜	
	34⅜	10,400	34⅛	12,400	34⅝	30,500	35½	27,300	35⅜	12,100
AMB	39¼		39¼		39⅜		39½		39½	
	38½		38½		38⅞		39		39⅛	
	38½	6,600	39⅛	10,900	39	9,000	39⅜	14,000	39½	6,800
BS	34		34⅛		34½		35⅜		36½	
	33½		33⅝		33⅞		34⅝		35¼	
	33¾	35,400	34	43,200	34½	39,400	35⅜	138,400	36⅛	113,500
C	10¼		10¼		10¼		10¼		10¼	
	10		10		10		9⅞		9⅞	
	10⅛	61,000	10⅛	23,100	10⅛	29,400	9⅞	87,700	10¼	168,000
DD	101		103½		107		111¾		113	
	100		101½		103½		107½		110⅝	
	101	22,100	103	40,300	107	86,200	109¾	132,900	113	108,000
EK	89⅝		90⅝		93		95		95¼	
	87⅞		89⅛		90⅛		93⅝		93¼	
	89½	51,400	89⅞	67,200	92¾	57,400	94¼	117,400	94⅞	66,800
ESM	25¾		25½		26		26⅞		26⅛	
	25⅜		24¾		24⅞		26⅛		25¾	
	25⅜	23,100	25⅛	31,400	25⅞	48,800	26¼	17,100	26	6,200

	04/07/75		04/08/75		04/09/75		04/10/75		04/11/75	
GE	44⅞		45¼		46¾		47¾		48½	
	44⅜		44⅜		45		46½		47⅛	
	44⅜	51,500	45⅛	60,200	46¾	64,100	47¾	106,600	48½	76,500
GF	22⅞		23		23¼		24		23⅞	
	22⅝		22⅝		22¾		23½		23⅝	
	22⅝	14,800	23	16,800	23¼	15,800	23⅞	25,100	23¾	16,100
GM	40½		40¾		41⅜		42¼		42½	
	39⅝		39⅞		40½		41⅜		41¾	
	39¾	74,200	40⅜	75,200	41⅛	48,600	42⅛	94,900	42½	75,300
GT	17⅛		17⅛		17¾		18¼		18½	
	16¾		16⅞		17		17⅝		17⅞	
	16⅞	34,800	17	14,500	17¾	71,200	18¼	103,600	18½	43,300
HR	24⅞		24⅞		25⅝		25⅞		25¾	
	24⅛		24¼		24¾		25¼		25¼	
	24½	19,900	24⅝	14,400	25¼	21,800	25½	31,100	25¾	20,200
IP	42⅛		43⅜		44⅛		45⅝		46¼	
	41¾		42⅝		43		44¼		44⅞	
	41⅞	9,600	43⅛	34,600	44⅛	37,300	44¾	97,300	46¼	36,600
JM	20¼		19⅞		20⅜		20½		20⅝	
	19¾		19⅛		19½		20		20⅛	
	19⅞	9,000	19¼	15,300	20⅜	13,800	20¼	25,700	20⅝	12,900

N	24⅞		25½		26¼		26¼		26⅞	
	24⅝		25		25¼		25⅞		26⅛	
	24¾	13,400	25½	20,600	26¼	14,300	26	28,400	26⅞	16,800
OI	39		38½		39¼		38¼		38½	
	38¼		38⅛		38⅛		37¾		37¾	
	38½	6,500	38⅜	7,700	38½	10,500	38	20,200	38½	8,200
PG	92		93¼		93¼		95¾		96⅜	
	90½		91⅝		91⅞		93		95¼	
	91½	18,200	91⅝	14,400	92⅝	22,300	95¼	32,700	96⅜	21,000
S	62⅞		63		63¾		65½		65⅜	
	62		62		62⅛		64⅛		64⅜	
	62⅛	50,900	62⅜	33,500	63½	33,700	65	46,600	65	26,700
SD	23¾		23⅞		24⅞		25⅝		25⅝	
	23⅛		23¼		23⅝		25		25	
	23½	49,300	23¾	36,000	24⅞	67,900	25⅛	63,000	25	37,700
T	48⅜		48⅝		49		49⅛		48⅞	
	48		48⅛		48½		48⅝		48⅝	
	48⅜	81,000	48½	96,700	49	111,200	48⅞	133,400	48⅞	88,500
TX	23⅞		24⅛		24½		24⅞		24⅜	
	23⅜		23½		23⅞		24¼		23⅞	
	23½	71,400	24⅛	73,000	24½	90,200	24⅜	104,600	24	99,300

	04/07/75		04/08/75		04/09/75		04/10/75		04/11/75	
UTX	40¾		42⅜		43¼		45¼		44⅞	
	39		40½		41⅜		43½		43⅝	
	40¾	9,300	41⅝	24,000	43	54,900	44¾	60,000	44¾	35,000
UK	55½		55⅜		57¾		60⅜		61	
	54⅝		54⅞		55¼		58½		59⅝	
	54¾	75,300	55	65,900	57⅝	100,200	60⅛	248,800	60¾	184,500
WX	13½		13¾		13⅞		14¼		14⅝	
	13¼		13¼		13½		13¾		14⅛	
	13½	43,300	13½	89,500	13¾	37,600	14¼	74,700	14½	140,600
X	55¾		56⅜		57½		59		60	
	54⅝		55⅜		55⅝		57⅞		58⅝	
	55⅜	66,600	55½	33,500	57⅜	41,500	58⅞	116,100	60	114,400
XON	71⅛		72		74		74⅜		75	
	70¼		70½		71⅝		73½		73¾	
	70⅜	59,400	71⅝	33,900	73½	46,600	74	39,100	75	31,300
Z	14		14		14⅛		14¼		14⅜	
	13¾		13⅞		14		14⅛		14	
	14	23,100	14	42,000	14⅛	51,700	14⅛	24,700	14⅜	24,000
	04/14/75		04/15/75		04/16/75		04/17/75		04/18/75	
Dow	806.95	1,626,500	815.08	2,461,600	815.71	2,043,900	819.46	2,350,700	808.43	1,674,500

NY		26,800,000		29,620,000		22,970,000		32,650,000		22,610,000
A	17⅝		18¼		19⅞		20¾		20¼	
	17¼		17½		18		19¼		19⅜	
	17⅜	18,600	18⅛	83,500	19¾	82,000	19½	86,700	19¾	30,200
AA	41⅞		43¼		43¼		46⅜		45⅜	
	39¾		41⅞		42¾		44½		44½	
	41½	75,000	43⅛	68,500	43¼	86,300	45⅛	78,100	45	74,000
AC	31⅜		31		30		29⅝		29⅞	
	30⅝		29¾		28¾		29		29⅛	
	31¼	15,600	30	50,900	29⅛	33,800	29¼	24,500	29⅜	59,600
ACD	36⅞		37		37⅜		37¾		37½	
	35⅝		36⅛		36⅛		37⅛		37	
	36½	17,500	36⅝	38,100	37¼	22,300	37⅛	31,600	37½	42,700
AMB	39⅞		39¾		39½		39¼		38⅝	
	39¼		39		38⅝		38⅜		38⅛	
	39¾	8,300	39⅜	13,400	39	12,300	38⅜	8,200	38¼	3,400
BS	37⅛		38		37⅝		38⅜		38	
	36¼		37¼		37⅛		37⅞		36¾	
	37⅛	116,400	37½	124,300	37½	77,900	37⅞	98,500	36⅞	54,200
C	10⅞		11¼		11		10⅞		10⅞	
	10⅜		10⅞		10⅝		10¾		10	
	10⅞	52,600	11	91,700	10⅞	41,300	10⅞	59,900	10⅞	32,000

	04/14/75		04/15/75		04/16/75		04/17/75		04/18/75	
DD	119		124¼		123¾		126¼		124	
	114		119¼		121		123		121¼	
	118½	128,100	124¼	173,500	123¾	73,400	124	71,700	122	70,100
EK	98¾		101⅛		102½		106¼		103¾	
	94¾		97¾		99		102⅞		100¾	
	98¾	102,600	100⅛	142,500	102½	126,100	103½	151,200	101⅞	81,700
ESM	26⅝		26¾		26⅜		27¼		27½	
	26		26¼		25⅝		26⅛		26½	
	26½	11,500	26⅝	14,000	26¼	16,600	27	16,100	26¾	23,700
GE	49		49		48		48		45¾	
	47⅞		48¼		46⅛		46		44½	
	48⅞	62,600	48⅞	123,500	48	161,200	46	150,800	44½	133,300
GF	24¼		24⅞		25⅛		25⅛		24¾	
	23⅝		24		24⅛		24½		23½	
	24	15,000	24½	22,700	24¾	41,800	24⅞	31,300	23½	32,900
GM	43½		44		43⅛		43⅛		42	
	42⅞		43⅜		42¼		41⅞		41⅜	
	43½	84,000	43½	140,600	42¾	93,800	41⅞	120,300	41⅝	99,500
GT	19⅛		19⅝		19		19		18⅞	
	18⅜		19		18⅝		18¾		18½	
	19⅛	27,800	19⅛	56,400	18¾	72,900	18⅞	70,100	18⅝	44,600

HR	26⅜		26¼		26		26⅛		26⅛	
	25⅝		25⅝		25¼		25⅝		25⅜	
	25⅞	19,100	25¾	26,000	25⅝	31,600	26	29,100	25⅝	20,100
IP	48		47½		46⅞		47¾		47½	
	47		46¼		46		47⅛		46½	
	47¼	54,300	46⅜	52,300	46½	55,100	47⅜	56,800	46⅝	47,500
JM	20⅞		20		20⅜		21⅛		20⅞	
	19⅝		19⅝		19⅞		20½		20⅜	
	20⅛	36,900	20	57,700	20⅜	38,000	20⅞	40,200	20⅜	14,100
N	27⅞		28⅛		27¾		27⅝		27¼	
	27¼		27⅝		27¼		27¼		27	
	27⅞	21,000	27⅝	38,400	27⅜	88,100	27¼	32,300	27⅛	29,700
OI	39		38⅞		38⅝		39		37⅞	
	38¼		38¾		38¼		38		37	
	38½	17,300	38¾	35,100	38½	14,700	38	32,100	37	10,900
PG	98¼		99⅞		100		100¾		97½	
	96¼		97		98⅜		97¾		95¾	
	98	27,600	99½	35,700	100	39,200	97¾	60,200	96¼	28,500
S	65⅞		66½		67¼		69⅜		67¾	
	65⅛		65⅜		65⅝		67⅜		65⅛	
	65⅞	36,400	66½	64,400	67¼	82,900	68	72,800	65½	111,700

	04/14/75		04/15/75		04/16/75		04/17/75		04/18/75	
SD	26		26		25¾		26⅞		25¾	
	25		25⅛		25		25¼		25¼	
	25¾	29,200	25¼	50,100	25½	37,500	25½	44,600	25¼	38,500
T	49⅛		49⅛		48¾		49⅛		48¾	
	48¾		48½		48⅜		48½		48¼	
	48⅞	57,100	48⅞	173,900	48⅜	124,200	48⅞	244,300	48⅜	163,000
TX	24⅜		24⅜		24⅞		25⅜		25	
	24		24		24⅛		24⅞		24⅜	
	24⅜	88,400	24¼	112,100	24¾	139,100	25	107,800	24⅝	89,100
UTX	45⅞		45⅞		45		46⅞		46⅜	
	44⅝		45⅜		44		45½		45¼	
	45⅞	48,700	45½	43,600	45	41,600	46¼	56,300	45¾	31,000
UK	61½		62		61⅝		63½		63½	
	60¾		60⅞		60⅜		62		61½	
	61⅜	113,600	61⅜	220,400	61½	132,700	62⅝	204,200	62½	91,100
WX	15		14⅞		14¾		15		14¾	
	14½		14⅝		14½		14½		14¼	
	14½	161,300	14¾	119,100	14⅝	68,300	14½	87,500	14¼	49,400
X	60⅞		62⅛		62¼		64⅛		62¾	
	60		60½		61⅛		62⅜		61	
	60⅝	95,800	61⅝	132,500	61⅞	99,700	62⅞	142,900	61⅞	79,300

XON	77		78⅞		77¾		78⅝		78⅜	
	76		76⅜		76⅝		77⅝		77	
	76⅛	54,600	77⅞	69,500	76⅞	42,400	78¼	75,200	77¾	58,100
Z	14⅞		15¾		15⅞		16⅜		16½	
	14⅜		14⅝		15⅜		16⅛		16⅛	
	14⅞	29,600	15¾	87,200	15⅞	67,100	16⅛	65,400	16½	30,600
	04/21/75		*04/22/75*		*04/23/75*		*04/24/75*		*04/25/75*	
Dow	815.86	1,216,600	814.14	1,695,000	802.49	1,498,300	803.66	1,502,700	811.80	1,655,000
NY		23,960,000		26,120,000		20,020,000		19,050,000		20,260,000
A	20¼		20⅜		18⅜		17⅝		17¾	
	19⅞		19¼		17½		17		17⅜	
	20¼	23,000	19¼	25,700	17½	57,400	17½	55,100	17½	19,900
AA	47½		48¼		46⅝		46		46	
	45¼		46½		45¼		45½		45⅛	
	47½	53,800	46⅝	51,200	45¾	67,600	45⅝	56,500	45⅝	18,600
AC	29⅜		29¼		28¾		29		29	
	29		28⅞		28¼		28⅜		28⅝	
	29⅛	13,000	29	18,800	28¾	13,800	29	14,200	29	10,100
ACD	37⅞		38		38		37⅜		37¾	
	37¼		37⅝		36¾		36¼		36⅝	
	37¾	17,300	37⅝	14,700	37⅛	18,500	37	19,000	37⅜	32,700

	04/21/75		04/22/75		04/23/75		04/24/75		04/25/75	
AMB	38¾		38⅞		38⅝		38⅞		39⅜	
	38		38¼		38		38⅛		38¼	
	38⅝	7,500	38¼	18,000	38½	5,600	38¾	2,700	38½	63,300
BS	37⅝		38⅛		38⅛		38¾		39½	
	36¾		37½		37½		37¼		38⅜	
	37¼	32,200	37¾	74,200	37½	78,700	38¼	69,900	39⅜	71,500
C	11		11⅜		11⅛		10¾		11⅛	
	10¾		10⅞		10⅞		10½		10½	
	11	54,400	11¼	95,100	11	54,000	10¾	28,800	10⅞	53,000
DD	123¼		124⅞		122½		120½		123	
	121½		121		120¼		119		120⅛	
	122⅞	17,000	122	52,900	120⅜	39,600	120	53,800	121⅞	22,500
EK	104¼		104⅞		103		101¾		102¾	
	101⅛		102⅜		99¾		99⅛		100½	
	103⅛	56,800	102⅜	44,700	99¾	59,600	100	80,500	101¾	70,800
ESM	27⅝		27¾		27¼		26⅞		27	
	26½		27⅛		26¾		26½		26⅝	
	27¼	13,700	27⅛	21,800	26¾	13,500	26⅝	8,200	27	5,600
GE	45½		46½		45½		45⅛		45⅜	
	44½		45½		44¾		44¼		44½	
	45⅜	73,300	45⅝	91,600	45	88,400	44⅞	132,900	44¾	85,700

GF	24		24¼		23⅞		23½		23¾	
	23¼		23⅜		23¼		23		22⅞	
	23¼	13,900	23¾	35,000	23¼	19,200	23	10,200	23⅜	11,900
GM	42		43⅝		43¼		43		44⅜	
	41⅝		42½		42⅜		42¼		42⅞	
	41⅞	87,400	42⅞	106,100	42¾	68,300	42⅝	62,700	44⅛	141,100
GT	18⅝		18¾		18½		18⅜		18½	
	18¼		18⅜		18⅛		17¾		18⅛	
	18½	55,400	18½	67,500	18⅛	105,600	18⅜	30,100	18⅛	37,800
HR	26⅛		27		26¾		26⅜		26⅛	
	25½		26½		26		25⅞		25¾	
	26⅛	24,300	26¾	68,200	26⅜	25,600	26⅜	20,700	25¾	23,500
IP	47¼		47⅜		46⅝		46⅞		47⅝	
	46⅜		46¾		46⅜		45⅞		47	
	47	40,800	46¾	28,900	46⅜	43,900	46⅞	36,500	47⅛	42,300
JM	21¼		22		21¾		21⅝		21⅞	
	20½		21⅜		21⅛		21¼		21¼	
	21¼	20,500	21⅝	21,700	21¼	7,200	21⅝	10,100	21¾	22,000
N	27¼		27¼		27⅛		26⅝		26¼	
	27		27⅛		26⅝		25⅞		25⅞	
	27	14,100	27⅛	35,900	26⅝	15,800	25⅞	71,600	26¼	12,100

	04/21/75		04/22/75		04/23/75		04/24/75		04/25/75	
OI	37		37		36¾		35¾		35⅞	
	36⅜		36⅝		35½		35⅛		35½	
	36⅜	26,200	36⅝	18,700	35½	8,600	35½	6,900	35½	16,800
PG	97½		98⅛		96¾		94¼		93⅞	
	96		96¾		94¾		93¼		92	
	96½	21,200	96½	24,100	94⅞	37,300	93½	51,300	92⅞	42,600
S	66⅝		66⅝		65⅜		64⅝		65⅞	
	65⅝		65⅛		64⅜		63		64¾	
	65⅝	45,900	65⅛	43,200	64⅜	38,800	64¼	48,500	65⅜	52,500
SD	25⅝		25⅝		24¾		24¾		25	
	25		24½		23⅝		23⅝		24⅜	
	25⅝	40,100	24½	73,600	23¾	75,100	24½	48,700	24⅝	89,200
T	49¼		49¾		49		48⅝		48¾	
	48½		49		48½		48⅜		47⅞	
	49⅛	118,000	49⅛	134,500	48⅝	117,900	48½	155,800	48	167,000
TX	25		24⅞		23¾		24¼		24⅝	
	24½		23½		23¼		23⅝		24⅛	
	24¾	65,700	23½	165,200	23¾	166,900	24¼	78,600	24⅜	109,600
UTX	45⅞		46¼		45⅞		45⅛		47	
	44⅝		45¾		44¾		43¾		45¼	
	45¾	15,800	45¾	32,900	44¾	16,400	45	30,900	46⅜	75,900

UK	63⅜		63⅜		62¾		62½		64¾	
	62½		62⅝		61⅞		61½		62⅛	
	63⅛	83,400	62⅝	89,000	62¼	87,000	62¼	97,100	64¼	113,000
WX	14⅝		14⅞		14⅞		14¾		14⅝	
	14¼		14½		14½		14¼		14⅜	
	14½	54,900	14⅝	90,900	14⅝	45,000	14¼	57,800	14½	53,300
X	63¼		63½		62½		64⅜		65¼	
	60½		62½		61⅞		61⅝		63⅛	
	63	70,300	62½	58,900	62¼	54,800	63¼	83,700	64½	105,100
XON	78¼		78⅞		78¾		79⅞		80⅜	
	77¼		77⅞		77⅞		78⅛		79⅝	
	77½	25,300	78⅝	52,700	78⅜	50,600	79⅜	57,800	80	66,100
Z	17		17¼		17		16¾		16⅞	
	16¼		16⅝		16⅜		16⅛		16⅛	
	16¾	31,400	17	39,300	16½	17,500	16½	21,100	16¾	19,500
	04/28/75		*04/29/75*		*04/30/75*		*05/01/75*		*05/02/75*	
Dow	810.00	1,533,500	803.04	1,477,400	821.34	1,433,200	830.96	1,824,400	848.48	2,133,100
NY		17,850,000		17,740,000		18,060,000		20,660,000		25,210,000
A	18		16⅞		16⅞		17⅜		17	
	17		16¼		16⅜		17		16⅜	
	17	30,700	16⅝	29,500	16⅞	17,800	17⅛	27,500	16⅝	41,200

	04/28/75		04/29/75		04/30/75		05/01/75		05/02/75	
AA	46		45¾		46		46¾		48½	
	45⅜		45¼		45		45⅞		47¼	
	45½	129,400	45¼	23,800	46	27,600	46¾	39,500	47¾	61,200
AC	29		28⅞		28¾		29⅛		30¼	
	28¾		28		28¼		28¾		29¼	
	28¾	17,300	28¼	30,600	28¾	8,400	29⅛	12,700	30	19,500
ACD	37¾		37½		37¼		38¾		39¼	
	37		36⅜		36¼		37¼		38¾	
	37¼	17,800	36⅜	10,900	37¼	17,300	38¾	26,300	39	31,100
AMB	38½		37½		38½		38¾		39⅛	
	37½		36⅝		37		38¼		38½	
	37½	8,300	37¼	13,200	38¼	14,900	38½	14,000	38⅞	10,600
BS	39⅝		39½		39½		40		40¼	
	39		38⅜		38¼		39½		39¾	
	39⅜	55,900	38½	79,500	39½	63,400	39⅞	127,800	40⅛	76,400
C	11		10½		10¼		10¼		10½	
	10½		10		10		10		10	
	10½	33,100	10	52,300	10⅛	32,000	10	35,600	10½	52,400
DD	121¾		122		126½		130		133½	
	120		119⅜		119⅞		125½		128¾	
	120¼	28,800	119⅞	38,400	126½	44,300	129	60,300	133	71,400

EK	103		101¼		104½		106¾		109	
	99⅞		97⅝		98		104		105¾	
	100⅛	103,800	98½	116,800	104½	67,000	106½	103,200	108⅛	105,500
ESM	28		27½		27½		27⅝		27¾	
	27		26⅝		26⅝		26¾		27¼	
	27	13,900	26⅝	8,000	27⅛	3,900	27¼	9,700	27⅜	7,600
GE	45⅜		45½		46		47½		48½	
	44¾		44⅜		44½		46½		46⅞	
	44¾	63,300	44⅞	51,300	46	51,700	47	115,600	48¼	134,000
GF	23⅞		23⅜		23⅛		23⅝		23⅞	
	23¼		22¾		22⅝		22¾		23	
	23¼	24,600	22⅞	11,500	22⅞	13,100	22⅞	11,900	23½	29,500
GM	44¼		43⅞		43		43½		44⅞	
	43⅝		42⅞		42⅛		42¾		43¾	
	43⅞	81,900	43	79,600	43	82,900	43½	94,900	44⅞	135,600
GT	18⅜		18⅜		18½		19		19⅛	
	17⅞		18		18⅛		18½		18¾	
	18	26,100	18⅛	21,000	18½	23,500	18⅝	35,200	18¾	55,000
HR	25⅞		26⅛		26⅜		26⅞		27¾	
	25⅜		25½		25⅞		26		27	
	25⅝	31,600	26⅛	16,000	26¼	17,500	26⅞	22,800	27½	41,800

	04/28/75		04/29/75		04/30/75		05/01/75		05/02/75	
IP	49⅞		51½		50½		51		52⅜	
	47⅝		49½		49		50¼		50⅝	
	49¾	40,600	49¾	70,200	50½	36,900	50¾	53,900	51½	48,800
JM	22⅛		21⅞		22½		22¾		23¼	
	21¾		21½		21⅝		22⅜		22½	
	22⅛	37,300	21⅝	9,000	22½	15,500	22½	12,000	23¼	29,100
N	27¼		27⅝		27⅜		27⅛		27⅜	
	26½		26⅞		26¾		26½		27	
	27¼	51,800	27¼	39,600	26⅞	68,300	27	75,600	27¼	19,700
OI	36¼		36¼		37		38		38¾	
	35⅛		35½		35		37¼		38¼	
	36	9,000	35½	6,000	37	33,100	37¾	18,400	38⅝	18,100
PG	93¼		93⅞		95¼		95¾		97⅛	
	92		91⅞		92⅞		94		94¾	
	92¼	17,300	92⅞	20,800	95¼	32,300	95	34,400	96¾	25,000
S	65¾		64⅛		63½		65¼		67⅝	
	63½		62⅝		62½		63		65⅜	
	63¾	42,900	63	43,600	63⅛	60,000	64¼	121,200	67⅝	58,900
SD	24⅝		24½		24⅞		25⅜		26⅛	
	23¾		24		23⅞		24⅝		25⅜	
	24½	57,900	24¼	53,100	24⅞	72,100	25	103,200	25⅞	71,300

T	48⅛		48⅜		49¼		49¾		50¼	
	47½		48		48¼		49¼		49¾	
	48⅛	170,000	48⅜	92,100	48⅞	107,100	49⅝	107,300	50⅛	126,000
TX	24⅜		24⅜		24		24⅛		23⅞	
	23⅞		23¾		23½		23½		23⅜	
	24	137,300	24⅜	101,600	24	141,300	23⅝	152,100	23½	178,300
UTX	47¼		47⅜		48⅛		48⅜		49¼	
	46¾		46⅝		45½		47⅜		48¼	
	47	39,800	46⅝	39,900	48	54,400	47¾	17,700	48¼	185,400
UK	64¼		64		64⅜		64⅝		66⅜	
	63⅜		63		62⅞		63⅞		64⅝	
	64	85,000	63⅛	93,100	64¼	106,600	64⅜	99,800	66⅜	157,500
WX	14⅞		14¾		14¾		14⅞		15½	
	14½		14⅜		14⅜		14⅝		14¾	
	14¾	42,700	14⅜	37,600	14⅝	33,400	14¾	77,800	15½	160,600
X	65⅝		65½		64¼		64⅝		64¾	
	64½		63½		63¼		63¾		63¾	
	65½	87,800	64⅛	225,300	64⅛	127,500	63⅞	121,100	64¾	82,800
XON	80¼		80¼		81		83⅞		84⅞	
	79¾		79⅝		79½		81		84⅛	
	80	31,300	79⅝	37,400	81	38,800	83½	75,900	84¾	73,300

	04/28/75		*04/29/75*		*04/30/75*		*05/01/75*		*05/02/75*	
Z	17		16¾		16⅛		16½		16¾	
	16⅝		16⅛		15¾		16⅛		16⅜	
	16⅝	15,800	16⅛	21,400	16	20,700	16⅜	17,000	16½	25,500
	05/05/75		*05/06/75*		*05/07/75*		*05/08/75*		*05/09/75*	
Dow	855.60	1,799,300	834.72	1,996,100	836.44	1,836,000	840.50	1,389,800	850.13	1,690,400
NY		22,370,000		25,410,000		22,250,000		22,980,000		28,440,000
A	16⅞		16⅝		16		15⅞		16⅜	
	16½		15⅞		15¾		15½		15¾	
	16⅝	18,100	16	33,700	15⅞	17,300	15⅝	23,500	16¼	16,500
AA	49⅜		50¼		49⅜		49⅛		48¾	
	47¾		49		38¾		47½		47¾	
	49	28,100	49¼	170,800	49⅛	62,900	48⅛	80,900	48	48,700
AC	30⅛		30½		30¼		30⅞		32¼	
	29¾		30		29⅞		29⅞		31	
	30	17,900	30¼	15,300	30⅛	13,500	30⅞	12,900	32¼	13,500
ACD	41		42		40½		40⅞		41	
	38⅞		40		39¾		39⅞		40⅛	
	40⅞	60,400	40	46,700	40¼	24,700	40⅛	22,300	41	16,300
AMB	38⅝		38⅜		38⅛		38½		39	
	38⅛		37⅜		36¾		38⅛		38⅛	

	38⅜	12,800	37⅝	17,800	38	9,700	38¼	10,900	39	19,100
BS	40⅛		40		37¾		37⅞		39⅜	
	39½		37⅝		36¼		36¾		37⅞	
	40	80,200	37¾	87,500	37⅛	70,600	37¾	48,800	39¼	64,300
C	10⅞		10⅞		10½		10¾		10⅞	
	10¼		10⅜		10⅜		10⅜		10⅝	
	10⅞	112,600	10⅜	47,900	10⅜	29,200	10¾	41,200	10¾	35,000
DD	133½		133		131		130⅝		132½	
	132		129¾		128		128⅞		130⅝	
	132¾	50,600	129¾	48,300	130⅜	42,800	130⅜	32,800	132	28,600
EK	109½		109⅛		106⅜		106½		107¼	
	106⅞		104⅝		103½		104⅜		105	
	109¼	92,200	104⅝	102,200	106⅛	130,400	105⅝	50,000	105	55,200
ESM	28		27¼		27⅛		27¼		27¾	
	27		26¾		26⅝		26½		27¼	
	27¼	47,900	26¾	10,800	26⅞	8,700	27	9,600	27½	7,100
GE	48¼		47⅞		47⅜		47⅝		48⅜	
	47¼		45⅜		46		46⅝		47⅜	
	47⅞	107,300	45⅞	70,300	47⅛	87,500	47⅝	63,200	47⅞	109,200
GF	23⅞		24¾		23½		23⅛		23⅝	
	23¼		23¾		22⅝		22⅝		22¾	
	23¾	12,300	23¾	43,400	22⅞	73,800	23⅛	23,300	22⅞	37,800

	05/05/75		05/06/75		05/07/75		05/08/75		05/09/75	
GM	45¼		45		44⅝		45		44⅞	
	44		43⅝		43½		44⅛		44¼	
	44⅞	148,300	43⅝	106,800	44½	80,200	45	98,500	44⅞	89,000
GT	18⅞		19⅛		19¼		19½		19⅜	
	18½		18½		18⅜		18⅞		18⅞	
	18¾	87,100	18½	32,700	19⅛	43,900	19	58,800	19¼	45,300
HR	28¾		29		28⅝		28⅞		29⅜	
	27⅝		27¾		27⅝		28		28¾	
	28½	48,400	27⅞	38,600	28¼	30,600	28⅞	27,200	29	43,200
IP	53		53⅜		52¾		53		53⅞	
	51⅛		52		51⅞		52⅛		52⅝	
	53	45,000	52⅛	45,900	52⅝	78,600	52½	24,300	53¼	47,200
JM	23¾		24¼		23½		23¼		23½	
	23		23		23		22⅞		22¾	
	23¼	23,600	23¼	33,800	23⅛	20,000	23¼	32,700	23¼	15,100
N	27¾		27¾		27½		27½		27⅞	
	27		27¼		27⅛		27¼		27⅝	
	27¾	19,900	27⅜	26,500	27⅜	27,700	27⅜	30,300	27⅞	7,500
OI	39		39		38⅜		38¾		39	
	38⅜		38¼		37¾		38		38⅜	
	39	10,800	38¼	5,300	38	12,000	38⅜	3,000	39	4,200

PG	98¼		98½		96⅜		96¼		96½	
	96¼		96		94½		95		95½	
	97½	22,900	96	36,400	96⅜	29,200	96	23,100	96½	28,900
S	69½		69⅞		68⅜		68¼		69⅝	
	66¾		67¾		66¾		67½		68¼	
	69½	46,700	67¾	62,300	67⅜	72,100	68	25,000	68⅞	40,500
SD	26⅝		26⅞		27		28⅛		29⅜	
	25⅞		26⅜		26		27		28⅛	
	26⅝	79,700	26⅜	80,900	26⅞	63,300	28	83,700	29	123,900
T	50⅝		51		50½		51⅛		51½	
	49⅞		50⅛		49⅞		50		51⅛	
	50⅝	99,700	50⅛	157,800	50½	131,600	51⅛	146,100	51⅜	93,900
TX	23⅞		24		24		24		25⅛	
	23½		23⅝		23½		23⅝		24	
	23⅞	114,800	23¾	116,200	24	113,100	24	99,000	24⅞	208,000
UTX	49⅜		48⅝		47¾		48¼		49½	
	48⅜		47		46¾		46		48⅛	
	48½	27,900	47⅛	50,300	47⅛	29,600	48	46,200	48⅞	67,700
UK	66½		66¼		64⅞		63⅝		63⅞	
	65⅝		64¾		63⅛		62¾		63⅜	
	66⅜	94,600	65	113,000	63⅜	128,400	63¼	79,100	63⅝	65,300

	05/05/75		05/06/75		05/07/75		05/08/75		05/09/75	
WX	15¾		16		15¾		16		17¼	
	15⅛		15⅝		15⅜		15½		16⅛	
	15⅝	129,100	15¾	111,600	15⅝	71,600	16	57,900	17⅛	185,700
X	64¼		62½		60⅜		61⅜		62	
	63		60		58½		60⅛		61¼	
	64⅛	87,600	60⅜	185,700	60	211,800	61	70,500	61⅜	94,500
XON	86⅝		86		82⅞		82⅝		82⅞	
	84½		82⅜		80⅞		81¾		82	
	86¼	58,800	82⅜	82,600	82⅛	93,200	81⅞	46,200	82⅛	66,200
Z	16½		16⅝		16¼		16¼		16½	
	16¼		16⅛		15⅞		15¾		16	
	16½	14,000	16¼	15,000	16	28,000	16¼	18,800	16½	13,000

	05/12/75		05/13/75		05/14/75		05/15/75		05/16/75	
Dow	847.47	1,550,300	850.13	2,297,700	858.73	3,386,100	848.80	2,514,500	837.61	1,473,300
NY		22,410,000		24,950,000		29,050,000		27,690,000		16,630,000
A	17¼		17⅛		17¼		17¼		17	
	16⅜		16¾		16⅞		17		16⅝	
	16⅞	16,800	16⅞	12,600	17⅛	15,900	17⅛	9,300	16⅞	13,200
AA	48⅛		48		48¾		48½		48	
	47		47½		47⅝		47¾		47⅝	

	47¾	23,600	47¾	17,300	48	34,300	47¾	41,400	47⅞	68,600
AC	32⅜		32⅜		32½		32½		32⅛	
	31¾		31⅝		32		31⅜		31	
	31¾	16,200	31⅞	9,100	32	9,200	31¾	10,800	31¼	10,800
ACD	41¼		41		40⅞		40⅞		39⅜	
	40½		40		40¼		39¾		37¾	
	41⅛	28,600	40¼	26,700	40½	18,000	39¾	20,000	38½	19,900
AMB	39½		39½		40½		40⅝		40	
	38¾		39		39⅜		39⅝		39½	
	39½	9,200	39½	17,200	40	31,700	39⅝	18,700	39⅝	7,000
BS	39¼		37⅝		38⅛		38⅛		37½	
	38¼		36⅞		37		37¼		36¾	
	38¼	39,400	37	67,700	38	61,100	37½	30,100	37¼	23,500
C	11¼		12½		12½		12⅜		11½	
	10¾		11		12		11¼		11¼	
	11	106,400	12¼	289,800	12⅛	204,100	11⅜	90,200	11⅜	47,700
DD	133		132⅞		133⅜		133		129⅛	
	131¼		131		131		129¼		125⅝	
	132½	37,500	131¼	42,300	132	27,000	129¼	25,700	126¼	31,700
EK	106¼		109½		110		109⅜		106¼	
	104½		105¾		107⅝		106		103¼	
	105¾	70,100	108⅝	75,400	108¾	82,900	106	52,700	104⅛	66,400

	05/12/75		05/13/75		05/14/75		05/15/75		05/16/75	
ESM	27½		26⅞		27		27⅜		27¼	
	26½		26½		26⅝		27⅛		27	
	26½	44,100	26⅝	9,600	27	6,900	27⅛	14,000	27	13,800
GE	48⅛		47⅝		47⅝		47⅞		47⅛	
	47¼		46¾		46⅞		46¾		46⅛	
	47⅜	57,400	46¾	152,000	47⅜	69,600	47⅛	100,900	46¼	69,900
GF	23⅜		23¼		22¾		22⅞		22¼	
	22⅞		22⅝		22¼		22		21½	
	22⅞	21,700	23⅛	19,300	22⅝	19,000	22	32,000	21¾	66,200
GM	45½		46⅜		47¾		48⅛		46	
	44¾		44⅞		47		46		45¼	
	44⅞	113,200	46⅛	177,600	47⅝	206,700	46	139,300	45½	112,600
GT	19⅛		18¾		18⅞		18⅝		18⅜	
	18¼		18¼		18¼		18¼		17½	
	18½	56,700	18½	34,900	18⅝	40,700	18¼	43,900	17⅞	83,500
HR	29½		29¼		29		29		28⅞	
	29		28⅞		28¼		28½		28¼	
	29	46,000	28⅞	41,900	28½	34,900	28½	42,400	28⅞	39,200
IP	53¾		54¾		54½		54¼		52¼	
	52¾		52⅞		53¼		52½		51⅜	
	52¾	28,800	54	27,500	53¾	30,800	52½	28,300	51⅝	36,200

JM	23¾		23¾		23¾		22⅞		22⅝	
	23¼		23⅜		22½		22½		22	
	23½	10,700	23⅜	11,600	22⅞	95,400	22½	7,300	22¼	8,300
N	28⅛		28⅜		28⅝		29⅛		28½	
	27⅞		27¾		27⅞		28½		27⅞	
	27⅞	30,700	28⅛	18,000	28⅝	61,500	28½	43,100	27⅞	22,100
OI	39		38¾		39½		40		38¾	
	38½		38⅝		38½		38¾		38¼	
	38¾	6,300	38⅝	3,700	39½	8,500	38¾	10,200	38¾	10,200
PG	97		96¾		97		98½		97⅜	
	96¼		95¾		96		96¾		95⅞	
	96¾	15,300	95⅞	50,200	97	53,700	97	43,800	95⅞	30,500
S	69½		69⅞		72⅞		73⅜		70⅜	
	68⅛		68⅛		70		70		68¾	
	68½	27,300	69⅜	36,300	71¾	105,200	70	82,500	69¼	50,500
SD	29		28½		28⅜		29⅛		28⅝	
	27¾		27¾		27⅝		28⅜		27⅞	
	28⅛	76,400	27⅞	70,900	28⅜	48,000	28¾	97,200	28¼	46,500
T	51½		52		51⅞		51⅞		50⅞	
	51¼		51¼		51⅞		51⅞		49⅞	
	51¼	132,700	52	729,900	51⅞	1,503,100	51⅞	990,400	50¼	161,900

	05/12/75		05/13/75		05/14/75		05/15/75		05/16/75	
TX	24⅞		25⅛		25		25		24¾	
	24½		24½		24⅝		24⅝		24⅜	
	24⅝	144,900	25	229,900	24¾	148,800	24⅞	117,200	24½	85,200
UTX	49¼		48½		49½		49½		48¾	
	48		47¾		48½		48⅞		47½	
	48⅛	34,900	48⅜	11,900	48⅞	24,800	49	54,400	47¾	41,400
UK	64⅜		64¼		65		66⅛		65⅜	
	63¾		63⅜		64		65⅛		64⅛	
	63⅞	92,800	63⅞	72,300	65	126,700	65⅜	96,100	65⅛	104,200
WX	17½		17⅛		17¼		17⅜		16⅞	
	16⅞		16½		16⅝		16⅞		16½	
	17	161,700	16⅞	84,600	17	98,700	16⅞	97,200	16⅝	100,200
X	61½		60⅜		63		63⅜		62⅛	
	60½		59⅝		59¾		62⅜		61⅜	
	60⅝	48,500	60⅛	88,000	63	126,600	62⅜	86,000	61⅝	46,100
XON	82⅞		83¾		84¼		84⅝		82⅝	
	82⅛		81⅞		83		82¾		82	
	82½	29,700	83⅜	55,700	83⅜	68,500	82¾	67,200	82½	37,300
Z	16⅝		16⅜		16½		16¼		16⅛	
	16¼		16⅛		16⅛		16		15¾	
	16⅜	16,200	16¼	15,200	16¼	23,800	16⅛	21,700	15⅞	18,100

	05/19/75		05/20/75		05/21/75		05/22/75		05/23/75	
Dow	837.69	1,463,500	830.49	1,391,600	818.68	1,510,600	818.91	1,674,700	831.90	1,386,200
NY		17,870,000		18,310,000		17,640,000		17,610,000		17,870,000
A	16⅞		16⅞		16⅝		16⅜		16¼	
	16½		16⅜		16		15⅞		15⅝	
	16⅝	7,500	16⅜	10,600	16	10,100	16	11,000	16	20,700
AA	47½		46¾		46¼		46⅝		48	
	46		45¾		45⅞		46		47¼	
	46	74,000	46	37,400	46	22,800	46½	26,100	48	25,300
AC	31⅞		31¾		31½		31⅜		31½	
	31⅛		31¼		31		31		31¼	
	31⅝	10,500	31⅜	25,400	31	7,700	31¼	6,600	31¼	9,200
ACD	38⅝		38¾		38⅝		37¾		37¾	
	37⅞		38⅛		37⅜		36⅞		37	
	38⅝	14,700	38⅛	7,700	37⅜	15,500	37¼	8,300	37⅛	28,000
AMB	40¼		40⅝		39⅝		39¼		39⅜	
	39⅝		39⅛		38¾		38¾		37½	
	40¼	8,100	39½	32,700	39⅛	10,600	39	3,100	38⅛	39,300
BS	37⅝		37⅞		37⅜		36⅝		35⅜	
	36¾		37⅝		36½		35		34¾	
	37½	36,800	37⅝	33,500	36½	68,900	35¼	107,100	34⅞	73,000

	05/19/75		05/20/75		05/21/75		05/22/75		05/23/75	
C	11⅝		11⅝		11⅛		10⅞		11	
	11⅛		11¼		10⅞		10½		10⅝	
	11⅝	30,700	11⅜	31,400	10⅞	46,100	10⅝	55,100	11	46,000
DD	128½		126⅛		123¾		124½		127¾	
	125		124½		122⅛		121½		124⅝	
	126	36,800	124⅝	44,000	122⅛	36,500	123⅞	28,900	127½	19,400
EK	106½		107		105		105½		107½	
	103⅜		104¾		103		102¼		105⅛	
	106	53,400	104¾	63,800	103⅛	83,200	104½	61,700	107½	56,700
ESM	27		27		27		28⅛		28¾	
	26¾		26⅝		26½		26½		28¼	
	26¾	12,600	26⅝	8,300	26⅝	9,200	28⅛	33,600	28¾	16,100
GE	47		46⅞		45⅝		45⅝		46	
	45⅝		45¼		44½		44¾		45⅜	
	46⅞	49,400	45½	62,100	44⅞	168,000	45¼	78,000	46	66,000
GF	21⅞		21⅝		21¾		21⅞		24⅛	
	21¼		21⅛		21¼		21		22	
	21⅝	32,800	21⅜	49,800	21¼	11,600	21⅞	84,700	24⅛	73,100
GM	45⅞		45¾		45¼		45		45¼	
	44¾		44½		44⅜		44¼		44⅜	
	45¾	76,800	44⅝	82,600	44½	105,000	44⅜	106,800	45¼	65,700

GT	18⅛		18⅛		17⅞		18⅛		18¼	
	17½		17¾		17½		17½		17⅞	
	18	56,100	18	35,200	17¾	27,700	18	47,700	18⅛	39,700
HR	29⅜		29¾		29⅜		29½		29½	
	28½		29¼		28⅝		28⅞		28⅞	
	29⅜	32,700	29½	30,200	29	31,200	28⅞	21,400	29½	16,900
IP	52⅜		52¼		51		51⅜		50	
	50		51⅜		50⅝		48⅝		49¼	
	52	51,500	51⅜	32,300	50⅝	48,700	48⅝	61,200	49⅞	26,000
JM	21¾		21⅝		20⅞		20½		21¼	
	20⅞		20½		20⅜		19⅝		20¼	
	21¼	17,600	20⅝	80,900	20½	16,800	20½	49,100	21	22,700
N	28⅛		28⅜		28		27⅝		28	
	27⅝		28⅛		27½		27⅜		27½	
	28⅛	14,300	28⅛	18,900	27⅝	36,000	27⅝	9,900	28	29,900
OI	39		39¾		39		38⅞		39	
	38⅜		38⅝		38¼		38		38⅝	
	38¾	4,000	39¼	11,400	38¼	7,500	38⅞	4,400	38⅝	9,100
PG	96⅞		96⅞		96		95½		96¼	
	94½		95⅜		95		94⅝		95⅜	
	96½	21,000	95¾	25,000	95⅜	16,800	95	29,600	96¼	14,700

	05/19/75		05/20/75		05/21/75		05/22/75		05/23/75	
S	68½		68⅞		67½		68⅛		67⅜	
	66¾		67¾		66½		66⅞		66½	
	67⅞	66,500	67¾	39,300	67⅛	58,500	67¼	33,800	67	62,600
SD	28½		28⅜		27⅞		27⅜		27⅜	
	27⅞		27⅞		27		26⅝		26¾	
	28⅜	60,900	27⅞	62,800	27½	37,700	26¾	41,900	27¼	30,400
T	49½		49⅞		49⅜		49⅛		49⅞	
	48¾		49¼		48⅝		48⅝		49	
	49½	352,700	49½	160,000	48⅝	195,700	49	226,600	49⅞	202,100
TX	24½		24½		24⅜		24¼		24⅜	
	24¼		23⅝		23⅝		23⅜		23¾	
	24⅜	79,900	23⅞	167,000	24⅜	100,100	24¼	143,800	24¼	120,500
UTX	48		48		47¼		47		48	
	46¼		47¼		46¼		46½		46⅞	
	48	26,600	47⅜	33,700	46⅞	21,300	46⅞	18,400	48	15,100
UK	65¼		65¼		64		63⅜		64⅛	
	64½		64⅛		63		62		63	
	64⅞	45,700	64⅜	52,400	63	108,500	62⅞	95,700	63¾	46,000
WX	16¾		17		16¾		16½		17	
	16¼		16⅝		16⅛		16¼		16½	
	16¾	47,600	16¾	56,300	16⅜	52,500	16½	46,800	17	58,400

X	62⅛		62¾		60¾		60⅜		58⅛	
	61		61⅞		60		56⅝		57	
	62	57,900	62⅛	41,900	60⅛	89,700	57⅜	131,500	57½	99,300
XON	82⅜		82⅜		81⅜		81¼		81⅞	
	81¼		81⅛		80		80		81⅛	
	81¾	45,700	81¼	38,900	80	49,400	80⅞	37,800	81⅞	32,600
Z	16		16		15⅞		15⅝		16⅛	
	15½		15⅝		15⅝		15⅜		15½	
	15⅞	38,200	15¾	16,100	15¾	17,300	15½	64,100	16	21,600
	05/26/75		*05/27/75*		*05/28/75*		*05/29/75*		*05/30/75*	
Dow	HOLIDAY		826.11	1,280,100	817.04	1,667,800	815.00	1,257,800	832.29	1,830,400
NY				17,050,000		21,850,000		18,570,000		22,670,000
A			16⅝		16⅜		15⅞		16	
			16		15¾		15¾		15⅝	
			16⅜	11,100	15⅞	17,500	15¾	6,500	15⅞	15,000
AA			47⅞		46¼		45⅝		46	
			46¼		45½		45		44¾	
			46¼	19,800	45½	45,600	45	25,300	46	31,300
AC			31½		31⅜		31¼		31⅜	
			30¾		30⅞		30⅝		31	
			31¼	10,800	31	82,000	30⅞	7,400	31⅛	10,100

	05/26/75	05/27/75		05/28/75		05/29/75		05/30/75	
ACD		37¼		37		36⅝		37	
		35½		36⅛		36		36⅜	
		36	36,500	36¼	19,700	36½	19,400	37	26,600
AMB		38⅛		37¾		38		39⅜	
		37⅛		37¼		37⅜		38⅛	
		37½	9,000	37½	14,700	38	10,300	39⅜	8,700
BS		35		34⅛		34⅛		35⅛	
		33½		33		33¼		34¼	
		34⅛	63,200	33⅝	75,800	34	43,700	35⅛	50,700
C		11½		10⅞		10⅞		11¼	
		10⅞		10⅝		10⅝		10¾	
		11⅛	46,600	10¾	42,000	10¾	25,700	11	93,700
DD		127⅜		126¾		124½		124¼	
		125⅛		123½		121⅝		121	
		126	19,100	123¾	29,900	122	32,900	123	30,400
EK		107⅛		106½		105⅝		105⅞	
		105		104⅝		103⅝		104⅜	
		105¾	41,100	105⅛	52,200	104⅛	46,900	105¼	41,400
ESM		29⅝		30⅝		29⅞		30⅛	
		29⅛		29⅞		29½		29⅝	
		29⅝	14,300	29⅞	21,400	29⅞	8,700	30⅛	11,100

GE	46		46		45⅝		45⅝	
	45¼		44¾		44¾		45	
	45½	69,700	44⅞	72,700	44⅞	41,800	45⅜	74,100
GF	25¼		25¼		25⅛		25½	
	24⅛		24¼		24¼		24¾	
	24¾	88,400	24½	52,000	24⅝	50,100	25⅜	96,900
GM	45½		44⅛		44		44	
	44⅞		43¼		43		43½	
	44⅞	65,200	43⅝	127,100	43½	107,600	44	68,500
GT	18⅜		18		17⅞		17⅞	
	18		17⅝		17½		17⅝	
	18	22,700	17⅞	30,400	17½	23,700	17⅞	26,300
HR	29⅞		30½		30		30¼	
	29½		29¾		29⅝		29¾	
	29⅞	21,200	30	44,500	29⅞	19,500	29⅞	16,700
IP	49⅝		49⅛		47		48⅞	
	48½		47½		46		46¼	
	48½	47,300	47½	41,500	46¼	75,500	48¾	53,900
JM	21		21⅛		20⅝		20½	
	20⅝		20½		19⅞		19⅞	
	21	12,600	20⅝	13,000	19⅞	36,000	20½	43,800

	05/26/75	05/27/75		05/28/75		05/29/75		05/30/75	
N		28⅛		27⅞		27¾		28⅛	
		27⅞		27⅝		27½		27¾	
		28	20,800	27⅝	20,800	27⅝	22,300	28⅛	18,600
OI		39¼		39¾		39½		39⅝	
		38⅝		39		39⅛		39¼	
		38¾	15,400	39	6,300	39⅛	1,300	39¼	6,700
PG		97¼		96		95⅛		97¼	
		95¾		94⅜		94		95¼	
		96	13,300	94½	26,800	94¾	33,400	97	12,000
S		67⅞		67		65¾		66⅞	
		66⅝		65		64¾		65¾	
		66⅝	49,100	65⅛	40,300	64¾	24,700	66⅞	37,200
SD		28¼		28¾		29⅜		30⅜	
		27½		28		28⅝		29⅝	
		28¼	81,500	28¾	54,200	29¼	74,900	29¾	140,900
T		49¼		48⅞		48⅞		49½	
		48½		48⅜		48½		48⅞	
		48½	112,200	48½	121,100	48⅝	62,200	49¼	164,300
TX		24⅜		24½		25⅜		26	
		23⅞		23⅞		24¼		25½	
		24⅛	151,500	24½	202,300	25⅜	167,600	25⅞	238,800

UTX	48¼		48½		48		48	
	47¾		47⅝		47⅛		47¼	
	47⅞	15,900	47⅞	60,800	47¼	11,500	48	36,500
UK	64¼		63⅜		59¾		62¼	
	63⅜		60		58½		59⅜	
	63⅜	31,600	60	114,900	58¾	120,700	61½	96,600
WX	17⅛		17⅛		16⅞		17⅞	
	16⅝		16¾		16⅝		16⅞	
	16⅞	64,500	16⅞	67,100	16⅞	44,900	17⅞	163,100
X	57½		57⅛		56⅞		59⅛	
	55⅞		55¾		56⅛		57½	
	56⅜	73,800	56	112,200	56¾	38,000	59	57,100
XON	83¼		84¾		85½		87¾	
	82⅜		83⅛		83½		86½	
	83⅛	36,400	83⅞	52,500	85⅜	52,800	87⅝	107,900
Z	16		15½		14⅝		14½	
	15⅝		14⅝		14⅜		14⅛	
	15¾	12,500	14¾	80,000	14½	21,600	14¼	51,100

	06/02/75		*06/03/75*		*06/04/75*		*06/05/75*		*06/06/75*	
Dow	846.61	2,045,000	846.14	1,963,400	839.96	1,774,600	842.15	1,541,200	839.64	1,360,800
NY		28,240,000		26,560,000		24,900,000		21,610,000		20,460,000

	06/02/75		06/03/75		06/04/75		06/05/75		06/06/75	
A	16⅜		17⅜		18¼		18¾		19	
	15⅞		16⅛		17¼		18		17⅞	
	16¼	41,700	17¼	40,800	17⅞	75,700	18⅝	87,600	18	57,000
AA	46¼		45¾		45¼		44		44¼	
	45¼		45		44⅜		43⅜		43	
	45½	16,200	45⅜	45,500	44⅜	18,800	44	22,300	43⅜	19,600
AC	32½		32⅞		33		32⅞		32⅞	
	31¼		32⅜		33½		32¼		32½	
	32¼	16,700	32½	8,300	32¾	7,900	32¾	11,100	32¾	8,000
ACD	37⅜		36¾		36⅞		37		37	
	37		36¼		36¼		36⅝		36⅜	
	37⅛	20,500	36⅜	38,100	36⅞	22,300	36⅞	25,800	36⅝	16,000
AMB	39⅝		39⅞		41		40¾		40⅞	
	39		39¼		39¾		40¼		39⅝	
	39⅜	14,100	39⅞	8,400	40⅞	29,800	40¾	11,700	39⅝	13,600
BS	36⅜		36⅜		35¾		34⅞		34⅜	
	35⅜		35⅜		34⅞		33⅞		33¾	
	35¾	60,600	35¾	49,200	34⅞	68,800	34⅜	45,800	33⅞	32,100
C	11½		11¼		11¼		11¼		11¼	
	11⅛		11⅛		11⅛		11		11	
	11⅛	58,600	11⅛	47,100	11⅛	22,800	11⅛	32,000	11	61,200

DD	125½		127		125¾		125½		126	
	123⅝		124¾		124⅝		124		124¼	
	124¾	16,600	125⅞	61,600	124¾	29,100	125½	25,100	124⅝	14,200
EK	106¾		106½		104⅞		103¾		105	
	105⅜		104⅜		103⅛		101½		103⅛	
	106⅜	66,100	104¾	69,300	103¼	45,500	103⅛	70,000	104⅜	74,600
ESM	32¼		32⅞		32⅛		32¼		32⅜	
	30½		31⅝		31¾		32		32	
	32	47,000	32	24,200	32	28,300	32	28,100	32¼	16,000
GE	47		47⅞		47½		47⅜		47½	
	45¾		46¾		46⅞		46¼		46¾	
	46⅞	59,400	47⅜	95,000	47¼	71,000	47⅜	79,800	47¼	59,600
GF	26		26¼		25⅞		26		26	
	25⅜		25⅜		25¼		25⅜		25½	
	25⅝	39,500	25⅜	64,300	25⅝	25,700	25⅞	30,100	25¾	20,200
GM	44¾		43⅞		44⅛		44½		44⅞	
	43⅛		43½		43¼		43½		44⅛	
	43½	105,300	43⅝	81,400	43⅞	204,600	44½	88,300	44½	103,400
GT	18		18⅜		18¼		18⅛		18⅜	
	17⅝		17¾		17¾		17¾		17⅞	
	17¾	54,800	17⅞	37,600	18	29,900	18	27,000	18	24,000

	06/02/75		06/03/75		06/04/75		06/05/75		06/06/75	
HR	30½		30⅜		30¼		30⅛		29⅞	
	29⅞		30		29⅝		29		29⅛	
	30¼	19,200	30⅛	24,700	29¾	19,400	30	28,900	29⅝	31,500
IP	50½		49⅞		49½		48½		48½	
	49¾		49¼		48⅛		48⅛		47⅛	
	50	58,300	49¾	33,500	48⅝	41,000	48½	25,900	47⅛	23,700
JM	21⅛		21¼		21⅛		21½		21½	
	20¾		20¾		20¾		20¾		21	
	20⅞	80,500	21⅛	49,400	20⅞	22,000	21½	41,500	21	16,300
N	28½		28¾		28⅝		28		28⅛	
	28¼		28⅜		28⅛		27¾		27⅝	
	28½	24,000	28½	53,200	28⅛	15,000	28	12,300	27⅞	9,500
OI	40⅞		41⅜		41¼		41¼		41	
	39¼		41		41		40¾		40⅝	
	40⅝	31,700	41¼	9,900	41	2,900	41¼	3,900	40⅝	7,500
PG	98¾		98½		98¼		97		97⅛	
	97⅝		98		96½		96		95⅞	
	98¼	25,500	98	10,500	97½	27,100	97	25,700	96⅜	17,200
S	68¾		69⅜		69⅛		68⅜		69½	
	67⅝		68¼		68¼		68		68¼	
	68	48,000	69	50,300	68½	34,400	68⅛	27,800	69⅜	54,900

SD	30⅞		31¼		31½		31½		32⅛	
	30		30⅜		31		30⅝		31⅜	
	30¾	272,100	30⅞	116,600	31¼	97,200	31⅛	80,700	31⅞	87,300
T	49½		49⅜		49⅜		49⅜		49½	
	49¼		49¼		49⅛		49⅛		49	
	49⅜	145,800	49¼	161,500	49⅜	103,400	49¼	175,800	49⅛	107,000
TX	26⅝		26⅛		26⅜		26⅛		26	
	26¼		25¾		25¾		25⅝		25⅝	
	26¼	141,200	26⅛	164,600	25	186,000	25⅞	128,500	25⅞	110,800
UTX	49⅞		51½		52¾		53½		54⅞	
	48		49¾		51		51¼		53⅝	
	49⅝	86,300	50¾	110,300	51¾	194,600	53⅜	65,800	54½	90,200
UK	63⅜		63¼		61⅛		59¾		60⅛	
	62¼		61⅝		59½		59		57½	
	63¼	101,800	61⅝	115,800	59½	90,700	59⅜	94,700	57⅞	68,500
WX	19		19¼		19⅛		19		19⅛	
	18⅛		18⅝		18¾		18⅝		18⅝	
	19	166,700	19⅛	181,800	19	101,800	19	76,700	18⅞	66,500
X	61¼		60		58½		57⅛		57	
	59¾		58⅞		55¾		56		55¾	
	60⅛	59,900	58⅞	102,600	56¼	68,900	56⅝	62,400	56¼	56,800

	06/02/75		*06/03/75*		*06/04/75*		*06/05/75*		*06/06/75*	
XON	89½		89		88⅛		87½		88⅜	
	88¼		87⅝		86½		85⅜		87⅝	
	89⅛	119,400	87⅞	70,600	86½	69,600	87⅛	89,700	88	72,200
Z	14⅝		14¾		14¾		14¾		15⅜	
	14¼		14½		14½		14½		14⅞	
	14⅝	47,500	14¾	37,300	14¾	17,100	14¾	16,200	15⅜	21,400
	06/09/75		*06/10/75*		*06/11/75*		*06/12/75*		*06/13/75*	
Dow	830.10	1,408,800	822.12	1,723,000	824.55	1,203,600	819.31	1,179,500	824.47	1,433,600
NY		20,670,000		21,130,000		18,230,000		15,970,000		16,300,000
A	18¼		17½		17¾		17½		17½	
	17½		17⅛		17¼		17⅛		17⅛	
	17½	30,100	17½	15,800	17⅜	31,400	17⅛	12,500	17⅜	13,800
AA	42¾		42⅛		42		42⅝		42¾	
	42		41⅛		41⅝		41⅝		41¼	
	42	30,600	41⅜	39,300	41¾	47,100	41⅝	25,500	42¼	48,800
AC	32⅝		32		31½		31¼		31¼	
	32⅛		31⅜		31⅛		31		31	
	32⅜	6,900	31⅝	10,700	31⅜	5,700	31⅛	5,400	31	8,400
ACD	37⅜		36⅝		36⅝		37		37⅜	
	36⅝		36		36¼		36½		36⅝	

	36⅞	23,800	36¼	22,000	36⅝	44,500	37	52,300	37⅛	19,800
AMB	39⅞		39⅞		40⅜		40⅜		40	
	39¼		39⅛		39⅝		39¾		39⅜	
	39½	6,200	39¾	8,500	40¼	10,900	40	4,800	39¾	10,400
BS	34		33⅝		34½		34½		34	
	33⅜		33⅛		33½		33¾		33⅜	
	33½	25,400	33⅝	75,100	34¼	27,800	34	17,800	33⅞	37,600
C	11⅛		10⅞		10⅞		10¾		10⅝	
	10¾		10⅝		10⅝		10½		10½	
	10⅞	56,500	10⅝	28,600	10¾	34,900	10⅝	28,000	10½	30,700
DD	124⅝		123		123½		121½		119¾	
	122¾		121½		121½		117		114½	
	122⅞	30,700	121⅝	30,200	121½	19,300	117½	27,900	119½	33,800
EK	104		102½		103¼		102⅝		101⅛	
	102⅛		100⅞		101¾		100		99¼	
	102¼	46,200	101⅞	68,500	102¼	71,500	100	74,200	99⅞	82,600
ESM	32		31¾		31¾		31⅝		31¼	
	31¾		31		31⅜		31⅛		30½	
	31⅞	10,500	31½	18,500	31⅜	6,300	31⅛	5,900	30½	9,800
GE	47¼		46¼		46⅝		46		46	
	46½		45¾		45¾		44¾		44½	
	46½	43,100	45¾	78,600	45¾	51,800	45	44,700	46	55,300

	06/09/75		06/10/75		06/11/75		06/12/75		06/13/75	
GF	25⅞		25¾		25⅞		25½		25½	
	25½		25⅜		25¼		25¼		25¼	
	25¾	20,500	25⅝	20,000	25½	43,900	25½	25,700	25⅜	14,100
GM	44⅝		43¼		43⅜		43⅞		43⅝	
	43½		42½		42⅝		43¼		42½	
	43½	71,400	42⅞	158,900	43¼	80,300	43⅜	59,000	43⅝	151,700
GT	18⅛		17½		17¾		17¼		17⅜	
	17⅝		17		17¼		16⅞		17⅛	
	17⅝	54,500	17¼	64,800	17⅜	45,100	17⅛	27,400	17¼	32,400
HR	29⅝		28½		28¼		28⅜		28¼	
	29		26⅞		27⅞		27¾		27⅞	
	29¼	20,400	27¾	81,200	28¼	15,500	28	15,000	27⅞	17,500
IP	47⅛		45⅜		45⅝		45⅞		46⅛	
	45⅝		44½		44¾		45⅜		45½	
	45⅝	48,000	44⅞	65,600	45½	38,600	45⅝	50,400	46⅛	21,800
JM	21½		20⅞		21		21		20⅞	
	20¾		20¼		20½		20½		20¼	
	20¾	68,800	20⅞	59,200	21	18,400	20⅞	11,900	20¼	74,600
N	27¾		27		26⅝		26¼		27	
	27¼		26⅜		26⅛		26⅛		26¼	
	27¼	19,400	26½	115,700	26¼	11,700	26¼	10,200	27	10,100

OI	40⅜		40⅜		40¾		41		41	
	40		40		40		40⅛		40½	
	40	5,900	40¼	3,100	40⅛	6,500	40¾	6,200	41	6,100
PG	96½		95		94¾		94⅞		93⅜	
	95¼		93¾		93⅝		93¼		92¼	
	95¼	16,700	93¾	32,500	93¾	21,100	93¼	20,900	93⅜	51,700
S	69½		68⅞		69¼		68⅝		68⅝	
	68⅜		68⅛		68		68		67¾	
	68½	36,100	68¾	38,600	68	36,900	68	36,000	68½	29,700
SD	32⅝		31⅞		31⅞		32¼		31⅜	
	31¾		31⅛		31½		31⅛		30⅝	
	32¼	90,900	31½	85,500	31¾	60,900	31⅛	73,100	31⅜	60,400
T	49⅜		49		49¼		49		49	
	48⅞		48¾		48¾		48¾		48¾	
	49	140,300	49	78,600	48⅞	66,300	48⅞	69,900	48¾	87,800
TX	26⅛		25¾		26		26		26⅛	
	25⅝		25⅜		25½		25½		25⅝	
	25¾	135,100	25⅝	101,900	25⅝	86,500	25⅝	188,800	26	280,800
UTX	57⅞		55⅛		54⅜		54⅛		55⅜	
	55¼		53¼		53¾		53½		53½	
	55⅜	103,300	54⅜	50,400	53⅞	50,100	53½	46,600	55⅛	33,800

	06/09/75		06/10/75		06/11/75		06/12/75		06/13/75	
UK	58¾		56⅝		57½		56⅞		57¼	
	57⅝		55½		55⅞		56		56⅛	
	57¾	72,000	56	116,200	56	85,200	56¼	47,500	57	62,000
WX	18¾		18⅛		18½		18⅜		18¼	
	18¼		17¾		18		17⅞		17⅞	
	18¼	76,100	18	114,500	18⅛	56,700	18¼	71,600	18⅛	40,100
X	57⅛		56⅜		57½		57¾		57½	
	55⅞		55½		56¾		56½		56⅜	
	56	39,300	56⅛	48,800	56¾	39,300	56⅞	29,400	57	36,100
XON	88½		88¼		89¾		90⅝		91⅛	
	87⅛		85⅞		88¾		89⅛		89½	
	87¼	64,900	88¼	76,100	89⅜	73,800	89⅝	79,400	91⅛	58,800
Z	15½		15⅛		15¼		15¼		15⅜	
	15⅛		14⅞		14⅞		15		14⅞	
	15¼	15,200	14⅞	15,600	15	15,800	15¼	11,500	14⅞	13,100

	06/16/75		06/17/75		06/18/75		06/19/75		06/20/75	
Dow	834.56	1,357,900	828.61	1,440,300	827.83	1,327,500	845.35	1,632,000	855.44	2,117,400
NY		16,660,000		19,440,000		15,590,000		21,450,000		26,260,000
A	17½		17		16⅞		16½		17	
	16¾		16¾		15⅞		16⅛		16⅛	

	16⅞	24,500	16⅞	10,000	16⅛	45,900	16⅜	28,300	16⅛	37,200
AA	43¾		44½		44½		45¼		46⅞	
	43⅜		44		43⅞		44		45⅝	
	43½	29,100	44	37,000	44¼	42,800	45¼	47,000	46⅜	101,600
AC	31¾		31⅞		31⅞		32		32¼	
	31		31½		31½		31⅝		31¾	
	31⅝	6,700	31½	7,600	31¾	7,400	31⅞	7,700	31¾	15,900
ACD	37⅛		36⅞		37⅛		37¼		38½	
	36¾		36¼		36⅛		36½		37⅝	
	36⅞	8,200	36½	13,800	37	19,200	37	9,400	38	33,900
AMB	39¾		39½		40¼		40⅝		41	
	39½		38¾		39		40⅛		40⅝	
	39½	16,900	38¾	9,100	40	6,200	40⅝	8,400	40¾	11,100
BS	35		35		34⅝		35½		36¼	
	33¼		34		34⅛		34		35⅛	
	34⅝	60,400	34⅛	49,700	34¼	19,000	35½	27,200	35⅝	40,300
C	11¼		11⅜		10⅞		11⅛		11⅜	
	10⅝		10¾		10⅝		10½		10⅞	
	11¼	45,400	10¾	39,000	10¾	20,400	11	46,500	11	39,900
DD	120¾		121½		117		120		124½	
	118½		116½		114		116½		121¼	
	120¾	39,800	116¾	19,600	116½	33,600	120	35,900	123½	47,300

	06/16/75		06/17/75		06/18/75		06/19/75		06/20/75	
EK	100		100⅞		100¾		103¾		105⅜	
	99⅛		99		98¾		100⅜		103¼	
	99⅞	87,100	99⅛	108,400	100	61,400	103¾	81,700	103¾	105,300
ESM	30⅞		31¼		31¼		32¾		33	
	30⅜		30⅝		30¾		31¼		32⅛	
	30⅝	11,900	31	6,800	31¼	6,200	32¼	22,600	32⅞	23,300
GE	46⅝		46⅝		46½		47⅞		48½	
	45¾		45⅞		45¾		46¼		47⅜	
	46⅝	59,900	45⅞	34,700	46⅜	39,900	47⅞	67,600	47¾	149,300
GF	25⅞		26		25¾		26⅜		27	
	25⅜		25⅝		25½		25½		26⅜	
	25¾	21,900	25⅞	43,400	25¾	39,500	26¼	76,000	27	77,500
GM	43¾		43¾		43½		45⅛		45⅞	
	43¼		43		43		43⅜		44⅞	
	43½	121,000	43½	163,200	43⅜	76,200	45⅛	131,800	45⅛	131,900
GT	17½		18		17½		17¾		18⅛	
	17		17¼		17⅛		17⅜		17¾	
	17⅜	44,300	17½	37,400	17½	24,700	17⅝	76,100	18⅛	36,900
HR	28⅛		27⅞		27⅝		27¾		28⅛	
	27¾		27¼		27⅛		27½		27⅝	
	28	22,800	27⅜	15,800	27½	16,800	27¾	17,100	28⅛	22,000

IP	46½		48¼		48		50		51	
	45⅝		46¾		47¼		48		50⅜	
	46½	42,700	48	28,300	47¾	15,000	49¼	36,600	50½	74,100
JM	20⅞		21¾		21⅞		22⅜		22¼	
	20½		20⅞		21⅛		21⅞		22	
	20¾	10,000	21⅜	33,700	21⅞	37,300	22	29,000	22⅛	72,700
N	27⅜		27⅜		27¼		27⅜		27½	
	26⅝		27		26¾		27⅛		27⅛	
	27¼	6,300	27⅛	8,300	27⅛	17,200	27⅜	8,600	27⅛	16,700
OI	41¾		41⅝		41½		41½		42⅜	
	41⅛		41¼		41⅛		41		41⅜	
	41½	8,400	41¼	7,800	41⅛	6,700	41¼	8,400	41⅝	21,600
PG	95½		96¼		93¼		94¼		95¼	
	93⅜		94¼		92		92⅛		93⅞	
	95	19,600	94⅜	27,800	92	24,300	93¼	29,100	94	34,900
S	69⅜		69⅜		68⅜		69⅛		70½	
	68⅛		68⅛		68		68¼		69⅝	
	69⅜	30,900	68⅛	29,900	68⅜	32,600	69	30,200	70¼	46,900
SD	32⅜		32⅝		31⅞		32		32⅛	
	31⅜		31⅞		31½		31½		31¾	
	32⅛	63,900	32	68,100	31⅝	54,600	31⅞	86,900	31¾	71,800

	06/16/75		06/17/75		06/18/75		06/19/75		06/20/75	
T	49		49⅛		49¼		50		50¾	
	48¾		48⅞		48⅞		49⅛		50⅜	
	48⅞	60,000	49	102,300	49⅛	84,100	49⅞	181,700	50½	288,300
TX	26⅝		27		26⅝		27		27¼	
	26		26¼		26⅛		26¼		26¾	
	26⅝	167,700	26¼	168,900	26¼	116,100	26⅝	121,800	27¼	195,400
UTX	56½		58¼		60		58½		59⅝	
	54⅞		56⅞		58⅛		57⅝		58¼	
	56½	33,700	58⅛	64,900	58¾	221,600	58¼	81,100	59¼	67,300
UK	58¾		59⅜		58⅛		60¼		62¼	
	56½		58		57⅜		57¾		60¾	
	58¾	95,600	58½	67,700	57⅝	52,800	60⅛	50,100	61½	77,800
WX	18¼		18⅛		17⅜		18		18⅜	
	17⅞		17½		17		17¼		18	
	18	72,100	17½	68,200	17¼	99,200	18	62,000	18⅛	75,000
X	58⅞		59		58½		60⅜		61¾	
	57		57⅝		57½		58⅛		60¾	
	58¾	39,700	58	50,200	58	25,500	60⅜	82,600	61	88,300
XON	92⅜		92⅛		90		90¾		91½	
	91⅝		89⅝		88¼		88⅜		90½	
	92	96,900	90¼	97,900	88⅞	72,300	90½	80,600	91	64,800

Z	15		15		14¾		15		15½	
	14¾		14¾		14⅝		14¾		15	
	14⅞	10,500	14¾	20,800	14¾	8,500	14⅞	60,000	15⅛	48,400
	06/23/75		*06/24/75*		*06/25/75*		*06/26/75*		*06/27/75*	
Dow	864.83	1,332,000	869.06	1,750,600	872.73	1,385,600	874.14	2,756,300	873.12	1,699,600
NY		20,720,000		26,620,000		21,610,000		24,560,000		18,820,000
A	17¼		17¾		18		18⅜		18⅜	
	16¼		17⅜		17⅜		17⅞		17⅝	
	17¼	51,800	17⅜	26,700	17⅞	32,800	18⅛	116,100	17¾	29,200
AA	46½		46⅞		47⅜		47⅝		47⅞	
	46		46¼		46½		47⅛		47⅜	
	46½	41,100	46½	73,800	47	41,500	47⅜	23,900	47½	14,600
AC	31⅞		31⅞		31¾		31½		31¼	
	31¼		31¼		31¼		31		31	
	31½	16,900	31½	10,800	31⅝	9,300	31	15,500	31¼	10,800
ACD	38¼		38⅝		38⅞		39¾		39½	
	38		38⅛		38¼		39		38⅞	
	38	13,000	38¼	30,600	38⅞	13,500	39	11,700	39⅛	27,200
AMB	40⅞		41		40⅞		40¾		40⅞	
	40⅜		40½		40⅛		40⅜		40½	
	40⅝	8,200	40¾	8,600	40⅜	14,800	40⅝	16,000	40⅝	9,400

	06/23/75		06/24/75		06/25/75		06/26/75		06/27/75	
BS	36		36⅝		35⅞		36¼		36¼	
	35		35⅝		35⅜		35⅝		35⅝	
	35⅞	33,600	35¾	41,500	35¾	32,000	35⅞	28,900	36⅛	22,800
C	11		11⅛		11		11⅝		12⅛	
	10⅞		10¾		10¾		10⅞		11½	
	11	24,800	10⅞	56,200	10⅞	28,500	11⅜	122,600	11⅞	137,200
DD	126½		129¾		129		129½		128½	
	122⅜		127¼		126¾		127½		127⅝	
	126½	33,500	127⅞	30,100	128	14,900	129⅛	40,100	127⅝	15,400
EK	105		105⅞		104⅝		104¾		104	
	102¼		103		103⅛		103½		102⅞	
	105	55,900	103¼	54,800	104¼	30,700	103⅞	46,200	103⅛	29,600
ESM	34		35		35⅝		36⅜		37	
	32⅞		34½		34½		35½		36⅛	
	34	18,300	34½	40,600	35½	16,300	35¾	26,500	36⅛	28,500
GE	48⅜		49¼		51		52⅜		52⅞	
	47⅛		48⅜		48½		50½		51½	
	48⅜	57,200	48⅞	111,100	50⅞	153,500	51⅞	155,900	52¼	118,000
GF	27⅛		27½		27⅜		27⅜		27⅛	
	26⅝		26⅞		27⅛		26½		26½	
	27	33,600	27¼	35,500	27⅜	22,300	26⅞	26,200	26⅞	26,200

GM	45¼		46⅛		46		47⅝		48	
	44⅞		45		45⅜		46¼		47¼	
	45¼	110,200	45½	117,100	46	69,000	47⅛	158,600	47¾	94,900
GT	18¼		18⅞		18⅞		18⅞		19	
	17⅝		18⅛		18⅜		18½		18¼	
	18⅛	46,500	18½	47,600	18⅝	34,800	18½	95,500	18¾	31,000
HR	28⅛		28¼		28⅛		28¼		28	
	27⅝		27½		27⅝		27⅝		27¾	
	28	23,700	28	26,500	28⅛	19,400	27⅞	15,400	28	12,800
IP	51¾		51¼		51⅝		52⅜		52⅜	
	49⅞		50⅝		50½		50⅞		51¾	
	50¾	32,700	51⅛	39,900	51⅛	15,200	52¼	41,600	52⅛	26,600
JM	22¼		22⅜		22⅜		22½		23½	
	21⅝		22		22		22		22⅝	
	22	38,300	22⅛	133,800	22⅛	25,200	22⅜	275,600	23½	48,500
N	27¼		27⅝		27¾		28⅛		28⅛	
	26⅞		27¼		27½		27⅝		27⅞	
	27¼	15,100	27⅝	24,200	27¾	21,100	27¾	15,900	27⅞	14,600
OI	42		42		41⅞		42⅜		42	
	41¼		40½		41¼		41⅝		41⅝	
	42	6,200	41¾	26,800	41⅝	7,800	42	77,800	41⅝	15,600

	06/23/75		06/24/75		06/25/75		06/26/75		06/27/75	
PG	97		97⅞		98¼		98¾		99¼	
	93½		96		97		97¼		97⅜	
	97	19,700	97	23,100	98	34,600	98	12,900	97⅜	23,900
S	71¼		73⅝		74⅜		74		73¾	
	69⅝		71½		73		73⅛		72¾	
	71⅛	49,000	73½	65,500	73½	47,400	73⅜	28,800	73	28,200
SD	32		32⅛		32⅜		33		32⅞	
	31½		31⅜		32		32⅛		32	
	32	35,400	32	68,800	32⅜	56,000	32½	60,800	32	32,500
T	50⅞		51⅛		51⅛		51⅛		51	
	50¼		50¾		50¾		50⅞		50¾	
	50⅝	155,200	51	195,000	51	99,600	51	126,600	50¾	107,500
TX	27½		27⅝		27½		26⅞		26⅞	
	26⅞		27⅛		27⅛		26½		26½	
	27½	108,100	27⅜	141,600	27⅛	109,900	26⅝	869,700	28¾	491,300
UTX	61		62⅛		60⅝		58⅞		55⅞	
	59⅛		61		58		56¾		54½	
	60⅞	7,000	61¾	38,800	59	130,200	56¾	55,500	55½	75,300
UK	62⅛		62⅜		62⅜		62⅜		61½	
	60⅞		61⅜		61⅜		61½		60⅞	
	62	50,000	61¾	50,700	62¼	63,600	61⅝	71,100	61½	34,700

WX	18½		19		19		19		18⅞	
	17⅞		18⅝		18¾		18⅝		18½	
	18½	57,500	19	71,200	18¾	87,600	18⅝	77,100	18⅝	65,300
X	61¼		61⅞		61		61⅞		61¼	
	60¼		60⅝		60½		60¼		60⅜	
	61¼	48,100	60⅞	56,500	60⅞	46,900	61	46,900	61¼	52,800
XON	91¼		92⅜		91⅝		92⅜		92⅛	
	89⅞		91⅜		90⅞		91⅛		91½	
	91¼	47,700	91⅜	68,000	91¼	52,000	91⅞	56,000	91⅞	58,900
Z	15¼		15⅞		16⅞		17		16⅞	
	14⅞		15¼		15¾		16¾		16⅜	
	14⅞	25,700	15¾	35,200	16¾	55,200	16¾	40,900	16¾	16,300

06/30/75

Dow	878.99	1,346,000
NY		19,430,000
A	18	
	17½	
	18	18,700
AA	49	
	47½	
	49	40,300

06/30/75

AC	31⅜	
	31⅛	
	31⅜	8,000
ACD	39⅛	
	38⅞	
	38⅞	11,700
AMB	40⅞	
	40½	
	40½	13,400

06/30/75

BS	37	
	36	
	36⅝	57,900
C	12⅜	
	11⅞	
	12⅜	119,800
DD	129	
	127	
	128⅛	11,600

	06/30/75			06/30/75	
EK	104		SD	32⅜	
	102½			31½	
	103¼	79,400		31¾	34,500
ESM	37⅜		T	51	
	35⅞			50⅞	
	37¼	17,800		50⅞	106,200
GE	52¾		TX	26¾	
	51¾			26½	
	52⅝	83,500		26⅝	113,400
GF	26¾		UTX	58¼	
	26			55½	
	26¾	42,400		58	39,000
GM	48⅞		UK	62¼	
	47⅞			61½	
	48¾	122,400		61⅞	29,700
GT	19¼		WX	18¾	
	18⅞			18⅜	
	19	62,500		18⅝	80,800
HR	28		X	61¾	
	27½			60⅞	
	27½	16,900		61⅜	24,700

IP	52	
	51	
	51	15,000
JM	25	
	23¾	
	25	63,600
N	28	
	27⅝	
	27⅞	33,300
OI	41¾	
	41¼	
	41¼	3,400
PG	99	
	96½	
	98⅛	18,400
S	73¾	
	72⅞	
	73⅜	24,800
XON	92½	
	91⅞	
	92½	38,700
Z	16¾	
	16¼	
	16⅜	14,200